CASTING THE FUTURE

The arcane keys to one of mankind's oldest ambitions—learning the future from celestial configurations—are offered to amateurs and professionals alike in this comprehensive and practical guide that combines the functions of a dictionary, textbook, and encyclopedia. This vast storehouse of wisdom, written in a clear, understandable style, includes:

- Step-by-step instructions for casting a horoscope
- Basic tools of chart interpretation
- Histories of Western, Hindu, and Chinese astrology
- Biographies of leading astrologers
- A comparative presentation of 20 different systems of house division
- A list of astrological symbols and abbreviations
- Signs of the zodiac, planets, houses, and aspects
- Transits, progressions, and solar returns
- Chart comparison, sample chart, and composite charts
- Horary, mundane, medical, electional, and locational astrology
- Sidereal, humanistic, and heliocentric astrology
- Uranian system, cosmobiology, and harmonics
- Statistics and computers
- Professional ethics
- 60 explanatory diagrams and tables

ABOUT THE AUTHORS:

JEAN-LOUIS BRAU is a highly regarded French author and astrological authority, while HELEN WEAVER and ALLAN EDMANDS are practicing astrologers. Consultants of the book include Charles Harvey, President of the Astrological Association of Great Britain; Charles Jayne, President of the Association for Research in Cosmecology; and Robert Hand, publications director of the National Council for Geocosmic research, and a computer expert whose works on technical astrology have a worldwide reputation.

LAROUSSE ENCYCLOPEDIA OF
ASTROLOGY

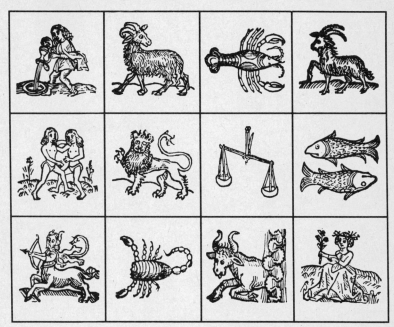

Jean-Louis Brau, Helen Weaver
and Allan Edmands

Edited and with a preface by Helen Weaver

CONSULTING AND CONTRIBUTING EDITORS:
Robert Hand, Charles Harvey, and Charles Jayne

A PLUME BOOK
NEW AMERICAN LIBRARY
TIMES MIRROR
NEW YORK AND SCARBOROUGH, ONTARIO

Design: BOOKGRAPHICS

Line Art: Allan Edmands and Gary Tong

Typography: Thomas D'Espinosa, DEKR Corporation

This is an authorized reprint of a hardcover edition published by
McGraw-Hill Book Company.

First Plume Printing, April, 1982

1 2 3 4 5 6 7 8 9

PRINTED IN THE UNITED STATES OF AMERICA

PREFACE

The resurgence of astrology in the twentieth century is a phenomenon unparalleled in the long history of this remarkably durable human activity. A recent Gallup poll found that 29 percent of Americans believe in astrology and think their lives are governed by the positions of the stars. Astrology columns are carried by 1,200 of the nation's 1,750 daily newspapers and a variety of popular magazines. The signs of the zodiac appear on many of the artifacts of modern civilization. New books on astrology, from mass market potboilers to serious works, are published regularly. Scholarly journals are issued by organizations devoted to the reintegration of astrology and science, and courses in astrology are being offered in a dozen American universities.

Some people see the current popularity of astrology as part of a rising tide of irrationality that is threatening the very foundations of Western civilization. To this group belong the 186 scientists who signed a statement issued by the *Humanist* magazine in 1975 condemning astrology as "a cult of unreason and irrationalism . . . being foisted on an unsuspecting public." Other people see the current renewal of interest in astrology and other occult subjects as part of an evolutionary process, a necessary balance to an overemphasis on reason that has characterized Western society since the Renaissance. However one views the phenomenon, there is no denying its reality.

Yet in spite of the extraordinary popularity of astrology and the proliferation of literature on the subject, to date there has been no reliable guide to the language of astrology written for the general reader. There are dictionaries and encyclopedias of astrology, of course, but most of them are so specialized or technical as to be of very little help to the beginner. The only really good one— Nicholas de Vore's *Encyclopedia of Astrology*—was published in 1947 and has never been updated. In those thirty years astrology has been in a state of rapid transition. De Vore's *Encyclopedia*, although it reflects the work of early twentieth-century modernizers like Alan Leo, is still very much grounded in the traditional principles of Ptolemy, the Greek astronomer who compiled and systematized the astrology of the ancients in the second century A.D. But the results of the latest research, both by astrologers working to bring the field up to the standards of an empirical science and by scientists working in related fields, are placing this traditional Ptolemaic astrology in a new perspective. Statistical tests are validating some parts of traditional doctrine and giving other parts a vote of no confidence. Some of this research is revealing correlations between planetary patterns and human behavior of which Western astrologers have been previously unaware.

The *Larousse Encyclopedia of Astrology* is designed to fill this gap: to provide an accurate, understandable, and interesting reference book that will be helpful not only to astrologers and students of astrology but also to the general reader.

Beginners will find step-by-step instructions for calculating a horoscope based on the time and place of birth, as well as descriptive articles on the signs of the zodiac, the planets, the houses, and the aspects that will provide them with the basic tools of chart interpretation. To show how an astrologer proceeds from the delineation of the separate parts of a birth chart to a synthesis of the whole, the editors have included a sample chart interpretation based on the horoscope of the anthropologist Margaret Mead. Those who wish to use this book as a textbook will find, immediately following this preface, a study guide in which entries are listed in order of increasing complexity. The study guide is followed by a list of abbreviations and symbols commonly used in astrology.

Students will find definitions of technical terms and explanations of the celestial geometry involved in chart calculation, with sixty diagrams and tables; a table of Standard Time meridians and information on Daylight Saving Time throughout the English-speaking world; and biographies of leading astrologers, complete with birth and death information, when available. Also included are introductions to branches such as electional, esoteric, horary, locational, medical, and mundane astrology; techniques such as transits, progressions, directions, solar returns, chart comparison, and composite charts; and approaches such as the sidereal zodiac, humanistic astrology, statistics, computers, the Uranian system, harmonics, and heliocentric astrology.

Professionals will find historical articles on such topics as Chinese, Hindu, Egyptian, and Pre-Columbian astrology; a comparative presentation of twenty different systems of house division, with diagrams showing how each is derived; information on two different dwad and decanate systems; an article on meaningful precision in astrological calculation, and one on professional ethics; a table of fixed stars; and a host of technical and astronomical information relevant to the theory and practice of astrology.

And skeptics—should this book fall into their hands—will find remarks on astronomy, relativity, the precession of the equinoxes, and statistics that might well challenge some of their cherished preconceptions.

In a real sense, then, this volume combines the functions of a dictionary, an encyclopedia, and a textbook. It defines the terms used in all the major branches of Western astrology, together with a good representation of those used in the East; it places those terms in historical perspective and explains how they fit into the theory of astrology; and it shows how they are used in practice by means of concrete examples and graphic illustrations. In using this threefold approach, the *Larousse Encyclopedia* reflects the spirit of Jean-Louis Brau's *dictionnaire de l'astrologie*, of which it is an expanded version.

The French text called itself a dictionary but was really a mini-encyclopedia. Not content with merely giving definitions, the author also gave delineations— that is, examples of the meaning of the planets in the signs and houses, a feature generally restricted to textbooks. Brau's book was also informed by a sense of history: There were articles on the contributions of various periods and peoples, from Chaldean astrology to the present, as well as biographies of astrologers and other figures important in the development of astrology. Furthermore, Brau did not limit himself to Western astrology but included instructions for finding one's sign according to the Chinese Buddhist zodiac and descriptions of the characteristics of each sign.

On the other hand, from the point of view of English-speaking readers, there were certain omissions in Brau's presentation. Thus, there were entries on Jean-Baptiste Morin and Paul Choisnard but none on Alan Leo or Dane Rudhyar. There was a perceptive analysis of the schools of modern astrology but no mention of Alfred Witte, Reinhold Ebertin, or John Addey, and only a passing reference to the pioneering research of French statisticians Michel and Françoise Gauquelin. The vexed question of house division was more or less avoided.

In keeping with the international spirit of the original, Allan Edmands and I have added entries on modern American, British, and German astrologers as well as scientists whose work has a bearing on astrology. In keeping with its inclusiveness, we have added material to reflect the multiplicity and controversy that characterizes modern astrology. And in keeping with its educational aims, we have expanded the interpretive entries to include more examples. The French edition contained 442 entries and 24 diagrams; the American edition contains 761 entries and 60 diagrams.

In the interests of clarity and organization, we have adopted some of the stylistic devices of standard reference works. For example, terms used within an entry that are defined elsewhere in entries of their own are set in small caps, thus: ASPECT. Additional cross-references appear in parentheses to guide the reader to related subjects, thus: (see ASPECT).

While we do not consistently give the derivations of words, we do include etymologies when they help to clarify meaning, make words easier to remember, or simply when they are interesting. Thus we noted that the word *cardinal*, which describes the signs of the zodiac that the Sun enters at the beginning of a new season, comes from the Latin word for "hinge" or "turning point."

Although the emphasis has been on the terms and concepts used in modern astrology, we have included some archaisms and near-archaisms—terms such as *affliction, besieged,* and *via combusta*—which readers might come across in the older textbooks.

But while we have included some archaic terminology, we have taken pains not to perpetuate certain outmoded assumptions, such as the sexism that continues to pervade much of modern astrology. We point out that the use of the words *masculine* and *feminine* to distinguish the more assertive fire and air signs from the more responsive earth and water signs often reflects a stereotyped view of sex roles that is increasingly being called into question. Whenever possible, we have tried to avoid the conventional use of *man* as a generic term for the human race. The medieval notion that "man is a microcosm of the universe" has been updated to include woman.

Another area subjected to scrutiny is the determinism that underlies much of classical astrology. We point out that terms such as *malefic* and *benefic* to describe planets or aspects are giving way to terms like *challenging* and *helpful*, or *hard* and *soft*. In general we have tried to avoid language that implies that the planets actually determine human behavior, a notion that is repellent to many people and to which, in fact, very few astrologers subscribe. Many modern astrologers view the planets in terms of information rather than influence and consider astrology to be a symbolic language rather than an empirical science. Others believe that there is an actual physical influence that has not as yet been understood or measured. But since there is no direct evidence of such influence, we have chosen not to speak in terms of causality. For example, it would be presumptuous to assert that "Saturn on the Ascendant makes a person serious, hard-working, and thrifty." We have tried to restrict ourselves to language such as "Saturn on the Ascendant is associated with seriousness, industry, and economy." Since the idea of causality is built into the English language, avoiding it sometimes makes for awkward sentence structure. Any causal terms that may have crept in should be taken with a grain of salt.

It may seem strange to some readers to find technical terms like *azimuth* and *right ascension* cheek by jowl with interpretive material on everything from the music of the spheres to the Age of Aquarius. Those not familiar with astrological literature—and some of those who are—may find this book a surprising mixture of astrology and astronomy, of philosophy and science. We would remind those readers that originally astrology and astronomy were a single discipline and that their separation is a relatively recent phenomenon when viewed from the perspective of history. The first astrologers were also the first astronomers, members of a priestly class who observed the motions of the heavenly bodies and interpreted those motions in terms of human affairs. The Greeks who modernized the ancient astrology of the Chaldeans made no distinction between philosophy and science. The medieval mind was dominated by the idea that each individual is a microcosm, a miniature version of the cosmos, and that everything in nature is linked together by a system of mysterious sympathies and correspondences. While not all astrologers were astronomers, a great many were; and some of the greatest astronomers the world has known, including Ptolemy, Brahe, Kepler, and Galileo, were practicing astrologers.

This situation of cooperation—or at any rate peaceful coexistence—between astrology and astronomy continued well into the seventeenth century. Then, for a variety of reasons, astrology fell into disfavor, first with scientists and then with educated people in general. With the new scientific discoveries, the development of the scientific method, and later, the invention of the telescope, science began to concern itself more and more with measurement and to leave questions of meaning to philosophy and theology. As science focused its attention outward onto measurable phenomena, human beings were thought of primarily as objective observers of nature rather than subjects of observation. Astronomy, the observation of the stars, began to separate itself from astrology, the interpretation of their significance to human beings. The organic model of the universe that prevailed in the Middle Ages—the concept of the microcosm within the macrocosm—was replaced in the eighteenth century by the mechanical model of the clock. Astrology, which retained the medieval idea that man is intimately connected to his cosmic environment, was dismissed as irrational superstition. Whereas in the Renaissance astrology had been an integral part of the curriculum, it was henceforth banished from the universities.

It was not until the twentieth century, when the new physics challenged the

Newtonian model of the universe and the social sciences reinstated human behavior as a fit subject for scientific inquiry, that the foundations were laid for a revival of serious astrology. (Popular astrology had survived, of course, but had been degraded to the level of fortune-telling, which made it all the more vulnerable to the contempt of science.) By mid-century Jung could write that astrology was once again knocking on the doors of the universities, and at this writing astrology is once again being taught at the university level, for the first time since the Renaissance.

After three hundred years of stagnation, during which it has been cut off from the mainstream of science, astrology is in the throes of rebirth. Current research has revealed the need to reassess traditional doctrine and, as Kepler once put it, to "separate the gems from the slag." At long last astrologers are coming out of their defensive isolation and developing a healthy respect for the scientific method. And although it cannot be said that scientists in general are developing a respect for astrology, there are a few scientists, impressed by research that reveals significant correlations between planetary motions and human behavior, who are beginning to listen. It may be only a matter of time before the gulf between astronomy, the science of observation, and astrology, the technique of interpretation, will be bridged and the two activities will seem no longer conflicting but complementary.

Such an integration can only be mutually enriching. For an astrology that refuses to submit to the rigors of controlled experiment is in danger of being overwhelmed by a mass of contradictory opinion; while a science that refuses to deal with questions of human value is in danger of being engulfed—and engulfing the world—in its own unbridled technology. So it is as a challenge to the imagination and as an act of faith in the ultimate reintegration of astrology and science that the language of quality and the language of quantity are here presented side by side. It is hoped that this book will not only provide readers with answers but will also raise some questions that had not occurred to them.

I would like to thank Pierre Larousse for his revolutionary idea of popularizing the encyclopedia in order to share elitist knowledge with ordinary people; Philip Rideout, my editor, for his imagination, sensitivity, and patience; Allan Edmands, without whose enthusiasm and expertise I could not have faced the task of revision; Dodie Edmands, for her eagle-eyed copy editing; and Mary Orser, for the use of her professional library. Also, the American Museum of Natural History, for supplying biographical information on Margaret Mead; the C. G. Jung Foundation, for their courteous assistance; Charles Emerson, for sharing his private files on Vernon Clark; Charles Jayne, for his generous help and encouragement; and Dane Rudhyar, for continued inspiration. I am especially grateful to Robert Hand and Charles Harvey, whose critical reading of the manuscript and many invaluable suggestions added significantly to the quality of the book.

Finally, I want to dedicate my work on this book to my father, the late Warren Weaver, a scientist who listened and who, at the end of his life, found the courage to open his mind to astrology.   —HELEN WEAVER

FOREWORD

The new *Larousse Encyclopedia of Astrology* is a masterly achievement on the part of all who shared in its creation. It has been translated from the French by Helen Weaver; but actually considerably more than a translation is involved, since she has greatly broadened the scope of the original edition. In this task she had the help of Allan Edmands, particularly on the technical and historical articles. There is very little that has not been included. It is also authoritative, for they consulted a number of experts in the field on all moot points. Hence disputed issues can usually be resolved.

Having had a hand in the creation of Nicholas de Vore's *Encyclopedia of Astrology* of 1947, I can appreciate the magnitude of their accomplishment. Excellent as that earlier encyclopedia was, much has happened in astrology in the interim, and there was an urgent need for updating. The *Larousse Encyclopedia* is a real contribution to modern astrology.

CHARLES JAYNE

How to Use This Book as a Textbook

The way to learn a language is to speak it; the way to learn astrology is to study your own birth chart. To master astrology, you must immerse yourself in the meanings of the signs, planets, houses, and aspects as you would the grammar and vocabulary of a new language. But at the same time, you must try to understand those meanings within the context of your own chart and the charts of the people you know best.

Within its alphabetized entries, the *Larousse Encyclopedia of Astrology* contains complete instructions for setting up birth charts as well as the basic tools for interpreting them. Thus, although it is organized as a reference book, it may also be used as a textbook. If you have little or no knowledge of astrology and would like to begin learning it, you may find it helpful to consult entries in the suggested order. On the other hand, you may prefer another order, or no order at all. If you do use the study guide, feel free to stop and explore related subjects by following up cross-references. (Cross-referenced terms are set in SMALL CAPS to indicate that they are discussed elsewhere in entries of their own.)

1. Read ASTROLOGY and ASTRONOMY.
2. Read SIGNS OF THE ZODIAC. Look up your Sun sign in the table and read the entry for that sign.
3. Read BIRTH CHART and ASCENDANT.
4. Read BIRTHTIME. Read and study TIME and determine from the table whether Daylight Saving Time was in effect at the time and in the locality of your birth. Read EPHEMERIS and TABLE OF HOUSES.
5. Obtain a table of houses and an ephemeris for the time of your birth. Assemble paper, pen, ruler, and compass or blank chart forms; read CHART

FORM. Read and study CHART CALCULATION and, following its step-by-step instructions, set up your own birth chart.

6. Read the entry for the sign on your Ascendant.
7. Read PLANETS, SUN, and MOON, and then read the entry for the sign occupied by your Moon. You now have a basic understanding of Sun, Moon, and Ascendant in your own chart and are ready to expand your knowledge.
8. Read QUALITIES, CARDINAL, FIXED, and MUTABLE; ELEMENTS, FIRE, EARTH, AIR, and WATER; and POLARITY. Then read the entries for the signs that are occupied by planets in your chart. Read RULERSHIP, DOMICILE, and EXALTATION.
9. Read and study HOUSES. Then read HEMISPHERE; DESCENDANT, MIDHEAVEN, and IMUM COELI; ANGULAR, SUCCEDENT, and CADENT; and DIGNITY.
10. Read BENEFIC and MALEFIC. Then read the entries for the planets in this order: MERCURY, VENUS, MARS, JUPITER, SATURN, URANUS, NEPTUNE, and PLUTO. Pay special attention to the suggested delineations for each planet in the sign and house it occupies in your chart.
11. Read and study ASPECT. Find the aspects in your chart. Next read CONJUNCTION, OPPOSITION, SQUARE, TRINE, SEXTILE, and the entries for any minor aspects you may have identified. Read RETROGRADE and APPLYING ASPECT.
12. Read MAJOR CONFIGURATION and check the entries for DOUBLE BIQUINTILE, DOUBLE QUINCUNX, GRAND CROSS, GRAND TRINE, KITE, MYSTIC RECTANGLE, and T-SQUARE to determine whether there are any major configurations in your chart.
13. Read PART OF FORTUNE. Calculate your Part of Fortune and enter it in your chart.
14. Read ECLIPTIC and NODES, and enter the Moon's nodes in your chart.
15. Read the entries for any remaining signs of the zodiac not occupied by planets in your chart.
16. Read the analysis of Margaret Mead's chart in CHART INTERPRETATION. Write an interpretation of your own chart.
17. Calculate and study the charts of your parents, teachers, friends, lovers, children, and other people you know well.
18. Read TRANSIT, PROGRESSION AND DIRECTION, SOLAR RETURN, CHART COMPARISON, COMPOSITE CHART, and ETHICS.

Abbreviations and Symbols Commonly Used in Astrology

Asc.	Ascendant	MC	*Medium Coeli*, or Midheaven
δ	declination	℞	retrograde

Desc.	Descendant	℞, α	right ascension
D	direct	SD	stationary direct
GMT	Greenwich Mean Time	S℞	stationary retrograde
GST	Greenwich Sidereal Time	ST	Standard Time or sidereal time
IC	*Imum Coeli*	SZ	sidereal zodiac
λ	longitude	TZ	tropical zodiac
β	latitude	d	day
LMT	local mean time	h	hour
LST	local sidereal time	m	minute of time
s	second of time	♈	Aries
+	north declination or latitude, or positive altitude	♉	Taurus
		♊	Gemini
−	south declination or latitude, or negative altitude	♋	Cancer
		♌	Leo
°	degree of arc	♍	Virgo
′	minute of arc	♎	Libra
″	second of arc	♏	Scorpio
☌	conjunction (0°)	♐	Sagittarius
☍	opposition (180°)	♑	Capricorn
□	square (90°)	♒	Aquarius
△	trine (120°)	♓	Pisces
✳	sextile (60°)	☉	Sun
⌄	semisextile (30°)	☽	Moon
⊼	quincunx (150°)	☿	Mercury
∠	semisquare (45°)	♀	Venus
⊡	sesquisquare (135°)	♂, ♂	Mars
★, Q	quintile (72°)	♃	Jupiter
±	biquintile (144°)	♄	Saturn
●	New Moon	♅, ♅	Uranus
☽	First Quarter	♆	Neptune
○	Full Moon	♇, ♇	Pluto
☾	Third Quarter	⊕	Earth or Part of Fortune
◕	eclipse of the Sun	☊	north node
◑	eclipse of the Moon	☋	south node

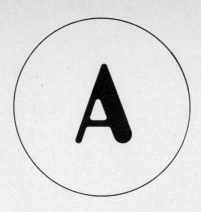

Absolute Longitude: See CELESTIAL LONGITUDE.

Acceleration: See LONGITUDE ACCELERATION; TIME ACCELERATION.

Accidental Dignity: See DIGNITY.

Adams, Evangeline: See ASTROLOGY AND THE LAW.

Addey, John (June 15, 1920, about 8:15 A.M., Barnsley, Yorkshire, England–): British philosopher and astrologer. Addey obtained his Master of Arts degree from Saint John's College, Cambridge. His serious interest in astrology began while he was still at school. In 1946 he joined the Astrological Lodge of the Theosophical Society, serving as its vice-president from 1951 to 1958. In 1951 he obtained the Faculty of Astrological Studies Diploma.

In the summer of 1955, his dissatisfaction with the confused and uncertain state of the art led him to try to find an acceptable and secure scientific approach to the subject. In his studies of 1956–57 on cases of longevity and polio, he perceived the beginning of a "wave theory" of astrology. Over the years his own experiments and observations, as well as his analysis of the statistical work of others, such as Donald Bradley, Brigadier R. C. Firebrace, and Michel GAUQUELIN, have led him to the conclusion that all astrological symbolism may be understood in terms of the fundamental concepts of cycle and number. He has demonstrated that all astrological effects—from signs, houses, aspects, and midpoints to such refinements as degree areas and the Hindu *shodasavargas*—can most fruitfully be understood in terms of the *harmonics of cosmic periods*. In the theory of HARMONICS he has uncovered a unifying principle—which in fact harks back to Pythagoras—capable of bringing together all schools and traditions of astrology and even of integrating astrology into the total spectrum of scientific thought, where, in Addey's own words, "astrology is destined to assume an almost central role."

In 1958 he inspired other astrologers to join him in founding the Astrological Association to promote the serious development and integration of astrology. From 1961 to 1973, as president of the Association, he

John Addey.

built it into the leading organization of its kind; he was also editor of the *Astrological Journal.* In 1970 he created the Urania Trust, an educational charity dedicated to the reintegration of astrology and astronomy into a single science.

Addey's quantitative work has not been motivated by a desire to incorporate astrology into the materialist world view, but rather by the aspiration "to get past the [materialist] scientists, who stand between astrology and its future supporters." For Addey the universe is a manifest expression of an inner and higher order of Truth, which may be revealed in part by the observation of the comos as the "written" Word of God.

Addey's major publications are *Astrology Reborn* (1972), *Harmonics in Astrology* (1976), *Harmonics Anthology* (1976), and *Selected Writings* (1976).
—Charles Harvey

Adjusted Calculation Date (ACD): See progression and direction.

Affliction: Condition of a planet that receives difficult aspects from other planets, especially the malefics, or that is in conjunction or parallel with the malefics. For example, the Moon is afflicted if it is squared by Venus and opposed by Jupiter; more so if it is squared by Venus and opposed by Mars; and even more so if it is conjunct Saturn and squared by Mars. Afflictions from benefics are considered to be easier to resolve. The most difficult afflictions are those that affect Sun, Moon, or Ascendant. A planet that receives many difficult aspects and few or no harmonious aspects is said to be heavily afflicted.

Afflictions in a birth chart represent psychological problems that require conscious effort if the native is to realize his or her full potential as a human being. The person with Moon conjunct Saturn and squared by Mars has to contend with very powerful emotions, especially anger, that he or she may be afraid to express, a situation that can generate tension and frustration, but also motivation for self-understanding and change. Heavily afflicted charts are sometimes associated with neurosis and psychosis, but they are often also the charts of highly creative people who accomplish a great deal, illustrating the truth of Blake's dictum, "Without contrarieties, no progression." (See benefic; malefic.)

Age of Aquarius: See Aquarian Age.

Ages, Astrological: See Precessional Age.

Ages of Man: An ancient theory according to which succeeding periods in the life of a human being are ruled by the planets, usually in the order of the length of their cycles. Thus infancy is ruled by the Moon, early education by Mercury, adolescence by Venus, early adulthood by the Sun, the prime of life by Mars, middle age by Jupiter, and old age by Saturn. (These planetary periods correspond roughly to the "Seven Ages of Man" described by Shakespeare in *As You Like It*, 2.7. 143–66, with the curious omission of the Sun.)

Authorities disagree on the length of these periods. The system that assigns 7 years to each planet fits in rather neatly with the quarter cycles of both transiting Saturn and the progressed Moon. It will also be noted that in the Catholic church, confirmation takes place at the canonical "age of discretion" (Mercury), at about age 7 years, thus ending the "age of innocence" (Moon); that the age of confirmation for Jews—an ancient rite of puberty (Venus)—is approximately 14; and that the age of legal majority (Sun) is still fixed at 21.

However, greater longevity and a slower aging process have caused the periods ruled by the outer planets, Jupiter and Saturn, to expand considerably; and the modern planets, Uranus, Neptune, and Pluto, have never been satisfactorily integrated into the scheme. But despite the lack of clear boundaries between one age and the next, these rulerships are still relevant. The Moon, standing for the unconscious and instinctual re-

Dutch copper engraving depicting the Seven Ages of Man. (The Bettman Archive.)

sponses, is still dominant in childhood; Mercury still rules the learning process, especially the acquisition of reading, writing, and arithmetic skills; and so on. The role of the modern planets—namely, the transformation of consciousness and the development of psychic ability—seems less geared to a temporal frame of reference of this kind. (See CYCLE.)

Agricultural Astrology: The branch of astrology that deals with the planting and harvesting of crops. This may be the oldest branch of astrology, because even before the invention of zodiacs or calendars, it was possible to observe the effects of planting or harvesting in relation to the phases of the Moon. Planting by the Moon is traditional in the East. In the West, astrological advice to farmers and gardeners is included in popular almanacs such as *Raphael's Almanac*, *The Farmer's Almanac*, and Llewellyn's *Moon Sign Book*. Raphael recommends sowing when the Moon is in the earth or water signs of the tropical zodiac. Llewellyn prefers the water signs for planting and pays attention to the phase of the Moon as well. For example, annuals and non-root crops are said to do better if planted under a waxing Moon; perennials and root crops under a waning Moon.

Orthodox studies of the relation of plant growth to lunar cycles tend to confirm the importance of phase rather than sign and suggest that response varies according to species. The American biologist Frank Brown has done extensive research on the response of various organisms to lunar cycles. Brown has found a consistent variation in a seed's capacity to absorb water, which is correlated with lunar phase and is unaffected by external magnetic fields.

Air: According to HERMETIC THEORY, one of the four ELEMENTS, under which the signs Gemini, Libra, and Aquarius, known as the *air triplicity* or *air trigon*, are classified. In astrology air stands for communication, relationship, and intellect. Alan LEO calls the air signs the "humane" signs. Originally they were all represented by human figures (the old symbol for Libra was a woman holding a scale).

An overemphasis of air signs in a chart may indicate a personality that is overly verbal or intellectual. A lack of air may be associated with difficulty in thinking clearly or expressing oneself, a disadvantage that may be considerably offset by a well-placed, well-aspected Mercury. (Also see CHINESE ASTROLOGY.)

Air Signs: See AIR.

Air Trigon: See AIR.

Air Triplicity: See AIR.

Albohali: See ISLAM, ASTROLOGY IN.

Albumazar (Latinized name of **abu-Mashar Ja'far ibn-Muhammad**; A.D. 805, Balkh, Khorasan province, Persia–886): Arab philosopher and astrologer of the school of Baghdad, pupil of Jacobus Alkindi (800–874). His writings were widely respected for several centuries. Among the most important are *The Book of the Astrologer* and *The Flowers of Astrology*, one of the first books to be printed by Gutenberg. Besides formulating the physical laws of the tides, Albumazar originated the theory of cycles, based on the geometrical symbolism of the Hermetists of the Neo-Alexandrine school, whereby great historical events are subject to the return of the *aduar* and the *akuar* (cycles of 360 solar years and 120 solar years, respectively).

Alcabitius System: See HOUSE DIVISION.

Allan, William Frederick: See LEO, ALAN.

Allen, Garth: See SIDEREAL ZODIAC.

Altitude: Angular distance measured in degrees, minutes, and seconds above or below the HORIZON of any locality, which is considered to have an altitude of 0°. Altitude above the horizon is positive; altitude below the horizon is negative. The ZENITH has the maximum altitude above (+90°), and the NADIR the maximum below (−90°). (See CELESTIAL COORDINATES; ELEVATION.)

Anareta (from the Greek *anairetes,* destroyer): The destroyer of life; a MALEFIC or other planet that is in unfavorable aspect to the HYLEG. The term is seldom used in modern astrology.

Androgynous (from the Greek *andros,* man, and *gyne,* woman): Having the characteristics of both sexes; a term used to describe the planet Mercury, which PTOLEMY classified as neither masculine nor feminine.

Angle: In a birth chart, one of the four cardinal points representing the places where the HORIZON plane of the birthplace and the MERIDIAN plane intersect the ECLIPTIC. The angles are referred to variously as ASCENDANT, DESCENDANT, MIDHEAVEN, and IMUM COELI; east, west, north, and south; or the cusps of the First, Seventh, Fourth, and Tenth Houses, respectively. The HOUSES of which these angles form the cusps are called *angular houses* (see CUSP; HOUSE DIVISION).

The four angles are the most sensitive points on the birth chart, and traditionally any planet on or near an angle, especially if it is in an angular house, will have a strong and conspicuous influence on the native's personality (Ascendant and Descen-

dant) or public image (Midheaven and Imum Coeli); but see ANGULAR, and GAUQUELIN, MICHEL AND FRANÇOISE.

Angular: A term used to describe the HOUSES in a horoscope that immediately follow the *angles,* proceeding in a counterclockwise direction, or the planets occupying such houses (see ANGLE). The angular houses are the First, Fourth, Seventh, and Tenth; they correspond to the CARDINAL signs, and planets in those houses are associated with initiation and leadership. A planet is said to be strengthened by being angular, just as it is weakened by being *cadent*— that is, placed in one of the houses immediately preceding the angles of the chart.

The angular houses are regarded as the strongest in the chart, the traditional order of strength being: First, Tenth, Seventh, and Fourth. Planets occupying these houses are thereby accidentally dignified and are believed to have a conspicuous influence on the native's personality, especially if they are on or near the angles (see DIGNITY). The traditional importance of angular planets (especially those near the First and Tenth House cusps) in influencing personality and profession has recently been confirmed by statistical evidence, although the traditional meaning of angular houses has not (see GAUQUELIN, MICHEL AND FRANÇOISE).

Angular Distance: 1. Any distance on an arc that can be expressed in degrees, minutes, and seconds. **2.** The distance in arc, expressed in degrees of CELESTIAL LONGITUDE, between two straight lines, each connecting a planet or other point with a hypothetical observer located at a point on the Earth, usually the birthplace of an individual. Angular relationships between planets, especially certain recognized divisions of the circle, are referred to in astrology as *aspects* (see ASPECT).

Angular Signs: See CARDINAL.

Annular Eclipse: See ECLIPSE.

Anomalistic Period: In the orbit of a satellite around a primary, the period between one closest approach to the primary and the next. The anomalistic period of a planet is measured from one PERIHELION to the next; of the Moon, from one PERIGEE to the next. There is very little difference in duration between an anomalistic period and a sidereal period. (See ORBIT.)

Antiscion: A point that is equidistant with a given planet from either *solstice point* (0° Cancer or 0° Capricorn) but on the opposite side. For example, if Mars is at 18° Gemini, its antiscion is at 12° Cancer; likewise if Saturn is at 23° Pisces, its antiscion is at 7° Libra. The *contrascion* is a point equidistant with a given planet from either *equinox point* (0° Aries or 0° Libra) but on the opposite side; it is always directly opposite the antiscion. When a planet is at the antiscion degree of another planet in a

natal chart or reaches that degree by progression, direction (see PROGRESSION AND DIRECTION), or TRANSIT, the two bodies have a relationship similar to an ASPECT. The antiscion has been compared to a CONJUNCTION and the contrascion to an OPPOSITION. If both planets related by antiscion have 0° CELESTIAL LATITUDE (that is, if both are on the ECLIPTIC), the aspect is actually a *parallel*; if both planets related by contrascion have 0° latitude, the aspect is a *contraparallel* (see PARALLEL). Some astrologers refer to antiscions as "solstice points"—an ambiguous usage which is best avoided.

Antivertex: See EAST POINT; VERTEX.

Aphelion (from the Greek *apo*, away, and *helios*, Sun): The point in a planet's ORBIT that is most distant from the Sun, or the moment when the planet is at that point. (See PERIHELION.)

Apheta: See HYLEG.

Apogee (from the Greek *apo*, away, and *gaia*, Earth): The point in the Moon's ORBIT that is most distant from the Earth, or the moment when the Moon is at that point. (See PERIGEE.)

Apparent Horizon: See HORIZON.

Apparent Motion: Motion observed from a geocentric point of view—that is, motion relative to the Earth, which is thought of as stationary. The Sun, Moon, planets, and stars have a daily apparent motion of rising in the east, culminating on the local MERIDIAN, and setting in the west. This apparent motion results from the Earth's rotation on its axis. The Sun has a yearly apparent motion around the entire zodiac along the ECLIPTIC, a motion that is actually the Earth's annual orbit around the Sun. A planet in its circuit through the zodiac apparently stops, travels backward for a while, stops again, and resumes forward motion—an illusion caused by the Earth's own motion relative to that of the planet (see RETROGRADE). All the constellations as a unit—the entire starry fabric of the heavens—appear to move slowly forward through the TROPICAL ZODIAC, but this appearance is due to another of the Earth's own motions, the "wobble" of its rotational axis about the ecliptic pole (see PRECESSION OF THE EQUINOXES).

That the Earth is not the stationary center of the universe around which all else moves was known to several observers in ancient Greece, but the geocentric concept continued to be dominant in the human imagination until it was challenged by Nicolaus COPERNICUS (1473–1543). Now most people are aware that apparent motion is really a result of the Earth's motion. Nonetheless, apparent motion is the motion actually observed and measured; "true" motion is calculated or derived from it by mathematics. Moreover, according to the theory of relativity, any given observational viewpoint, including that of the Earth considered as stationary, is as valid as any other and may be use-

ful in describing circumstances in the vicinity of the observer.

Apparent Solar Time: See TIME.

Applying Aspect (or **Approaching Aspect**): An ASPECT in which one planet is approaching the point of exactitude; an aspect that has not yet become exact. For example, if the Moon is at 10° Cancer and Pluto is at 16° Libra, the Moon is said to be applying to a square with Pluto. The faster-moving body is said to be applying to the aspect with the slower one. A *doubly applying* (or *doubly approaching*) aspect is one in which both planets are moving toward the aspect point. In the foregoing example, if Pluto were RETROGRADE, the aspect would be doubly applying.

A *separating aspect* is one in which the faster-moving planet is moving away from the aspect point. For example, if the Moon is at 18° Cancer and Pluto is at 16° Libra, the Moon is said to be separating from a square with Pluto. A *doubly separating* aspect is one in which both bodies are moving away from the aspect point, as would be the case in the example just cited if Pluto were retrograde. An applying aspect is said to be stronger than a separating one, and its strength is said to be greatest immediately before it becomes exact.

Applying and separating should not be confused with *dexter* and *sinister aspects*, which indicate the phase of an aspect in the complete 360° cycle (see DEXTER ASPECT).

Approaching Aspect: See APPLYING ASPECT.

Aquarian Age: The next great PRE-CESSIONAL AGE after the *Piscean Age*; the post-Christian era. Many astrologers believe that the human race is currently in a state of transition between the Piscean Age and the Aquarian Age. Evidence for this belief includes the accelerating rate of social and cultural change; the decline of many of the institutions of Western society, such as orthodox religion in general and Christianity in particular; the changing role of women; the collapse of the economy; the rise of violence and the threat of global extinction by nuclear war or ecological disaster or both—a total picture that is interpreted by some observers as a general collapse of Western civilization as we know it.

During the Piscean Age, Western culture has been dominated by Christianity, a religion of salvation that offers the promise of eternal life in exchange for self-denial in this life. The Piscean model of human perfection is Christ, the son of God, who agreed to become human and to suffer death in exchange for the potential salvation of the human race. Piscean virtues are renunciation, self-sacrifice, otherworldliness, deferred pleasure, the accumulation of credit for the future (capitalism) rather than enjoyment of the present. Curiously, the early symbol for Christianity was the fish, which is also the symbol for the sign of Pisces; and Jesus told the twelve apostles that they were "fishers of men."

Indications often given for the imminence of the Aquarian Age include the rise of group consciousness, as evidenced by communism, socialism, communes, intentional and spiritual communities, nonbiological families, tribalism, Woodstock Nation, group therapy, and group sex; internationalism; the rise of technology, including computers and space travel; television, which turns the planet into a small town; the trend toward social planning and equal distribution of wealth instead of resigned acceptance of an unjust social and economic hierarchy; and in general, an emphasis on science and reason rather than religion and faith.

Since constellations have invisible, nebulous, and overlapping boundaries, there is no agreement as to the exact location of this critical cusp; but some astrologers believe the "eye of the storm" will be experienced before the year 2000. The entrance of Pluto, planet of profound collective transformation, into its own sign of Scorpio in 1984, and the conjunction of Saturn, Uranus, and Neptune in Capricorn in 1988–89 are sometimes cited as decisive. Some astrologers regard the entrance of the star Alcyone into tropical Gemini in 2001 as marking the change; others look forward to Regulus's entry into Virgo in 2012 (see STAR). However, calculations by astrologers using the SIDEREAL ZODIAC would place the beginning of the Aquarian Age far into the future. For example, Robert de Luce would place the beginning in A.D. 2157, Cyril FAGAN in A.D. 2374. (See PRECESSION OF THE EQUINOXES.)

Aquarius (glyph ♒): The eleventh sign of the zodiac, which the Sun

 Aquarius

transits during the second month of winter, from about January 21 to about February 20. The symbol for this sign is the water bearer. Its PO-LARITY is positive, its element is air (see ELEMENTS), its quality is fixed (see QUALITIES), its ruling planet is Uranus (see RULERSHIP), its traditional ruler is Saturn, and its NATU-RAL HOUSE is the Eleventh.

In Aquarius the intellectuality of air and the persistence of fixity are combined with the innovating force of Uranus to create an individual who can be liberal and opinionated at the same time. The symbol for Aquarius is a human figure holding a jug of water; yet Aquarius is an air sign. The water here does not represent emotion, but truth. Aquarians—who include not only Sun-sign Aquarians, but all in whose charts the sign is emphasized—are seekers and disseminators of truth. This is the same truth of which the Bible says, "And ye shall know the truth, and the truth shall make you free" (John 8:32). They are dedicated to the realization of the ideal society, characterized by liberty, equality, and fraternity. Where Leo, the opposite sign on the zodiac wheel, believes in monarchy and the divine right of kings, Aquarius believes in democracy and the divine right of human beings.

Rulership of Aquarius was traditionally assigned to Saturn, a planet that accords with the sign's rationality and interest in government and science. After the discovery of Uranus, that planet became the modern ruler of Aquarius, as appropriate to its unconventionality and interest in social reform and progress. Guided by reason rather than convention, Aquarians reject the prevailing norms, now reaching into the future to discover the new technology of tomorrow, now delving into the past to revive the simpler ways of yesterday. Either way, these independent thinkers seem slightly "out of synch" with their time. Aquarius can produce cranks, agitators, and fanatics—"rebels without a cause"—or humanitarian leaders and inspired geniuses of the highest kind.

All the air signs are concerned with relationship, but while Gemini is the sign of brothers and sisters and Libra of husbands and wives, Aquarius is the sign of friends. Most Aquarians feel more at home in a group of people with like interests than in an intimate situation.

Even Aquarian babies come to life in company and delight in cutting into adult conversations with their own babbling comments. Parents are sometimes troubled by their Aquarian offsprings' unpredictable sleeping and eating patterns, not to mention their frequent insurrections. Aquarian children have minds of their own and will not react well to an arbitrary show of authority. But their originality and ingenuity will make their parents proud.

Aquarians are capable of love, but their version is somewhat impersonal. Much of their energy is likely to go into group activities, public life, or some absorbing project of value to mankind, and their partners must give them freedom to pursue their distant goals. Though seldom passionate, they are faithful and can be highly imaginative lovers. Uranus rules unconventionality, and Aquarius is associated with homosexuality, bisexuality, and group sex. Their most compatible signs are Gemini, Libra, Sagittarius, and Aries; Capricorn, Pisces, Cancer, and Virgo are neutral; Taurus and Scorpio are likely to be difficult. With another Aquarius, there is a good basis for friendship. With Leo there will be both attraction and tension; but ultimately the question of COMPATIBILITY can be answered only by careful comparison of two whole birth charts.

Aquarians like to work in groups, or if alone, they must feel that their work makes a contribution to mankind. The sign is associated with intellectual activity, especially writing, inventing, and science; politics, usually liberal; and the arts, especially music. Because it is a group effort demanding technical skill, film making seems to be a natural. Famous Sun-sign Aquarians include Susan B. Anthony, Francis Bacon, Colette, Charles Darwin, James Dean, Charles Dickens, Thomas Edison, Sergei Eisenstein, Federico Fellini, W. C. Fields, John Ford, D. W. Griffith, Abraham Lincoln, Charles Lindbergh, Thomas More, Wolfgang Amadeus Mozart, Thomas Paine, Franklin Delano Roosevelt, Franz Schubert, Gertrude Stein, and Adlai Stevenson. (See BIRTHSTONES; COLORS; DAYS OF THE WEEK; METALS.)

Aquinas, Saint Thomas (1225?–74): Italian scholastic philosopher and theologian, author of the systematization of Catholic doctrine known as Thomism. Aquinas acknowledged the influence of the planets but believed that human beings could modify that influence by the use of reason. In reconciling astrology with the Christian doctrine of free will, Aquinas arrived at a position that is very close to that of modern esoteric astrologers. In *Summa Theologica,* he wrote, "Are the celestial bodies the cause of human action? I reply that one must say that the celestial bodies exert a force upon men directly and through themselves . . . but they only act indirectly and by accident on the forces of the soul which animate the bodily organs. . . . Most men follow their corporal passions; their actions therefore for most of the time are subject to the influences of the celestial bodies. There are but a few wise men alone who moderate these influences by their reason. This is why in many cases astrologers announce true things, especially for events which depend on humans in groups." (See CHRISTIANITY AND ASTROLOGY.)

Arabian Parts: A group of points used by Arabian astrologers, obtained by adding the difference in CELESTIAL LONGITUDE between two planets to the celestial longitude of the Ascendant. For example, the longitude of the Ascendant plus the longitude of the Moon minus the longitude of the Sun equals the PART OF FORTUNE. The Part of Love is the Ascendant plus Venus minus the Sun; the Part of Spirit is the Ascendant plus the Sun minus the Moon. According to some authorities, the Arabian parts should be calculated in RIGHT ASCENSION rather than longitude and then brought back to the ecliptic.

Ancient astrologers attributed considerable importance to these Arabian parts; modern astrologers generally ignore them, with the exception of the Part of Fortune. It should also be noted, however, that the URANIAN SYSTEM of astrology, with its use of mathematical formulas, midpoints, and planetary pictures, owes a great deal to the Arabian theory of parts. For example, the midpoint between the Moon and Ascendant is also the midpoint between the Sun and the Part of Fortune; thus a square or opposition to the Part of Fortune makes a complete planetary picture. (See ISLAM, ASTROLOGY IN.)

Arc of Direction: See PROGRESSION AND DIRECTION.

Arcturan System: See HOUSE DIVISION.

Aries (glyph ♈): The first sign of the zodiac, which the Sun transits during the first month of spring, from about March 21 to about April 20. The symbol for this sign is the ram. Its POLARITY is positive, its element is fire (see ELEMENTS), its quality is cardinal (see QUALITIES), its ruling planet is Mars (see RULERSHIP), and its NATURAL HOUSE is the First.

The Sun's entrance into Aries marks the first day of spring and the beginning of the astrological year. Aries is essentially a sign of beginnings, of boundless creativity and pure energy. Arians—who include not only Sun-sign Arians, but all in whose charts the sign is emphasized—must be up and doing for the sheer joy of it, especially if the activity involves adventure, the exploration of unknown territory, and even danger. The rulership of Mars bestows strength and courage, and a strong desire nature, which means both sexual desire and the drive to conquer and possess material things, power, and fame. The incredible Aries energy in initiating new projects is a blend of the enthusiasm and self-confidence of fire and the outgoing activity of cardinality. The polar opposite of indecisive Libra, Arians seldom have time to look before they leap; they simply rush forward headlong, for it is their business to lead and to inspire.

Aries babies are in such a hurry to advance that they may walk at nine months. But walking won't suffice

♈ Aries

for long; almost all Aries children prefer running. Aries children are sometimes labeled "hyperactive" by their teachers, but their parents become accustomed to their fights with friends, frequent accidents from which they quickly rebound, and noisy resistance to bedtime. Their overflowing energy finds a healthy outlet in competitive sports.

The Aries personality has the virtues of its defects: An unconscious egotism, which may express itself as arrogance, aggression, and even violence, can coexist with a childlike innocence, a total absence of guile, and a devout love of freedom. The essence of Aries is the life force itself, the desire to be born and the will to survive, and the intensity of the Aries energy makes both the primitive and the evolved types virtually unstoppable. In contrast to legalistic, diplomatic Libra, Aries is a law unto itself, responsible only to its own unpredictable impulses.

Aries natives' strong sex drive makes them passionate lovers, but their desire for conquest and love of novelty can lead to a Don Juan or *femme fatale* syndrome that is ultimately unsatisfying. As the sign of individualism, Aries does not have a natural instinct for partnership. However, Aries natives have a great love of children, with whom they identify as primitive beings, and they are capable of forming stable relationships with those who respect their need for independence. Their most compatible signs are Leo, Sagittarius, Gemini, and Aquarius. Taurus, Virgo, Scorpio, and Pisces are neutral, while Cancer and Capricorn are likely to be difficult. A pair of Arians would probably compete for dominance. With Aries and Libra there is both attraction and tension, the outcome depending, as with all combinations, on other factors in the two charts (see COMPATIBILITY).

Before the feminist movement Aries was thought to be an unfortunate sign for women, but recently the powerful Aries woman has started coming into her own. Pearl Bailey, Joan Crawford, Bette Davis, Billie Holiday, Erica Jong, Clare Booth Luce, Bessie Smith, Gloria Steinem, and Gloria Swanson all have Sun in Aries.

Aries people are drawn to such diverse occupations as explorer, adventurer, military leader, athlete, actor, musician, researcher, and artist. The influence of Mars, which rules metals and firearms, gives them a natural affinity for metallurgy, mechanics, surgery, butchery, and policework. A few famous male examples of the indomitable Aries spirit are Johann Sebastian Bach, Otto von Bismarck, Marlon Brando, Giovanni Casanova, Charles Chaplin, Charlemagne, César Chavez, Thomas Jefferson, Wilhelm Reich, John D. Rockefeller III, Ravi Shankar, and Vincent van Gogh. (See BIRTHSTONES; COLORS; DAYS OF THE WEEK; METALS.)

Armillary Sphere: An instrument consisting of an assemblage of rings, or *armils* (from the Latin *armilla*, bracelet), representing the CELESTIAL EQUATOR, two parallels of DECLINATION (corresponding to the Tropics of Cancer and Capricorn), the ECLIPTIC, the HORIZON, and the MERIDIAN, with which ancient astronomers made approximate observations, calculated house cusps, and so on. It is said to have been invented by Thales or Anaximander (sixth century B.C.). (See COSMOGRAPHY.)

Ascendant (from the Latin *ascendere*, to rise; often abbreviated **Asc.**): The degree of the zodiac rising at the eastern horizon of the birthplace at the moment of birth—that is, the eastern point of intersection of HORIZON and ECLIPTIC—usually the cusp of the First House (see COSMOGRAPHY; HOUSE DIVISION). Historically, *Ascendant* has been synonymous with *horoscope* (from the Greek *hora*, hour, and *skopos*, watcher), but the two words have come to have different meanings.

Knowledge of the Ascendant is of the utmost importance in interpreting a birth chart. Since it expresses the exact moment when the native begins independent existence, it is very specific and personal, indicating the first impression made on other people, the native's distinctive style of interacting with them, his or her outward personality and mannerisms—even physical appearance. Combined with Sun sign and Moon sign, the Ascendant can provide much preliminary information about the native's personality.

One sign of the zodiac may take from less than ½ hour to over 3 hours to cross the horizon, but within 24 hours, all twelve signs will have risen. Thus, the average time it takes for a sign to rise is 2 hours. Since there are 30° in a sign, a new degree appears on the horizon on the average of every 4 minutes. It follows that in order to determine an accurate Ascendant, an astrologer must have, in addition to the TERRESTRIAL LONGITUDE and LATITUDE of the birthplace, a reasonably precise time of birth. Without this information he cannot determine a true Ascendant, and without a true Ascendant, the horoscope has approximately the value of a negative that is out of focus: better than nothing, but leaving much to be desired.

In most systems of HOUSE DIVISION the Ascendant is identical with the CUSP of the First House. The sign on that cusp is known as the Ascendant sign, or rising sign. A person with the Sun in Taurus who has the cusp of the First House at 20° Gemini, for example, is said to be "Taurus, with Gemini rising."

The planet that rules the sign on the Ascendant is regarded as the ruler of the Ascendant (see RULERSHIP). Many astrologers regard this planet as the ruler of the entire chart. In the example cited, the ruler of the Ascendant is Mercury, because Mercury rules Gemini, the sign on the Ascendant, or First House cusp.

Any planet that is close to the Ascendant—some astrologers use an ORB of 15° in either direction—exerts a powerful influence on the Ascendant. This is true to a lesser degree of any planet POSITED in the First House. If there are several planets in the First House, the one that most strongly colors the Ascendant is the one closest to the cusp.

The Ascendant was once regarded as more important than the Sun, the reverse of the situation in the twentieth century, in which media-fed consumerism and the desire for instant knowledge has given rise to commercialized Sun-sign astrology. Thus tradition has it that Louis XIV was a Sun-sign Virgo with Leo rising, the qualities of despotic Leo outweighing those of modest Virgo and earning him the nickname of "Sun King." Even today some astrologers believe that the Ascendant is more immediately revealing of the native's personality than is the Sun sign. In any case, the importance of the Ascendant is one reason why the ready-made horoscopes published in newspapers and magazines are misleading.

Ascendant Arc: See PROGRESSION AND DIRECTION.

Ascendant House System: See HOUSE DIVISION.

Ascending Node: See NODES.

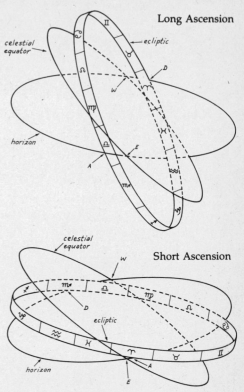

Figure 1. The distinction between long and short ascension. The changing signs on the Ascendant **(A)** is a phenomenon of the Earth's diurnal rotation, expressed as a continuous unvarying motion of the celestial equator relative to the horizon. The ecliptic is "tied" to the celestial equator. Thus, when the angle between the ecliptic and the horizon is small, signs will cross the Ascendant rapidly. When the angle is large, signs will cross the Ascendant slowly. The two situations illustrated here are for midlatitudes north of the Equator. In the Southern Hemisphere the situation is reversed, since Aries through Virgo are on the portion of the ecliptic that is *below* the celestial equator, while Libra through Pisces are *above* it. **A** = Ascendent, **D** = Descendent, **E** = East Point, **W** = West Point.

Ascension, Long or Short: Because of the obliquity of the ecliptic, in midlatitude regions the angle between the HORIZON and the ECLIPTIC varies hour after hour, causing some signs to move across the Ascendant faster than others. The faster-moving signs are called *signs of short ascension*; the slower-moving signs are called *signs of long ascension*. In the Northern Hemisphere signs of short ascension are Capricorn through Gemini (with Pisces and Aries being the shortest); signs of long ascension are Cancer through Sagittarius (with Virgo and Libra being the longest). In the Southern Hemisphere midlatitudes the situation is reversed. (See figure 1.)

Aspect (from the Latin *aspicere, aspectum,* to look at): Angular relationship between two planets or important points on the zodiac; one of a set of specific angles. In a birth chart, aspects are the building blocks of character, and the interpretation of a chart depends to a great extent on the study of aspects. It is worth noting that the archaic meaning of *aspect* was "glance," "gaze," or "appearance." Its use in astrology is part of an anthropomorphic legacy in which planets are "lords" and "rulers" and have "domiciles" and "mansions." Thus the planets' aspects were how they "looked at" each other—that is, in a friendly or unfriendly manner. This may explain why classical astrologers did not consider the conjunction, when two planets occupy the same degree, as an aspect but rather as a position.

The German astronomer Johannes KEPLER was the first to formulate a general theory of aspects and to divide them into major and minor. Major aspects include the *conjunction,* when two planets have the same CE-LESTIAL LONGITUDE; the *opposition,* when they are opposite each other on the zodiac, that is, when they form an angle of 180°; the *square,* when they form an angle of 90°; the *trine,* when they form an angle of 120°; and the *sextile,* when they form an angle of 60° (see figure 2).

Minor aspects include the *semisquare* (45°), sometimes called the *octile,* and the *sesquisquare* (135°), also called the *sesquiquadrate* or *sesquare;* the *semisextile* (30°) and the *quincunx* (150°); the *quintile* (72°), the *biquintile* (144°), and the *decile* (36°). The minor aspects are a fairly modern innovation. PTOLEMY recognized only the major aspects; he did not consider the conjunction an aspect, although he treated it as one, and dismissed the quincunx as the "inconjunct." The minor aspects, including the quintile group, were introduced by

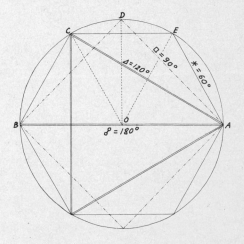

Figure 2. Aspects. **O** is the point of reference—usually the Earth. **A, B, C, D,** and **E** are possible directions for planets or other important points. Planets **A** and **B** are opposed; angle **AOB** is 180°. Planets **A** and **C** are trine; angle **AOC** is 120°. Planets **A** and **D** are square; angle **AOD** is 90°. Planets **A** and **E** are sextile; angle **AOE** is 60°.

Kepler; the semisextile and quincunx may have been introduced by Jean-Baptiste MORIN. (See ANTISCION; PARALLEL.)

Classical astrologers characterized aspects as *benefic* or *malefic*, that is, good or bad. Most modern astrologers find these terms antiquated and feel that they convey an unfortunate determinism; they prefer to use such words as *helpful* and *challenging*, or *soft* and *hard*, to distinguish the two general categories of aspects. It will be noted that the hard aspects all derive from repeated division of the circle by two, whereas the soft aspects represent division of the circle by three, five, six, or twelve.

The quality of the conjunction is regarded as dependent on the nature of the planets it brings together. For

Architectural "sextant" of sixty steps at the observatory at Samarkand. Each step enabled astrologers to observe the sky from a different angle. (Photo by Boudot-Lamotte.)

example, a conjunction of Moon and Venus would be helpful, whereas a conjunction of Mars and Saturn would be difficult. The trine, which combines signs of the same element, is considered helpful; the sextile, which combines signs of harmonious elements, perhaps even more so. The sextile seems to require a little more effort on the native's part; the trine is sometimes associated with laziness and lack of motivation. The opposition and square are deemed difficult, although the stress they indicate may also be a spur to personal growth. The general consensus of modern astrologers is that the square is harder to resolve than the opposition. This may be because in an opposition the two planets are usually in signs of harmonious elements, whereas this is usually not the case in the square (see COMPATIBILITY).

In interpreting a birth chart, the different aspects are not given the same strength. Most astrologers find that the closer an aspect is to being exact, the stronger it is; but its strength also depends on the orbs of the planets involved. An *orb* is a spherical space of variable size surrounding a planet or sensitive point within which its influence or receptivity with respect to other bodies is considered to operate. The exact size of the orbs of the planets has never been established, but the general rule is the faster the planet or point is moving—and thus the sooner it will form a given aspect with another planet—the wider its orb. Thus the Moon or Ascendant may have orbs of up to 15°, whereas Uranus, Neptune, or Pluto may be assigned only

2°. An exception to this rule is the Sun, which is granted an orb comparable to the Moon's by virtue of its importance. Orbs for aspects between Sun, Moon, or faster-moving planets and slower-moving planets are an average of the greater and the lesser orb.

By the same token, orbs for applying aspects are greater than those for separating aspects (see APPLYING ASPECT). Orbs also vary according to the strength of the aspect. Thus the orb allowed for a major aspect, such as the conjunction or opposition, is wider than that permitted for a minor aspect, such as the quintile or sesquisquare. Orbs are increased in cases where there is TRANSLATION OF LIGHT. Finally, orbs vary according to the strength and importance of a planet within a particular chart. Thus a slow-moving planet such as Saturn may be given a wider orb than usual if it is the ruler of the Ascendant, dignified by sign or house position, CULMINATING or on an ANGLE, the ruler of a STELLIUM, part of a MAJOR CONFIGURATION, or emphasized in some other way.

With all these factors to consider, there can be no hard-and-fast rules, but many astrologers allow 8° to 10° for the conjunction, 6° to 8° for the opposition, 5° to 6° for the square, 4° to 6° for the trine and sextile, and 2° for the minor aspects.

The strength of an aspect is decreased if it is "out of sign," that is, if the planets are within orb of aspect but their respective signs do not correspond to the aspect involved. For example, if Mercury is at 27° Gemini and Jupiter is RETROGRADE at 3°

Pisces, the two planets are within orb of a trine, but their signs are in square. The trine is said to be "out of sign." The aspect "works," especially since it is doubly applying, but is weaker than it would be if Mercury were in 0° Cancer, and in trine to Jupiter by sign as well as by longitude. Out-of-sign aspects are less conspicuous than in-sign aspects and hence are easily overlooked, even by experienced astrologers.

The foregoing discussion of aspects represents a blend of traditional and modern ideas. The major aspects are traditional, the minor aspects modern; the idea of good and bad aspects is traditional, the more neutral approach implied by *hard* and *soft* is modern. The idea of orb is a fairly recent one; there is good reason to believe that in defining the major aspects, Ptolemy was really talking about the relationship between signs: In other words, any two planets in water signs would be in trine, regardless of degree. This is still the approach taken by Hindu astrology (see INDIA, ASTROLOGY IN).

The latest trend in aspect theory, which reflects the impact of NELSON'S work in weather forecasting and ADDEY'S work in HARMONICS, is toward more aspects and smaller orbs. The study of harmonics has introduced the possibility that all divisions of the circle may be relevant—or at least many more than have been considered in the past. And Nelson's success in predicting radio disturbances by observing patterns in the heliocentric positions of the planets (what he—independently of Addey—calls "simultaneous multiple harmonics") suggests that aspects are more powerful in groups than singly. Nelson's findings provide a heliocentric parallel to the Uranian use of "planetary pictures" (see URANIAN SYSTEM). The importance of major configurations in the work of heliocentric astrologers Michael and Margaret Erlewine is part of the modern trend to consider aspects in combination rather than in isolation.

Amid the current uncertainty over such questions as HOUSE DIVISION, RULERSHIP, and even the validity of the zodiac itself, aspect theory stands out as one of the few areas where astrological tradition is being both supported and refined by research. The exploration of aspects may well be the wave of the future. (See CONJUNCTION; MUNDANE ASPECT; OPPOSITION; PARALLEL; SEXTILE; SQUARE; TRINE; and so on. Also see HARMONICS.)

Aspectarian: A section included in most EPHEMERIDES that lists all the major planetary aspects for a given period, usually a month, in order of formation (see ASPECT). The time when an aspect reaches exactitude is generally given in *Ephemeris Time* or *Greenwich Mean Time* (see TIME), either of which may be converted to the desired local time by adding (east of Greenwich) or subtracting (west of Greenwich) the appropriate number of hours. (See sample page from an ephemeris, page 48.)

Asteroids (also called **Minor Planets** or **Planetoids**): Thousands of small bodies invisible to the naked eye, nearly all of whose orbits lie between Mars and Jupiter (but see CHIRON). The four largest—CERES, PALLAS, JUNO, and VESTA—were discovered in 1801, 1802, 1804, and 1807, respectively. Because of the difficulty in obtaining accurate positions, the asteroids were ignored by most astrologers until 1973, when Eleanor Bach undertook to have an astronomer prepare an ephemeris of the first four. Her pioneering work led to greater use of the asteroids among serious astrologers, especially those with a humanistic orientation. A more accurate ephemeris for these bodies was published under the direction of Dr. Zipporah Dobyns in 1977.

Bach assigns all the asteroids to Virgo. She believes that they are related to the general welfare of humankind and have a civilizing or humanizing influence that is peculiarly feminine. She associates them with women's liberation, ecology, nutrition, birth control, and abortion reform. Dobyns assigns Ceres and Vesta to Virgo and Juno and Pallas to Libra. She associates Ceres and Vesta with the work ethic and service and Juno and Pallas with justice and equality, especially women's liberation.

Astrocartography: See LOCATIONAL ASTROLOGY.

Astroeconomics: The application of astrological principles to the world of business and finance. Astrologers specializing in this area may study the charts of large corporations or corporation executives (NATAL ASTROLOGY) or correlate the motions of the planets with trends in international trade and the stock market (MUNDANE ASTROLOGY). Fluctuations in the Dow Jones Average have been linked to the cycles of Jupiter and Saturn: Jupiter, the principle of expansion, is associated with optimism, rising prices, and inflation; Saturn, the principle of contraction, with caution, falling prices, and scarcity. The great technical astrologer L. E. JOHNDRO supported himself partly by playing the stock and commodity market; he also advised prominent business people about their investments.

Astroflash: See BARBAULT, ANDRÉ; COMPUTERS AND ASTROLOGY.

Astrolabe (from the Greek *astron*, star, and *lambanein*, to take): A compact instrument said to have been invented by HIPPARCHUS (second century B.C.) for observing the positions of the heavenly bodies and determining their elevation above the horizon. Astrologers used the astrolabe in or-

Astrolabe of Abu Bakr ibn Iusuf. Each disk corresponds to a season. (Musée Paul-Dupuy, Toulouse; photo by Lauros-Giraudon.)

der to erect horoscopes before the publication of EPHEMERIDES. PTOLEMY gave the name to the ARMILLARY SPHERE, a usage that persisted until the twelfth century. Certain astrologers of the late nineteenth century, including Julevno, used the term to refer to a kind of protractor with movable arms that was used to determine aspects.

Astrological Age: See PRECESSIONAL AGE; PRECESSION OF THE EQUINOXES.

Astrology (from the Greek *astron*, star, and *logos*, discourse): Literally, the science of the stars; the parent of ASTRONOMY and, among the ancients, synonymous with it. Astrologers generally recognize four broad stages in the history of astrology: preliterate astrology, which preceded recorded history; ancient astrology, from the dawn of history to about the second century A.D.; classical, or traditional, astrology, from the second century A.D. to 1700; and MODERN ASTROLOGY, from 1700 to the present. Modern astrology might be defined as the study of the movements of the Sun, Moon, and planets in relation to events on Earth, especially human personality and behavior; or, conversely, as the study of human affairs in relation to their cosmic environment. The central assumption of astrology is that the positions of the Sun, Moon, and planets at the birth of an individual or the beginning of an enterprise are related in a significant and observable manner to the intrinsic character and later development of that individual or enterprise.

Herodotus' remark that "by observing the day of a person's birth, one can predict his destiny" implies a deterministic conception of astrology that was already being opposed by the beginning of the Christian era. The adage *astra inclinant, non necessitant* ("the stars incline, they do not compel") has by now become a commonplace. Indeed, there are few astrologers who have denied that human beings have the ability to exercise free will.

Although astrology was long considered a means of divination and is still associated in the public mind with prediction, many contemporary astrologers are less interested in predicting the future than in exploring the psyche and revealing the multiple facets of a personality. They regard the BIRTH CHART as a complex mass of information pertaining to the individual's potential rather than a blueprint of his fate, and the stars as descriptive symbols rather than determining causes of his temperament.

Astrology has several different branches and subbranches. The most familiar, and the one that is the primary focus of this volume, is *natal* (or *genethliacal*) *astrology*, which involves the calculation and interpretation of birth charts for individuals (known as *natives*), as well as the study of transits, progressions, and directions to such charts (see PROGRESSION AND DIRECTION; TRANSIT), and their comparison with other charts (CHART COMPARISON, or *synastry*). Under natal astrology are also included MEDICAL ASTROLOGY, which uses the birth chart as an aid in anticipating potential health problems and diagnosing physical or mental illness, and ESOTERIC ASTROLOGY, which sees the birth chart as a guide to spiritual awareness and evolution.

MUNDANE (or *judicial*, or *political*) ASTROLOGY focuses on collective rather than personal history and attempts to anticipate the course of public events and cultural trends by studying the positions of the planets at EQUINOXES, SOLSTICES, lunations, eclipses, and major planetary conjunctions, as well as planetary patterns and cycles seen at long range. Under mundane astrology are also included ASTROECONOMICS, the application of astrology to the world of business and finance, ASTROMETEOROLOGY, or *meteorological astrology*, the application of the theory of aspects to the forecasting of weather conditions and earthquakes and undoubtedly the oldest branch of all, AGRICULTURAL ASTROLOGY, the application of astrological principles to the planting and harvesting of crops. (See CYCLE; ECLIPSE; LUNATION.)

HORARY ASTROLOGY is a form of divination in which a horoscope is cast for the moment a question is asked. ELECTIONAL ASTROLOGY is the study of transits (see TRANSIT) with a view to choosing a favorable moment for initiating a new enterprise— for example, starting a business, going on a trip, or getting married. LOCATIONAL ASTROLOGY is the application of astrological principles to the choice of a new location.

Overlapping these basic branches of astrology, there are various schools of thought on specific elements of astrological theory, reflecting the current state of the art. Thus there is the GEOCENTRIC versus the HELIOCENTRIC approach; the TROPICAL ZODIAC versus the SIDEREAL ZODIAC; the scientific or statistical school versus the humanist approach or the symbolist school; the URANIAN SYSTEM versus the classical, or *Ptolemaic, system*—not to mention the several different systems of HOUSE DIVISION. Ideally all these different approaches ought eventually to form part of one integral astrology, once the underlying principles of the subject are fully understood. (See ADDEY, JOHN; HUMANISTIC ASTROLOGY; MODERN ASTROLOGY; STATISTICS AND ASTROLOGY.)

Astrology and the Law: Astrology was outlawed in England in 1736 under the Witchcraft Act and again in 1825 under the Vagrancy Act, which classified astrologers with "rogues and vagabonds." As late as 1964 astrologers were still liable to prosecution under these laws as "fortune-tellers," but few cases have been brought to trial. A famous exception is the case of astrologer Alan LEO (1860–1917). Leo was tried and acquitted in London in 1914; in 1917 he was arrested again on a charge of "pretending and professing to tell fortunes." His lawyers argued that he was not an imposter, since he made no claims to predict the future with certainty, but merely indicated tendencies. A skeptical judge fined him £30.

In America, however, astrologer Evangeline Adams won a major victory in the battle for astrological respectability. Arrested in New York

Evangeline Adams. (The Bettman Archive.)

City in 1914 on a charge of fortune-telling, Adams insisted on standing trial. She came to court armed with reference books, expounded the principles of astrology, and illustrated its practice by reading a blind chart that turned out to be that of the judge's son. The judge was so impressed by her character and intelligence that he ruled in her favor, concluding that "the defendant raises astrology to the dignity of an exact science." Fortune-telling is still illegal in New York, but thanks to Evangeline Adams, astrology is no longer regarded as fortune-telling.

In France the legal status of astrologers is unclear. Some jurists maintain that vendors of horoscopes are liable to prosecution under a law designed to punish "all persons who make a profession of predicting the future or interpreting dreams." However, the majority of jurists disagree, pointing out that this article, broadly interpreted, could apply equally well to psychoanalysts. Another article designed to curb fraud has occasionally been cited, but its application would oblige the judge to exceed his rights in denying the validity of astrology. As Robert Amadou points out, "Even if a wise judge decided that only the authors of identical printed horoscopes that are sent out to all customers are liable to conviction, the court would then find itself in the position of having to formulate the rules for sound divination." In the absence of precise legislation, French law ordinarily prosecutes only astrologers who sell talismans or who publish offers that fall under the heading of false advertising. Reputable astrologers in all countries are only too happy to see these individuals brought to justice. (See ETHICS.)

Astrometeorology (or **Meteorological Astrology**): The study of planetary positions in relation to weather conditions and earthquakes. Although meteorology is a comparatively recent science, meteorological astrology may well be one of the oldest branches of astrology. The earliest zodiacs were devised partly to anticipate changes in the weather, such as the annual flooding of the Nile.

In the 1950s and 1960s the American sidereal astrologer Donald Bradley did extensive statistical research on the relationship between record rainfalls and the positions of the planets—especially Jupiter, traditionally associated with rain—at the time of lunar ingresses. Bradley also joined a group of orthodox scientists at New York University who conducted a comprehensive computerized survey of weather patterns, including a study correlating lunar phase and rainfall.

Traditionally astrologers have based weather forecasts on the geocentric positions of the planets, whereas meteorologists, who are just beginning to explore the relationship between planetary patterns and conditions in the Earth's atmosphere, work within a heliocentric framework. The scientist who has had the most success in predicting sunspots and the disturbances in radio reception that are associated with them is radio engineer John NELSON. Nelson's system, which is based on a complex system of heliocentric planetary patterns he calls "simultaneous multiple harmonics," enables him to predict storms with 90 percent accuracy.

Weather prediction, like the prediction of human behavior, is an extremely complex undertaking because of the number of variables. Any attempt to forecast weather conditions should take into account not only planetary patterns but also climate, geography, and season.

Astronomical Year: See TROPICAL YEAR.

Astronomy (from the Greek *astron*, star, and *nomos*, law): The science that studies the heavenly bodies in order to formulate the natural laws that govern them and to comprehend the physical structure and evolution of the universe. The earliest astronomical study—observations of the motions of the Sun, Moon, stars, and planets—probably arose from the need of agricultural societies for an accurate calendar. Astronomy was once synonymous with astrology, and the observation and interpretation of the heavens was originally the province of priests. Current speculations of astronomers investigating such bizarre phenomena as quasars and black holes are beginning to sound more and more like metaphysics and religion. But most ordinary astronomical investigations aim simply to quantify the macrocosm— that is, to determine the distance, size, density, temperature, brightness, speed, and age of objects and phenomena in the heavens. Modern astronomers, using huge optical and radio telescopes, make their measurements with the aid of visible light and its analyzed spectra, radio waves, infrared rays, X rays, cosmic rays, and radar beams.

For thousands of years and until the last two or three centuries, astronomy was a part of astrology. The relationship of astronomy to astrology was similar to that of the eyes to the brain: Astronomy provided the visual data; astrology interpreted the data as they related to human beings. According to Ralph Waldo Emerson, "astrology is astronomy brought to earth and applied to the affairs of men"; according to Emily Dickinson:

Nature assigns the Sun—
That—is Astronomy—
Nature cannot enact a Friend—
That—is Astrology.

All the great astrologers of antiquity were also capable astronomers in their day; conversely, the individuals responsible for some of the greatest advances in astronomical knowledge—for example, Tycho BRAHE, Johannes KEPLER, Galileo GALILEI, and Isaac NEWTON—were practicing astrologers or at least took astrology seriously.

The present schism between astrology and astronomy began in the sixteenth century with COPERNICUS's displacement of the Earth as the center of the universe, and expanded with the telescopic discovery in 1781 of Uranus, which overthrew the venerable symmetry of astrology's seven planets (see MODERN ASTROLOGY). Contemporary astronomers typically consider astrology a quaint superstition, a laughable pseudoscience with no basis in fact. A statement issued by *Humanist* magazine in 1975 and signed by 186 scientists, including many astronomers, condemned astrology as a "cult of unreason and irrationalism . . . being foisted on an unsuspecting public."

Most astronomers' objections to astrology are based on two principal arguments: (a) that the signs of the zodiac do not coincide with the constellations after which they were named; and (b) that planetary "action at a distance" is impossible. The first argument is known and accounted for by most astrologers (see TROPICAL ZODIAC), and the second has recently been seriously questioned by scientific investigations (see NELSON, JOHN; RELATIVITY, THEORY OF); but these facts are largely ignored by astronomers intent on discrediting astrology.

Astrologers, for their part, have

been guilty of the most profound ignorance of astronomy. Many of them seem to regard the physical structure of the universe, especially anything beyond our solar system, as irrelevant, and quantification in any form as a threat to the human and spiritual significance of astrology. There are exceptions. For example, Theodor Landscheidt finds astrological significance in quantum mechanics, the space-time continuum, and .the evolution and structure of the galaxy (see GALACTIC CENTER; GALAXY); and Michael and Margaret Erlewine integrate into their HELIOCENTRIC ASTROLOGY the most recently discovered astronomical phenomena, including quasars, pulsars, and black holes.

Augustine, Saint: See CHRISTIANITY AND ASTROLOGY; MIDDLE AGES, ASTROLOGY IN THE.

Autumnal Equinox (or **Autumn Equinox**): See EQUINOXES.

Autumnal Ingress (or **Autumn Ingress**): See INGRESS.

Axial Rotation: The spinning of any celestial body around its axis. The axial rotation of the Earth causes the apparent diurnal motion of the Sun, Moon, planets, and stars from their rising at the eastern HORIZON to their culmination on the local MERIDIAN to their setting at the western horizon. One complete axial rotation of the Earth takes 23 hours 56 minutes 4.09 seconds of mean solar time, a period known as the *sidereal day* (see TIME).

Axis: 1. A straight line about which rotation occurs and which is perpendicular to the direction of rotation. For example, the Earth's axis extends from the North Pole to the South Pole (also from the north celestial pole to the south celestial pole) and is perpendicular to the Equator (also to the CELESTIAL EQUATOR). The Earth rotates about this axis in the plane of the Equator. Any plane can have an axis perpendicular to it. For example, the ECLIPTIC has an axis perpendicular to its plane about which the Earth's rotational axis revolves in 25,800 years (see PRECESSION OF THE EQUINOXES). **2.** One of the two intersecting lines, or *axes,* of a birth chart—the HORIZON and the MERIDIAN—that divide it into four *quadrants.* **3.** Any line connecting polar opposites; for example, the opposition from Cancer to Capricorn is along the Cancer-Capricorn axis. The term is sometimes used to mean POLARITY. **4.** A term used in cosmobiology to refer to (a) a factor that stands at the midpoint of two other factors and thereby activates the midpoint; or (b) the actual midpoint itself.

Ayanamsa (or **Ayanamsha**) (from the Sanskrit for precession): The difference in CELESTIAL LONGITUDE between the Indian sidereal sign and its corresponding Western tropical sign. The ayanamsa used by Western siderealists is that of FAGAN and Bradley. Its precise value was arrived at by empirical and statistical methods; in 1950 it was approximately 24°. In India there are several different ayanamsas in use. Because of PRECES-

SION OF THE EQUINOXES, the value of an ayanamsa increases by about 1.4° every hundred years. (See INDIA, ASTROLOGY IN; SIDEREAL ZODIAC.)

Azimuth (from the Arabic *al-sumut*, plural of *al-samt*, the way, direction, arc): Angular distance measured in degrees, minutes, and seconds along the HORIZON, usually in an eastward direction from the North Point. The azimuth of the North Point is 0°, the East Point 90°, the South Point 180°, and the West Point 270°. However, azimuth is sometimes considered to increase in a westward direction from the North Point, or eastward from the South Point; and sometimes in both directions, in which case there is an east (or positive) azimuth and a west (or negative) azimuth. An *azimuth circle*, or *vertical circle*, labeled by a specific number of degrees is a GREAT CIRCLE perpendicular to the horizon at a point that number of degrees from the azimuth starting point. (See CELESTIAL COORDINATES.)

Azimuth Circle: See AZIMUTH.

Babilius: See ROMANS, ASTROLOGY AMONG THE.

Bach, Eleanor: See ASTEROIDS.

Bacon, Francis (1561–1626): English philosopher, statesman, and essayist; regarded as the father of modern science and, with Descartes, of modern philosophy. Bacon was an ardent believer in and champion of astrology. In *Astrologia Sana*, he expressed the opinion that astrology had rule over the fates of princes and nations.

Bacon, Roger: See MIDDLE AGES, ASTROLOGY IN THE.

Bailey, Alice: See ESOTERIC ASTROLOGY.

Barbault, André (October 1, 1921, 5:00 P.M., Champignelles/Yonne, France–): French astrologer, author, and popularizer of astrology. An autodidact, Barbault was collecting and studying birth charts by the age of fifteen. His discovery of Freud at the age of nineteen convinced him that the symbolic language of astrology can only be understood in the light of Freudian concepts, especially the unconscious. In 1961 he published

two books, *de la Psychanalyse de l'Astrologie*, a psychological interpretation of astrology, and *Traité pratique d'Astrologie*, a textbook widely used in France, Belgium, Switzerland, Italy, and Spain.

Barbault was a leading force in the Centre International d'Astrologie from its formation in 1946 and served as its vice president from 1953 to 1967. In 1967 he caused a sensation by opening, on the Champs-Elysées in Paris, the first computerized astrology service, Ordinastral-Astroflash, which turned out thousands of horoscopes a day, complete with interpretations. Barbault's colleagues criticized him for engaging in this commercialized form of astrology, but Astroflash quickly spread to seventeen other countries of Europe, America, Africa, and Australia. In the same year Barbault founded the serious quarterly journal *l'Astrologue*, now in its fiftieth issue, whose contributors have included numerous scientists and academicians, and such notables as Jean Cocteau, André Breton, and C. G. Jung.

Although it is his psychoanalytic approach to astrology that has been most influential in shaping modern

French astrological practice, much of Barbault's work as a serious astrologer has been devoted to MUNDANE ASTROLOGY. Concentrating his attention on the nineteenth and twentieth centuries, he began by correlating series of related events with the synodic cycles of pairs of planets. His analysis of the great trends of modern history is set forth in *les Astres et l'histoire* (1967). His efforts to verify his correlations led to a systematic technique of prediction with which he successfully forecast crises in French government as well as a dozen of the milestones in the international history of the last quarter century (see *le Pronostic experimental en astrologie*, 1973). In his latest work, *l'Astrologie mondiale* (1979), he turns from individual synodic cycles to the solar system as a whole and reconciles some of the concepts of traditional cosmology with those of modern geophysics.

Generally considered France's greatest living astrologer and widely read in Europe, Barbault is known in the United States chiefly as the author of the programs for Astroflash, and not one of his thirty-odd books has been translated into English. (See COMPUTERS AND ASTROLOGY.

Benefic: Literally, "doing good"; a term applied by ancient and classical astrologers to planets or aspects regarded as having a favorable influence; the opposite of MALEFIC. PTOLEMY classifies Jupiter, Venus, and the Moon as benefic planets and the trine and sextile as harmonious aspects. Modern astrologers are moving away from the categorization of planets and aspects as good or bad and the outmoded determinism this implies. They tend to regard the planets as energies that can operate for either good or ill, depending on how they are used. Thus Jupiter is a principle of expansion and Venus is a principle of magnetism, either of which can lead to excess. Similarly, in referring to aspects, the words *benefic* and *malefic* are being replaced with such terms as *helpful* and *stressful,* or *soft* and *hard.*

Berosus: Babylonian priest, historian, and astrologer born around 330 B.C. A contemporary of Alexander, he left Mesopotamia and settled on the Greek island of Cos, where he taught astrology. Around 280 B.C. he wrote a history of Babylonia, of which only fragments remain. It was through his teaching that CHALDEAN ASTROLOGY spread to Greece. (See GREEKS, ASTROLOGY AMONG THE.)

Besieged: A somewhat archaic term used to describe a planet or other SIGNIFICATOR located between, and within orbs of, two other planets, especially two malefics, in which case it was held to be severely afflicted; but also two benefics, in which case it was held to be "favorably besieged."

Bicorporeal Signs: See DOUBLE SIGNS.

Biquintile (symbol ±): A minor aspect of 144°, introduced by KEPLER, based on the division of the circle by five (i.e., 144° equals two-fifths of

360°). It is regarded as indicative of talent.

Birth Chart (also called **Natal Chart** or **Nativity**): A stylized diagram of the heavens showing the positions of the Sun, Moon, planets, and important points on the zodiac in degrees of CELESTIAL LONGITUDE with respect to the horizon of a given birthplace at the time of an individual's birth. The above terms are distinguished from the terms *horoscope, map, sky map,* and *figure,* which can also be applied to the chart of a moment, event, or phenomenon other than the birth of an individual (see HOR-OSCOPE). The erection and interpretation of birth charts is the primary technique of NATAL ASTROLOGY, as distinguished from such secondary techniques as progressions, directions, transits, and solar returns. (See CHART CALCULATION; CHART INTER-PRETATION; PROGRESSION AND DIREC-TION; SOLAR RETURN; TRANSIT.)

Birthday Locality Chart: See LOCA-TIONAL ASTROLOGY.

Birthplace System: See HOUSE DIVI-SION.

Birth Sign: See SUN SIGN.

Birthstones: According to HERMETIC THEORY, certain precious or semiprecious gems were associated with certain signs of the zodiac and were regarded as beneficial and even therapeutic for natives of those signs, who sometimes wore them as talismans. Unfortunately, there have been several sets of these correspondences; hence, there is no agreement as to which gems correspond to which signs. The following list is suggestive, if not definitive:

Aries	diamond, ruby, bloodstone, carnelian, garnet
Taurus	emerald, jade, moss agate
Gemini	agate, cat's eye, crystal, aquamarine
Cancer	jacinth, pearl, moonstone, opal, quartz
Leo	sardonyx, chrysolite, topaz
Virgo	sapphire, agate, jacinth, opal
Libra	coral, emerald, opal
Scorpio	beryl, obsidian, ruby, sardonyx, topaz
Sagittarius	turquoise, amethyst, lapis lazuli
Capricorn	gems in general; onyx, jet, garnet
Aquarius	white coral, amber, chalcedonyx, amethyst, pearl
Pisces	aquamarine, ivory, sardonyx, jade

Rings engraved with astrological symbols, used as talismans. (After Abraham Gorlaeus.)

Birthtime: An accurate time of birth is essential for the calculation of a satisfactory birth chart, yet even with the current revival of interest in astrology it is sometimes hard to come by. Most birthtimes are rounded off to the nearest quarter hour, half hour, or even hour. Many hospitals now record time of birth, but they do so without any great concern for precision and often, one suspects, several minutes after delivery has occurred. But even under ideal circumstances—an astrologer husband or midwife standing by with one eye on the mother and the other on an accurate timepiece—the question arises, When does birth occur—crowning (first appearance of the baby's head), delivery, first cry, first breath, or the severing of the umbilical cord? All of these stages in the birth process are surely of vital importance, but the consensus of astrologers seems to be that the beginning of the infant's independent existence coincides with the first intake of breath that normally follows his or her first cry.

The natural source of birth information is the mother, but unfortunately her memory is often no more accurate than that of the father, sister, or other relatives. Time of birth is often shown on the birth certificate. If it is not, it may still be on file at the hospital or, in the United States, at an office of the Department of Health in each of the fifty states. Hospitals usually supply the information free of charge; the state agency will send a copy of the document for a small fee. For a pamphlet entitled *Where to Write for Birth and Death Records* which lists the addresses of these agencies, write to: The Superintendent of Documents, U.S. Government Printing Office, Washington, D.C. 20402.

If you were adopted, born at home, or for some other reason are unable to obtain an accurate birthtime, you should explore the possibility of having your chart rectified by a competent astrologer. In the meantime, you can work with a SOLAR CHART. (See PRECISION; RECTIFICATION.)

Bonati, Guido: See MIDDLE AGES, ASTROLOGY IN THE.

Bonaventura: See MIDDLE AGES, ASTROLOGY IN THE.

Borrowed Light: See TRANSLATION OF LIGHT.

Bradley, Donald: See SIDEREAL ZODIAC.

Brahe, Tycho (April 13, 1546, Kundstorp, Denmark–October 21, 1601, Prague): Danish astrologer and astronomer. Under the patronage of King Frederick II, he taught astronomy at the University of Copenhagen and founded an observatory on the island of Hven, which he received as a fief from the king. After Frederick's death, he moved to Prague, where he was received by Emperor Rudolf II and took as his assistant Johannes KEPLER. Tycho Brahe was the greatest astronomer since HIPPARCHUS, and to him we owe the most precise

Tycho Brahe. (The Bettman Archive.)

observations that were made before the invention of the telescope. He designed accurate metal instruments and discovered exploding novae. The accuracy of his observations, which was unprecedented, led Kepler to the discovery of the laws governing the motions of the planets. An enthusiastic practitioner of MUNDANE ASTROLOGY, he developed the theory of aspects, with special attention to the relationship between the great conjunctions and natural cataclysms (see ASPECT).

Brown, W. Kenneth: See JOHNDRO, L. E.

Buffalo: See Ox.

Byzantium, Astrology in: Crossroads of many civilizations, Byzantium inherited the use of magic and sorcery from the Orient. As for astrology, the new contributions of Islam, known through Latin translations, were gradually, over the centuries, added to the teachings of the Greeks, especially PTOLEMY.

At first astrology was regarded with suspicion by the temporal and spiritual powers of Christian Byzantium. In the fourth century the Eastern Church formally condemned its determinism, a position that was upheld four centuries later by Saint John of Damascus. But these efforts were in vain, and from the eighth century until the capture of Constantinople by the Ottoman Turks in 1453 astrology flourished in Byzantium.

Michael Psellus (1018–78), a Byzantine philosopher who reformed the university, taught astrology, along with rhetoric, philosophy, and cosmogony. His belief in astrology influenced two of his friends, Michael Caerularius, author of the schism between the Greek Church and Rome, and John Xiphilin, both of whom held the post of patriarch of Constantinople. In the last years of the empire, the Platonic philosopher Gemistus Pletho (ca. 1355–1450), a pioneer in the revival of learning in Western Europe who had visited the Muslim court of Adrianople before heading a school of philosophy at Nistra, was convinced of the scientific validity of astrology. He traveled to Florence, where he met Petrarch and played an important role in spreading Byzantine astrology in Renaissance Italy.

In the golden age of Byzantium, however, astrology was not available to the common people. The astrologers were philosophers, mathematicians, and often priests, and they had no dealings with the magicians, vendors of amulets and potions, fortune-tellers, and mountebanks who abounded in the marketplaces of all the cities of the empire. Their services were expensive, and it was mostly among the aristocracy that they recruited their clientele. There were also many emperors who called in astrologers to advise them, even if their predictions sometimes proved to be false. In 792 Pancratos, astrologer to Constantine VI, predicted that his master would win a certain battle, whereas he suffered a crushing defeat. And in 1154 Manuel Comnenus, who was at war with the king of Sicily, consulted his astrologers before preparing his fleet, which was nevertheless beaten. This did not prevent him from commissioning Michael Glykas to write a *Defense of Astrology* in answer to a monk who had attacked it. During the twelfth century, Byzantine astrology reached its peak. It was then that two important astrological poems were written, one by Theodore Prodrome, the other by John Kamateros, a sort of keeper of the seals to the emperor, dedicated to Manuel Comnenus. Although Alexius Comnenus was somewhat skeptical about astrology, his daughter, Anne, one of the few educated women in the empire, practiced it herself and wrote a history of it in which she erroneously concluded that it was a recent phenomenon. (See DAYS OF THE WEEK.)

Cabala (also **Cabbala, Cabbalah, Kabala, Kabbala, Kabbalah, Qabbala,** or **Qabbalah**): A system of philosophy, at first handed down orally and later committed to writing, based on mystical interpretation of the Scriptures and practiced by ancient Jewish rabbis and certain medieval Christians. Cabalist thought had a profound impact on all the occult teachings, particularly those concerned with divination, such as numerology and the Tarot. Cabalists shared with astrologers the medieval idea that man is a microcosm. (See HEBREWS, ASTROLOGY AMONG THE; MICROCOSM.)

Cadent (from the Latin *cadere,* to fall): Term used to describe the HOUSES in a horoscope that "fall away" from the ANGLES, or the planets occupying such houses. The cadent houses are the Third, Sixth, Ninth, and Twelfth; they correspond to the MUTABLE signs, and planets in those houses are associated with distribution and service. According to traditional astrology, a planet is weakened by being cadent, just as it is strengthened by being *angular*—that is, placed in one of the houses following the angles of the chart. However, the work of Michel and Françoise GAUQUELIN demonstrates that cadent houses, particularly the half adjoining the angles, give exceptional strength to a planet; for example, Mars is at its most "combative" and "self-willed" in this position.

Calendar Year: See TROPICAL YEAR.

Campanus, Johannes (also known as **Giovanni Campanella**; d. ca. 1297): Italian mathematician and geometer of the thirteenth century. He translated Euclid's *Elements* from the Arabic. He is also reputed to have perfected a method of HOUSE DIVISION that is still used by some astrologers, although there is some uncertainty as to the identity of this person.

Campanus System: See HOUSE DIVISION.

Cancer (glyph ♋): The fourth sign of the zodiac, which the Sun transits during the first month of summer, from about June 21 to about July 22. The symbol for this sign is the crab. Its POLARITY is negative, its element is water (see ELEMENTS), its quality is cardinal (see QUALITIES), its ruling

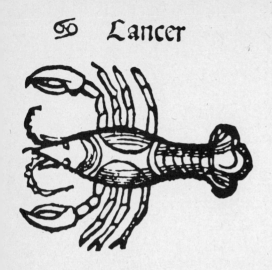

♋ Cancer

planet is the Moon (see RULERSHIP), and its NATURAL HOUSE is the Fourth.

In Cancer, the activity of cardinality, the emotionality of water, and the instability of the Moon combine to produce a paradoxical creature whose extreme sensitivity does not always show on the surface. Like the crab that is their animal symbol, Cancerians develop a tough outer shell to protect the vulnerability within. This shell may be their home, a place they can retreat to, full of familiar treasures they have collected to console their psyche in an alien world. It may also be a system of psychological defenses they have created in order to avoid pain. Also like the crab, Cancerians will move sideways to avoid a confrontation, but when attacked, they will hang on tenaciously: Crabs will risk losing a claw before they will release their prey.

The Moon rules infancy and motherhood, and Cancerians—who include not only Sun-sign Cancers, but all in whose charts the sign is emphasized—remain deeply connected to the early part of their lives, even though it may not have been especially tranquil. As babies they are given to inexplicable crying jags and seem more subject than other infants to visceral discomfort. Cancer children are famous for their protective attitude toward younger siblings and their worried concern for the well-being of every family member, and as they grow older, this maternal quality becomes more conspicuous.

Even adult Cancerians are deeply connected to their mother. They crave the total intimacy of the baby at the breast, and since no adult relationship can re-create the perfect fulfillment of those moments, they may often feel unsatisfied. They may hold on to old hurts and resentments simply out of fear of the unknown. And yet in their very sensitivity, there is a great source of strength. Once Cancerians can overcome their shyness, their passivity, and their preoccupation with themselves and can learn to master their turbulent moods, there is almost nothing they cannot accomplish. With their gifts of imagination, intuition, and insight and their ability to get in touch with their inner experience, they can reverse the tide of negativity and turn suffering into success.

Because relationships are so important to them, Cancerians in love can be both demanding and generous. They are passionate and possessive, sometimes holding on to a relationship long after it has proved unrewarding. Since Cancerians like to perpetuate the mother-child bond, they often pick partners they can mother or whom they can look up to as a parent figure or, better yet, partners with whom they can alternate between the two roles, playing the child today and the mother tomorrow, as the mood strikes them. Their sensitivity to others' moods is a two-edged sword, making them both impossibly touchy and wonderfully sympathetic. But Cancerians will atone for their moodiness by their loyalty to their mates and will make their home and family the center of their life. Their most compatible signs are Scorpio, Pisces, Taurus, and Virgo; Gemini, Leo, Sagittarius, and Aquarius are neutral; and Aries and Libra are likely to be difficult. With Capricorn, their polar opposite in the zodiac, there is both attraction and tension. With another Cancer, there may well be too much feeling for one home to withstand. But in all cases, the success of the relationship will depend on how the two charts interact and not on the COMPATIBILITY of Sun signs alone.

With their acute perceptions and psychic ability, Cancerians can succeed in many professions, but they are at their best in activities where they can express their imagination and their need to nurture. The sign is associated with such diverse fields as homemaking, advertising, interior decorating, antiques, cooking, counseling, nursing, teaching, editing, writing, and the arts. Contrary to popular opinion, Cancerians can be very successful at business: cautious, conservative, and with keen antennae for changing public tastes and trends. The list of famous Sun-sign Cancerians includes Ingmar Bergman, John Calvin, Jean Cocteau, Mary Baker Eddy, Stephen Foster, Buckminster Fuller, Hermann Hesse, Franz Kafka, Helen Keller, Reinhold Niebuhr, George Orwell, Marcel Proust, Rembrandt van Rijn, Nelson Rockefeller, Jean-Jacques Rousseau, Peter Paul Rubens, Georges Sand, and Henry David Thoreau. (See BIRTHSTONES; COLORS; DAYS OF THE WEEK; METALS.)

Capricorn (glyph ♑): The tenth sign of the zodiac, which the Sun transits during the first month of winter, from about December 22 to about January 20. The symbol for this sign is the mountain goat. Its POLARITY is negative, its element is earth (see ELEMENTS), its quality is cardinal (see QUALITIES), its ruling planet is Saturn (see RULERSHIP), and its NATURAL HOUSE is the Tenth.

The old symbol for Capricorn is a mythological creature with the head of a goat and the tail of a fish, an image that contains the idea of evolution: the long, slow climb of animal life out of the primordial slime and upward toward the stars. The idea of ascent is echoed by Capricorn's rulership of the knee, which must bend in order for the body to climb. The Sun is also climbing northward in Capricorn, for it enters the sign at the winter solstice, the longest night of the year. Thus Capricorn is the sign of hope, ambition, and aspiration.

The practicality of earth, the initiating energy of cardinality, and the sobering influence of Saturn combine

℣ Capꞧicoꞧnus

to make up a nature that is oriented toward leadership and excellence. Capricornians—who include not only Sun-sign Capricorns, but all in whose charts the sign is emphasized—are serious people. Capricorn children are in a hurry to grow up and assume responsibility. They feel a strong connection with older people, especially their fathers, whose approval they seek and whom they look up to as teachers.

As adults, Capricorns continually seek to improve themselves, whether by making more money, furthering their education, or choosing a spiritual path, usually one involving discipline or where they follow the teachings of a master. Saturn rules the limitations of the material world, especially time and space, and the Capricorn awareness of time takes the form of anticipating the future rather than living in the present. This makes them wonderful organizers

and planners, but it sometimes limits spontaneity.

Contrary to popular belief, and the influence of Saturn notwithstanding, Capricorn is not necessarily a sexually cold sign. All the earth signs are sensual, and once Capricorns overcome their anxieties about not being good enough and learn to relax, they can be lusty and imaginative lovers. The women often have the type of classic beauty based on good bone structure that is sometimes seen in the pages of high-fashion magazines. Both sexes are often attracted to older partners and are capable of marrying for money or prestige. Their most compatible signs are Taurus, Virgo, Scorpio, and Pisces; Sagittarius, Aquarius, Gemini, and Leo are neutral; and Aries and Libra may be difficult. With another Capricorn, there is often mutual respect. With Cancer, their polar opposite on the zodiac, there will be both attraction and tension; but ultimately the question of COMPATIBILITY can be answered only by careful comparison of two entire charts.

With their love of work, patience, and high standards, Capricorns can rise to the top of almost any field. With their understanding of money, power, and timing, they have a natural flair for business, but with their intuitive sense of form and their tireless pursuit of quality, they can achieve wonders in the arts. Their fascination with the structure of the universe may take them far in science, and their sense of responsibility may inspire them to assume the role of religious leader or even martyr. As the sign ruling government,

Capricorn has an affinity for politics, and here we may see statesmen who devote their lives to their convictions, as well as ruthless opportunists who will stop at nothing in their compulsive drive for power. This sign is also associated with teaching, masonry, excavation, construction, clockmaking, jewelry making, mining, geology, real estate, accounting, and photography. The list of Sun-sign Capricorns who have "made it" is endless; here is a representative sample: Muhammad Ali, Joan of Arc, Pablo Casals, Carlos Castaneda, Paul Cézanne, Marlene Dietrich, Benjamin Franklin, J. Edgar Hoover, Johannes Kepler, Martin Luther King, Jr., Henri Matisse, Sir Isaac Newton, Richard Nixon, Louis Pasteur, Elvis Presley, Helena Rubinstein, Albert Schweitzer, Joseph Stalin, Mao Tse-Tung, Swami Vivekananda, and Woodrow Wilson. (See BIRTHSTONES; COLORS; DAYS OF THE WEEK; METALS.)

Caput Draconis: The Dragon's Head, or north node of the Moon (see NODES).

Cardinal (from the Latin *cardo,* hinge or turning point): One of the three *qualities*, or modes, that characterize the signs of the zodiac, the other two being FIXED and MUTABLE. The cardinal quality has been compared to centrifugal force in physics, or to energy itself. The cardinal signs of the zodiac (also called angular, intiating, leading, moving, or movable signs) are the four signs whose cusps coincide with the cardinal points of the ecliptic, that is, the two EQUINOXES and the two SOLSTICES. The cardinal signs are Aries, Cancer, Libra, and Capricorn. The Sun's entrance into any of these signs marks the beginning of a new season. The cardinal signs are characterized by outgoing energy, initiative, and activity; on the negative side, they are associated with lack of staying power.

In classical astrology, the cardinal signs were known collectively as the *cardinal quadruplicity*, since there are four of them. They are also sometimes referred to as the *cardinal cross,* since if planets in them are connected by straight lines, they form a cross. A *grand cardinal cross* is a major configuration in which two pairs of opposing planets, all in cardinal signs, are in square aspect to each other, forming a cross (see GRAND CROSS).

Carter, Charles Ernest Owen (January 31, 1887, 10:55 P.M., Poole, Dorset, England–October 4, 1968, 4 P.M., London): English astrologer and author. Carter came to astrology in 1910 at the age of twenty-three after seeing an advertisement of Alan LEO's for "shilling" horoscopes. In 1913 he married Gwendoline Phyllis Collet. In 1920 he revived the Astrological Lodge of the Theosophical Society, which had virtually become defunct when Alan Leo died three years before. He was elected president, a post he held until 1952. In 1923 his magazine *Uranus* appeared; in 1926 he initiated the printed quarterly *Astrology,* which he edited until 1959. His many articles and editorials show broad and deep interests in all branches of astrology, scientific and holistic.

Charles Carter.

Carter was not primarily an astrological initiator, in spite of the considerable originality of his thought; his contribution was rather in bringing a greater unity, clarity, and depth to existing concepts. His first book, published in 1924, was *The Encyclopaedia of Psychological Astrology.* His most popular book was his *Astrological Aspects,* which was first published in 1930 and by 1970 had run into ten editions. Others were *The Principles of Astrology* (1925), a textbook; *The Seven Great Problems of Astrology* (1927); *The Zodiac and the Soul* (1928); *Symbolic Directions* (1929); *The Astrology of Accidents* (1932); *Some Principles of Horoscopic Delineation* (1934); and *Essays on the Foundations of Astrology* (1947). In 1948 the Faculty of Astrological Studies was formed with his

encouragement, and he became its first president. In 1951 he published his last book, *An Introduction to Political Astrology*—the outcome of a great deal of observational and statistical work during World War II.

Charles Harvey writes of Charles Carter, "He was a man of intellect who brought real standards and a splendid measure of sound common sense to an area previously awash with vague assertions. His mixture of observation, experiment, and a keen sense of first principles was an extremely important influence both on the development of the Faculty of Astrological Studies and the Astrological Assocation, and personally on the work of John ADDEY and many other less well known figures in British astrology. His influence is still very much alive."

Cat: The fourth sign of the Chinese zodiac, including all persons born between

January 29, 1903, and February 16, 1904 (water)
February 14, 1915, and February 3, 1916 (wood)
February 2, 1927, and January 23, 1928 (fire)
February 19, 1939, and February 8, 1940 (earth)
February 6, 1951, and January 27, 1952 (metal)
January 25, 1963, and February 13, 1964 (water)
February 11, 1975, and January 31, 1976 (wood)
January 29, 1987, and February 17, 1988 (fire)

Talkative, theatrical, endowed with a rich imagination, the Cat is also vain and somewhat superficial. On the other hand, natives of this sign have amazing self-control and are neither envious nor jealous, qualities that, added to their good taste and refinement, help to atone for their faults. Money does not interest them, but they are very good at busi-

ness; they are particularly successful in professions requiring diplomacy and a gift for getting along with people.

Frivolous and fun-loving, in relationships they prefer a light flirtation; the grand passion is not their cup of tea. Their sense of family is not particularly strong, although they are affectionate.

Compatible signs: Cat, Dog, Dragon, Goat, Horse, Monkey, Ox, Serpent, and Tiger.

Neutral sign: Pig.

Incompatible signs: Cock, Rat.

The list of famous Cats includes Fidel Castro, Marie Curie, Albrecht Dürer, Albert Einstein, W. C. Fields, Garibaldi, Joan of Arc, John Keats, Martin Luther, George Orwell, Eva Perón, Joseph Stalin, Leon Trotsky, Queen Victoria, Orson Welles, and Walt Whitman. (See CHINESE ASTROLOGY.)

Cauda Draconis: The Dragon's Tail, or south node of the Moon (see NODES).

Cazimi: Literally, "the heart of the Sun"; a term used by Arabian astronomers to refer to the center of the solar disk. In astrology it is used to describe a planet whose celestial longitude is within 17' of that of the Sun. Being cazimi was once thought to strengthen the planet's influence as much as being COMBUST the Sun weakened it. Modern astrologers tend to disagree, although as in all conjunctions, the positive or negative nature of the influence will vary according to the nature of the planet involved.

Celestial Coordinates: A pair of numbers used to determine the position of an object on the CELESTIAL SPHERE relative to a central reference plane (or GREAT CIRCLE) and the two poles of that plane. The coordinates may be specific to a particular location on the Earth's surface (the alt-azimuth system), the axial rotation of the Earth (the equatorial system), the Earth's orbital revolution around the Sun (the ecliptic system), or some other scheme.

The *alt-azimuth system* is useful in surveying and navigation. The central reference great circle is the local HORIZON, which is divided into 360° of *azimuth*, usually measured from the North Point in an eastward direction. The poles of the horizon plane—that is, the two points most remote from the horizon—are the *zenith* and the *nadir*. Angular distance away from the horizon is measured in degrees, minutes, and seconds of *altitude*. Positive altitude is above the horizon, negative altitude below; maximum positive altitude occurs at the zenith ($+90°$), maximum negative altitude at the nadir ($-90°$). The altitude of the horizon is 0°. The alt-azimuth coordinates of heavenly bodies are valid only for a specific place on

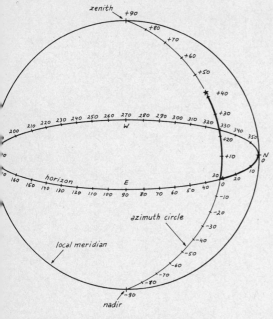

Figure 3. The alt-azimuth system. The star Capella has recently risen over the eastern horizon. At this moment it has an azimuth of 30°, measured from the North Point along the horizon in an eastward direction; and an altitude of +40°, measured from the horizon along the azimuth circle of 30°. The local meridian is an azimuth circle.

the Earth; the coordinates change from moment to moment—a great disadvantage for locating them. In figure 3 we see the alt-azimuth position of the star Capella from the viewpoint of Puttalam, Sri Lanka, at 12:12 A.M. on November 15, 1980: Capella has 30° of azimuth and +40° of altitude, expressed as 30°, +40°. Azimuth is sometimes measured from the South Point; and sometimes in both directions from the South Point (180° of east, or positive, azimuth; 180° of west, or negative, azimuth).

The *equatorial system* is the favorite of astronomers; it is useful for locating celestial bodies at specific times, since it is keyed to the Earth's rotation. The central reference great circle is the *celestial equator*, divided into 360° of *right ascension* (or 24 hours of sidereal time), measured from the VERNAL POINT in an eastward direction. The points most remote from the equatorial plane are the north and south *celestial poles*. Angular distance away from the celestial equator is measured in degrees, minutes, and seconds of *declination*; north declination is toward the north celestial pole, south declination toward the south celestial pole. Each pole has

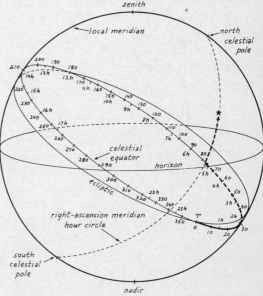

Figure 4. The equatorial system. The star Capella has a right ascension of 78°48' (5h 15m 12s), measured from the vernal point along the celestial equator; and a declination of 45°59' north (45N59) measured from the celestial equator along the right-ascension meridian of 78°48', which is also the hour circle of 5h 15m 12s. The local meridian is the right-ascension meridian that is at any moment connecting the zenith and nadir.

maximum declination (90N and 90S, respectively); the declination of the celestial equator is 0°. The equatorial coordinates of a celestial body change very slowly, averaging no more than 1° every 72 years for right ascension and much less for declination. Unlike alt-azimuth coordinates, they are applicable to every location on the Earth. In figure 4 we see the equatorial coordinates of Capella.

The *ecliptic system*, which is keyed to the Earth's orbit around the Sun, or *ecliptic*, is used by astrologers to locate planets, since the planets never stray far from the ecliptic. Its central reference great circle is the

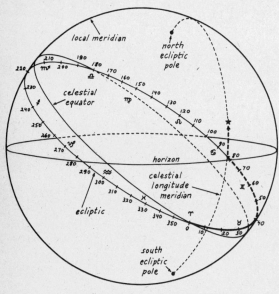

Figure 5. The ecliptic system. The star Capella has a celestial longitude of 81°34′ (21°34′ Gemini), measured from the vernal point along the ecliptic; and a celestial latitude of 22°55′ north (22N55), measured from the ecliptic along the longitude meridian of 81°34′. Longitude meridians extend from the north ecliptic pole to the south ecliptic pole, neither of which is situated on the local meridian.

ecliptic, divided into 360° (or twelve signs of 30° each) of *celestial longitude*, measured from the vernal point in an eastward direction. The points most remote from the ecliptic plane are the north and south *ecliptic poles*. Angular distance away from the ecliptic is measured in degrees, minutes, and seconds of *celestial latitude*; north latitude is toward the north ecliptic pole, south latitude toward the south ecliptic pole. Each pole has maximum celestial latitude (90N and 90S, respectively); the latitude of the ecliptic is 0°. The ecliptic coordinates of a celestial body change very slowly, celestial longitude about 1° every 72 years and celestial latitude hardly changing at all. Like equatorial coordinates and unlike alt-azimuth coordinates, they are applicable to every location on the Earth. In figure 5 we see the ecliptic position of Capella.

Celestial Equator: The Earth's Equator projected onto the CELESTIAL SPHERE; the GREAT CIRCLE perpendicular to the Earth's axis of rotation. (See CELESTIAL COORDINATES.)

Celestial Latitude: Angular distance measured in degrees, minutes, and seconds north or south of the ECLIPTIC, which is considered to have a latitude of 0°. Maximum celestial latitude is at the north ecliptic pole (90° north) and the south ecliptic pole (90° south). Celestial latitude does *not* correspond to terrestrial latitude (see DECLINATION). The celestial latitude of the Sun, which is on the ecliptic by definition, is always 0°. Most

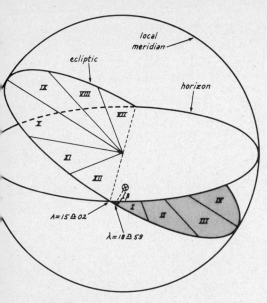

Figure 6. The importance of celestial latitude. Pluto's celestial longitude (λ) is 18°59' Libra. The longitude of the Ascendant **(A)** is 15°02' Libra. Thus it would seem that Pluto is below the horizon in the First House, as is the ecliptic after 15°02' Libra. But Pluto is not on the ecliptic. It is 17°12' of celestial latitude (β) above it, which makes its position (⊗) well above the horizon in the Twelfth House.

planets stay within 4° of latitude north or south of the ecliptic, but the Moon can achieve a maximum latitude of 5°18', Mercury of 7°0', and Pluto of 17°19'. Comets or stars can have any latitude. The daily latitude of the planets is often included in EPHEMERIDES (see sample page from an ephemeris, page 48).

Celestial latitude may either be *geocentric*, in which case it is calculated as if the object were being seen from the center of the Earth, or *heliocentric*, in which case it is calculated as if from the center of the Sun.

Many astrologers ignore celestial latitude, confining themselves to one

dimension in the heavens—that of CELESTIAL LONGITUDE. This can lead to errors in the determination of aspects involving stars or such large-latitude planets as Mercury or Pluto. Disregard of latitude can also lead an astrologer to place a planet in the wrong house. For example, consider a birth chart cast for July 4, 1980, at 35° north terrestrial latitude, in which the Ascendant has a celestial longitude of 15°02' Libra (see figure 6). Since Pluto has a longitude of 18°59' Libra that day, most astrologers would place Pluto in the First House. But actually Pluto, with a celestial latitude of 17N12 (17°12' north) that day, is well into the Twelfth House. (See CELESTIAL COORDINATES.)

Because of latitude the body of a planet can rise at a degree some distance removed from its zodiacal position. In large parts of the world there can be differences between the *Rising Point* and the Ascendant of up to 20° for the Moon and Mars, up to 10° for Saturn, and up to 5° for Jupiter. In the case of Pluto, which can have over 17° latitude, the difference can be very much greater.

Celestial Longitude: Angular distance measured in degrees, minutes, and seconds along the ECLIPTIC in an eastward direction from the VERNAL POINT, whose longitude is 0°. Celestial longitude does *not* correspond to TERRESTRIAL LONGITUDE. Most astrologers reckon longitude in degrees of signs (each of the twelve signs having 30°), but some astrologers—and all astronomers—reckon longitude in cumulative degrees from 0° to 360°, called *absolute longitude*, as follows:

Sign	Absolute Longitude
0°–29° Aries	0°– 29°
0°–29° Taurus	30°– 59°
0°–29° Gemini	60°– 89°
0°–29° Cancer	90°–119°
0°–29° Leo	120°–149°
0°–29° Virgo	150°–179°
0°–29° Libra	180°–209°
0°–29° Scorpio	210°–239°
0°–29° Sagittarius	240°–269°
0°–29° Capricorn	270°–299°
0°–29° Aquarius	300°–329°
0°–29° Pisces	330°–359°

Thus the longitude of Margaret Mead's Sun (see CHART CALCULATION) can be expressed as either 23°57′ Sagittarius (usually written 23♐57) or 263°57′. Absolute longitude is invaluable to the astrologer when calculating the Part of Fortune, midpoints, and harmonic charts, or when using an electronic calculator.

A *longitude circle*, or *longitude meridian*, is a great circle perpendicular to the ecliptic at a point a certain number of longitude degrees from the vernal point (compare RIGHT ASCENSION). For example, as of 1980 the star Alphecca is on the longitude circle of 222° (or 12° Scorpio), even though it is remote from the ecliptic (its celestial latitude is 44N20—that is, 44°20′ north).

Celestial longitude may be either *geocentric*, in which case it is calculated as if the object were being seen from the center of the Earth, or *heliocentric*, in which case it is calculated as if from the center of the Sun.

Most available astrological EPHEMERIDES list the positions of the planets in geocentric longitude expressed in sign degrees, minutes, and (for the Sun and Moon) seconds. (See sample page from an ephemeris, page 48.)

Celestial Meridian: See MERIDIAN.

Celestial Sphere: The sky as it appears to an observer, who sees the heavenly bodies as though they were displayed on the inner surface of a sphere—or dome, since the lower half of the sphere is hidden beneath the local HORIZON. The observer seems to be in the center of the sphere. Of course, it is now nearly universally accepted that (a) the stars and planets are at varying distances from the Earth; and (b) the Earth—not to mention any specific location on its surface—is no more the center of the universe than any other place. Nonetheless, the celestial sphere remains a useful concept for orienting oneself to objects in the sky and for measuring the motions of those objects (and the motions of the Earth as well). (See CELESTIAL COORDINATES; COSMOGRAPHY.)

Ceres (glyph ⚳): The largest of the ASTEROIDS, discovered in 1801. Zipporah Dobyns associates it with personal service and nurturing; Eleanor Bach with fertility, nourishment, and health.

Chaldean Astrology: For centuries the discovery of astrology has been attributed to the Chaldean priests. Translations of the cuneiform tablets, especially those in the library of Ashurbanipal, king of Assyria from 669 to 626 B.C., reveal that astrologers were making periodic reports to their sovereign, advising him about the likelihood of war or bumper crops. They based their forecasts on such phenomena as the Moon having extreme south DECLINATION ("When the Moon is low in appearance, the submission [of the people] of a far country will come to the king"), which happens about once a decade, or a conjunction of Mars and Jupiter ("When Mars approaches Jupiter, in that year the king of Akkad will die and the crops of that land will be prosperous"), which occurs once every 2 years. These interpretations echo those traditionally believed to have been supplied the Akkadian king Sargon in the middle of the third millennium B.C.

The word *Chaldean* is the source of considerable confusion. We learn from Genesis (11:31) that Abraham emigrated from "Ur of the Chaldees"; since Ur was the principal city of the Sumerians, and since Abraham's departure was early in the second millennium B.C., when the Sumerians were still flourishing, we see that the Hebrews regarded the Sumerians as Chaldeans. In Mesopotamian records, however, the first mention of the Chaldeans is in the seventh century B.C. Herodotus identifies the Chaldeans as the people who took over Mesopotamia in 606 B.C. and ruled from Babylon, and it is these "new" Babylonians (as distinguished from the Amorite Babylonians, whose empire flourished in the first half of the second millennium B.C.), particularly the priests, who are famous for developing astrology, which was then indistinguishable from astronomy. They mapped the entire sky, improved methods for recording time, successfully forecast eclipses, and determined the precise length of the solar year to within 26 minutes. After the Persians conquered Babylon in 538 B.C., the word *Chaldean* came to mean the native priesthood in Babylon, as distinguished from the Persian priesthood, who were called *magi*. After the Macedonians conquered the area in the late fourth century B.C., the word *Chaldeans* was used to describe Greeks who had studied in the Babylonian schools of astrology. The Romans referred to all astrologers as Chaldeans, no matter what their nationality (see ROMANS, ASTROLOGY AMONG THE).

Actually, all the Mesopotamian peoples—that is, all those living between the Tigris and Euphrates rivers—were involved in the development of astrology, and ultimately the total contribution of the "Chaldeans" cannot be separated from that of the Sumerians, the Amorite Babylonians, or the Assyrians. Astrology, obviously, was not made in a day. The Sumerians of the early third millennium B.C. identified the four *royal stars*—Aldebaran, Regulus, Antares, and Fomalhaut—as marking the position of the EQUINOXES and SOLSTICES. A thousand years elapsed between these first empirical observations and the general astrological theology advanced by the Amorite Babylonians in the early second millennium B.C. That theology was further refined by the Chaldeans, or "new" Babylonians, a thousand years later.

Mesopotamian theology was very

conducive to the development of astrology. Fundamental to it was the conviction that conditions in heaven corresponded exactly to conditions on Earth, which is the sense of the astrological adage "as above, so below." Overall, this correspondence was viewed pessimistically, for if the world of the gods was just as capricious as the world of mankind, where was there room for hope? Mesopotamian theology was, of course, a product of its environment: a land subject to unpredictable, famine-producing floods and droughts and totally vulnerable to military invasion. Astrology was a way of discovering the will of the perverse gods and the law of Necessity, which even the gods had to obey, and it was more scientific than interpreting dreams or examining sheep livers.

The Babylonians believed that one day a female monster named Tiamat was brought forth by the primordial waters that covered the sky as well as the Earth. The god Marduk (Bel), or Ashur, sliced her in two with his sword and turned the two halves into two superimposed vaults, both immobile: the rounded dome of the heavens and the flattened arch of the Earth. In the celestial dome certain stars were led by the gods along regular paths, under the omnipotent eye of Marduk: These were the fixed stars. Others, however, were not subject to a regular course fixed by Marduk, but to a vaster trajectory subject to Anu, the universal Father. These privileged stars, which were in fact the planets, were five in number: Dapinu (Jupiter), ruled by Marduk; Kilbat (Venus), ruled by Ishtar; Kai-

manu (Saturn), ruled by Ninib; Bibu (Mars), ruled by Nergal; and Mustabarru (Mercury), ruled by Nebu. To these were added the two luminaries, Sin (the Moon), who was a masculine god, and Shamash (the Sun).

Thus out of the observation of the sky by the shepherds of the desert and attempts to interpret the phenomena observed by the priests, there arose a *cosmogony*, that is, a theory of the celestial system that is the origin of modern astrology, although at the time it was primarily mythological. But what of the condition of man, so small and weak in comparison with this cosmic infinity? For the Chaldeans, the answer to this question was self-evident: "The seven stars subject to Anu foretell future events and reveal to men the benevolent plans of the gods," according to the Greek historian Diodorus Sicilus (first century B.C.), who studied Chaldean civilization.

Astrology was born. But before the new science could become more precise, it was necessary to define the zodiac and to build up a body of correspondences between celestial and terrestrial events through painstaking observation. It was to this task that the Chaldean astrologer-priests—there was no distinction between the two functions at this time—devoted themselves for centuries.

The apparent motion of the Sun always takes place in the same part of the sky, the narrow zone we now call the *ecliptic*. By observing at night the part of the sky through which the Sun apparently traveled during the day, the Chaldean priests noticed that every month the Sun travels across a different background of fixed stars. This observation was the origin of the SIDEREAL ZODIAC, which was divided into twelve parts, each one bearing the name of the constellation across which the Sun traveled. Although the Greeks later gave them other names, corresponding to their own mythology, these early astrological signs were rather similar to our own.

Kusarikkut (Aries), the first sign of the zodiac, was a transitional phase, for some stars of the constellations of Pisces and Cetus appear in this part of the ecliptic. It was the sign of agriculture. Te-te (Taurus), represented by a bull harnessed to a chariot, suggests the bull that was used by the goddess Ishtar to fight Gilgamesh, the legendary hero. Tua-mu or Masmasu (Gemini) corresponds to the two brother gods Nebu and Marduk, whom the Greeks called Castor and Pollux. The dual nature of this sign is a vestige of the struggle between the two warring brothers.

Nangaru, or Al-lul (Cancer), is a sign charged with symbolism. Al-lul means "the claw of the crab," which suggests the crescent shape of the Moon, ruler of this sign. Nanguru means "carpenter," but it also stands for the cradle with curved rockers used by the Aramaeans. The cradle of Jesus, born the son of a carpenter, must have been of this kind. Many astrologers have speculated that the birth chart of Jesus had Cancer on the Midheaven, no doubt due to the tradition that he was born at midnight on December 25. Hence the analogy often seen by *Cabalists* be-

tween Christ and the Moon god of the ancient Chaldeans.

A-ru (Leo) was identified with the star Regulus, which appeared when the Sun was as ferocious as the king of beasts. Shi-ru, or Ki (Virgo), whose Chaldean name means "ear of wheat," was the archetypal symbol of the mother (the worship of Mary considerably antedated Christianity). Zibanitu, or Nuru (Libra), suggests the balance between day and night as well as between life and death.

Akrabu (Scorpio), corresponding at that time to the autumn equinox, represented the snake man who was said to have helped Tiamat resist the attack of Marduk. Pabilsag (Sagittarius) is an extension of the previous sign; indeed, some authorities believe that the arrow of Sagittarius is really the sting of the scorpion.

Sakhu, or Enzu (Capricorn), had the same symbolism as today, a remarkable case of persistence. Gu, or Mulgula (Aquarius), means "the great man" and stood for Gilgamesh, who corresponds to the Greek Hercules.

Finally, Nunu, or Zib (Pisces), the twelfth and last sign of the zodiac, completed the soli-lunar year of the Chaldeans with the death of nature before the resurrection of spring (see LUNAR YEAR).

Chart: See BIRTH CHART.

Chart Calculation: The birth chart is the foundation of all astrological procedure. It is the basis on which an astrologer can make a preliminary interpretation of the native's personality and character and then go on to calculate progressions, directions, and transits, or engage in chart comparison.

The interpretation of a birth chart requires considerable expertise, including knowledge of a body of rules, many of them centuries old, that constitute astrological tradition. An introduction to that tradition is one of the main purposes of this volume. On the other hand, the operations involved in calculating and drawing up a birth chart for a given moment are within reach of everyone, provided he or she proceeds carefully and pays attention to details.

A few tools are essential. You will need an EPHEMERIS and a TABLE OF HOUSES; an atlas (or any other reference work that gives longitudes and latitudes); and a source of determining local time zones and whether or not Daylight Saving (or Summer) Time was in effect. (Examples are Neil Michelsen's *American Atlas* or Doris Chase Doane's *Time Changes in the USA, Time Changes in Canada and Mexico,* and *Time Changes in the World;* for abbreviated information on time zones and time changes, see TIME.) As an aid in calculation some astrologers use a four-operation calculator, others use proportional logarithms, others use tables of diurnal motions, and still others use a slide rule. We will explain how to proceed with a calculator and with logs. In addition to paper, pen or pencil, and ruler, you may want to use one of the styles

Note 1: The procedure described in this entry is the so-called direct method. The editors have selected it because it is the method preferred by the majority of those astrologers who acted as consultants on this book. However, it is not the only possible procedure for calculating accurate birth charts. The traditional, or "LMT," method, still used by most astrologers in the United States, differs from the direct method in a few essential steps in the calculation of house cusps, yet it produces the same results. According to the LMT method, one converts the Standard Time of birth (step 2) to *local mean time* (LMT), the actual solar time at the birthplace (see TIME). Then one adds the following values: the listed Greenwich sidereal time (GST) in the ephemeris; the time elapsed since GST (that is, the LMT, plus an additional 12 hours only if the LMT is P.M. and one is using a midnight ephemeris, or if the LMT is A.M. and one is using a noon ephemeris); TIME ACCELERATION, and LONGITUDE ACCELERATION. The result is the local sidereal time of birth (LST). This will be the same quantity arrived at in step 12 by the direct method, which converts Standard Time to Universal Time and then back to local time. Astrologers using either method employ Universal (or Greenwich) time in the calculation of the planets' positions.

Note 2: Students who have some experience with astrological calculations may be surprised to find instructions to round off values in steps 1, 10, 13, 14, 15 (note), and 18. There may be some who will point out, in step 8, that the amount to subtract from GST to correct a noon ephemeris to midnight is really 12 hours 1 minute 58 seconds, not 12 hours 2 minutes; or, in step 9, that the solar-sidereal correction is really 9.86 seconds per hour, not 10 seconds per hour; or, in steps 16 through 20, that Universal Time (UT) is used instead of Ephemeris Time (ET). The editors of this encyclopedia feel that such precision is excessive if a birthtime has been rounded to the nearest minute. It may be objected that rounding off other entry values (such as longitude and latitude) and intermediate values (such as LST) tends to compound whatever error is introduced by the approximated birthtime. But this compounding at worst only amounts to a matter of seconds. Naturally, very precise values are needed in order to obtain accurate indications from such techniques as primary directions and solar and lunar returns. If such precise values are desired, we recommend that the student have his or her chart *rectified* by an experienced astrologer (see RECTIFICATION). For a more extensive discussion of the reasons for rounding, see PRECISION.

of blank chart forms available at many astrological bookstores (see CHART FORM).

For our example we are using the birth data of Margaret Mead, who was born at 9:00 A.M., December 16, 1901, in Philadelphia, Pennsylvania. (For the source of this birthtime, see CHART INTERPRETATION.) We will first assume, for purposes of instruction, that the time of 9:00 A.M. is accurate to the minute. Later, we will indicate shortcuts for cases where the birthtime is more vague.

BIRTHTIMES ACCURATE TO THE MINUTE
Houses

1. Find the terrestrial coordinates (latitude and longitude) of the birthplace, round the values to the nearest quarter degree, and enter on your worksheet. The coordinates given for Philadelphia in Michelsen's *American Atlas* are 39N57 (latitude) and 75W10 (longitude), which can be rounded to 40N and 75¼W.

2. Determine whether or not Daylight Saving (or Summer) Time was in effect. If so, subtract 1 hour from the given birthtime to arrive at Standard Time. (If Double Summer Time was in effect, subtract 2 hours. Some localities only advance ½ hour for Daylight Saving Time; for these subtract ½ hour.) We see on page 285 that the United States did not observe Daylight Saving Time before 1918. Thus, we know that the 9:00 A.M. birthtime is already Standard Time.

3. Express the Standard Time according to the 24-hour clock. If the time is midnight, express it as 0:00. If it is between 12:01 and 12:59 A.M., change the 12 to 0 and drop the A.M. If the time is 1:00 to 11:59 A.M., simply drop the A.M. If the time is noon, express it as 12:00. If the time is between 12:01 and 12:59 P.M., simply drop the P.M. If the time is between 1:00 and 11:59 P.M., add 12 hours to it and drop the P.M. According to the 24-hour clock, Mead's 9:00 A.M. birthtime is expressed simply as 9:00.

4. Find the Standard Time meridian for the birthplace. On page 283 we see that the Standard Time meridian for the Eastern time zone in the United States is 75W.

5. Divide the value of the Standard Time meridian by 15. In Mead's case, this is 75 ÷ 15 = 5.

6. If the Standard Time meridian is west, add the value from step 5 in hours to the Standard Time (from step 3). If the Standard Time meridian is east, subtract. This is the *Universal Time* (UT). If the result is more than 24 hours, subtract 24 hours and add 1 day: In this case the UT is for the day *after* the recorded birthday. Write the UT and the UT date (either the recorded birthday or the day after) on your worksheet. Be sure to write the letters *UT* next to the time.

In Mead's case, the Standard Time meridian is west, so we add 5 hours to her birth Standard Time of 9:00, obtaining a UT of 14:00, still on December 16.

7. Find out whether your ephemeris gives data for Greenwich midnight (0 hours) or Greenwich noon (12 hours). This fact is usually given on the title page or somewhere nearby. (If not, use the following

DECEMBER 1901

LONGITUDE

DECLINATION and LATITUDE

DAILY ASPECTARIAN

Figure 7. Sample page from *The American Ephemeris 1901–1930*. (Reprinted by permission of Astro Computing Services.)

14ʰ 36ᵐ 0ˢ MC 219° 0′ 0″ ♏ 11° 25′ 58″					N LAT	14ʰ 40ᵐ 0ˢ MC 220° 0′ 0″ ♏ 12° 26′ 45″				
11	12	Ascendant	2	3		11	12	Ascendant	2	3
♐10 35.9	♑ 8 16.1	≈ 6 36.6	♓ 7 17.7	♈ 9 47.7	0	♐11 32.1	♑ 9 11.4	≈ 7 35.4	♓ 8 21.7	♈10 52.7
9 33.9	6 42.2	4 55.3	5 56.1	9 9.0	5	10 30.5	7 38.2	5 55.2	7 1.5	10 15.3
8 32.5	5 5.9	3 7.9	4 27.2	8 26.4	10	9 29.4	6 2.6	4 8.9	5 34.2	9 34.1
7 30.8	3 25.9	1 12.4	2 48.4	7 38.5	15	8 28.0	4 23.2	2 14.3	3 57.1	8 47.8
7 18.3	3 5.3	0 48.1	2 27.3	7 28.2	16	8 15.6	4 2.7	1 50.2	3 36.3	8 37.7
7 5.8	2 44.5	0 23.3	2 5.5	7 17.5	17	8 3.1	3 41.9	1 25.7	3 14.9	8 27.4
6 53.2	2 23.4	♑29 58.1	1 43.2	7 6.5	18	7 50.5	3 20.9	1 0.6	2 52.9	8 16.8
6 40.5	2 2.0	29 32.4	1 20.2	6 55.1	19	7 37.9	2 59.7	0 35.0	2 30.3	8 5.8
6 27.8	1 40.4	29 6.1	0 56.6	6 43.4	20	7 25.2	2 38.1	0 8.9	2 7.0	7 54.4
6 14.9	1 18.5	28 39.2	0 32.2	6 31.2	21	7 12.4	2 16.2	♑29 42.3	1 43.1	7 42.6
6 2.0	0 56.2	28 11.8	0 7.2	6 18.6	22	6 59.5	1 54.1	29 15.0	1 18.3	7 30.5
5 48.9	0 33.7	27 43.7	≈29 41.3	6 5.6	23	6 46.4	1 31.5	28 47.1	0 52.8	7 17.8
5 35.8	0 10.7	27 15.0	29 14.5	5 52.0	24	6 33.3	1 8.7	28 18.5	0 26.5	7 4.7
5 22.5	♐29 47.4	26 45.5	28 46.9	5 38.0	25	6 20.0	0 45.4	27 49.2	≈29 59.2	6 51.1
5 9.0	29 23.7	26 15.3	28 18.2	5 23.3	26	6 6.6	0 21.7	27 19.1	29 31.0	6 36.9
4 55.4	28 59.6	25 44.4	27 48.6	5 8.0	27	5 53.0	♐29 57.6	26 48.3	29 1.7	6 22.1
4 41.7	28 35.0	25 12.5	27 17.8	4 52.0	28	5 39.3	29 33.1	26 16.6	28 31.3	6 6.6
4 27.7	28 9.9	24 39.8	26 45.8	4 35.3	29	5 25.3	29 8.1	25 44.0	27 59.8	5 50.5
4 13.6	27 44.4	24 6.2	26 12.6	4 17.8	30	5 11.2	28 42.5	25 10.4	27 26.9	5 33.5
3 59.3	27 18.3	23 31.6	25 38.0	3 59.4	31	4 56.9	28 16.5	24 35.9	26 52.7	5 15.7
3 44.8	26 51.7	22 55.9	25 1.9	3 40.1	32	4 42.4	27 49.9	24 0.3	26 17.0	4 57.0
3 30.1	26 24.5	22 19.1	24 24.2	3 19.7	33	4 27.6	27 22.6	23 23.6	25 39.8	4 37.3
3 15.1	25 56.7	21 41.1	23 44.8	2 58.2	34	4 12.6	26 54.8	22 45.6	25 0.8	4 16.4
2 59.9	25 28.2	21 1.9	23 3.6	2 35.5	35	3 57.4	26 26.3	22 6.4	24 20.0	3 54.4
2 44.4	24 59.0	20 21.3	22 20.4	2 11.4	36	3 41.9	25 57.0	21 25.9	23 37.1	3 31.0
2 28.6	24 29.1	19 39.4	21 35.0	1 45.8	37	3 26.1	25 27.0	20 43.9	22 52.2	3 6.2
2 12.5	23 58.4	18 55.9	20 47.3	1 18.5	38	3 9.9	24 56.3	20 0.4	22 4.9	2 39.7
1 56.1	23 26.9	18 10.8	19 57.1	0 49.3	39	2 53.5	24 24.7	19 15.2	21 15.0	2 11.4
1 39.3	22 54.5	17 24.1	19 4.2	0 18.0	40	2 36.7	23 52.2	18 28.4	20 22.4	1 41.0
1 22.2	22 21.2	16 35.5	18 8.2	♓29 44.4	41	2 19.5	23 18.8	17 39.7	19 26.8	1 8.4
1 4.7	21 47.0	15 45.0	17 9.1	29 8.2	42	2 1.9	22 44.4	16 49.0	18 28.0	0 33.3
0 46.8	21 11.7	14 52.4	16 6.4	28 29.1	43	1 44.0	22 8.9	15 56.2	17 25.5	♓29 55.2
0 28.4	20 35.3	13 57.6	14 59.8	27 46.6	44	1 25.5	21 32.3	15 1.2	16 19.1	29 13.9
0 9.6	19 57.7	13 0.5	13 49.0	27 0.2	45	1 6.6	20 54.5	14 3.8	15 8.5	28 28.9
♏29 50.3	19 18.9	12 0.9	12 33.6	26 9.5	46	0 47.2	20 15.5	13 3.9	13 53.2	27 39.5
29 30.5	18 38.8	10 58.7	11 13.1	25 13.8	47	0 27.3	19 35.1	12 1.2	12 32.7	26 45.2
29 10.1	17 57.3	9 53.6	9 47.1	24 12.2	48	0 6.7	18 53.3	10 55.6	11 6.6	25 45.2
28 49.1	17 14.3	8 45.5	8 15.0	23 3.8	49	♏29 45.6	18 10.0	9 47.0	9 34.3	24 38.4
28 27.5	16 29.7	7 34.1	6 36.2	21 47.4	50	29 23.8	17 25.1	8 35.0	7 55.1	23 23.8
28 5.2	15 43.5	6 19.3	4 50.1	20 21.5	51	29 1.3	16 38.4	7 19.4	6 8.5	21 59.8
27 42.1	14 55.5	5 0.8	2 56.1	18 44.3	52	28 38.1	15 49.9	6 0.1	4 13.7	20 24.7
27 18.3	14 5.5	3 38.4	0 53.3	16 53.5	53	28 14.1	14 59.4	4 36.7	2 9.8	18 36.0
26 53.6	13 13.5	2 11.8	♑28 41.0	14 46.4	54	27 49.2	14 6.9	3 9.0	♑29 56.2	16 31.0
26 28.0	12 19.4	0 40.8	26 18.4	12 19.1	55	27 23.4	13 12.1	1 36.8	27 31.9	14 5.9
26 1.5	11 22.9	♐29 5.0	23 44.7	9 27.3	56	26 56.5	12 14.9	♐29 59.7	24 56.1	11 16.1
25 33.9	10 23.9	27 24.3	20 59.2	6 5.0	57	26 28.7	11 15.2	28 17.4	22 7.9	7 55.5
25 5.2	9 22.3	25 38.3	18 1.1	2 5.2	58	25 59.6	10 12.7	26 29.7	19 6.6	3 56.5
24 35.3	8 17.8	23 46.7	14 49.9	≈27 19.2	59	25 29.3	9 7.3	24 36.2	15 51.7	≈29 10.0
24 4.1	7 10.3	21 49.3	11 25.3	21 37.2	60	24 57.7	7 58.7	22 36.7	12 22.8	23 25.4
23 31.4	5 59.5	19 45.9	7 47.4	14 49.9	61	24 24.5	6 46.8	20 31.0	8 39.9	16 32.0
22 57.1	4 45.2	17 36.1	3 56.5	6 51.4	62	23 49.8	5 31.3	18 18.7	4 43.5	8 22.8
22 21.2	3 27.2	15 20.0	♐29 53.5	♑27 44.4	63	23 13.3	4 11.9	15 59.8	0 34.5	♑28 59.8
21 43.4	2 5.1	12 57.2	25 40.1	17 45.7	64	22 34.8	2 48.3	13 34.0	♐26 14.8	18 41.0
21 3.5	0 38.8	10 27.8	21 18.2	7 26.7	65	21 54.2	1 20.3	11 1.4	21 46.5	8 1.1
20 21.4	♏29 7.8	7 51.7	16 50.5	♑27 26.0	66	21 11.2	♏29 47.5	8 22.0	17 12.5	♑27 42.6
5	6	Descendant	8	9	S LAT	5	6	Descendant	8	9
		♉ 11° 25′ 58″						♉ 12° 26′ 45″		
2ʰ 36ᵐ 0ˢ		MC	39° 0′ 0″			2ʰ 40ᵐ 0ˢ		MC	40° 0′ 0″	

Figure 8. Sample columns from *AFA Table of Houses: Koch System*. (Reprinted by permission of the American Federation of Astrologers.)

rule: If the sidereal time given for January 1 of any year is 6+ hours, it is a midnight ephemeris; if it is 18+ hours, it is a noon ephemeris.) The ephemeris we will be using to calculate Mead's chart is a midnight ephemeris.

8. Turn to the page in your ephemeris for the UT date (from step 6) and find the column giving the *Greenwich sidereal time* (GST) for each day of the month. (GST is generally given on the left, as it is in the sample page [figure 7], and is usually headed simply *sidereal time* or *Sternzeit*.) If you are using a midnight ephemeris, directly under the UT you wrote down in step 6 write the GST given for the UT date. Write *GST—0h* next to it. The GST given in our sample ephemeris page for December 16, 1901, is 5h 35m 45s, or 5:35:45.

(For a noon ephemeris, subtract 12 hours 2 minutes from the GST given for the UT date in order to obtain the GST corrected to midnight. To do this subtraction, it may first be necessary to add 24 hours to the given GST.)

9. Calculate the *solar-sidereal correction*. This amounts to 10 seconds for every hour, or 1 second for every 6 minutes, of UT. Express the result in minutes and seconds and write under the ephemeris GST. (Be sure to keep minutes under minutes and seconds under seconds!) The solar-sidereal correction for Mead is 14 hours × 10 seconds/hour = 140 seconds, or 2 minutes 20 seconds.

10. Add the UT, the ephemeris GST, and the solar-sidereal correction. The result is the *birth GST*. Ex-

press in its simplest form and round to the nearest minute. If the GST is greater than 24 hours, subtract 24 hours. In Mead's case:

$$
\begin{array}{ll}
14:00 & UT \\
5:35:45 & GST\text{—}0h \\
+\quad 2:20 & s\text{–}s\ correction \\
\hline
19:37:65, &
\end{array}
$$

which simplified is

19:38:05   *birth GST*,

which we round to 19:38.

11. Multiply the value of the birth longitude by 4 and express in minutes of time. Simplify this result, if necessary, to hours and minutes. This is the *longitude correction*. Multiplying Mead's birth longitude of 75¼ by 4, we obtain 301 minutes, which can be simplified to 5 hours 1 minute.

12. If the birth longitude is west, subtract the longitude correction from the birth GST. If the birth longitude is east, add the longitude correction. The result is the *local sidereal time* (LST). Mead's birth longitude is west, so we subtract.

$$
\begin{array}{ll}
19:38 & birth\ GST \\
-\ 5:01 & longitude\ correction \\
\hline
14:37 & LST
\end{array}
$$

(For birthplaces of south latitude, add 12 hours to the LST to arrive at the adjusted LST. If the result is more than 24 hours, subtract 24 hours.)

You are now ready to find the Midheaven and the other house cusps. Write the roman numerals corresponding to the houses on your worksheet, one under the other, in this order: *X, XI, XII, I, II, III.*

13. Open your table of houses. (See sample page from the Koch table, figure 8.) Observe that there are main columns divided into subcolumns corresponding to the Eleventh, Twelfth, First (Ascendant), Second, and Third Houses. Running across these columns are rows corresponding to latitudes, usually from 0° to 66°. At the top of each main column three values are normally given: a specific sidereal time on the left; the corresponding celestial longitude on the Midheaven (here abbreviated *MC*) in the center, and the corresponding right ascension on the right.

Find the main column with the sidereal time that is closest to the LST of birth. If the sidereal time at the top of one of the main columns is the same as the LST of birth and if the birth latitude was rounded to the nearest whole degree, you can copy the house cusps directly from the table of houses. (If the latitude was not rounded to the nearest whole degree, see note on page 52.) For the Tenth-House cusp, take the value given in the center at the top of the main column. For the other house cusps, take the values given in each house subcolumn for the birth latitude, and round them to the nearest quarter degree. Find the appropriate sign by reading upward from the latitude; do not simply take the sign at the top of the subcolumn. (For birthplaces of south latitude, use the opposite sign for each house cusp; see SIGNS OF THE ZODIAC.)

If no sidereal time at the top of a main column corresponds exactly to the LST of birth, find the two adjacent main columns for the sidereal times *before* and *after* the LST. Since Mead's LST is 14:37, we need the columns with 14:36 and 14:40 at their upper-left corners.

Round the sidereal time given in the earliest main column to the nearest minute. In our sample this has already been done. The sidereal time for the earlier main column is 14:36.

Subtract this earlier time from the LST and divide by 4, disregarding the unit. In Mead's case, 14:37 (LST) − 14:36 = 1 minute, or—disregarding the unit—1. Dividing by 4, we get ¼.

14. Calculate the Midheaven, or Tenth-House cusp. To do this, find the difference in minutes between the MC in the earlier column and that in the later column. Both values should be rounded to the nearest minute. Multiply the result by the fraction found at the end of Step 13, round the result, and add to the figure in the earlier column, rounding to the nearest quarter degree. In Mead's case, the MC in the earlier column is 11°25′58″ Scorpio, which we round to 11°26′; the MC in the later column is 12°26′45″ Scorpio, which we round to 12°27′. The difference between them is 1°1′, or 61′. Multiplying this by ¼, we get 15¼′, which we round to 15′. When we add this to the figure in the earlier main column, 11°26′ Scorpio, we get 11°41′ Scorpio, which we then round to 11¾° Scorpio, which is Mead's Midheaven. (For birthplaces of south latitude, use the opposite sign; see SIGNS OF THE ZODIAC.)

15. Repeat the operation for the Eleventh-, Twelfth-, First-, Second-, and Third-House cusps, using the values given for the appropriate latitude degrees in each house subcolumn. (If the latitude was not rounded to the nearest whole degree, see note after this step.) Remember that the appropriate sign on the cusp is found by reading upward from the latitude; do not simply take the sign at the top of the subcolumn. Write the results opposite the roman numerals corresponding to the houses on your worksheet, rounding to the nearest quarter degree. (Remember to use the opposite signs for birthplaces of south latitude.) Here are the results for Mead's chart:

X   11¾° ♏
XI   2° ♐
XII 23¼° ♐
I   17¾° ♑
II   19½° ♒
III 0¾° ♈

The cusps for the Fourth through Ninth Houses have the same degrees as those for the Tenth through Third Houses, but they have the opposite signs. All cusps can now be copied onto a chart form and the houses drawn on the chart, if necessary.

Note: The foregoing system for calculating house cusps is appropriate in cases where latitude of birthplace has been rounded to the nearest whole degree. In cases where the latitude has *not* been rounded to the nearest whole degree, in figuring cusps for all except the Tenth House, it is necessary to interpolate. To do this for the Eleventh-House cusp, turn to the earlier main column, and in the subcolumn for the Eleventh-House figure the difference between the value given for the whole-number latitude degree *less* than the birth latitude and the value given for the whole-number latitude degree *greater* than the birth latitude. (For birthplaces with south latitude, use the corresponding north latitude.) Multiply this difference by the remaining fraction of a degree in the birth latitude and round to the nearest minute. For example, the latitude of New York City is 40°45′ north (40N45), which is rounded to 40¾N. In the Eleventh-House subcolumn, the difference between the value for latitude 40N (1°39.3′) and that for latitude 41N (1°22.2′) is 17.1′, rounded to 17′. Multiplying by ¾, we get ⁵¹⁄₄, or 12¾, which can be rounded to 13. Put a plus sign (+) in front of this number if the values increase going down the subcolumn and a minus sign (−) if the values decrease going down the subcolumn. Write this number to the left of the roman numeral *XI* on your worksheet. Repeat for the Twelfth, First, Second, and Third Houses. Then repeat step 14 for these five houses, using the values given for the smaller whole-number latitude degree in each subcolumn. Add or subtract (as indicated) the number of minutes you wrote to the left of the roman numeral for each house cusp, and round the result to the nearest quarter degree. Write the results to the right of the roman numerals and copy onto the chart.

Planets

16. In calculating the positions of

the planets, we will be working with two different dates in the ephemeris, a *prior date* and a *following date*. For a midnight ephemeris, as in our example, the prior date is the UT date.

(For a noon ephemeris, if the UT is greater than 12:00, subtract 12 hours from it; the prior date is the UT date. If the UT is less than 12:00, add 12 hours to it; the prior date is the day preceding the UT date. In either case, you will be working with an *adjusted UT* in subsequent steps. If the UT is exactly 12:00, the planets' positions can be read directly from the UT date.)

17. On your worksheet, write out the glyphs for the planets, one under the other, in this order: ⊙ (Sun), ☽ (Moon), ☿ (Mercury), ♀ (Venus), ♂ (Mars), ♃ (Jupiter), ♄ (Saturn), ♅ (Uranus), ♆ (Neptune), and ♀ or ♇ (Pluto).

18. Find the *daily motion* of each planet and write it to the left of the corresponding glyph. The daily motion is the difference between the longitude given for the prior date and the longitude given for the following date. As with the table of houses, always read upward from the date to find the sign; do not simply use the sign at the top of the column. If the longitude for the prior date is greater than that for the following date, the planet is RETROGRADE: Write the symbol ℞ after the planet's glyph and insert a minus sign (−) in front of the daily motion. If you will be using a calculator, express the daily motion in minutes; if you will be using logarithms, express it in degrees and minutes. If you use a calculator, the Sun's motion should be rounded to

the nearest tenth of a minute; otherwise round it to the nearest minute. The motion of the Moon and the planets should be rounded to the nearest minute.

For example, let us consider the daily motion of Mead's Sun. The longitude given for the prior date is 23°21'19" Sagittarius, which we round to 23°21.3'. The longitude for the following date is 24°22'24" Sagittarius, which we round to 24°22.4'. The difference is 1°1.1', or 61.1'.

We can round the longitude of the Moon to the nearest minute. The Moon's prior-date longitude is 18°35'51" Aquarius, which we round to 18°36'. The following-date longitude is 1°31'20" Pisces, which we round to 1°31' Pisces and then express as 31°31' Aquarius so that we can subtract the prior-date longitude. The difference is 12°55', or 775'.

Here are the calculated daily motions for all Mead's planets:

1°1.1' = 61.1' ⊙
12°55' = 775' ☽
1°33' = 93' ☿
56' ♀
47' ♂
14' ♃
7' ♄
4' ♅
−1' ♆ ℞
−1' ♀ ℞

Note that Neptune and Pluto are retrograde.

19. Find the longitudes of the planets for the UT (or adjusted UT). *To do this by calculator,* divide the UT (or adjusted UT) in hours and decimals of hour by 24. Store this decimal

Hours or Degrees

Min.	0	1	2	3	4	5	6	7	8	9	10	11
0	3.1584	1.3802	1.0792	9031	7781	6812	6021	5351	4771	4260	3802	3388
1	3.1584	.3730	.0756	07	63	6798	09	41	62	52	3795	82
2	2.8573	.3660	.0720	8983	45	84	5997	30	53	44	88	75
3	.6812	.3590	.0685	59	28	69	85	20	44	36	80	68
4	.5563	.3522	.0649	8935	10	55	73	10	35	28	73	62
5	2.4594	1.3454	1.0614	8912	7692	6741	5961	5300	4726	4220	3766	3355
6	.3802	.3388	.0580	8888	74	26	49	5289	17	12	59	49
7	.3133	.3323	.0546	65	57	12	37	79	08	04	52	42
8	.2553	.3258	.0511	42	39	6698	25	69	4699	4196	45	36
9	.2041	.3195	.0478	19	22	84	13	59	90	88	38	29
10	2.1584	1.3133	1.0444	8796	7604	6670	5902	5249	4682	4180	3730	3323
11	.1170	.3071	.0411	73	7587	56	5890	39	73	72	23	16
12	.0792	.3010	.0378	51	70	42	78	29	64	64	16	10
13	.0444	.2950	.0345	28	52	28	66	19	55	56	09	03
14	.0122	.2891	.0313	06	35	14	55	09	46	49	02	3297
15	1.9823	1.2833	1.0280	8683	7518	6600	5843	5199	4638	4141	3695	3291
16	.9542	.2775	.0248	61	01	6587	32	89	29	33	88	84
17	.9279	.2719	.0216	39	7484	73	20	79	20	25	81	78
18	.9031	.2663	.0185	17	67	59	09	69	11	17	74	71
19	.8796	.2607	.0153	8595	51	46	5797	59	03	09	67	65
20	1.8573	1.2553	1.0122	8573	7434	6532	5786	5149	4594	4102	3660	3258
21	.8361	.2499	.0091	52	17	19	74	39	85	4094	53	52
22	.8159	.2445	.0061	30	01	05	63	29	77	86	46	46
23	.7966	.2393	.0030	09	7384	6492	52	20	68	79	39	39
24	.7781	.2341	1.0000	8487	68	78	40	10	59	71	32	33
25	1.7604	1.2289	0.9970	8466	7351	6465	5729	5100	4551	4063	3625	3227
26	.7434	.2239	.9940	45	35	51	18	5090	42	55	18	20
27	.7270	.2188	.9910	24	18	38	06	81	34	48	11	14
28	.7112	.2139	.9881	03	02	25	5695	71	25	40	04	08
29	.6960	.2090	.9852	8382	7286	12	84	61	16	32	3597	01
30	1.6812	1.2041	0.9823	8361	7270	6398	5673	5051	4508	4025	3590	3195
31	.6670	.1993	.9794	41	54	85	62	42	4499	17	83	89
32	.6532	.1946	.9765	21	38	72	51	32	91	10	77	83
33	.6398	.1899	.9737	00	22	59	40	23	82	02	70	76
34	.6269	.1852	.9708	8279	06	46	29	13	74	3995	63	70
35	1.6143	1.1806	0.9680	8259	7190	6333	5618	5003	4466	3987	3556	3164
36	.6021	.1761	.9652	39	74	20	07	4994	57	79	49	57
37	.5902	.1716	.9625	19	59	07	5596	84	49	72	42	51
38	.5786	.1671	.9597	8199	43	6294	85	75	40	64	35	45
39	.5673	.1627	.9570	79	28	82	74	65	32	57	29	39
40	1.5563	1.1584	0.9542	8159	7112	6269	5563	4956	4424	3949	3522	3133
41	.5456	.1540	.9515	40	7097	56	52	47	15	42	15	26
42	.5351	.1498	.9488	20	81	43	41	37	07	34	08	20
43	.5249	.1455	.9462	01	66	31	31	28	4399	27	01	14
44	.5149	.1413	.9435	8081	50	18	20	18	90	19	3495	08
45	1.5051	1.1372	0.9409	8062	7035	6205	5509	4909	4382	3912	3488	3102
46	.4956	.1331	.9383	43	20	6193	5498	00	74	05	81	3096
47	.4863	.1290	.9356	23	05	80	88	4890	65	3897	75	89
48	.4771	.1249	.9330	04	6990	68	77	81	57	90	68	83
49	.4682	.1209	.9305	7985	75	55	66	72	49	82	61	77
50	1.4594	1.1170	0.9279	7966	6960	6143	5456	4863	4341	3875	3455	3071
51	.4508	.1130	.9254	47	45	31	45	53	33	68	48	65
52	.4424	.1091	.9228	29	30	18	35	44	24	60	41	59
53	.4341	.1053	.9203	10	15	06	24	35	16	53	35	53
54	.4260	.1015	.9178	7891	00	6094	14	26	08	46	28	47
55	1.4180	1.0977	0.9153	7873	6885	6081	5403	4817	4300	3838	3421	3041
56	.4102	.0939	.9128	54	71	69	5393	08	4292	31	15	35
57	.4025	.0902	.9104	36	56	57	82	4799	84	24	08	28
58	.3949	.0865	.9079	18	41	45	72	89	76	17	01	22
59	.3875	.0828	.9055	00	27	33	61	80	68	09	3395	16

Figure 9. Table of proportional logarithms. (Reprinted by permission of the American Federation of Astrologers.)

Hours or Degrees

Min.	12	13	14	15	16	17	18	19	20	21	22	23
0	3010	2663	2341	2041	1761	1498	1249	1015	0792	0580	0378	0185
1	04	57	36	36	56	93	45	11	88	77	75	82
2	2998	52	30	32	52	89	41	07	85	73	71	79
3	92	46	25	27	47	85	37	03	81	70	68	75
4	86	41	20	22	43	81	34	0999	77	66	64	72
5	2980	2635	2315	2017	1738	1476	1229	0996	0774	0563	0361	0169
6	74	29	10	12	34	72	25	92	70	59	58	66
7	68	24	05	08	29	68	21	88	66	56	56	63
8	62	18	00	03	25	64	17	84	63	52	52	60
9	56	13	2295	1998	20	60	13	80	59	49	48	57
10	2950	2607	89	1993	1716	1455	1209	0977	0756	0546	0345	0153
11	45	02	84	89	11	51	05	73	52	42	42	50
12	38	2596	79	84	07	47	01	69	49	39	39	47
13	33	91	74	79	02	43	1197	65	45	35	35	44
14	27	85	69	74	1698	38	93	62	42	32	32	41
15	2921	2580	2264	1969	1,694	1434	1189	0958	0738	0529	0329	0138
16	15	75	59	65	89	30	85	54	34	25	26	35
17	09	69	54	60	85	26	82	50	31	22	22	32
18	03	64	49	55	80	22	78	47	27	18	19	29
19	2897	58	44	50	76	17	74	43	24	15	16	25
20	2891	2553	2239	1946	1671	1413	1170	0939	0720	0511	0313	0122
21	85	47	34	41	67	09	66	35	17	08	09	19
22	80	42	29	36	63	05	62	32	13	05	06	16
23	74	36	23	32	58	01	58	28	09	01	03	13
24	68	31	18	27	54	1397	54	24	06	0498	00	10
25	2862	2526	2213	1922	1649	1393	1150	0920	0702	0495	0296	0107
26	56	20	08	17	45	88	46	17	0699	91	92	04
27	50	15	03	13	40	84	42	13	95	88	90	01
28	45	09	2198	08	36	80	38	09	92	85	87	0098
29	39	04	93	03	32	76	34	05	88	81	83	94
30	2833	2499	2188	1899	1627	1372	1130	0902	0685	0478	0280	0091
31	27	93	83	94	23	68	26	0898	81	74	77	88
32	21	88	78	90	19	63	23	94	78	71	74	85
33	16	83	73	85	14	59	19	91	74	68	71	82
34	10	77	68	80	10	55	15	87	70	64	67	79
35	2804	2472	2164	1875	1605	1351	1111	0883	0667	0461	0264	0076
36	2798	67	59	71	01	47	07	80	64	58	61	73
37	93	61	54	66	1597	43	03	76	60	54	58	70
38	87	56	49	62	92	39	1099	72	56	51	55	67
39	81	51	44	57	88	35	95	68	53	48	51	64
40	2775	2445	2139	1852	1584	1331	1092	0865	0649	0444	0248	0061
41	70	40	34	48	79	27	88	61	46	41	45	58
42	64	35	29	43	75	22	84	57	42	37	42	55
43	58	30	24	38	71	18	80	54	39	34	39	52
44	53	24	19	34	66	14	76	50	35	31	35	48
45	2747	2419	2114	1829	1562	1310	1072	0846	0632	0428	0232	0045
46	41	14	09	25	58	06	68	43	29	24	29	42
47	36	09	04	20	53	02	64	39	25	21	26	39
48	30	03	2099	16	49	1298	61	35	21	18	23	36
49	24	2398	2095	11	45	94	57	32	18	14	20	33
50	2719	2393	2090	1806	1540	1290	1053	0828	0614	0411	0216	0030
51	13	88	85	02	36	86	49	24	11	08	13	27
52	07	82	80	1797	32	82	45	21	08	04	10	24
53	02	77	75	93	28	78	41	17	04	01	07	21
54	2696	72	70	88	23	74	37	14	01	0398	04	18
55	2691	2367	2065	1784	1519	1270	1034	0810	0597	0394	0201	0015
56	85	62	61	79	15	66	30	06	94	91	0197	12
57	79	56	56	74	10	61	26	03	90	88	94	09
58	74	51	51	70	06	57	22	0799	87	84	91	06
59	68	46	46	65	02	53	18	95	83	81	88	03

quotient in the calculator memory so that it can be recalled by pressing the constant function key, which we here label *K*. Multiply each planet's daily motion in minutes by *K*. *By logarithms*, from the table (see figure 9), find the log of the UT (or adjusted UT) in hours and minutes and mark it *PL* (for permanent log). Add to it the log for the daily motion of each planet in degrees and minutes. Find the sum in the log table and convert it back into degrees and minutes of longitude (this is called finding the *antilog*).

Finally, add the result—whether derived by calculator or by logarithms—to the prior-date longitude of the planet (subtract if the planet is retrograde).

For example, to find the longitude of Mead's Sun by calculator, divide 14.000 (the UT) by 24 and store in the memory. This quotient—.5833333—can now be recalled by pressing *K*. Clear the display window. Now multiply 61.1' (the Sun's daily motion) by *K*. The result is 35.641664', which is rounded to 35.6'. By logarithms, add the log of 14 hours (the UT), or .2341, to the log of 1°1' (daily motion), or 1.3730. The result is 1.6071, the antilog of which rounds to 0°36'. Adding the result by either method to the prior-date longitude of 23°21.3' Sagittarius (calculator) or 23°21' Sagittarius (logs), gives the Sun's position as 23°56.9' Sagittarius (calculator) or 23°57' Sagittarius (logs).

To find the longitude of Mead's Moon by calculator, multiply 775' (daily motion) by *K*. The result is 452.0833', which is rounded to 452', or 7°32'. By logarithms, add the log

of 14 hours (the UT), or .2341, to the log of 12°55' (daily motion), or .2691. The result is .5032, the antilog of which is 7°32'. Adding the result by either method to the prior-date longitude of 18°36' Aquarius, gives the Moon's position as 26°08' Aquarius.

The calculated longitudes for all Mead's planets are as follows:

☉	23♐56.9 or 23♐57
☽	26♒08
☿	14♐41
♀	10♒44
♂	17♑12
♃	17♑52
♄	15♑56
♅	17♐31
♆ ℞	00♋15
♇ ℞	17♊28

20. The birth longitude of the mean north node is determined in the same way as the longitudes of the planets. Assume a daily *retrograde* motion of 3'. Mead's north node, then, is 11°20' Scorpio. The south node (which is always exactly opposite the north node) is at 11°20' Taurus.

Now the planets and nodes can be entered on the chart form in their appropriate houses, as determined by their longitude. After entering the planets, many astrologers draw colored lines between any planets that form aspects so that these may be easily identified. For a graphic illustration and interpretation of Margaret Mead's chart, see CHART INTERPRETATION.

BIRTHTIMES NOT ACCURATE TO THE MINUTE

When the birthtime is not accurate

to the minute, it is pointless for the astrologer to calculate the chart with a precision appropriate for an exact birthtime. If the birthtime is accurate to the nearest quarter hour, round off the latitude and longitude of the birthplace to the nearest whole-number degree. Use the main column in the table of houses that is closest to the LST, and take the house cusps directly from that column. Round the longitudes of the house cusps to the nearest degree, and understand that there is a 3°–4° margin of imprecision. Round the Sun's longitude to the nearest minute and the Moon's to the nearest tenth of a degree.

If the time is accurate only to the nearest hour, do not use UT in calculating the houses. Use UT (or adjusted UT) only in calculating the planets' positions. For the houses obtain an approximate sidereal time by adding the GST given in the ephemeris for the birthday to the Standard Time of birth expressed according to the 24-hour clock (see step 3). If you are using a noon ephemeris, correct the given GST to midnight (see step 8). Determine the signs on house cusps, but not the degrees, and understand that there may be a margin of imprecision of one sign. Round the longitudes of the Sun, Mercury, and Venus to the nearest tenth of degree, and round the longitude of the Moon to the nearest degree. Consider seriously the possibility of having the chart rectified (see RECTIFICATION).

If only the birthdate is known, rectification is strongly urged. Use none of the foregoing steps. Take the planets' positions directly out of the ephemeris, without correcting for time or place. Display the planets on a chart form using the format described under SOLAR CHART or SUNRISE CHART.

—ALLAN EDMANDS

Chart Comparison (also called **Synastry**): The comparative study of two or more charts of individuals, nations, corporations, and so on, for the purpose of determining compatibility, improving communication, or illuminating problems within a personal, political, or professional relationship. In chart comparison particular attention is paid to major ASPECTS between charts, especially conjunctions and oppositions, and especially those between Sun, Moon, and Ascendant. In addition relative ELEMENT dominance and HEMISPHERE emphasis, MAJOR CONFIGURATIONS, heavily afflicted planets, and other factors important in interpreting single charts are also brought into play.

For example, a Sun-Mercury conjunction between charts—one person's Sun within orb of conjunction of another person's Mercury—indicates ease of communication, mental stimulation, and possible business contact. The two people "speak the same language," can discuss their relationship openly and deal rationally with any differences that may arise. They may give each other important information, especially about business matters, act as go-betweens for each other, or have an employer-employee relationship, the Sun representing the employer and Mercury the employee.

Aspects between Venus and Mars are important in the charts of lovers, since Venus rules affection and Mars sexuality. Jupiter contacts indicate possibilities for growth and expansion, while Saturn contacts are associated with seriousness and stability. Uranus may show a sudden meeting or unorthodox arrangement; Neptune, mutual confusion or illusion; and Pluto, intense feelings or a power struggle.

Chart comparison is very ancient; PTOLEMY writes in the *Tetrabiblos* that "marriages for the most part are lasting when in both the genitures the luminaries happen to be in harmonious aspect, that is, in trine or in sextile with one another . . . and even more when the husband's Moon is in such aspect with the wife's Sun." The positions of the luminaries and Ascendant in the charts of marriage partners were studied in the 1950s by the Swiss psychologist JUNG, who used astrology in connection with his clinical work.

Chart comparison is widely practiced in India, where even the poorest families would not consider contracting a marriage without first consulting an astrologer. Hindu methods place special emphasis on the Moon's LUNAR MANSION in each partner, there being tables of compatibility for different placements. Many factors are considered and, for example, where a daughter's chart shows the danger of widowhood, a husband is sought with suitable contraindications.

Chart comparison is commonly used, in conjunction with ELECTIONAL ASTROLOGY, to choose a favorable day for a marriage or to make a decision regarding a business partnership or professional collaboration.

In MUNDANE ASTROLOGY, the techniques of chart comparison can be applied to the study of a political situation, such as a war or peace treaty between two nations, by setting up and comparing the charts of the founding of the respective entities.

Authorities differ as to the orbs for major aspects between charts, but many astrologers would agree with Margaret Hone and Robert Hand in allowing 2° to 3°. (Also see COMPOSITE CHART.)

Chart Form: A graphic model designed to be used by astrologers to display the positions of the Sun, Moon, planets, and other important points in a horoscope. The chart form is thus a two-dimensional frame of reference for representing a moment of time in the three-dimensional solar system. The form generally used by modern astrologers is circular, with the circumference of the circle representing the ECLIPTIC. There are three basic styles of circular ecliptic

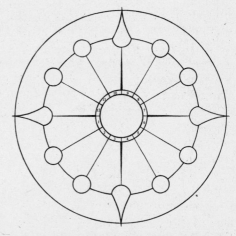

Figure 10. An equal-house chart form. (Reprinted by permission of Arcane Publications.)

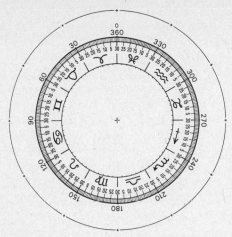

Figure 11. A calibrated chart form with printed glyphs, designed by Paul Choisnard.

forms: the equal-house, the calibrated 360° wheel, and the harmonic.

The *equal-house style* of chart form (not to be confused with the Equal House system of house division) stresses the perspective of the birthplace (see figure 10). The horizontal line represents the actual HORIZON, or ground, of the birthplace, and the vertical line represents the local MERIDIAN, local north and south, and local up and down. Seen from the birthplace, the houses are equal (provided the house system is specific to the birthplace and is not based on direct division of the ecliptic; see HOUSE DIVISION); it is the ecliptic that may appear distorted.

The *calibrated 360° wheel* displays the heavens from the perspective of the Earth as a whole (or, in a heliocentric chart, from the perspective of the Sun). Here the ecliptic is not distorted; it is the birthplace and its local horizon, meridian, and houses that may appear askew. The great advantage of this style over the equal-house style is that it makes it

easier to see and identify the aspects: A square really looks like a square. In most 360° forms the circle is divided into twelve 30° segments representing the signs of the zodiac. In one type (figure 11) the segments are identified by printed glyphs beginning with Aries on the left and proceeding counterclockwise around the wheel. In another type, useful with the Uranian Earth House system (again see HOUSE DIVISION), the printed zodiac begins with Libra on the left. A third type (figure 12) has no printed glyphs; these are filled in by the astrologer.

In the *harmonic style* of chart form the positions of the planets and points are displayed on a circle calibrated into a number of degrees that is a factor of 360°, such as 90°, 72°, 60°, 45°, 30°, or 7½°. Such a harmonic format is useful for instantly making a particular aspect visible, and for displaying midpoints (see HARMONIC CHART, HARMONICS). For example,

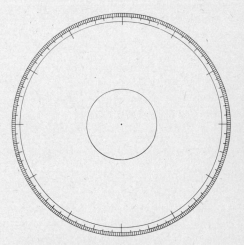

Figure 12. A calibrated chart form without printed glyphs. (Reprinted by permission of Arcane Publications.)

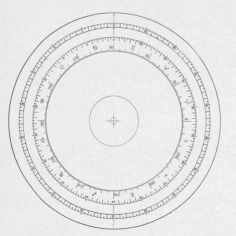

Figure 13. A 90° dial chart form. (Reprinted by permission of Ebertin Verlag.)

the 90° format—called the *90° dial*—consists of four superposed sectors, each of 90° (see figure 13). Positions that are approximately 0°, 180°, or 90° apart on the ecliptic will appear on the 90° dial as conjunct; positions that are 45° or 135° apart will appear as oppositions; positions that are 22½° or odd-number multiples thereof will appear as square. The 90° dial is widely used in COSMOBIOLOGY and the URANIAN SYSTEM of astrology.

With any of these circular forms larger concentric circles can be added to show the positions of progressed or transiting planets. In addition to the ecliptic forms, there are circular forms based on the CELESTIAL EQUATOR (useful for primary directions; see PROGRESSION AND DIRECTION), the PRIME VERTICAL, or the horizon. A few astrologers spurn the circle and prefer to use a linear form. At the other extreme, there have been a few attempts to design a form utilizing CELESTIAL LATITUDE, extending the chart out of the two-dimensional ecliptic plane (which in the ordinary form is really one-dimensional, since no attempt is made to represent planetary distances).

The use of printed chart forms is comparatively recent. In antiquity and the early part of the Christian era, there were no fixed rules for drawing up the horoscope. Each school of astrologers had its own way of representing the positions of the planets at the time of a nativity. Often the information was simply recorded in linear fashion, and the astrologer relied on a mental image of the heavens at the moment in question.

In the Middle Ages, two styles of charting were commonly used. In the first, twelve triangles corresponding to the twelve houses were placed inside a ring formed by two concentric circles, and the time and place of birth were written inside the smaller circle. The second style, which was the one most often used until the early twentieth century, consisted of three squares inscribed one inside

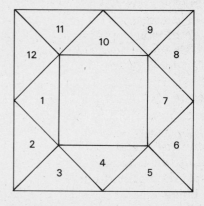

Figure 14. A medieval chart form.

the other so as to form twelve triangles (see figure 14). Each triangle corresponded to a house, as in the first style, and in it the astrologer noted the sign included in that house and the planets with their longitudes. Sometimes lines were drawn between the houses to indicate aspects.

Chart Interpretation: The art of translating the symbols contained in a horoscope into statements about human experience. Interpretation includes *delineation*—the translation of a specific piece of information such as a planet's sign or house position, an aspect, and so on—and *synthesis*, the weaving of all these separate pieces into a whole. While the calculation of a birth chart involves operations that can be performed almost immediately by anyone with an elementary understanding of mathematics and a little patience, its interpretation is a skill that is acquired gradually. It is difficult to teach and can best be learned by calculating the charts of people one knows well, starting with oneself, and studying them over a period of time.

Let us take as an example the chart of anthropologist Margaret Mead, born December 16, 1901, at 9 A.M. in Philadelphia, Pennsylvania (see figure 15). The source of the birthtime is a letter from Dr. Mead to the author of this entry. Her horoscope was cast in 1918 by a certain Dr. Twing, a physicist friend of the family who was also an astrologer. Dr. Mead had misplaced the chart but remembered the time.[1]

One cannot help wondering what Dr. Twing saw when he looked at

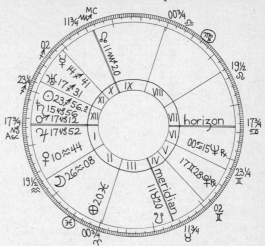

Figure 15. Geocentric birth chart of Margaret Mead.

the chart of this sixteen-year-old girl who was to become an international celebrity and who at her death would be hailed by the *New York Times* as "a pioneer whose innovations in research method have helped social anthropology to come of age as a science."[2] In the first place, his eye would immediately have been drawn to that trio of planets in Capricorn closely flanking the ASCENDANT: Mars and Saturn rising, and Jupiter just about to rise. The Ascendant has traditionally been regarded as the most sensitive point in the chart and any planets there as strongly influencing the personality. Jupiter on the Ascendant indicates self-confidence, broad interests, expansiveness, and a tendency to be stout; Mars, physical energy, courage, and self-assertiveness; Saturn, seriousness, organizing ability, ambition, and a tendency to short stature. The *Times* obituary reads, "The slight but sturdy Dr. Mead was possessed of virtually boundless energy, an unquenchable curiosity, a tenacious memory, and a genius for organizing her time."[3] As for courage, a woman who lived with equanimity among cannibals and headhunters surely possessed that quality in abundance; and as for self-assertiveness, Mead's feistiness was legendary, and the way she had of banging her forked stick on the floor for emphasis earned her such epithets as "stormy petrel."

Capricorn gives a liking for responsibility and is often emphasized in the charts of first children who assume a parental role with their younger siblings. Margaret was the oldest and by the age of eight was taking over preparations for family festivities, filling the stockings and trimming the Christmas tree. Saturn occupies its own sign of Capricorn, and since that sign is on the Ascendant, Saturn is also ruler of the chart. Chart ruler conjunct the Ascendant gives a powerful ego, and Saturn there gives an air of authority. Saturn conjunct the Ascendant can also give a strong sense of mission and urgency, of serious work to be done and time running out. Mead writes that when she was a graduate student, she used to wake up saying to herself, "The last man on Raratonga who knows anything about the past will probably die today. I must hurry."[4]

The statistical research of the GAUQUELINS has shown a strong correlation between planets rising just above the Ascendant at birth and later choice of profession; specifically, Mars and Saturn were found rising in the charts of scientists with a frequency significantly above the chance level.

The placement of Mars, Saturn, and the Sun in the Twelfth House shows a person who needs a certain amount of solitude and will probably spend some time in isolation from the world. Mead had a lifelong addiction to attic retreats. Her family was perpetually moving, and as soon as they arrived at a new house, "I ran ahead to find a room for myself as far away as possible from everyone else."[5] The Twelfth House also describes the long, lonely stretches of time spent in the field, totally cut off from her family and friends with little or no news of the world; and the famous "tower office" on the fifth floor of the American Museum of Natural History, which she occupied during her entire 52-year association with the museum.

The conjunction of Mercury, Uranus, and the Sun in Sagittarius, ruled by Jupiter, repeats and swells the Jupiterian theme announced by that planet's placement on the Ascendant and underlines its qualities of openness, curiosity, and broad perspective. Sagittarius is associated with the professions, teaching, and travel; it indicates an interest in abstract ideas and systems of values and a tendency to relate single experiences to larger wholes. There is a strong attraction to philosophy and religion; indeed, Mead was criticized by her colleagues in anthropology for overstepping the traditional limits of scientific observation and "preaching" about the lessons to be learned from certain so-called primitive societies.

It is interesting to note that Mead's Sun is within 1½° of the point on the zodiac that corresponds to the center of our galaxy. Theodor Landscheidt regards this point as an information center and associates it with emotional equilibrium, personal magnetism, and spiritual aspiration. The Sun conjunct Uranus shows unpredictability and unconventionality, traits that Mead manifested in both her professional and her domestic life. A strong Uranus breaks up marriages; asked to comment on her three divorces, Mead replied rather smugly that all three marriages were successful.

Mercury in aspect to Uranus indicates an original and independent thinker; here the two are in applying conjunction, a strong indication of genius. Mercury is the most elevated planet in the chart, forms aspects to every other planet, and stands at the MIDPOINT between Ascendant and MIDHEAVEN, indicating exceptional gifts of self-expression. Mead's powerful Mercury was manifested in the speed and ease with which she mastered seven different languages, not to mention her enormous output both as a writer (she wrote twenty-four books, coauthored or edited eighteen, and turned out vast numbers of scientific papers, monographs, and popular articles) and as a public speaker (in a sample year her scientific and popular lectures totaled 110).

The Mercury-Uranus conjunction is in the Eleventh House of friends, brotherhood, and the future, the natural house of Aquarius. If in Mead's incredible range of interests one thread could be found to predominate, it was her passionate interest in change and her deep sense of concern for the future. Her high school graduation speech was about the future, and her lifelong goals were mobility within one generation and building a world where "the valuable unit is a human being and not simply membership in one kind of culture rather than another."[6]

This Aquarian emphasis is repeated on a personal level by her Moon and Venus in Aquarius. Her Aquarian Venus in the First House in sextile to Uranus also gave her an enormous, if somewhat eccentric, charm. With Moon and Venus in the sign of groups, she was able to relate to every person in each of the eight villages she lived in and to remember them all later, sometimes after gaps of many years. Aquarius is an impersonal sign; one searches her autobiography and letters in vain for introspection or revelations about her private life. She scorned intimate journals; her diaries contained the bare bones of events and records, in case her work should be interrupted.

The Moon in Aquarius describes her mother, a woman of advanced ideas and egalitarian principles who danced for joy at the outbreak of the Russian Revolution. It also stands for her paternal grandmother, whom she loved deeply and acknowledged as the most decisive influence in her life. The Moon in the Second House of values and resources in trine to Neptune in Cancer indicates a deep womanliness that was expressed by her love of children, her interest in child rearing, and her insistence on being a mother, in spite of a tipped uterus that caused several miscarriages. The Moon's close sextile to the Sagittarian Sun made it possible for her to integrate the responsive side of her nature with her need to contribute something of value to the world. "She wanted to be a mother to the world," commented one of her friends, and indeed, in 1969, *Time* magazine named her "Mother of the World."

Mead's impact not only on her generation but on her age is suggested by the many aspects from personal points to Uranus, Neptune, and Pluto. Uranus is near the midpoint between Sun and Mercury, tying both into its close opposition to Pluto. In addition, Uranus forms aspects to every other planet in the chart, including close semisextiles to the three flanking the Ascendant. Neptune in the Sixth House of service is in out-of-sign but doubly applying trine to the Moon, denoting both compassion and a sense of mission. It not only opposes the Sun (idealism and self-sacrifice—Mead worked for a full year knowing she was dying of cancer), but its midpoint with Pluto is exactly opposite the Sun, which meant that Mead consciously identified with everyone alive on the planet. An example of this planetary consciousness is her reaction to the dropping of the first atomic bomb on Hiroshima in summer 1945, which caught her in the midst of writing. "I tore up every page of the book I had nearly fin-

ished. Every sentence was out of date. We had entered a new age."[7] Pluto is also heavily aspected, and its close quincunx to the Ascendant suggests a powerful personality and the possibility of influencing large numbers of people.

The Part of Fortune in Pisces in the Second House indicates considerable talent, material success, and a personality that best expresses itself by selfless devotion to the enduring values of civilization and culture. The north node conjunct the Midheaven describes a person the thrust of whose life is toward professional recognition and achievement. The sign on the Midheaven shows the qualities the native aspires to and will be remembered for. Scorpio stands for power, insight, and research; it is also the sign of sexuality. Mead achieved instant fame with *Coming of Age in Samoa* (1928), a study of puberty rites among adolescent girls; and with *Sex and Temperament in Three Primitive Societies* (1935) and *Male and Female: A Study of Sexes in a Changing World* (1949), her name became permanently associated with sexual theory. She is known for her open criticism of sexual repression in our society and her championing of sexual equality.

The total picture that emerges from this chart is one of tremendous energy, breadth of outlook, and concentration of purpose. Eight of the ten planets are clustered within a close quintile between the elevated Mercury and the Second-House Moon; the other two are tied in closely by aspect. The almost total absence of squares (except for Venus to the Midheaven and the north node) together with the Sun-Moon sextile conveys a sense of opportunities rather than obstacles, which is borne out by Mead's self-confidence, clear sense of vocation, and early success; but the presence of Saturn near the Capricorn Ascendant denotes unremitting industry. The majority of planets rising is the signature of the self-made person.

Margaret Mead's chart has not been chosen at random. It was selected to illustrate this book because Mead herself represents that integration of science and human values that the editors feel is—or should be—the goal of astrology. As a social scientist, Mead combined careful observation with a profound concern for people.

Not surprisingly, this independent thinker was also free of the usual scientific prejudice against astrology. In one of her columns in *Redbook* she recalled her introduction to horoscopes. "I was impressed then with the way a whole constellation of personality traits could be expressed in these astrological terms and how they became a language in which people could think about their own and other people's lives. . . . Whether there is anything further than this in horoscopes, we do not know. The scientific attitude is always to keep an open mind."[8]

—HELEN WEAVER

Chinese Astrology: Chinese astrology has its roots in Taoism, the name given to the doctrines of Lao-tse, the great philosopher who lived during the sixth century B.C. According to Lao-tse, the Tao is the intelligence, inaccessible to human understanding, that governs the natural course of things, including the movement of the stars. All the sciences, whether exact or conjectural, are part of the Tao. In fact the same word *tch'eou* is used to refer to scientists, astronomers, and astrologers.

Astrology flourished in ancient China. Marco Polo claims in his *Voyages* that there were five thousand

[1] A birthtime that is given on the hour is always regarded with suspicion. Every effort is being made to confirm the information with Mead's survivors, and should any discrepancy come to light, future editions of this book will be corrected accordingly.

[2] Boyce Rensberger in *The New York Times,* November 16, 1978.

[3] Alden Whitman in *The New York Times,* November 16, 1978.

[4] *Blackberry Winter: My Earlier Years* (New York: William Morrow, 1972), p. 338.

[5] Ibid., p. 10.

[6] *Letters from the Field 1925–1975* (New York: Harper & Row, 1977).

[7] *Blackberry Winter,* p. 313.

[8] "Margaret Mead Answers," *Redbook,* January 1965, p. 6.

Chinese astrological equipment built about 1880. (The Bettman Archive.)

astrologers living at the court of Kublai Khan. Over the years there arose several schools that differed greatly in their conception of the universe. Three of these schools claimed the majority of astrologers.

For the first group the Sun, the Moon, and all the stars floated freely in space according to the whims of the divine winds. The second group, who belonged to the school of Huen t'ien, believed that the sky was a solid area on which there were paths that the planets had to follow according to a precise itinerary. This solid sky was in the shape of an egg inside whose shell the Earth floated like the liquid mass of the yolk. The egg turned on its axis like a wheel, causing the Sun to dip below the horizon every evening, which explained the alternation of night and day. The third school, that of T'ien kai, conceived the sky to be a moving dais hanging over the Earth, which remained motionless in the position of an overturned bowl. The succession of the four seasons was caused by the Sun's following different itineraries on the dais of the sky.

Regardless of their conception of the universe—and we can see that they were very dissimilar—all Chinese astrologers followed the same procedure. They recorded the positions of the stars at the time of a person's birth and interpreted the chart on the basis of correspondences accumulated over centuries of observation. It mattered little whether the stars were drawn on a sky buffeted by divine winds, on the shell of an egg, or on a moving dais. Later, Chinese astrologers incorporated the discoveries of astronomy into their cosmology, but these discoveries did not alter the basic principles of interpretation.

The Chinese calendar is essentially based on the lunar cycle—that is, the Moon's SYNODIC PERIOD, whose duration is the period between New Moons. Each day the Moon occupies a different LUNAR MANSION, or *sieu*, similar to a constellation. There are twenty-eight *sieu*, grouped into four superconstellations—the Azure Dragon, the Black Warrior, the White Tiger, and the Red Bird—of seven *sieu* apiece. The Moon completes a circuit of the twenty-eight *sieu* in one SIDEREAL PERIOD, approximately. An extra day or two is needed for the Moon's synodic period to be completed; thus, some months have 29 days and some 30. The *sieu* in which the New Moon occurs gives its name to the month. Each year begins on the second New Moon after the winter solstice and usually consists of 12 months, although it is necessary for some years to have an extra, intercalary month (see LUNAR YEAR).

Chinese astrology, like Western astrology, has twelve signs. The main difference between the two systems is that the Chinese signs do not correspond to a month but to a year and that *all* bear the names of animals. (The twelve signs of Western astrology include animals, human beings, and mythological creatures.) The twelve signs of Chinese astrology are RAT, OX (or Buffalo), TIGER, CAT, DRAGON, SERPENT (or Snake), HORSE, GOAT, MONKEY, COCK (or Rooster), DOG, and PIG.

There is an old legend that one

New Year's Day, Buddha summoned all the animals in the creation to his court. Twelve of them, more civilized than the rest, turned up on time, and Buddha rewarded these twelve by naming the years after them in the order of their arrival. So in the Chinese calendar a new cycle of signs begins every 12 years.

In addition to the signs, Chinese astrology considers five elements: metal, water, wood, fire, and earth, whereas Western astrology has only four: earth, water, air, and fire (see ELEMENTS). Each element corresponds to 2 successive years, so that the entire elemental cycle takes 10 years. The combined sign and element cycle is 60 years, and the current combined cycle (1924–84) is the seventy-seventh since the adoption of the Sino-Vietnamese calendar in 2637 B.C.

The element *metal* is ruled by Venus and corresponds to the Western interpretation of that planet: cheerful, artistic, amorous, affectionate, harmonizing, flirtatious, lazy, self-indulgent, and obstinate.

The element *water* is very different from what it represents in Western astrology. It is ruled by and corresponds to Mercury: mental, humorous, witty, adaptable, studious, tricky, nervous, impressionable, worrisome, quibbling, and unscrupulous.

The element *wood* is ruled by and corresponds to Jupiter: enthusiastic, generous, respectful, optimistic, boastful, pretentious, vacillating, and fanatical.

The element *fire* is ruled by and corresponds to Mars: active, dynamic, courageous, high-spirited, adventurous, intemperate, rash, argumentative, and lustful.

The element *earth* is ruled by and corresponds to Saturn: sober, responsible, realistic, enduring, patient, reserved, inhibited, stern, pessimistic, and melancholy.

The current sign cycle of the Chinese calendar is as follows:

1980: year of the metal Monkey
1981: year of the metal Cock
1982: year of the water Dog
1983: year of the water Pig
1984: year of the wood Rat
1985: year of the wood Ox
1986: year of the fire Tiger
1987: year of the fire Cat
1988: year of the earth Dragon
1989: year of the earth Serpent
1990: year of the metal Horse
1991: year of the metal Goat

To find your sign according to the Chinese zodiac, add multiples of 12 to the year you were born until you arrive at one of the years listed above. For example, if you were born in 1930, your sign will recur in 1942, 1954, 1966, 1978, and 1990; thus you were born under the sign of the Horse.

Note: Since the traditional Chinese calendar is lunar, the day of the New Year is not fixed, as it is in the West, on January 1. Chinese New Year is always on the day (determined according to time in the Far East) of the second New Moon after the winter solstice. Western astrologers recognize this as the New Moon in Aquarius, which can occur in January or February. So if you were born during those 2 months, you may need to refer to the tables under the entries for each of the twelve signs to determine whether the animal for the previous year is applicable.

The Chinese zodiac has been adopted by the majority of Far Eastern peoples, with occasional variations. In Vietnam the Cock becomes the Chicken, and in Japan the Cat is replaced by the Hare; but the basic principles are the same.

To determine your element, find the year in the foregoing list whose last digit is the same as the last digit in your birth year. For example, if you were born in 1930, the last digit of your birth year is 0, so you would look at 1980 or 1990 on the list: Your element is metal. Again, be wary if your birthday is in January or February, for your element might be that of the previous year. Check the tables under the entries for each sign of the Chinese zodiac to be sure.

Astrologers were once very highly regarded by the Chinese, who accorded them a fearful respect. From the emperor's court to the common people, no one made a decision without consulting these interpreters of the celestial messages. Today in the People's Republic of China the profession of astrologer is forbidden by law. Nevertheless, a great many Chinese have their horoscopes cast secretly. A curious example of this persistence is the case of the fire Horse year, which was traditionally regarded as extremely malefic. During those years, the Chinese refrained from undertaking any new projects, assuming that they would be doomed to failure; many even avoided having children. In 1966, the most recent fire Horse year, a record number of abortions were reported in China, evidence of the survival of ancestral beliefs despite the official propaganda (see HORSE).

Chiron (glyph ⚷ or ⚷): A tiny planet (diameter 100–400 miles) or asteroidal body orbiting between Saturn and Uranus, discovered November 1, 1977, by Charles Kowal. Chiron was named by its discoverer after the wise centaur of Greek mythology who tutored many heroes in the military, medicinal, and cultural arts. Its orbit crosses that of Saturn regularly and that of Uranus occasionally, and has an inclination of 6°55.8′ and a mean sidereal period of 50.68 years. Its size and unexpected location have led many observers to classify it as an asteroid, and to suggest that it represents the first member of a trans-Saturnian asteroid belt.

Chiron's orbit was determined by Dr. Brian Marsden in late 1977 by examination of photographs of the object dating back as far as 1895. By early 1978 these photographs permitted the calculation of an astronomer's ephemeris from 1937 to 1977. Two groups of astrologers have published ephemerides on the new body, one led by Canadian writer Malcolm Dean, editor of *Phenomena,* and the other by American astrologer Al Morrison, editor of *CAO Times.* The *Ephemeris of Chiron 1890–2000,* published by Phenomena Publications, is calculated directly from orbital elements in heliocentric and geocentric longitude and latitude, right ascension, and declination. The *Ephemeris of Chiron 1890–1979,* published by

CAO Times, is based on Marsden's orbital calculations and gives longitude and latitude only. Never before has such a wealth of positional data been available so soon after the discovery of a celestial body.

The discovery of a new planet or planets orbiting between Saturn and Uranus was predicted by both Dane RUDHYAR in *The Astrology of Personality* and Charles JAYNE in the Spring 1961 issue of *In Search*. In addition, Jayne predicted that its period would be "fifty years, plus or minus two years" and that its orbit would "swing inside the orbit of Saturn."

At least five symbols have been proposed for Chiron; the two pictured above are those suggested by Dean and Morrison, respectively. As for Chiron's astrological significance, Dean suggests that the tiny planet may be related to the signs of Scorpio and Sagittarius, a view that accords with Jungian psychologist Tony Joseph's interpretation of Chiron as representing the archetype of the teacher and healer. The Association for Studying Chiron, initially under the guidance of Al Morrison, feels that the asteroid may have no sign rulership and describes its nature by such keywords as "maverick," "doorway," and "passage."

Choisnard, Paul (February 13, 1867, 10:45 P.M., Saint-Denis de Saintonge, France–February 9, 1930, 11:55 P.M.): French astrologer and author, at first under the pseudonym of Paul Flambard, later under his own name. A graduate of the famed Ecole Polytechnique and an excellent mathematician, he reformed the method for calculating the positions of the planets. Choisnard is one of the founders of the scientific movement that is concerned with finding statistical proof for astrology. His *Preuves et bases de l'astrologie scientifique* (1921), although later invalidated by the GAUQUELINS as based on faulty methods and insufficient samples, remains a pioneering work in its field. Choisnard is responsible for several innovations, including the use of standardized chart forms. He wrote some thirty books, the most important of which is *le Langage astral*. (See STATISTICS AND ASTROLOGY.)

Christianity and Astrology: In the early days of the Christian Church there was no official position on astrology, although some theologians—for example, Tertullian (160?–230)—were suspicious of its pagan origin. Origen (185?–254?), on the other hand, believed that celestial phenomena announced terrestrial events, though without causing them.

Through the ages the conflict between Christianity and astrology has focused on the issue of free will and grace. The determinism implicit or explicit in much early astrological thinking deprives man of his free will, so that he cannot choose between good and evil. This led some of the Church Fathers, notably Saint Augustine (354–430), to condemn astrology formally. Others, however, such as Synesius of Cyrene and Julius Maternus, who lived around the time of Augustine, believed that astrology could lead to a better understanding of theological problems.

The fact that according to Christian tradition it was a star that had guided the three Wise Men (who in the original Greek are called astrologers) to Bethlehem was a powerful argument. How was one to condemn the study of the stars when the Holy Spirit itself had used a star to announce the birth of Christ? The consensus of opinion among modern astrologers is that the "star" of Bethlehem was in fact a conjunction of Jupiter and Saturn in Pisces in 6–7 B.C., an exceptional phenomenon that the Wise Men would have considered a major omen.

During the turmoil of the early Middle Ages, Christian monasteries were the sole repositories of ancient literature, including works on astrology. At the same time, most of the secular clergy were condemning astrology because of its fatalism. But by the twelfth and thirteenth centuries astrology was taught in the universities; and Thomas AQUINAS (1225–74) reconciled the opposing views by proposing the doctrine that although celestial phenomena exerted a powerful influence over unevolved natures, who "follow their corporal passions," it was possible to rise above these influences through the proper use of reason. This idea is sometimes echoed by modern astrologers, who speak of the possibility of transcending difficult planetary configurations through greater self-awareness.

Christian fundamentalists have attacked astrology on the grounds that it is condemned in a number of passages in the Bible, particularly Deut. 18:9–14, where astrologers are called "an abomination before the Lord." However, Jesuit professor of philosophy Fr. Laurence L. Cassidy points out the danger of quoting translated passages out of context, and reminds us that the medieval Church doctors, who were thoroughly familiar with the Bible, had no trouble reconciling its testimony with their belief in astrology. (See BYZANTIUM, ASTROLOGY IN; MIDDLE AGES, ASTROLOGY IN THE; ROMANS, ASTROLOGY AMONG THE.)

Civil Year: See TROPICAL YEAR.

Clark, Vernon (August 29, 1911, 1:24 P.M. EST, 39N18 76W30–1967): American psychologist, author of a famous series of experiments testing the validity of astrology. One of the few orthodox scientists who have studied the subject, Clark held a diploma from the British Faculty of Astrological Studies. In 1959 he decided to test the ability of astrologers to distinguish between individuals by working with material derived from birth data alone. He designed three blind trials, which were given to a total of fifty astrologers from the United States, Britain, Europe, and Australia.

In the first test twenty astrologers each had to match ten birth charts of real people, five male and five female, with ten brief biographies describing career, hobbies, marriage, and health. To eliminate possible clues, subjects of biographies were chosen who were all born in the United States over a 20-year time span; each subject was established in his or her profession and had a reliable birthtime.

In the second test twenty astrologers were each given ten *pairs* of charts and ten short case histories and asked to pick the chart that fitted the case history. They were not told that one of the pair was a genuine chart and the other a chart erected for a random time and place. In the third test thirty astrologers had to distinguish between each of ten pairs of birth charts, one for a person of high intelligence and the other for a victim of brain damage. (The third test was double blind, since the data were supplied by independent physicians and psychologists, and Clark himself had no knowledge of the answers.) All three tests were also given to a control group of twenty psychologists and social workers with no knowledge of astrology.

The results of all three tests showed that astrologers performed at an extremely high level of significance, whereas the control groups performed at exactly chance level. The results of Clark's first and second tests, with slight variations, were replicated by both Dr. Zipporah Dobyns and Joseph Ernest Vidmar in the 1970s, the latter with results at a high level of significance.

The importance of Clark's work is in providing a model on which later experiments can be based. He is the pioneer of what might be called the holistic approach to astrological testing, as distinguished from the statistical approach, in which one factor of a complex totality is isolated for study, as in the work of Michel and Françoise GAUQUELIN.

Classical Astrology (or **Traditional Astrology**): According to most as-

trologers, astrology as it was practiced from the time of PTOLEMY (second century A.D.) to about the sixteenth century.

Clock Time: See TIME.

Cock (or **Rooster**): The tenth sign of the Chinese zodiac, including all persons born between

January 22, 1909, and February 10, 1910 (earth)
February 8, 1921, and January 28, 1922 (metal)
January 26, 1933, and February 14, 1934 (water)
February 13, 1945, and February 2, 1946 (wood)
January 31, 1957, and February 16, 1958 (fire)
February 17, 1969, and February 6, 1970 (earth)
February 5, 1981, and January 25, 1982 (metal)

The Cock, dedicated in Japan to the goddess of the Sun, Amaterasu, whom he is said to have saved one day from the wrath of the gods, is the symbol of courage. Natives of the sign are sincere, brilliant, and well spoken and very successful in society, although their candor is sometimes annoying. Among their intimates, however, they may become melancholy. Neither savers nor spenders, they cannot decide what life-style to adopt and may go from penny-pinching to extravagance at a moment's notice. Their lack of organization and discipline are no help to their career, but since they are clever

and stubborn, success is not out of the question. Their best fields are agriculture and professions requiring contact with the public.

In love, Cocks are not romantics. However, they are faithful, have a sense of family, and are often able to form lasting relationships.

Compatible signs: Horse, Ox, Serpent.

Neutral signs: Dragon, Pig, Rat, Tiger.

Incompatible signs: Cat, Cock, Dog, Goat, Monkey.

Famous Cocks include Francis Bacon, Amelia Earhart, Sergei Eisenstein, William Faulkner, Joseph Goebbels, J. P. Morgan, Samuel Pepys, Emily Post, Wilhelm Reich, Richard Wagner, and Edith Wharton. (See CHINESE ASTROLOGY.)

Colatitude: See VERTEX.

Colors: According to HERMETIC THEORY, all things in the universe had secret affinities with man. Thus classical astrologers believed that there were certain colors proper to each sign of the zodiac. The tradition has survived, although with some difference of opinion as to which colors correspond to which signs. While almost all astrologers would agree that red belongs to Aries and orange to Leo, other signs are more elusive. The following list is typical, if not definitive:

Aries: red
Taurus: pale green, pastels
Gemini: turquoise, iridescent shades, silver
Cancer: silver, pale blue
Leo: gold, orange, yellow
Virgo: brown, navy blue, gray, white

Libra: blue
Scorpio: dark red
Sagittarius: purple
Capricorn: red, black
Aquarius: electric blue, multicolor, rainbow
Pisces: sea green, violet, indigo

Combust: In classical astrology, the condition of a planet whose CELESTIAL LONGITUDE is very close to that of the Sun; the ORB of combustion varies from 3° to 8°30'. A planet "combust the Sun" was believed to be considerably weakened by this position. However, de Vore says that some authorities made an exception in the case of Mars, whose influence was said to be intensified; Mercury is also often considered to be an exception. (Also see CAZIMI.)

Comet: A luminous body, usually of small mass, generally irregular in shape and often with a long tail, that follows an orbit around the Sun. Comets consist of three parts, visible to the naked eye: nucleus, envelope (also called coma), and tail. Little is known about these celestial bodies; some have regular periods, whereas some do not, and their behavior is difficult to predict. In 1973, for example, 611 comets were counted. Of this number, a quarter had orbits that appeared truly elliptical, while the rest followed parabolas and even hyperbolas. In the latter case, they must have left the solar system altogether.

Ancient astronomers were aware of comets. The first observation reported in Chinese annals dates from the year 2349 B.C. In Rome, Pliny describes comets, classifying them according to their appearance. Traditionally comets have been very im-

Woodcut from a seventeenth century French book showing various types of comets. (The Bettman Archive.)

portant in MUNDANE ASTROLOGY, whereas their role in NATAL ASTROLOGY has been negligible. Until the eighteenth century, the appearance of comets in the sky made a great impression on the public, who regarded them as marvels heralding great events; thus comets were said to have accompanied the deaths of Caesar, Constantine, Attila, and Muhammad. Comets have always been associated with war, invasion, assassination, and catastrophe, and the concurrence of such events with the appearance of a comet is cited as evidence. In fact, such events also occur quite frequently in years without a spectacular comet. De Vore writes that the history-making events associated with comets are presumed to be effected by those whose birth co-

incided with the comet's appearance; thus the events occur many years after the comet.

"The year that Mithridates was born," writes Justin (third century A.D.) in his *Philippic History*, "as well as the year that he ascended the throne, there appeared for seventy days a comet of such great brilliance that the sky seemed on fire. It was so big that it occupied a quarter of the heavens, and so bright that it eclipsed the light of the sun. Four hours elapsed from its rising to its setting." It is possible that this description is not exaggerated; in 1910 the tail of Halley's comet extended the full width of the sky, visible from one horizon to the other.

Halley's comet is the best-known comet in modern times. In 1705 the astronomer Edmund Halley (1656–1742) noticed a similarity in the orbits of the comets observed in 1531, 1607, and 1682, concluded that they were really a single comet, and predicted that it would return in 1758. Halley's comet has a SIDEREAL PERIOD of 76.019 years, and its next appearance will be in 1986.

It is possible, though not customary, to include the position of a comet in a birth chart. One method is simply to use the CELESTIAL LONGITUDE of the comet at its exact moment of PERIHELION. This moment need not coincide with the individual's birthtime (or even birthday); its perihelion identifies that particular comet on that particular passage near the Sun. What matters is that the comet is visibly approaching, completing, or leaving perihelion. Another method is to use the comet's actual celestial longitude at the time of birth. Either way, a comet's longitude position should not be considered in the same way as that of a planet, for it is extremely likely that its CELESTIAL LATITUDE will be very great—that is, that the comet will be remote from the ECLIPTIC. Celestial longitude is sufficient in determining which sign the comet is transiting, but it may not reveal which house it falls in; depending on which system of HOUSE DIVISION is used, rigorous trigonometric calculations may be necessary. Moreover, an aspect between a comet and a planet is quite different from an aspect between two planets. Planetary aspects occur very close to a plane and can be thought of in two-dimensional terms, but an aspect from a high-latitude comet to a planet occurs in three dimensions. It is probably for these reasons that comets are usually ignored in natal astrology.

The traditional method of interpreting comets was to judge the moment when they were first sighted. If they were first seen in Leo this would augur badly for monarchs; if in Virgo, for the harvest, and so on. The interpretation of a comet in a chart should take into account its color, its shape, the duration of the phenomenon, the sign and DECANATE in which it appears, its probable house position, and its three-dimensional aspects to planets. A comet rising before the Sun is said to accelerate the manifestation of the events it portends, whereas a *vespertine*, or evening, comet delays it.

Spectacular comets of the past include De Cheseaux's comet of 1744 (nonperiodic), which had six tails; the Great Comet of 1811 (nonperiodic), whose nucleus appeared larger than the Sun and whose appearance was given as the reason for the excellent French wine of that season; the Great Comet of 1843, whose tail was 200 million miles long; Donati's comet of 1858, whose tail was curved; the Great Comet of 1861 (nonperiodic), through whose tail the Earth passed and which was so bright that it could easily be seen at midday; and Morehouse's comet of 1908, whose appearance changed dramatically from day to day.

Commercial Astrology: See SUN-SIGN ASTROLOGY.

Common Planet: According to PTOLEMY, Mercury was common because neither BENEFIC nor MALEFIC, neither MASCULINE nor FEMININE, and neither DIURNAL nor NOCTURNAL, its nature varying according to its condition by sign, house, and aspect.

Common Signs: See MUTABLE.

Compatibility: While it is obviously impossible to judge the compatibility of two individuals on the basis of their Sun signs alone, this information can provide some preliminary clues as to their chances for a good relationship. Because of the regular recurrence of the four ELEMENTS around the zodiac wheel, signs of the same element will always be in trine. Thus a Sun-sign Taurus will share a certain practical and workmanlike approach with the other two earth signs, Virgo and Capricorn. Similarly, signs of harmonious elements will be in sextile (earth and water are harmonious elements; so are air and fire). Hence, Taurus and Cancer are compatible; so are Gemini and Leo.

Signs of inharmonious elements, such as earth and fire, or air and water, will form semisextiles, quincunxes, and squares: The first two aspects are ambiguous; the third is difficult. Aries natives may feel compatible with Pisces and Taurus, their neighboring signs (semisextile), or they may not; likewise with Virgo and Scorpio, across the zodiac, at a peculiar angle (quincunx); but with Cancer and Capricorn, ego problems may well arise. However, Robert Hand believes that the semisextile and quincunx connections can be more difficult than the squares because the signs have nothing in common, whereas the squares are related by QUADRUPLICITY. Note that oppositions bring together harmonious elements—Aries (fire) and Libra (air), for example. There is tension between Aries and Libra, but it can be resolved more easily than in the case of Aries and Cancer or Aries and Capricorn.

Thus Sun signs can furnish a rule-of-thumb guide to compatibility, and such indications are included in the articles describing the characteristics of the individual signs. However, the complexity of human behavior cannot be reduced to any such simple formulas. A valid astrological assessment of the potential for any relationship would require a careful comparative study of the birth charts of the individuals involved. (See CHART COMPARISON; individual signs).

Composite Chart: The chart of a relationship between two or more persons, obtained by using midpoints between the planets, nodes, and other elements in the individual charts (see MIDPOINT). In calculating the houses of a composite chart, the MIDHEAVEN is the midpoint between the Midheavens of the charts in question. The Ascendant can either be the midpoint of the two Ascendants, or can be calculated for the latitude of the locality where the relationship is taking place. The composite chart is distinguished from the *relationship chart*, which is erected for the midpoint in time and space between the two sets of birth data, a technique developed by Ronald Davison. The interpretation of a composite chart is similar to that of a birth chart; and like the birth chart, it can be used as the basis for progressions, transits, and solar returns in order to follow events and stages in the development of the relationship (see PROGRESSION AND DIRECTION; SOLAR RETURN; TRANSIT).

As a tool in the study of human relationships, the composite chart supplements the much older technique of CHART COMPARISON, or *synastry*. Where chart comparison studies the relationships between two charts, the composite chart introduces a third element, the chart of the relationship itself. Many modern astrologers find that the composite chart helps them to understand the dynamics of a relationship more easily and more precisely than the conventional techniques of synastry.

The origin of the composite chart is obscure. Although sometimes said to have been developed in Germany in the 1920s, it may well predate that time. The definitive works to date are John Townley, *The Composite Chart*, and Robert Hand, *Planets in Composite*.

Computers and Astrology: On November 16, 1967, in Düsseldorf the German women's magazine *Constanze* offered its readers, for the first time, horoscopes cast by computer. This electronic invasion of the realm of astrology was soon imitated in France and the United States. One of the first and most popular services of this kind was Astroflash, whose program was written by the well-known French astrologer, André BARBAULT.

In the United States comprehensive calculation services were soon offered to astrologers by Astro-Numeric and by Neil Michelsen's Astro-Computing. These services and others like them have raised the standards of accuracy in astrology. Michelsen's widely used *American Ephemeris 1931–1980* was printed directly from the printout of his minicomputer, thus saving thousands of dollars in typesetting. Centralized computers are proving to be an invaluable tool for statistical research projects requiring the calculation of large numbers of charts. Eventually the computer may add substantially to our understanding of the meanings of the signs, planets, houses, and aspects.

Meanwhile, though, in the area of interpretation and prediction, the computer's role has been more commercial than serious. However intelligent the programs on which computerized forecasts are based—those of ParaResearch are among the best—there are certain built-in limitations. The computer can string together separate delineations, but it cannot synthesize them into a whole. In those areas where such faculties as judgment and intuition come into play, it is doubtful that the computer will ever replace the competent and experienced astrologer.

The advent of the microcomputer in 1977 marked a new phase in the computer revolution. Astrological programs written, largely by Michael Erlewine, for the Commodore Pet, Apple II, and TRS-80 have made it possible for astrologers with no knowledge of programming to have a variety of complex operations performed in seconds at the touch of a key. Erlewine's magazine *Matrix* is the main source of information for all aspects of astrocomputing. A major contributor is James Neely, who has made it possible to calculate the planets' positions from scratch with an accuracy to the nearest second of arc—an achievement for which he won the 1978 Johndro Award. Thus microcomputers have put reasonably accurate chart-casting facilities within reach of the average astrologer. At this point certain elaborate calculations still require large computers, but this situation will probably change within the next few years. Even after microcomputers become more elaborate, however, centralized computers will continue to be useful for research.

Conception Chart: A chart showing the positions of the Sun, Moon, and

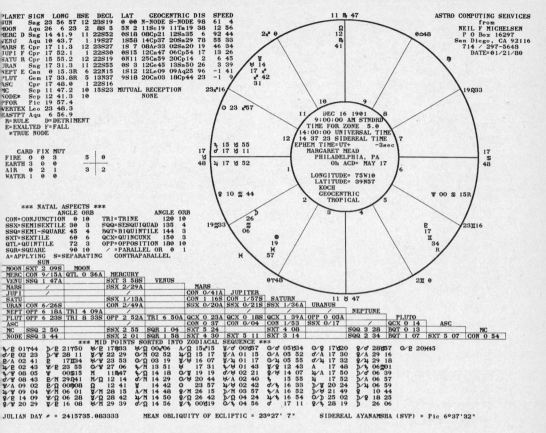

Geocentric computer chart of Margaret Mead. (Reprinted by permission of Astro Computing Services.)

planets at the time of an individual's conception. Since the period of gestation in humans is not invariable, this moment is difficult to determine; hence, such charts are usually hypothetical. All astrologers agree that, should precise information concerning the moment of conception become available, the resulting charts would be extremely valuable.

The problem was not unknown to the ancients. In his *Centiloquy*, PTOLEMY describes the *trutine* of Hermes, a formula for casting a horoscope for the time of conception. The trutine states that at or near the time of conception the Moon must be in conjunction or opposition to the natal Ascendant and the Ascendant must be in conjunction or opposition to the natal Moon. The *prenatal*, or *lunar epoch*, chart based on this theory was introduced to modern astrology in the early twentieth century by Sepharial (Walter Gornold) in *The Solar Epoch* and E. H. Bailey in *The Prenatal Epoch*. Both Sepharial and Bailey insisted that these interchanges must be exact; other astrologers could not agree, so the chart fell out of favor.

However, L. E. JOHNDRO and his partner, W. Kenneth Brown, made considerable use of the conception chart. In a study of 200 obstetrical cases from Flower Hospital in New York City, Johndro found that while the interchanges were valid, they need not be exact; that is, the usual orbs for conjunctions and oppositions were admissible. Johndro's findings were confirmed by Eleanor Hesseltine and Charles JAYNE. Johndro and Jayne, codiscoverers of the VERTEX, found that when the gestation period is less than eight months, the interchanges involve the Vertex instead of the Ascendant.

Johndro and Jayne believe that the conception chart shows how people think or "conceive" things; thus, it is more important for thinkers and innovators than for the average person. Jayne believes that all conception charts are ruled by Uranus and all birth charts by Saturn. Johndro and Brown found that the relationship between the conception chart and the birth chart reveals how successfully the native actualizes concepts.

The conception chart is currently used by Ronald C. Davison in England and Barbara Watters and Charles Jayne in the United States. Davison and Watters still use exact interchanges. Jayne, developing Sepharial's ideas, has found other epochs, both prenatal and postnatal; see his *A Primer of Prenatal and Postnatal Charts* (1959), *A Preface to Prenatal Charts* (1978), and *Paths to High Consciousness* (1979).

Configuration: In classical astrology, an aspect of two or more planets. (See MAJOR CONFIGURATION.)

Conjunction (symbol ☌): The strongest aspect in astrology, in which two or more planets occupy, or are within orb of, the same degree of CELESTIAL LONGITUDE.

Older authorities regard the conjunction as a position rather than an aspect; Sepharial defines it as "two planets within distance of half the sum of their orbs." To a modern astrologer, the distinction seems largely semantic, a vestige of the anthropomorphic language used to describe the planets. The word *aspect* comes from a Latin verb meaning "to look at," and its archaic meaning was "look, glance, or appearance." Thus the planets' aspects were how they "looked at" each other, a concept that did not apply when the planets were actually conjoined.

The conjunction has traditionally been regarded as neither BENEFIC nor MALEFIC, its quality depending on the nature of the planets involved, a view with which modern astrologers would agree. Thus a conjunction of the Moon and Venus in a birth chart would be an indication of a warm and affectionate nature, whereas a conjunction of the Moon and Saturn would suggest coldness and difficulty expressing emotion. The conjunction of the Sun and Moon, which occurs at New Moon and unites the two luminaries in the same sign of the zodiac, was traditionally considered unfortunate, especially for health and longevity. It is associated with a certain freshness, naïveté, and subjectivity, the opposite of the dialectical sophistication, tension, and objectivity associated with the OPPOSITION, which occurs at Full Moon. A chart with many conjunctions and few or no oppositions is character- ized by narrowness of outlook and concentration of effort, whereas a chart with no conjunctions is associ- ated with breadth of viewpoint and variety of experience.

Conjunctions are extremely impor- tant in directions and transits. In- deed, of all the aspects, they are the most powerful triggers of moods or events when formed by transiting, progressed, or directed planets to planets or sensitive points in a natal chart (see PROGRESSION AND DIREC- TION; TRANSIT). For example, a con- junction of transiting Mars to natal Ascendant would be accompanied by conspicuous changes in the native's personality, which would become more aggressive, more energetic, or more sexually oriented than usual, or all three, depending on the general complexion of the chart.

Orbs for conjunctions vary (see ORB), but since it is the strongest as- pect, a conjunction may operate within orbs of up to 10° or even more, especially if the Sun or Moon is in- volved. (See ASPECT; INFERIOR CON- JUNCTION; SUPERIOR CONJUNCTION.)

Constellations: Groups of fixed stars that have, since antiquity, been as- signed names suggestive of the pat- terns they supposedly form in the sky. Actually in the modern four-di- mensional universe the stars of a constellation have no physical rela- tionship with one another except that they belong to the same galaxy. Also, most of the constellations bear no re- semblance, at least to the modern ob- server, to the figures they are sup- posed to represent, and different cultures have assigned the same stars to different groupings representing different images.

Whatever groupings are used, however, constellations helped an- cient peoples organize their universe. Not only did they make it possible to track the Sun, Moon, and planets against a definite background of stel- lar patterns, but they provided illus- trations for myths about the gods in which the culture transmitted its morals to the young. Thus the con- stellation Leo represented the Ne- mean lion that was slain by Hercules and raised into the heavens by Zeus in his honor, showing that bravery is rewarded. Scorpius was the scorpion sent by the goddesses Artemis and Leto to kill Orion, who had boastfully threatened to kill all the animals on Earth, showing how hubris is pun- ished.

The SIGNS OF THE ZODIAC have the same names as the constellations that occur in the vicinity of the ecliptic, but here the resemblance ends. Un- like the signs, the constellations are not of equal length, and the bound- aries between them are indefinite. (It is true that in 1930 astronomers adopted boundaries for the conven- ience of cataloguing stars, but these boundaries are totally arbitrary.) Also, there is no consensus that the number of zodiacal constellations is twelve. The most important distinc- tion, however, is that the constella- tions and the signs have an approx- imate alignment only once in about 25,800 years. (See INDIA, ASTROLOGY IN; PRECESSION OF THE EQUINOXES; SIDEREAL ZODIAC; TROPICAL ZODIAC.)

Contraparallel: See PARALLEL.

Contrascion: See ANTISCION.

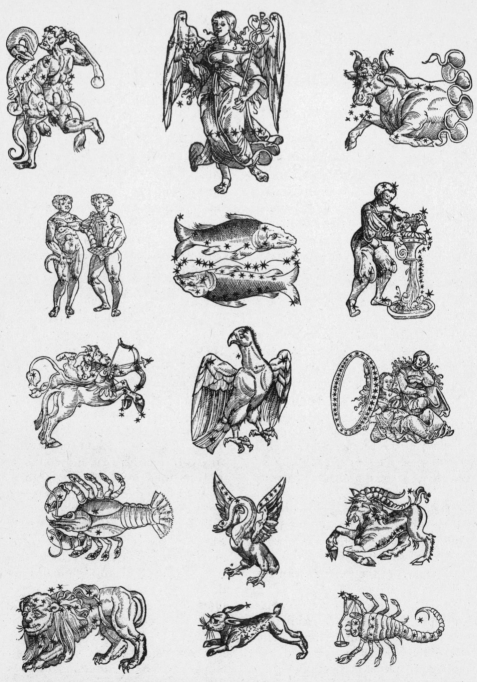

Hercules, Virgo, Taurus, Gemini, Pisces, Aquarius, Sagittarius, Aquila, Corona Borealis, Cancer, Cygnus, Aries, Leo, Lepus, Scorpio.

Converse Progression: See PROGRESSION AND DIRECTION.

Copernicus, Nicolaus (February 19, 1473, Toruń, Poland–May 24, 1543, Frombork, Poland): Polish astronomer, regarded as the founder of modern astronomy for establishing the theory that the Earth rotates daily on its axis and the planets revolve in orbits around the Sun. The heliocentric view of the universe was anticipated by the Greeks, notably Aristarchus of Samos, but was generally ignored until Copernicus's definitive statement in *De Revolutionibus Orbium Coelestium*. The book was completed about 1530 but was not printed until 1543, just in time for printer's proofs to reach the author on his deathbed.

Although the success of the Copernican system is generally believed to be a decisive factor in the decline of astrology, there is no fundamental contradiction between the two. Astrology studies the mutual relationships between the planets and the Earth, and its principles may be applied equally well in a geocentric or heliocentric frame of reference. The idea that Copernicus dealt the deathblow to astrology is ironic, for although it is not known with certainty whether Copernicus himself believed in astrology, it is known that he made no effort to deny it, erected birth charts, and gave his masterwork to an astrologer, his friend and disciple Joachim Rheticus, to publish.

Corona: See ECLIPSE.

Cosmobiology: An empirical school of astrology defined by the German

Nicolaus Copernicus. (The Bettman Archive.)

astrologer Reinhold Ebertin (February 16, 1901–), its foremost exponent, as "a scientific discipline concerned with the possible correlations between the cosmos and organic life, and the effects of cosmic rhythms and stellar motion on man." The term seems to have been introduced by the German H. A. Strauss in 1928, when the first *Cosmobiological Yearbook* was issued. Cosmobiology developed out of the work of another German astrologer, Alfred Witte, founder of the URANIAN SYSTEM of astrology, in the 1930s. Cosmobiology employs many of the same techniques as Uranian astrology, including the 90° dial, but it does not make use of the hypothetical Uranian planets. Cosmobiologists believe that specific interpretations can derive only from combinations of two or more planets: The more planets in a combination, the more specific the interpretation. They make systematic use of all the MIDPOINT combinations in their charts. Prediction of future events utilizes the technique of *solar arcs* (see PROGRESSION AND DIRECTION).

Cosmobiology emphasizes the observational, quantitative, and statistical approaches to research and pays considerable attention to the comparative method, in which small collections of similar cases are studied intensively in order to isolate common factors and elements. A major contribution of this school is the development of graphic techniques such as the 45° ephemeris, and the midpoint ephemeris. The center of its activities is the Ebertin Cosmobiological Academy in Aalen, West Germany, which draws together scholars and academics in all areas of astrological research. However, the term *cosmobiology* is sometimes used as a euphemism by astrologers unconnected with Ebertin.

Cosmography (from the Greek *kosmos*, the world, and *graphein*, to write): Literally, "a description of the world"; the science of the structure of the universe and the relationships between its parts. A knowledge of cosmography is useful, though not necessary, in learning to set up a birth chart, because chart erection is based on the cosmographic representation of the birthplace.

For example, let us consider a birthplace at terrestrial latitude 45° north, usually expressed 45N (for example, Salem, Oregon; Minneapolis, Minnesota; Pavia, Italy; Harbin, Manchuria). Figure 16 shows a *topocentric* cosmography, in which the idealized "plane" of the HORIZON (mountains and valleys leveled out) is tangent to the Earth's sphere at 45N. The cardinal directions are shown on the plane, which could be extended outward indefinitely, and *O* is the precise location of the birthplace.

For convenience' sake we can simplify our cosmography and make it *geocentric*, that is, with *O* at the Earth's center. This will create some error due to parallax, but for our purpose—plotting the planetary positions in the chart—the distortion is negligible, since the planets are so distant. (There is a parallax distortion in the Moon's position, however,

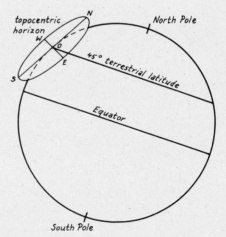

Figure 16. A topocentric cosmography.

that can in certain circumstances exceed 1°.) The advantage of the geocentric cosmography over the topocentric is that we can easily picture our horizon as one of the GREAT CIRCLES of the CELESTIAL SPHERE. This is essential, since the horizon's intersection with four other such circles is the basis for the HOUSES, which connect the solar system to the birthplace. In figure 17 we see the intersection of two great circles, horizon and MERIDIAN, the *axes* of the birth chart in most systems of HOUSE DIVISION. On a line drawn perpendicular to the horizon, straight up in the sky from the birthplace is the *zenith,* and straight down through the Earth is the *nadir.* (In figure 17 the zenith-nadir axis is not vertical because we are still representing the horizon as a tangent on latitude 45N.) The meridian is the great circle that connects due north on the horizon (*North Point*), zenith, due south on the horizon (*South Point*), and nadir.

In figure 18 we have made the ho-

rizon horizontal and thus positioned zenith and nadir up and down, respectively. We can do this because any position is relative. Showing the horizon as tilted is helpful for the topocentric view; showing it as horizontal conforms to our sensations of walking about on a "flat" earth. Now we can add a great circle in the third dimension: the *prime vertical,* which connects due east on the horizon (EAST POINT), zenith, due west on the horizon (*West Point*), and nadir.

We have pictured our local position in three dimensions, but we need to orient that position with respect to the rotation of the Earth and the zodiac of signs. We can accomplish this by inserting two other great circles, the *celestial equator* and the ECLIPTIC. The celestial equator is the Earth's Equator extended out into space and projected onto the starry background of the celestial sphere. An axis perpendicular to the plane of

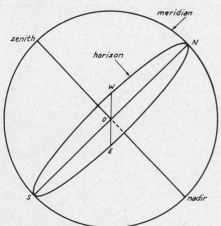

Figure 17. Horizon and meridian.

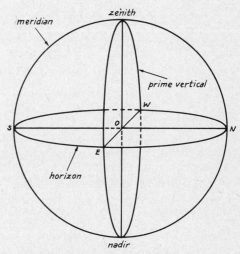

Figure 18. Horizon, meridian, and prime vertical.

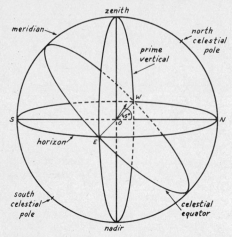

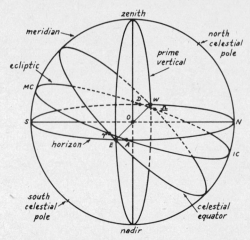

Figure 19. Horizon, meridian, prime vertical, and celestial equator.

Figure 20. Horizon, meridian, prime vertical, celestial equator, and ecliptic.

this circle coincides with the Earth's rotational axis and extends upward to the *north celestial pole,* which would be the zenith if we were standing at the North Pole of the Earth. Extending downward, the axis reaches the *south celestial pole,* the South Pole's local zenith. The north celestial pole is quite close to the North Star (Polaris) these days (see PRECESSION OF THE EQUINOXES), and from our 45N birthplace we would see that star at an ALTITUDE of 45° from the northern horizon (see figure 19). The celestial equator meets the eastern horizon at the East Point; it meets the western horizon at the West Point.

In figure 20 we have inserted the fifth great circle, the ecliptic, whereon is placed the zodiac. The point where the ecliptic meets the meridian above the horizon in the southern sky (it would be the northern sky if the birthplace were south of the Equator) is the MIDHEAVEN, or MC. The opposite point, where the ecliptic meets the meridian below the

horizon in the northern sky (southern sky in the southern hemisphere) is the IMUM COELI, or IC. The point where the ecliptic meets the eastern horizon is the ASCENDANT; where it meets the western horizon is the DESCENDANT. The two points where the ecliptic intersects the celestial equator are the EQUINOXES—0° Aries and 0° Libra. At the birth moment represented, 0° Aries is shown having just risen above the eastern horizon and 0° Libra having just set below the western horizon. Of course the equinox points, like all points on the zodiac, make a complete circuit of the sky (above and below the horizon) in 24 hours.

The foregoing geocentric cosmography can be compared with the *heliocentric* cosmography in figure 21. Note the points at which each of the four seasons begins. At each *solstice* the Sun is giving more light to one hemisphere than it is to the other. The favored half is experiencing its longest day and shortest night, whereas in the other half the situation is reversed. At both equinoxes, however, day and night are equal. (See HELIOCENTRIC SYSTEM.)

Culminating: Term used to describe a planet or star when, because of the apparent movement of the sky due to the Earth's rotation, it arrives at the upper MERIDIAN of the birthplace, attaining its greatest possible elevation. A planet is said to be culminating when it reaches the *Midheaven*. Such a planet is considered very powerful in the life of the native and will have a conspicuous influence on his or her public image.

Culmination: See CULMINATING; MERIDIAN.

Cusp: 1. The degree of the ECLIPTIC marking the beginning of a sign of the zodiac and thus dividing that sign from the one that preceded it. For example, if the Sun in a birth

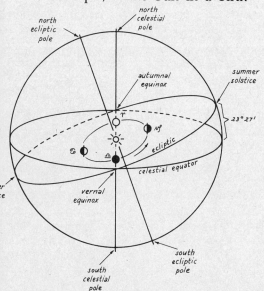

Figure 21. The heliocentric system.

chart is between 29° Pisces and 0° Aries, the native is said to be "on the cusp of Aries," or sometimes, "on the Pisces-Aries cusp."

2. The point regarded by most astrologers as the imaginary boundary that marks the beginning of a house in a birth chart and thus distinguishes it from the preceding house, although most Hindu astrologers and some Western astrologers—for example, Cyril FAGAN—consider the middle point of a house to be its cusp. (According to this view, the middle of the First House by the commoner method would be the beginning, or cusp, of the Second.) In the general opinion, however, the cusp of a house always precedes the house, moving around the wheel in a counterclockwise direction. Thus the Ascendant is the cusp of the First House, the line dividing the First House from the Second House is the cusp of the Second House, and so on around the wheel. Traditionally, house cusps have been used to time events—that is, when a planet transits a house cusp, an event associated with the affairs of that house should take place. But owing partly to the current state of confusion over systems of HOUSE DIVISION, most contemporary astrologers allow an ORB of 2° to 5° for house cusps. Thus a natal planet posited in the Fourth House but within 2° to 5° of the cusp of the Fifth House probably "works" for both houses. An orb of up to 15° is often allowed for ANGULAR houses. The vagueness of the boundaries between houses lends credence to the idea that the cusp is the middle part of the house.

Cycle: A regularly recurring period of time during which an event or series of events can be expected to occur and upon which predictions can be based. There are cycles of business activity, floods on the Nile, the population of grasshoppers, the sale of sweet potatoes, and the emotions of human beings. There are also cycles of celestial phenomena, such as the orbits of the planets around the Sun, the observation of which has made it possible to compile EPHEMERIDES.

Any demonstrated correspondence between planetary cycles and terrestrial events indirectly supports the underlying assumption of astrology: that the motions of the planets are related to, and thus a guide to, the understanding of the behavior of human beings. One as-yet-unproved astrological hypothesis is that the tidal effects of recurring planetary patterns provoke activity on the Sun, such as sunspots and solar wind, causing electrical changes in the Earth's ionosphere, which in turn affect the weather, our state of mind, and ultimately our behavior. To demonstrate the validity of this hypothesis, it would be necessary to prove each link in the chain of causation. The impact of solar activity on our ionosphere has been demonstrated by John NELSON; the relation of the sunspot cycle to planetary cycles has been demonstrated by Geoffrey Dean. Also significant is the observed correspondence of the Moon's cycle not only to oceanic tides but to the tides in the human body: In a 3-year study involving over one thousand patients, Dr. E. J. Andrews observed a regularly recurring increase in postoperative hemorrhaging during the Full Moon.

Astrologers pay close attention to phase within a planetary cycle. During the first half (*waxing*) the energies represented by the cycle are in a process of growth; during the second half (*waning*) the energies are released. The cycle can be further divided into quarters and even eighths, and the moments in the cycle that correspond to the boundaries of these divisions, or *phases*, are considered critical. There are two types of planetary cycles, sidereal (or tropical) and synodic.

The *sidereal cycle* (or period, or revolution) of a planet is the length of time it takes to complete one revolution around the Sun (see SIDEREAL PERIOD). In the case of the Moon, the *sidereal month* is the period of one complete revolution around the Earth, measured by recurring alignment to a star. For planets outside the Earth's orbit astrologers normally regard the planet's cycle as the time it takes it to make one complete circuit of the zodiac—really a TROPICAL PERIOD, not a sidereal period—although this introduces some irregularity due to our geocentric viewpoint (see RETROGRADE). The irregularity is regarded by most astrologers as part of the cycle's meaning. A planet's completion of its cycle is known as its *return*.

Many astrologers use the sidereal or tropical cycles of the planets—that is, the time it takes them to return to their natal positions in a given birth chart—in the study of personality development. Each phase of a planet's cycle is a turning point in the development of the individual born at the beginning of that (or a prior) cycle.

The sidereal or tropical cycles most often studied in natal astrology are those of the progressed Moon and transiting Saturn, both of which, curiously, are approximately 28 years. It takes Saturn about that length of time to transit all twelve signs of the zodiac and arrive at its natal position in an individual's chart (the *Saturn return*). It takes the Moon about 28 days to transit all twelve signs, and since progressions operate on the principle "a day for a year," the cycle of the progressed Moon is also about 28 years. Thus both progressed Moon and transiting Saturn will be at half-cycle, or in opposition to their natal positions, at approximately age 14, a time characterized by the tensions and self-consciousness of adolescence. Both cycles will be completed at about age 28, a time characterized by awareness of the passing of time and a new sense of responsibility and often experienced as the end of youth and the beginning of maturity.

The planetary cycle perhaps most conspicuous for its effects is the Uranus cycle. Since it takes Uranus approximately 84 years to make a complete circuit of the zodiac, it will oppose its natal position at about age 42. Uranus rules rebellion, the unexpected, the sudden breaking of long-standing habits. The Uranus opposition is a time characterized by that last fling at freedom, which may mean switching professions, getting divorced, or moving to California, and which has given rise to the popular expression "life begins at forty."

The cycles of Uranus, Neptune, and Pluto are more properly associated with changing trends in society as a whole than with the development of an individual. For example, Dane RUDHYAR has correlated Pluto's cycle of nearly 250 years with the duration of a style within a culture. The most comprehensive work on cycles to date is Alexander Ruperti's *Cycles of Becoming* (1978), which considers the whole spectrum of solar, lunar, and planetary cycles.

The *synodic cycle* always involves two planets, and is defined as the interval between one conjunction and the next. When astrologers refer to the *synodic period* of a single planet, it is understood that the other body is the Sun. Thus the synodic period of Jupiter is the interval between one Sun-Jupiter conjunction and the next. The synodic period of the Moon is the interval between one Sun-Moon conjunction and the next. The classic work on the soli-lunar relationship is Dane Rudhyar's *The Lunation Cycle*.

The synodic-cycle of Jupiter and Saturn is very important in MUNDANE ASTROLOGY. The mean interval between two heliocentric conjunctions of these two bodies is 19.859 years. These progressive conjunctions do not take place in the same region of the zodiac, but advance an average of 243° of CELESTIAL LONGITUDE, or a little over eight signs, which maintains the cycle in the same element for slightly less than 200 years. Table 1 shows the heliocentric longitudes of all Jupiter-Saturn conjunctions from 1802 to 2000. Not until the 1842 conjunction did the cycle finally establish itself in the earth element, where it remained for the following six conjunctions. The conjunction of 1981 marks the cycle's first foray into air, but it will not be firmly established there until the conjunction of 2019. The change of element was called *trigonalis* by the ancients and was considered extremely important both politically and economically. It is now generally known as the *great mutation conjunction*. It is a curious fact that no U.S. president elected to a term during which one of the seven conjunctions established in earth was to occur, managed to survive the presidency.

Every third conjunction occurs in the same area of the zodiac, with an advance averaging about 9°. This period, which has a mean interval of 59.577 years, is the *first-order recurrence cycle* of Jupiter and Saturn. The ancients regarded it as the lag interval between the appearance of any innovation and its widespread use in the culture. Every fortieth conjunction again occurs in the same area of the zodiac, this time with an advance of less than 1°. This period, which had an interval of almost 800 years, is the *second-order recurrence cycle*, and has been associated with the cyclical recurrence of civil strife in China.

The synodic cycle of Neptune and Pluto has an interval of approximately 493½ years. This cycle has been associated with major cultural expressions, alternating between a rational, aggressive, extraverted culture and one that is spiritual and introverted. The conjunction of 1892, the "closing of the frontier," marked the end of five centuries of Western aggressive expansion and rational inquiry and the beginning of an age in which the Western powers are declining, science is beginning to resemble mysticism (relativity and quantum mechanics), and astrology has once again emerged from obscurity.

Table 1. Conjunctions of Jupiter and Saturn.

Year	Heliocentric Longitude	Element
1802	07 Virgo	earth
1821	22 Aries	fire
1842	08 Capricorn	earth
1862	17 Virgo	earth
1881	01 Taurus	earth
1901	16 Capricorn	earth
1921	26 Virgo	earth
1940	11 Taurus	earth
1961	23 Capricorn	earth
1981	08 Libra	air
2000	21 Taurus	earth

Daily Motion: The angular distance along the ECLIPTIC, measured in degrees, minutes, and seconds of CELESTIAL LONGITUDE, that is traveled by a planet or luminary in a 24-hour period. It is necessary to know a planet's daily motion for a particular day in order to calculate the planet's position at the time of birth. (See CHART CALCULATION.)

Daylight Saving Time: See TIME.

Days of the Week: It was in Rome, in the reign of Augustus, that the days of the week were named after the planets that were believed to rule them. The first day corresponded to the Sun, the second to the Moon, the third to Mars, the fourth to Mercury, the fifth to Jupiter, the sixth to Venus, and the seventh to Saturn.

The Old Testament used the Roman week, and the Christians also adopted the Roman system. However, for the Lord's day of rest they chose not the seventh, the traditional Jewish day of rest, but the first, in memory of the resurrection of Jesus. Only in a few Germanic languages is the Lord's day still called "the day of the Sun" (English Sunday, German

Sonntag or Dutch *Zondag*). The astrologers of the Byzantine Empire believed that each day was lucky for natives of the sign ruled by its planet. Thus Wednesday is lucky for Geminis and Virgos because all three are ruled by Mercury. The complete list of rulerships follows:

Sign	Ruling Planet	Lucky Day
Aries	Mars	Tuesday
Taurus	Venus	Friday
Gemini	Mercury	Wednesday
Cancer	Moon	Monday
Leo	Sun	Sunday
Virgo	Mercury	Wednesday
Libra	Venus	Friday
Scorpio	Mars	Tuesday
Sagittarius	Jupiter	Thursday
Capricorn	Saturn	Saturday
Aquarius	Saturn	Saturday
Pisces	Jupiter	Thursday

Dean, Malcolm: See CHIRON.

Debility: A term describing the condition of a planet that is weakened by sign or house position; the opposite of DIGNITY. A planet in DETRIMENT or FALL is in a state of debility, as is a planet in a CADENT house or in a house opposite the house of which it is natural ruler (see NATURAL

HOUSE). Hence the Moon is in debility in Capricorn, the sign of its detriment, and in Scorpio, the sign of its fall; in the Ninth House, because it is cadent, and in the Tenth House, because the Moon is the natural ruler of the Fourth House. The term is seldom used by modern astrologers; and the statistical research of Michel and Françoise GAUQUELIN seems to indicate that in fact those with the Moon in the Ninth and first part of the Tenth House possess a very strong lunar component in their psychology.

Decanate (also **Decan**; from the Latin *decem*, ten): One of thirty-six 10° subdivisions of the signs of the zodiac. Each 30° sign is divided into three such segments, referred to as the first, second, and third decanates. Each decanate has been assigned a planetary ruler. There are at least two such rulership systems, the Chaldean (or Western) and the Oriental. According to the Chaldean system, the first decanate of Aries is ruled by Mars, the second by the Sun, the third by Venus; the first decanate of Taurus is ruled by Mercury, the second by the Moon, and the third by Saturn; the first decanate of Gemini is ruled by Jupiter, the second by Mars, and the third by the Sun; and so on around the wheel, in the Chaldean order of the planets, ending with the last decanate of Pisces ruled by Mars.

The Oriental system, which is the one preferred by modern astrologers, assigns the first decanate of each sign to the planet that rules that sign, and the second and third decanates to the planets that rule the other two signs in the same element, in the order in which the signs occur in the zodiac. Thus the first, or "Aries," decanate of Aries is ruled by Mars; the second, or "Leo," decanate by the Sun; the third, or "Sagittarius," decanate by Jupiter. Similarly the first, or "Taurus," decanate of Taurus is ruled by Venus; the second, or "Virgo," decanate by Mercury, the third, or "Capricorn," decanate by Saturn; and so on. (See RULERSHIP.)

In interpretation, the decanate system allows for greater subtlety in assessing planetary emphasis in a chart. Thus an already existing Uranus emphasis in a chart would be further heightened if, for example, the Sun were in the third, or "Aquarius," decanate of Gemini, that is, the decanate ruled by Uranus.

Decile (or **Semiquintile**): A minor aspect, introduced by KEPLER, formed when two planets are 36° apart, or separated by one-tenth of the 360° zodiac. It is half a QUINTILE, an aspect of 72° that is associated with talent, and thus has a mildly favorable influence.

Declination: Angular distance measured in degrees, minutes, and seconds north or south of the CELESTIAL EQUATOR, which is considered to have a declination of 0°. Declination has a correspondence to TERRESTRIAL LATITUDE but on the CELESTIAL SPHERE. For example, any object that reaches the ZENITH at a location 42° north terrestrial latitude has a declination of 42° north, expressed 42N. The declination of the Sun reaches a maximum of 23°27' north or south (at the summer and winter SOLSTICES, respectively) and has 0° declination at both spring and autumn EQUINOXES. The declination range of the planets does not exceed that by very much, but the Moon sometimes reaches a declination of nearly 29° north or south.

Just as there are parallels of terrestrial latitude on the Earth's surface, there are parallels of declination on the celestial sphere. There is also an aspect known as *parallel of declination* used by many astrologers. For this reason the daily declination of the planets is often included in an EPHEMERIS. (See CELESTIAL COORDINATES; PARALLEL; and the sample page from an ephemeris, page 48.)

Degree Meanings: Intrinsic meanings assigned to individual degrees of the zodiac, in the absence of a planet occupying or aspecting the degree. Traditionally, such meanings have often been attributed to fixed stars located at those degrees, but the question of whether these meanings are subject to PRECESSION has never been satisfactorily answered. Other possible sources of degree meanings are planetary NODES or perihelia, radio sources, and HARMONICS. There are at least thirty different sets of degree meanings in existence, of which fourteen are currently in print. One of the best known systems is the Sabian Symbols, which were obtained through a medium and adopted by Marc Edmund JONES and Dane RUDHYAR. Other important systems include Carelli's, Charubel and Sepharial's, Kozminsky's, and Gordon's.

Since there is very little agreement among these systems, and since the majority of them were arrived at through nonastrological means and are presented in symbolic language, the field is, as Geoffrey Dean puts it, "one of total confusion." However, a few empirical studies have been made, the most extensive one by E. C. Matthews, and more limited ones by CARTER, Wemyss, and Ebertin. Carter, Ebertin, and Wemyss working independently all found a correlation between malfunction of the pancreas and the Cancer-Capricorn axis (17° according to Carter; 16° according to Ebertin). The fact that there is scant evidence to date for the validity of degree areas does not rule out the possibility of such effects. Degree meanings is an area that calls out for clarification and that should lend itself admirably to the kind of statistical research made possible by the use of the computer. (See COMPUTERS AND ASTROLOGY; STAR; STATISTICS AND ASTROLOGY.)

Delineation: The interpretation of a piece of astrological information, such as a planet's sign or house position, an aspect, or a MAJOR CONFIGURATION. For example, the delineation of Mars in Virgo in the Sixth House might be a tendency to put a great deal of energy into work. If Mars were conjunct Neptune, this could amount to an obsession that could endanger the person's health, especially if Mars were afflicted from another house (see AFFLICTION). If Mars were the focal point of a T-SQUARE, for example, the delineation would be expanded accordingly.

The term *delineation* is sometimes applied to the interpretation of the chart as a whole, but this putting together of the pieces is more properly called *synthesis*. (See CHART INTERPRETATION.)

Depression: Archaic term for FALL.

Descendant: On a birth chart, the point opposite the ASCENDANT—that is, the western point of intersection of HORIZON and ECLIPTIC; usually the cusp of the Seventh House. The Descendant represents the point on the horizon of the birthplace where the Sun appears while setting. Any planet on the Descendant (and thus in opposition to the Ascendant) will strongly color and complicate the personality of the native and probably increase his or her self-awareness.

Descending Node: See NODES.

Detriment: In classical astrology, the condition of a planet when placed in the sign opposite the sign or signs it rules; the opposite of DOMICILE. Since the Moon rules (or has its domicile in) Cancer, it is in detriment in Capricorn; since Venus rules both Taurus and Libra, it is in detriment in both Scorpio and Aries. The ancients held that a planet in detriment is like a person in someone else's home: It operates at a disadvantage and expresses its own nature only with effort. Thus since it is the nature of the Moon to respond, a person with the Moon in Capricorn will find it harder to express his or her feelings than someone with the Moon in Cancer. The detriments of the other planets are as follows: Mercury in Sagittarius and Pisces, Sun in Aquarius, Mars in Taurus and Libra, Jupiter in Gemini and Virgo, Saturn in Cancer and Leo, Uranus in Leo, Neptune in Virgo, and Pluto in Taurus.

De Wohl, Louis: See OFFICIAL ASTROLOGERS.

Dexter Aspect (from the Latin *dexter*, right): According to PTOLEMY, an aspect formed by a planet to a slower-moving planet to the right of it as observed in the sky, or behind it in the zodiac. It is distinguished from a *sinister aspect* (from the Latin *sinister*, left), an aspect formed by a planet to a slower-moving planet to the left of it, or ahead of it in the zodiac. Dexter corresponds to *waxing* and sinister to *waning* (see CYCLE). Ptolemy considered a dexter aspect to be more powerful than a sinister one. Theodor Ram, a modern Dutch astrologer, regards the dexter aspect as more extraverted than the sinister, while Dane RUDHYAR considers dexter aspects to be more subjective. Nicholas de Vore compares the dexter aspect, with its increasing interval, to the Doppler red shift; and the sinister aspect, with its decreasing interval, to the Doppler violet shift; and suggests that the first is ruled by Mars and the second by Venus or Jupiter. The terms *dexter* and *sinister* should not be confused with *applying* and *separating*, which distinguish between aspects approaching or leaving exactitude (see APPLYING ASPECT).

Dignity: A somewhat antiquated term describing the condition of a planet that is strengthened by either sign position (*essential dignity*) or house position (*accidental dignity*). A planet is essentially dignified by being placed in the sign it rules (that is, in DOMICILE); in a sign of the same ELEMENT, or TRIPLICITY, as the sign it rules, in which case it is said to be "in dignity of triplicity" (unless it is in FALL in that sign); or in the sign of its EXALTATION. Thus the Moon is essentially dignified in Cancer, the sign it rules; in Pisces, one of the other two water signs (but not in the remaining water sign, Scorpio, where the Moon is in fall); and in Taurus, the sign of its exaltation.

A planet is accidentally dignified by being highly elevated (see ELEVATION); on an ANGLE, or in an ANGULAR house (unless it is a house where the planet is in natural DETRIMENT); or in a house of which it is the natural ruler (see NATURAL HOUSE). Thus the Moon is accidentally dignified if on the Midheaven or Ascendant, or in the First, Fourth (both because it is an angular house and because the Moon is its natural ruler), or Seventh House. (Although the Tenth House is angular, the Moon is not dignified there, since it is in natural detriment.)

A planet that is dignified, whether essentially or accidentally, is thereby made stronger, but this added strength was not necessarily considered an advantage. Thus the Moon in Cancer (domicile) may manifest as deep sympathy or defensive hypersensitivity; Moon in Taurus (exaltation) may indicate fine perceptions or emotional rigidity; and Moon on the Ascendant (angle) may mean great openness and flexibility or extreme vulnerability to the slightest change in external surroundings. (See RULERSHIP.)

Direct: A term used to describe a planet that appears from the perspective of the Earth to be moving forward through the zodiac from west to east, in order of the signs; the opposite of RETROGRADE. In chart interpretation, a planet's influence is regarded as stronger, more conspicuous, and more understandable when it is direct, and as weaker, more elusive, and more confusing when it is retrograde. (Also see STATIONARY.)

Direction: See PROGRESSION AND DIRECTION.

Direct Midpoint: See MIDPOINT.

Dispositor: In classical astrology, the ruler of the sign in which another planet is placed. For example, if Mercury is in Taurus, Venus (which rules Taurus) is said to be Mercury's dispositor. If Mercury is in one of the two signs it rules, Gemini or Virgo, it is its own dispositor; it "disposes of itself," which makes it stronger than if it were disposed of by another planet. In many birth charts there is a *final*, or *ultimate, dispositor*, a planet that disposes of all the other planets, sometimes at two or three removes, as well as of itself. Being the final dispositor adds considerably to a planet's importance in a chart.

Diurnal Arc: See HOUSE DIVISION.

Diurnal Planets (from the Latin *dies,* day): According to PTOLEMY, Sun, Jupiter, and Saturn. The Sun and Jupiter were classified as diurnal because they were MASCULINE PLANETS, and "the day is more masculine because of its heat and active force." Saturn was classified as diurnal by the principle not of affinity but of complementarity, so that its coldness would be offset by the warmth of day. Later the term was extended to include those planets in a birth chart that were placed above the HORIZON. The term is seldom used in modern astrology.

Diurnal Signs: In classical astrology, the MASCULINE SIGNS: Aries, Gemini, Leo, Libra, Sagittarius, and Aquarius. (See POLARITY.)

Dobyns, Zipporah: See ASTEROIDS; CLARK, VERNON.

Dodecile: See SEMISEXTILE.

Dog: The eleventh sign of the Chinese zodiac, including all persons born between

February 10, 1910, and January 30, 1911 (metal)
January 28, 1922, and February 16, 1923 (water)
February 14, 1934, and February 4, 1935 (wood)
February 2, 1946, and January 22, 1947 (fire)
February 16, 1958, and February 8, 1959 (earth)
February 6, 1970, and January 27, 1971 (metal)
January 25, 1982, and February 13, 1983 (water)

Anxious, withdrawn, intransigent, demanding of others as well as of themselves, natives of the sign of the Dog are antisocial creatures. However, their sense of duty and their

fidelity are proof for any test. They can be counted on in any situation, for they keep their promises. Methodical workers, shrewd, practical, they use their talents in the service of an ambition that is sometimes unbridled. They have a natural vocation for industry, research, and politics, especially union organizing and revolution.

Love at first sight is unknown to them, but when they have chosen a partner, they can be tender and sentimental and as jealous as they are faithful.

Compatible signs: Cat, Dog, Pig, Tiger.

Neutral signs: Horse, Monkey, Ox.

Incompatible signs: Cock, Dragon, Goat, Rat, Serpent.

Famous Dogs include Al Capone, Winston Churchill, Claude Debussy, Judy Garland, Victor Hugo, Akira Kurosawa, Sophia Loren, Norman Mailer, Molière, Ralph Nader, Elvis Presley, Bessie Smith, Socrates, and Voltaire. (See CHINESE ASTROLOGY.)

Domicile (from the Latin *domus,* home): In classical astrology, the condition of a planet when placed in the sign it rules, and where it is therefore "at home"; the opposite of DETRI-

MENT. (The sign of a planet's domicile was also known as its *sign of election*—that is, the sign in which it had "elected domicile.") The Sun is in domicile in Leo, the Moon in Cancer, Venus in Taurus and Libra, and so on. (See RULERSHIP.)

The ancients held that a planet in domicile is like a person in his or her own home: It operates freely and easily and expresses its nature without restraint. Thus, since it is the nature of the Sun to radiate energy, to create, and to rule, for example, people with the Sun in Leo will feel at home when they are in the center of their world, whether it be the artist's studio, the stage, or the arena of life.

Double Biquintile: A MAJOR CONFIGURATION in which two planets are in QUINTILE to each other, with a third planet at inverse MIDPOINT, forming BIQUINTILES to both ends of the quintile. Quintiles and biquintiles belong to the fifth harmonic (see HARMONICS) and are associated with talent. All major configurations tend to provide focus for the chart and hence to be integrative. Michael Meyer associates this configuration with unique self-expression and inspiration. An example of the double biquintile is the birth chart of William Blake, in which a Fifth-House Sun-Jupiter conjunction in Sagittarius ("Bring me my arrows of desire!") is in quintile to a Seventh-House Saturn in Aquarius, with a Twelfth-House Moon in Cancer at inverse midpoint: creative self-expression, moral responsibility, mystic receptivity, and the impulse to communicate brought into perfect potential harmony.

Double-Bodied Signs: See DOUBLE SIGNS.

Double Quincunx (also called **Eye of God, Finger of God, Hand of God,** and **Yod**): A MAJOR CONFIGURATION in which two planets are in SEXTILE to each other, with a third planet at inverse MIDPOINT, forming QUINCUNXES to both ends of the sextile. Since the quincunx itself is controversial, the double quincunx is likewise something of a mystery. The sextile is associated with opportunity, and the quincunx, lying as it does midway between the trine and the opposition, may represent a kind of offbeat wisdom. Any major configuration tends to focus the energies of the chart and provide a sense of purpose. The double quincunx is often associated with a strange or unusual destiny; humanistic astrologer Michael Meyer associates it with spiritual sensitivity, citing the example of Meher Baba.

Another example of the double quincunx is the chart of Lenny Bruce, in which a Tenth-House Sun-Mercury conjunction in Libra is in sextile to a Ninth-House Neptune in Leo, and a Third-House Uranus in Pisces forms quincunxes to both ends of the sextile. The qualities of iconoclasm, wild imagination, and obsession with justice and the law that characterized the tormented comic are accurately described in this configuration. With close aspects of Sun and Mercury to the outer planets, he became a spokesman for rebellious elements of his generation.

Double Signs (also called **Double-bodied Signs** and **Bicorporeal**

Signs): Gemini, Sagittarius, and Pisces; so called because of the dual nature of their symbols, which are the twins, the centaur, and the fishes, respectively.

Double Summer Time: See TIME.

Draconic Period (or **Nodical Period**): The period between one transit of a planet or the Moon over its ascending node with the ECLIPTIC and the next. The Moon's draconic period, the *nodical month*, is 27 days 5 hours 5 minutes 35.8 seconds—almost 3 hours shorter than the Moon's SIDEREAL PERIOD. (See NODES.)

Dragon: The fifth sign of the Chinese zodiac, including all persons born between

February 16, 1904, and February 4, 1905 (wood)
February 3, 1916, and January 23, 1917 (fire)
January 23, 1928, and February 10, 1929 (earth)
February 8, 1940, and January 27, 1941 (metal)
January 27, 1952, and February 14, 1953 (water)
February 13, 1964, and February 2, 1965 (wood)
January 31, 1976, and February 18, 1977 (fire)
February 17, 1988, and February 6, 1989 (earth)

The earthy nature of the Dragon gives natives of this sign strength, will power, and perseverance in the realization of their ideals. Outspoken and totally incapable of meanness, they abhor the vanities of this world. What makes them happy are small circles of intimates with whom they can communicate in a warm, congenial atmosphere. Their sometimes brutal frankness often arouses the hostility of those around them. Intelligent, obstinate, and industrious, they will rise in almost any profession, but their vocation is more likely

to be for architecture, medicine, or the law. If they go into politics, they are more at home behind the scenes of the party machinery than in the public eye.

They are great lovers, but their possessiveness sometimes causes them to suffer from jealousy. The females of the sign are particularly sensual and seductive. But both sexes prefer the single state to the bonds of matrimony.

Compatible signs: Cat, Goat, Monkey, Serpent, Tiger.

Neutral signs: Cock, Pig, Rat.

Incompatible signs: Dog, Horse, Ox.

Famous Dragons include Louisa May Alcott, Sarah Bernhardt, Salvador Dali, Marlene Dietrich, Sigmund Freud, Immanuel Kant, Helen Keller, Martin Luther King, Jr., Abraham Lincoln, Friedrich Nietzche, Edgar Allan Poe, Jean-Jacques Rousseau, George Bernard Shaw, Shirley Temple, Marshall Tito, and Oscar Wilde. (See CHINESE ASTROLOGY.)

Dragon's Head: The north, or ascending, node of the Moon; the point where the Moon's orbit intersects the plane of the ECLIPTIC when the Moon is moving in a northerly direction. (See NODES.)

Dragon's Tail: The south, or descending, node of the Moon; the point where the Moon's orbit intersects the plane of the ECLIPTIC when the Moon is moving in a southerly direction. (See NODES.)

Dwad (from the Sanskrit *dwadasamsa*, 12-division): One of twelve 2°30′ subdivisions of a sign of the zodiac. Each dwad is allocated to a different sign, according to one of two systems. The first system allocates the first dwad of a sign to that sign, the second dwad to the sign that follows it in the zodiac, and so on. For example, the first 2½° of Gemini is allocated to Gemini, the second 2½° to Cancer, and so on around the wheel. The second system allocates the first dwad of a sign to Aries, the second dwad to Taurus, and so on, so that each sign becomes a mini-zodiac. The second system corresponds to the twelfth harmonic (see HARMONICS). In Hindu astrology, from which the concept derives, the dwads are sometimes assigned to the traditional ruling planets of the signs instead of to the signs. The use of dwads is similar to that of decanates. (See DECANATE; INDIA, ASTROLOGY IN.)

Earth: 1. According to HERMETIC THEORY, one of the four ELEMENTS under which the signs Taurus, Virgo, and Capricorn, known as the *earth triplicity* or *earth trigon,* are classified. In astrology earth stands for practicality, sensuality, and caution. An overemphasis of earth signs in a birth chart is associated with sluggishness, materialism, and lack of imagination. A lack of earth is associated with impracticality, unreliability, and carelessness, qualities that may be considerably offset by a well-placed, well-aspected Saturn. (Also see CHINESE ASTROLOGY.)

2. The planet we inhabit; once thought to be flat and the center of the universe, now known to be spherical and to revolve in an elliptical orbit around the Sun together with the other planets in our solar system, of which it is fifth in size (7,900 miles in diameter) and third in distance from the Sun (93 million miles). The Earth's axis is tilted with respect to the plane of the ECLIPTIC at an angle of 66°33', causing our seasons (see COSMOGRAPHY). The Earth has one satellite, the Moon.

The discovery of the Earth's rotation on its axis, which causes the al-ternation of night and day, and of its revolution around the Sun, which causes our year, is attributed to COPERNICUS (1473–1543), although his ideas were anticipated by ancient astronomers—in particular, Aristarchus of Samos (third century B.C.). The *heliocentric* (Sun-centered) system of Copernicus replaced the *geocentric* (Earth-centered) system of PTOLEMY, which most people had accepted unquestioningly for almost 1,500 years.

Most astrological charts are geocentric, that is, they are calculated for a given location on the Earth's surface and show the positions of the planets from the perspective either of that location or of the center of the Earth. Such charts do not include the Earth as a planet, but use it rather as a point of observation—the specific terrestrial longitude and latitude of the birthplace. The continued use of geocentric charts does not invalidate astrology, which studies the angular relationships between the planets with respect to Earth, nor does it mean that astrologers are unaware of the Copernican revolution. The geocentric chart is a convention the validity of which is confirmed by Einstein's theory of relativity, which refutes the older notion that space and time are absolute entities independent of each other. Instead, each moving system conditions its own space and time, and each is a frame of reference as valid as any other.

Some astrologers do use heliocentric charts, and in such charts the Earth appears as a planet, represented by the astronomical symbol ⊕, which also happens to be the astrological symbol for the PART OF FORTUNE. (See GEOCENTRIC SYSTEM; HELIOCENTRIC ASTROLOGY; HELIOCENTRIC SYSTEM; RELATIVITY, THEORY OF.)

Earth House System: See HOUSE DIVISION.

Earthshine: See ECLIPSE.

Earth Signs: See EARTH, 1.

Earth Trigon: See EARTH, 1.

Earth Triplicity: See EARTH, 1.

Eastern Point: See EAST POINT.

East Point (also called **Equatorial Ascendant**): The point where the eastern HORIZON intersects the PRIME VERTICAL and the CELESTIAL EQUATOR; in some systems of HOUSE DIVISION, the cusp of the First House. The East Point should not be confused with the ASCENDANT, which is the point where the eastern horizon intersects the ECLIPTIC. Nor should it be confused with the *Eastern Point*, a name used by C. E. O. CARTER to describe the eastern intersection of the ecliptic with the "east-west me-

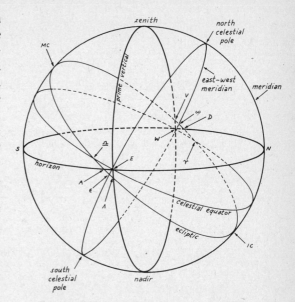

Figure 22. Eastern and western great-circle intersections. **E** = East Point; ε = "Eastern Point"; Λ = Antivertex; **W** = West Point; ω = "Western Point"; **V** = Vertex; **A** = Ascendant; **D** = Descendant; **N** = North Point; **S** = South Point; ♈ = vernal equinox; ♎ = autumnal equinox.

ridian," the GREAT CIRCLE passing through the celestial poles at right angles to the MERIDIAN; or the *Antivertex*, the eastern intersection of the ecliptic and prime vertical (see figure 22). The *West Point* corresponds to the East Point in the west; the *Western Point* to the Eastern Point; and the VERTEX to the Antivertex. (See COSMOGRAPHY.)

East-West Meridian: See EAST POINT.

Ebertin, Reinhold: See COSMOBIOLOGY.

Eclipse: The partial or total blocking of the light, or *occultation*, of one heavenly body by another. Astrology is concerned with eclipses that involve the Sun, the Moon, and the Earth; the two types of such eclipses are the *solar eclipse* and the *lunar eclipse*.

The solar eclipse occurs during any New Moon, or conjunction of the Sun and the Moon, in which the Moon passes directly between the Earth and the Sun and casts its shadow on the surface of the Earth. (During most New Moons, the luminaries are not in complete alignment: The Moon has the same CELESTIAL LONGITUDE as the Sun but a different CELESTIAL LATITUDE.) If, during an eclipse, the Moon is particularly close to the Earth—that is, near its *perigee*—the eclipse is *total* in the band of the Earth that is touched by the Moon's shadow cone. At that time the Sun's *corona*, its extremely hot outer atmosphere, which is normally invisible, can be seen. If the distance between the Moon and the Earth is greater, the eclipse may be *annular*: The Moon only blocks the central portion of the Sun, and a ring of the Sun's light may be observed around the edge of the Moon. An eclipse is *partial* when only part of the Sun is blocked by the Moon. This occurs when the Moon has sufficient latitude, as well as in those regions of the Earth that are near the band of totality of total eclipse but not in it. Since the Moon has no atmosphere, the edge of its shadow during any solar eclipse is sharply defined. (See figure 23.)

The lunar eclipse occurs during any Full Moon in which the Earth passes directly between the Moon and the Sun and casts its shadow on

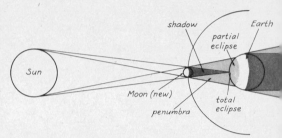

Figure 23. A solar eclipse.

the surface of the Moon. If the Moon is particularly close to the Earth, the eclipse is *total*. If the distance between the Moon and the Earth is greater, the eclipse may only be *penumbral*: The Moon is passing through the *penumbra*, or half shadow, of the Earth. If the Moon has sufficient latitude, the eclipse will be *partial*: Only a portion of its surface is occulted by the Earth. Because of the Earth's atmosphere, the edge of its shadow on the Moon is very vague. Also, there occurs a refraction of certain wavelengths of light in the Earth's atmosphere that gives a deep red appearance to the fully eclipsed Moon. It is usually possible to discern *earthshine*, infrared radiation refracted around the Earth by the atmosphere, on the eclipsed Moon. (See figure 24).

Either type of eclipse is possible only when the Sun and Moon are near the lunar NODES—that is, the points where the Earth's orbit, or the ecliptic, intersects the orbit of the Moon. Since the Moon's orbital speed is more than twelve times as great as the Sun's APPARENT MOTION, we need consider only those lunations when the Sun is close to one of the two nodes—that is, twice a year, approximately 6 months apart.

Lunar eclipses can be observed from anywhere that the Moon is visible above the horizon. Total eclipses of the Sun, on the other hand, are rare for any given location, occurring about once every 361 years. The maximum number of eclipses possible in a year is seven: either five solar and two lunar, or four solar and three lunar.

The *Saros cycle,* discovered by the ancient Chaldean astrologer-priests, is a period of 6,585 days (18 years, 10 to 12 days, depending on which of the years are leap years) in which the Sun, Moon, and lunar nodes return so nearly to the same relative positions that the eclipses of the following cycle occur in approximately the same order, for the same length of time, and so forth. This cycle enabled the priests to predict the next eclipse with great precision.

Eclipses have always had a prominent place in MUNDANE ASTROLOGY. The ancients believed they portended some dire calamity—a crucial battle or the death of a great leader—or the beginning of some important undertaking. In NATAL ASTROLOGY eclipses have traditionally been regarded as MALEFIC, especially when they fall on an angle or a planet in

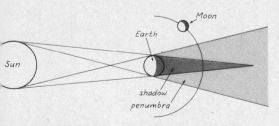

Figure 24. A lunar eclipse.

the chart; but modern astrologers tend to see them in a more positive light. The effects of an eclipse transiting Sun, Moon, Ascendant, or Midheaven may not be felt until another planet, particularly Mars or Saturn, transits the same degree and triggers the release of the pent-up energy.

Some astrologers believe that the last eclipse prior to birth is of importance to the native and that its path may mark areas on the Earth that will be of significance in the life. For example, the eclipse of February 29, 357 B.C., prior to the birth of Alexander the Great, was on the Midheaven at his birthplace, Pella in Macedonia. Its path of totality swept through the very lands which he was later to conquer: Egypt, Mesopotamia, and Persia. Similarly, the path of the eclipse that occurred on the day of Karl Marx's birth (May 5, 1818) swept right across the then Russian Empire. The subject of eclipses has been studied by Sepharial, L. E. JOHNDRO, Charles JAYNE, Charles Emerson, and Robert Jansky. Jayne believes that an eclipse is an energizer whose basic qualities are intensity, fatality, and unpredictability.

A total eclipse of the Sun has a profound impact on living creatures. When their circadian rhythm is thus interrupted, many animals will react to the drop in temperature and the sudden twilight by settling down for a night's sleep. In contrast, human beings—astronomers in particular—tend to become extremely excited, and an astronomer who realizes, only seconds from totality, that he or she has left an important camera lens at home may suffer extreme depression or temporary insanity.

Ecliptic: The Sun's apparent path around the Earth, also called *via solis*, or the Earth's orbit as viewed from the Sun; a GREAT CIRCLE used by astrologers, so named because it is on this circle that eclipses of the Sun and Moon occur. In the course of its APPARENT MOTION along the ecliptic, the Sun passes through the twelve signs of the zodiac; one such revolution constitutes a year. The plane of the ecliptic is tilted with respect to the plane of the CELESTIAL EQUATOR by approximately 23°, an angle that has been decreasing steadily for over 2,000 years. The ecliptic intersects the celestial equator at the two points the Sun transits at the spring and fall EQUINOXES.

Distance along the ecliptic circle is measured in degrees and minutes of CELESTIAL LONGITUDE, beginning with the VERNAL POINT; the entire ecliptic has 360° of longitude. Distance above or below the ecliptic is measured in degrees and minutes of CELESTIAL LATITUDE; the latitude of the north ecliptic pole is 90° north. The paths of the Moon and the planets do not coincide with the ecliptic, but they are all reasonably close. Pluto's orbit has the greatest inclination to the ecliptic; Pluto can reach a latitude of 17°. Mercury, with the next greatest inclination to the ecliptic, can reach a latitude of 7°. (See CELESTIAL COORDINATES; COSMOGRAPHY.)

Egypt, Astrology in: We have very little precise knowledge about astrology as it was practiced in ancient Egypt. The traditional view that Egyptian astrology began several thousand years ago has recently been challenged by scholars. Yet it has been extremely well documented that the Egyptians, at least as far back as the fourth millennium B.C., had a thorough understanding of basic astronomical principles. For example, the Great Pyramid of Khufu, built ca. 2600 B.C., had long sighting tubes accurately oriented toward Thuban, the first star in the constellation of the Dragon, which would have been the North Star at that time (see PRECESSION OF THE EQUINOXES). In *The Case for Astrology* John Anthony West and Jan Gerhard Toonder point out how unique the Egyptians would have been among all other ancient peoples if they had studied astronomy without applying it to their earthly situation. In fact it is well known that Egyptian priests had a monopoly on knowledge of the universe and kept it a secret from ordinary people, who were considered too profane. In order to maintain this secrecy, the knowledge was transmitted orally to the next generation of priests; very little of this tradition was committed to writing and thus made available for scrutiny by modern scholars. Nonetheless, hints abound concerning the antiquity of Egyptian astrology. Imhotep, the architect who designed the "stepped" pyramid of Zoser (Third Dynasty, ca. 2700 B.C.), was renowned not only as the father of medicine but as "Chief of the Observers," an epithet that probably refers to his role as an astrologer. The Great Sphinx at Gi-

Carved zodiac on the ceiling of the vestibule of the Temple of Hathor, Egypt. Begun in the reign of Ptolemy IX, this temple was completed under Nero, or between 80 B.C. and A.D. 68. (Louvre, Paris; photo by Giraudon.)

zeh (third millennium B.C.) embodies the fixed signs: It has the body of a bull (Taurus), the paws of a lion (Leo), the wings of an eagle (Scorpio), and the head of a human being (Aquarius). And the *Calendar of Favorable and Unfavorable Days*, which dates from the beginning of the New Empire (ca. 1570 B.C.), tells how the subjects of Pharaoh Ahmosis I, founder of the Eighteenth Dynasty, made predictions that resembled astrological horoscopes.

According to the Egyptologist Schwaller de Lubicz, the Egyptians regarded the universe as a conscious whole in which all the parts were interrelated. (This concept would later appear as HERMETIC THEORY, tradi-

tionally believed to have arisen about 2000 B.C. from the worship of Thoth, god of healing, intelligence, and writing. Modern scholars, however, have insisted that this theory was an invention of Greeks living in Egypt about the time of Christ.) Astrology was a part of the larger body of sacred knowledge—including architecture, medicine, and alchemy—that attempted to translate cosmology into guidelines for daily life.

The *Calendar of Favorable and Unfavorable Days* assigns every hour and every day to the control of a god, who intervened directly in the lives of humans. Thus a birth taking place on the fifth of the month of Phaophi was inauspicious (risk of death by a bull), whereas the sixth and ninth were particularly auspicious. The tenth of the month of Choiak, the twentieth of the month of Thoth, and the fourth of the month of Athyr were associated with presages of violent death. The twenty-sixth of the month of Thoth, the anniversary of the titanic battle between Seth and Horus, was a day of evil omen. Nothing undertaken on that day could come to good, and most Egyptians abstained from work.

The priests learned over the centuries to determine the positions of the constellations, including Orion, Cassiopea, and the Great Bear, and of various stars, including Sirius. They divided the stars into two categories. The first group they called the "indestructible" (*khemu-sek*), that is, those that were always visible in the same place. The second group they called the "indefatigable," (*khemu-urz*), those that wandered incessantly through the sky on their paths: Mercury, Venus, Mars, Jupiter, and Saturn.

The Egyptians assigned particular importance to thirty-six stars in all, each of which governed one of thirty-six 10-day periods in the year. The very accurate Egyptian year began on the day of the HELIACAL rising of Sirius. The priests came to believe that each star had a certain influence over the destiny of those born during the 10-day period it ruled.

The postimperial period (ca. 1090 to 332 B.C.) was characterized by an expansion of trade between Egypt and the Middle East. Mesopotamian influence in Egypt dramatically increased after the Persian conquest in 525 B.C. Mesopotamian influence may have begun somewhat earlier; perhaps it was Babylonian star worship (see CHALDEAN ASTROLOGY) that inspired Pharaoh Amenhotep IV (Ikhnaton, reigned 1377–60 B.C.) to impose on Egypt his short-lived monotheistic worship of the Sun (Aton), Lord of Heaven and Earth. But after the Persian conquest large numbers of Chaldeans took up residence in Egyptian towns, among them soothsayers and astrologers who soon built up a flourishing business while refusing, of course, to reveal their secrets. (Tradition has it that it was a priest named Manetho who popularized Mesopotamian astrology in the third century B.C.) About 150 B.C. the esoteric treatises of the mythical King Nechepso and his priest Petosiris were written, glorifying the Egyptian version of star worship. These treatises, pretending to a much greater antiquity, were highly regarded in the Roman world for centuries.

Einstein, Albert: See RELATIVITY, THEORY OF.

Election, Sign of: In classical astrology, the sign in which a planet has "elected domicile," that is, the sign that it rules. (See DOMICILE; RULERSHIP.)

Electional Astrology: The branch of astrology concerned with choosing the most favorable moment to begin any undertaking, such as getting married, going on a trip, starting a business, signing a contract, building a house, or moving into a new home. In electional astrology the principles of NATAL and especially of HORARY ASTROLOGY are applied in reverse. Instead of starting with a time and a configuration of planets and interpreting the results, the astrologer starts with a desired result and tries to find a time and a configuration of planets that will help to bring it about.

In preparing an electional chart (once called an *inceptional figure*), the astrologer must first make a careful study of the birth chart in question, in order to avoid times when any afflictions therein would be activated. He or she must also determine if the desired result may be beyond its potential, for nothing can take place that is not promised in the natal chart. Next the astrologer studies the sign positions and aspects of the transiting planets within the period of time available. Of particular importance in an electional chart are the

Ascendant and Midheaven, the house positions of the planets, and the condition of the Moon by sign, house, and aspect, since these are the fastest-moving elements in a chart and hence those over which the astrologer has the most control. Classical astrologers believed that the Moon should be not only free from any serious affliction but also swift in motion and increasing in light (waxing). There is a vast literature of rules and aphorisms relating to elections; PTOLEMY, Guido Bonatus, Roger Bacon, Jerome Cardan, and William LILLY all contributed to the subject.

Electional Chart (or **Electional Figure**): See ELECTIONAL ASTROLOGY.

Electrical Ascendant: See JOHNDRO, L. E.

Elements: The four fundamental substances—fire, air, water, and earth—which provide one of the two primary classifications of the signs of the zodiac, the other being the QUALITIES, or modes. The *fire signs* are Aries, Leo, and Sagittarius; the *air signs* are Gemini, Libra, and Aquarius; the *water signs* are Cancer, Scorpio, and Pisces; and the *earth signs* are Taurus, Virgo, and Capricorn. The common attributes of the fire signs are energy and enthusiasm; of the air signs, intellect and communication; of the water signs, emotion and sensitivity; and of the earth signs, practicality and stability. (See COMPATIBILITY; and entries under individual elements.)

The early Greek philosophers sought a single fundamental principle to which all forms of matter could be reduced. For Thales, this element was water; for Anaximander, it was the "moist"; for Anaxagoras, it was air; and for Heraclitus, it was fire. Empedocles (fifth century B.C.) recognized four primary elements, fire, air, water, and earth, and maintained that there was no hierarchy among the four. His theory was accepted almost unanimously by the thinkers of ancient Greece; Plato propounded it in *Timaeus*.

The Pythagoreans (sixth century B.C.) adapted the theory of the four elements to human physiology as the theory of the four HUMORS, fluids whose proportions in the body determined health and temperament: blood (air); phlegm (water); choler, or yellow bile (fire); and melancholy, or black bile (earth). This idea continued to dominate medicine until after the Renaissance.

Claudius Ptolemy (second century A.D.) applied the theory of the four elements to astrology, assigning to each element three signs which together made up the "triangle" (triplicity) of that element.

The Chinese have five elements: metal, water, wood, fire, and earth. (See CHINESE ASTROLOGY.)

Elements, Harmonious: See COMPATIBILITY.

Elevation: The distance of a celestial object above the horizon; altitude. The planet most highly elevated in a chart is thereby strengthened, especially if it is in the Tenth House or conjunct the Midheaven. Elevation is one of the ways a planet may be accidentally dignified. In classical astrology, the elevation of a malefic (Mars or Saturn) in a chart, especially above the Sun or Moon, was held to be highly unfavorable. A modern astrologer would make a careful study of the aspects of the elevated planet in relation to the chart as a whole before becoming alarmed.

Elongation: The angular distance of an inferior planet from the Sun, as seen from the Earth. The maximum elongation of Mercury is 28°; of Venus, 48°. This means that Mercury and Venus can never be in square, trine, or opposition to the Sun. The only aspects they can form to the Sun are the conjunction and the semisextile (Mercury and Venus) and the semisquare (Venus). The fact that these two planets form conjunctions with the Sun with much greater fre-

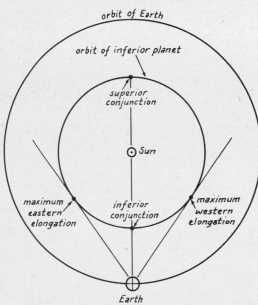

Figure 25. Conjunctions and elongations of an inferior planet.

quency than the other planets makes these conjunctions far less significant in a birth chart. The term *elongation* was also once a synonym for APHELION. (See figure 25.)

Ennius: See ROMANS, ASTROLOGY AMONG THE.

Ephemeris (plural **Ephemerides**; from the Greek *ephemeros*, existing no longer than a day): A publication giving the computed positions of the Sun, Moon, and planets for each day of the year, or for other regular intervals, in CELESTIAL LONGITUDE, CELESTIAL LATITUDE, and DECLINATION, as well as other data such as sidereal time, positions of the lunar NODES, aspects, lunations, ingresses, eclipses, and so on. Most ephemerides give the geocentric positions of the planets, although a few include heliocentric positions as well. Astronomers' ephemerides tend to use RIGHT ASCENSION rather than celestial longitude. An ephemeris including the year of the birth in question is an indispensable tool in setting up a chart.

Ancient astrologers determined the positions of the planets for a given moment by direct observation, using various instruments, such as the ARMILLARY SPHERE. With the advent of the ephemeris, such primitive methods are no longer necessary. First devised by astrologers to facilitate the casting of horoscopes, ephemerides came to be used by navigators and astronomers as well. The *Ephemerides of Raphael*, published every year since 1800 in Great Britain, were until recently the most widely used ephemerides in the world. Other well-known ephemerides available in English include the *Rosicrucian,* and the new *American Ephemeris,* which is produced with the aid of a computer. The Swiss *Ephemeriden* (1890–1950) and the 10-year *Deutsche Ephemeride* are perfectly comprehensible to English readers and widely available in America. Some older ephemerides lack positions for Pluto, even after its discovery in 1930. To fill in these gaps the American *Omega Pluto Ephemeris for 1773–2000* is highly recommended.

Beginners should beware that some ephemerides give the planets' positions for noon on a given day, while others give it for midnight. It is important to verify this point before attempting to set up a chart. For a demonstration of the use of an ephemeris, with a sample ephemeris page, see CHART CALCULATION.

Ephemeris Time (ET): See TIME.

Equal House System: See HOUSE DIVISION.

Equatorial Arc: See PROGRESSION AND DIRECTION.

Equatorial Ascendant: See EAST POINT.

Equinoctial Signs: Aries and Libra; see EQUINOXES.

Equinoctial Year: See TROPICAL YEAR.

Equinoxes (from the Latin *aequus,* equal, and *nox,* night): The two moments during the year when the Sun, in its apparent path along the ECLIPTIC, crosses the Equator, and day and night are of equal length all over the Earth. These two moments occur when the Sun enters the sign of Aries, at the beginning of spring, on or near March 21, called the *vernal,* or *spring, equinox,* and when the Sun enters the sign of Libra, at the beginning of fall, on or near September 22, called the *autumnal equinox.* At the spring equinox the Sun apparently passes from the Southern Hemisphere (where subsequent days are shorter) to the Northern Hemisphere (where subsequent days are longer). At the autumnal equinox, the situation is reversed.

The term *equinoxes* also refers to the two points where the ecliptic intersects the CELESTIAL EQUATOR. The equinoctial points are known by astrologers and astronomers alike as 0° Aries, also called the VERNAL POINT, and 0° Libra. Aries and Libra are sometimes called the *equinoctial signs.* Charts cast for the Sun's entry, or *ingress,* into the equinoctial signs are considered of great importance in MUNDANE ASTROLOGY. (See ANTISCION; COSMOGRAPHY; PRECESSION OF THE EQUINOXES; SOLSTICES.)

Erlewine, Michael and Margaret: See ASPECT; ASTRONOMY; COMPUTERS AND ASTROLOGY; HELIOCENTRIC ASTROLOGY.

Esoteric Astrology (from the Greek *esoteros,* inner; from *eso,* within): The study of the planets, signs, and houses as a guide to spiritual evolution. The term *esoteric* means intended for the initiated, as distinguished from *exoteric*, which means suitable for the general public, and hence more comprehensible. Alan LEO defines esoteric astrology as "the study of natural astrology, or *astrologia sana*, plus the eastern teachings concerning reincarnation and karma"; Alice Bailey calls it "the astrology of the soul."

Bailey, who wrote prolifically on occult subjects, believed that modern astrology had erred in laying undue emphasis on the personal horoscope, on the Earth (that is, the houses), and on individual differences. In esoteric astrology the emphasis is on the transpersonal, the underlying unity of the cosmos, and above all, on the soul. Esoteric astrologers tend to underplay the Ascendant, the most personal point on the chart. They pay more attention to the signs of the zodiac than to the houses, but less to the signs than to the planets, which are regarded as the vehicles of supreme intelligences, or angels. Although it generally uses the geocentric positions of the planets, esoteric astrology anticipates the new heliocentric astrology in that it is philosophically Sun-centered. To Alan Leo, God was the solar logos; Alice Bailey stresses the Sun at the expense of the Moon, which she dismisses as purely symbolic, a dead form possessing no emanation or radiation and therefore no effect.

Esoteric astrology has been much influenced by theosophy, from which it inherited a mixture of Oriental and Christian theology. Important Oriental features are the belief in REINCARNATION, the use of the doctrine of KARMA to explain the good and bad aspects, the correlation of the seven planets with the seven *chakras*, or energy centers, of the human body, and the use of the five elements of Eastern philosophy (the four Western elements, plus ether). Examples of Christian symbolism include relating the three qualities—cardinal, mutable, and fixed—to the trinity and referring to the angles of the chart as the cross of matter on which the native is crucified. The two great traditions are combined in the esoteric approach to astrology as a means of unification with the divine will. Like Saint Thomas AQUINAS, esoteric astrologers believe that "the wise man rules his stars, the fool obeys them." To them, the purpose of astrology is to help the individual achieve freedom from illusion by contacting the higher vibrations of the energies represented by the planets.

Essential Dignity: See DIGNITY.

Ethics: The question of ethics has special importance in astrology, because of its persistent association in the mind of the public with fortune-tellers and charlatans. Many astrological organizations (for example, the British Faculty of Astrological Studies, the Astrologers Guild of America, and the American Federation of Astrologers) have codes of ethics, and many of the authors of books on astrology refer implicitly or explicitly to the astrologer's moral responsibilities to his or her clients. Such codes of ethics can be traced back through William LILLY's famous "Epistle to the Astrologer" at least as far as Firmicus Maternus (fl. 330 A.D.), who devotes a chapter of his *Mathesis* to the "Life and Training of an Astrologer."

Some of the principles most often cited are the use of, and adherence to, a horoscope cast for the time and place of the client's birth, and the clear identification of any other techniques brought into play; the confidentiality of the horoscope itself and of any personal information provided by the client in consultation, in accordance with the standard professional practice of physicians, psychoanalysts, and attorneys; and the avoidance of claims to precise prediction of future events; of any emphasis on impending accident, illness, death, or disaster; or of any approach that tends to encourage in the client a psychological dependence on the astrologer or an abdication of personal responsibility for his or her own life.

The code of ethics of the Astrologers Guild of America states that the proper use of astrology is as "a technique for determining the probabilities in human events" and sternly reprimands "a pretense of powers to predict specific future events with absolute certainty." Although there are famous cases of astrologers predicting their own death or that of their clients, the modern tendency is to regard predictions concerning the time or manner of death as both unethical and irrelevant.

Dane RUDHYAR sees the special knowledge of the astrologer as a profound moral responsibility and warns against giving any information unless there is reason to believe that the client can assimilate it and use it constructively. He writes that "prediction has value only as it contributes to the person's development and essential welfare." The role of astrologers is not to impress clients with their power but to help them release their own potential; not to play on their fear of the unknown but to help them face the inescapable phenomenon of change. Rudhyar advises the astrologer to approach the chart with full acceptance of personal responsibility, "and indeed, in an attitude of prayer, asking for inner guidance and the bestowal of wise understanding."

Other responsibilities of astrologers include educating the public on the proper use of astrology, with a view to establishing professional standards and eliminating charlatans; helping to spread serious astrology through teaching, writing, and the media; supporting open-minded research and interdisciplinary study with a view to healing the rift between astrology and science; and collecting accurate birth information, especially on persons of interest to research and on the leading personalities of their time.

Evil Aspects: An antiquated classification for the OPPOSITION (180°), SQUARE (90°), SEMISQUARE (45°), and SESQUISQUARE (135°).

Exaltation: In classical astrology, the condition of a planet when placed in a specific sign in which it is held to be strengthened dramatically, a placement that is sometimes, but not necessarily, an advantage. For example, Venus, the planet of love and beauty, is exalted in Pisces, the sign of universal compassion and aesthetic sensitivity. Tradition has it that whereas a planet in DOMICILE is like a person in his or her own home, a planet in exaltation is like a person in someone else's home where he or she is an honored guest: It may be conspicuous and important, but it is not as comfortable or efficient as it would be in its own sign. Thus someone with Venus in Pisces may have highly refined sensibilities but may also be unusually gullible or carry self-sacrifice to dramatic extremes. The exaltations of the other planets are as follows: The Moon in Taurus, Mercury in Aquarius (or Virgo), Sun in Aries, Mars in Capricorn, Jupiter in Cancer, and Saturn in Libra. According to some authorities, a planet's exaltation is limited to specific degrees—for example, Sun in 19° Aries, Moon in 3° Taurus, Mercury in 15° Virgo, Venus in 27° Pisces, Mars in 28° Capricorn, Jupiter in 15° Cancer, and Saturn in 21° Libra.

Some modern astrologers prefer the exaltation to the domicile; Charles CARTER writes, "Generally, a planet in its own sign is thought to be stronger . . . rather than necessarily better in operation. On the other hand, a body in its exaltation is said to be purified and inclined to express itself well." The idea of purification works well for the Moon in Taurus and Mars in Capricorn, where the energy of the planet is restrained in its sign of exaltation, but not so well for the Sun in Aries or Saturn in Libra, where the energy of the planet is exaggerated.

There is some disagreement as to the signs of exaltation of the modern planets, and indeed, not all modern astrologers find the concept useful. Many of those who do, believe that Uranus is exalted in Scorpio, Neptune in Cancer (or Leo), and Pluto in Aries.

The sign (or degree) opposite the place of a planet's exaltation is the sign (or degree) of its FALL.

Extra-Saturnian Planets (also called TRANS-SATURNIAN PLANETS): See MODERN PLANETS.

Eye of God: See DOUBLE QUINCUNX.

Ezra, Abraham ben: See HEBREWS, ASTROLOGY AMONG THE.

Face (or **Facet**): A subdivision of a sign defined either as half a decanate or 5° of CELESTIAL LONGITUDE, in which case there are seventy-two faces in a chart (Alan LEO), or as a synonym for DECANATE, in which case there are thirty-six (Sepharial). The term is seldom used by modern astrologers.

Factor: A convenient blanket term used, particularly by cosmobiologists, to refer to any of the thirteen commonly used elements in a chart: Midheaven, Ascendant, Sun, Moon, Mercury, Venus, Mars, Jupiter, Saturn, Uranus, Neptune, Pluto, and the north node of the Moon.

Fagan, Cyril (May 22, 1896, 12:14:28 P.M., Dunsink, Dublin–January 5, 1970, 3–5:00 A.M., Tucson, Arizona): Irish astrologer, generally known as the father of modern sidereal astrology (see SIDEREAL ZODIAC). Fagan came to astrology at the age of twenty and for nearly twenty-five years applied his lively and fertile mind to it within the framework of the TROPICAL ZODIAC. In the late 1930s, however, the study of Egyptology and ancient astronomy began

to convince him that the earliest astrologers worked with the signs of the constellations and that this must therefore be the correct zodiac, a theory he finally accepted in 1944. The fundamental problem he set himself to solve was the value of the AYANAMSA—the difference between the two zodiacs—for any period.

Believing that the exaltation degrees of the planets as given by PTOLEMY offered an important clue to the problem, he searched for historical periods when the planets would in fact have been seen in those degrees at their HELIACAL rising or setting. He concluded that within recent millennia only during one year, 786 B.C., had all of the planets had their heliacal rising or setting in their exaltation degrees. Having made this remarkable discovery, he was able to give a close approximation to the value of the ayanamsa (see INDIA, ASTROLOGY IN), which was later refined by the statistical studies of Donald Bradley. A full account of this discovery is given in his *Zodiacs Old and New* (1950).

Whatever the intrinsic worth of this work—and it has been seriously questioned—there is no doubt that

Fagan launched one of the most productive debates in modern astrology. The statistical studies of Bradley, Firebrace, and others in pursuit of the "correct" zodiac and ayanamsa were soon being analyzed and repeated, spurring on the astrological community to develop a greater awareness of quantitative methods of research. In particular, the "zodiacal question" gave impetus to ADDEY's work on HARMONICS, which put sidereal studies into a wider perspective and allowed for the possibility of different zodiacs, each with its own starting point. At the same time the Western sidereal movement that grew up around Fagan's work, most notably in Britain through Brigadier Firebrace's journal *Spica*, touched off a wealth of research into new predictive techniques that allow for the precessional factor in calculating such things as solar and lunar returns and transits (see PRECESSION OF THE EQUINOXES; SOLAR RETURN; TRANSIT).

Fagan's *Primer of Sidereal Astrology* is still the standard textbook in its field. Many of the important and innovative ideas that originally appeared in his humorous "Solunar" column in *American Astrology* from 1953 on are summarized in the posthumous work *Astrological Origins* (1971). (See HOUSE DIVISION; SIDEREAL ZODIAC.)

—CHARLES HARVEY

Fall: In classical astrology, the condition of a planet when placed in the sign opposite the sign of its EXALTATION. Since Mars is exalted in Capricorn, it is in fall in Cancer. The ancients held that a planet in fall is like a person in exile: It is considerably weakened, and the energies it represents are distorted dramatically. Thus since Mars stands for goal-directed energy and action, someone with Mars in Cancer may find that too much of his or her energy is drained by emotions, that dwelling on old hurts prevents the native from getting on with the business at hand. The falls of the other planets are as follows: Moon in Scorpio, Mercury in Leo (or Pisces), Venus in Virgo, Sun in Libra, Mars in Cancer, Jupiter in Capricorn, and Saturn in Aries. According to some authorities, a planet's fall is limited to specific degrees—for example, Sun in 19° Libra, Moon in 3° Scorpio, Mercury in 15° Pisces, Venus in 27° Virgo, Mars in 28° Cancer, Jupiter in 15° Capricorn, and Saturn in 21° Aries.

There is some disagreement as to the signs of exaltation and fall of the modern planets, but many astrologers believe that Uranus is in fall in Taurus, Neptune in Capricorn (or Aquarius), and Pluto in Libra.

Fall Equinox: See EQUINOXES.

Fall Ingress: See INGRESS.

Feminine Planets: According to PTOLEMY, Moon and Venus; modern authorities often include Neptune and the asteroids.

Feminine Signs (also called **Negative**, **Nocturnal**, or **Unfortunate Signs**): The signs of the earth and water triplicities, namely, Taurus, Cancer, Virgo, Scorpio, Capricorn, and Pisces. The *masculine signs* belong to the fire and air triplicities. (See POLARITY.)

Fiducial: See SIDEREAL ZODIAC.

Figure: An antiquated term for horoscope.

Final Dispositor: See DISPOSITOR.

Finger of God: See DOUBLE QUINCUNX.

Fire: According to HERMETIC THEORY, one of the four ELEMENTS, under which the signs Aries, Leo, and Sagittarius, known as the *fire triplicity* or *fire trigon*, are classified. In astrology fire stands for energy, enthusiasm, and optimism. An overemphasis of fire signs in a chart is associated with egotism, arrogance, or even violence, depending on other factors in the chart. A lack of fire might manifest as listlessness, apathy, or lack of self-confidence, qualities that may be considerably offset by a well-placed, well-aspected Sun or Mars. (Also see CHINESE ASTROLOGY.)

Fire Signs: See FIRE.

Fire Trigon: See FIRE.

Fire Triplicity: See FIRE.

Fixed: One of the three *qualities*, or modes, that characterize the signs of the zodiac, the other two being CARDINAL and MUTABLE. The fixed quality has been compared to centripetal force in physics, or to matter. The fixed signs of the zodiac are the four signs immediately following the car-

dinal signs, namely, Taurus, Leo, Scorpio, and Aquarius. The Sun transits these signs when the season that began in the cardinal signs is at its most intense. Fixed signs are characterized by persistence, resourcefulness, and magnetism; on the negative side, they are associated with rigidity and resistance to change.

As archetypes of matter and duration, the fixed signs have a special significance in occult teachings. They appear in the Bible as the four beasts of the Apocalypse: "And the first beast was like a lion, and the second beast like a calf, and the third beast had a face as a man, and the fourth

WHEEL of FORTUNE.

beast was like a flying eagle" (Rev. 4:7). They are also represented on two of the Major Arcana of the Tarot, the tenth, the Wheel of Fortune, and the twenty-first, the World.

In classical astrology, the fixed signs were known collectively as the *fixed quadruplicity*, since there are four of them. They are also sometimes referred to us as the *fixed cross*, since if planets in them are connected by straight lines, they form a cross. A *grand fixed cross* is a major configuration in which two pairs of opposing planets, all in fixed signs, are in square aspect to each other, forming a cross (see GRAND CROSS).

Fixed Star: See STAR.

Fixed Zodiac: See SIDEREAL ZODIAC.

Forming Aspect: See APPLYING ASPECT.

Fortuna: See PART OF FORTUNE.

Fortunate Signs: See MASCULINE SIGNS; POLARITY.

Fortunes, the (also called **the Two Fortunes** or **the Benefics**): In classical astrology Jupiter and Venus, known as the *Greater Fortune* and the *Lesser Fortune*, respectively. Both were believed to bring wealth and favors, especially if ANGULAR and well aspected by the luminaries or PART OF FORTUNE. Modern astrologers tend to regard them as energies that can be used either creatively or destructively, depending on the individual's degree of self-awareness and self-control. (See BENEFIC.)

Full Moon: See LUNATION; MOON.

Gabirol, Solomon ben: See HE-BREWS, ASTROLOGY AMONG THE.

Galactic Center: The nucleus of our GALAXY, around which our solar system revolves at about 135 miles per second in a 225-million-year period known as the *cosmic year*. According to the most recent astronomical estimates, the 1980 position of the Galactic Center on the CELESTIAL SPHERE was 26°35′ Sagittarius (266°35′ of absolute CELESTIAL LONGITUDE) and 5°15′ of south CELESTIAL LATITUDE (5S15), in the constellation of Sagittarius. The Galactic Center is about 26,000 light-years distant from the Earth. It appears to move along with all the surrounding stars at a rate of about 1° of celestial longitude every 72 years because of PRECESSION OF THE EQUINOXES. The Center appears to move in relation to the surrounding stars at a rate of about 1° of longitude every 556,000 years because of our solar system's changing view of it during the cosmic year.

The Galactic Center is really the Sun of our Sun. It is certainly the source of most of the gravitational energy prevalent in the galaxy and possibly the ultimate source of the energy interactions whose effects are studied by astrology. According to Theodor Landscheidt, the radiation emanating from the Galactic Center is intercepted by our solar system and interpreted by it according to the ASPECT pattern of the planets at that moment, much as radio signals are interpreted in a particular way by an antenna of a particular shape. Landscheidt associates the Galactic Center with equilibrium of the personality structure, the power of attraction that the individual exerts on the environment, and his or her spiritual aspirations.

Galaxy (from the Greek *gala*, milk): An "island universe" composed of billions of stars together with gas and dust, held together and usually compressed into a plane by gravitation. The universe may contain many billions of individual galaxies, some of them gathered together in clusters. The closest galaxy to ours is the Andromeda galaxy, some 1.5 million light-years away.

Our galaxy is called the Milky Way. It contains between 30,000 and 100,000 million stars, is about 100,000 light-years in diameter and 5,000 to

10,000 light-years thick. The Milky Way rotates like a giant pinwheel; our solar system, located about 26,000 light-years from the GALACTIC CENTER, completes one revolution in about 225 million years.

The astrologer Theodor Landscheidt regards our galaxy as a system similar to a living organism, radiating information from its center in the form of gravitational and electromagnetic energy. This information is received by stellar systems throughout the galaxy, including our own, where it is a cybernetic program for the personality traits and events astrologers associate with planetary patterns.

Galilei, Galileo (known as **Galileo**; February 15, 1564, Pisa–January 8, 1642, near Florence): Italian astronomer and physicist. Galileo is responsible for the final public acceptance of the Copernican theory of a heliocentric universe. He invented one of the earliest refracting telescopes, with which he made some major astronomical discoveries, including sunspots, the pockmarked surface of the Moon, the Moon's reflected light, the moons of Jupiter, the rings of Saturn, and the fact that the Milky Way is made up of countless stars. He conceived the three laws of motion later formulated by Sir Isaac NEWTON. Like Johannes KEPLER, the other great exponent of the Copernican system, Galileo was a practicing astrologer. In 1609 he drew up the horoscope of his patron, the grand duke of Tuscany.

Galileo's attempt to reconcile the Copernican system with Christian

Galileo. Galilei (The Bettman Archive.)

theology brought him into conflict with the Church, which denounced the heliocentric view as contrary to Holy Scripture and forbade him to "hold, teach, or defend" the condemned doctrine. After 16 years' silence he published his *Dialogo dei due massimi sistemi del mondo* (1632), in which his support for Copernican principles was masked in dialogue form. Summoned to Rome by the Inquisition, he recanted. He died on the day Isaac Newton was born. (See COPERNICUS, NICOLAUS.)

Gauquelin, Michel (November 13, 1928, 10:20 P.M., Paris–) and **Françoise** (née Marie Schneider, 1929–): French statisticians and pioneers in the scientific investigation of astrology. Michel Gauquelin holds a Ph.D. in psychology and statistics from the Sorbonne; Françoise Gauquelin holds a degree in statistics from the University of Paris. The Gauquelins have devoted their life together to the reexamination of astrological concepts in the light of modern scientific

Michel and Françoise Gauquelin.

knowledge and methodology.

Gauquelin found that earlier statistical work in astrology that seemed to confirm the validity of signs, houses, and aspects was unsound due to inadequate size of samples and lack of proper controls. Between 1949 and the present, the Gauquelins have collected the birth data of many thousands of people from registrars all over Europe, and have studied the positions of the planets at their birth in relation to such effects as later choice of profession and personality traits.

They found that for certain groups of successful professionals—that is, sports champions, scientists, and writers—the diurnal distribution of certain planets followed a consistent pattern that differed significantly from chance. For example, in the charts of 1,553 sports champions the planet Mars was found to be rising or culminating—that is, just past the HORIZON or MERIDIAN of the birthplace—with a frequency whose probability of occurring by chance was 1 in 1,000. Similarly, there was a marked tendency for eminent scientists to have a rising or culminating Saturn and for successful writers to have a rising or culminating Moon. In all these studies, the Gauquelins used the charts of ordinary professionals in the same field as controls. Their results with sports champions were replicated by a highly skeptical group of Belgian scientists, the Committee for the Scientific Investigation of Claims of the Paranormal, using a different sample of 535 French and Belgian athletes. Indeed, their results were so similar to the Gauquelins' that the shocked scientists spent 4 years studying all possible objections and organizing numerous control experiments.

The Gauquelins' methodology for work of this kind is set out in a brief but important standard work, *Méthodes pour étudier la Répartition des Astres dans la Mouvement Diurne* (1957).

In statistical tests conducted during 1959–65, the Gauquelins found a planetary effect in heredity. Analysis of the birth charts of 30,000 parents and children (in a study published in 1966) revealed that children of parents with Moon, Venus, Mars, Jupiter, or Saturn ANGULAR tended to have those planets angular too, with a frequency whose probability of occurring by chance was 1 in 100,000. When both parents had the same angular planet, the effect was doubled, which accords with the laws of genetics. Curiously, the effect did not occur when birth was induced. These results were confirmed by a second study published in 1976 involving 37,000 new birth data.

In their later work the Gauquelins have focused on isolating the personality traits that underlie choice of profession, since their findings suggested that the true correlation is not between planet and occupation but between planet and character. The results of all their studies, including all the birth data, are published in a massive 23-volume series by their Laboratoire d'Etude des Relations Entre Rythmes Cosmiques et Psychophysiologiques, founded in 1969. In addition, Michel Gauquelin has written many books, of which the best-known available in English are *The Cosmic Clocks* (1967), *The Scientific Basis of Astrology* (1969), and *Cosmic Influences on Human Behavior* (1973).

Although the Gauquelins' results tend to confirm some parts of astrological doctrine, such as the traditional correlation between planets and temperament, they lend no support to others, such as the correlation between choice of profession and the sign position of the Sun. Also, it should be noted that the positions "preferred" by certain planets in the charts of successful professionals are not on the horizon and meridian, but just *past* them—that is, in the Twelfth and Ninth Houses, not in the First and Tenth Houses, the sensitive "angular" positions of traditional astrology.

Like John ADDEY in England, the Gauquelins are laying the foundations for a new astrology in which many of the ideas that have been accepted more or less unquestioningly since PTOLEMY may be eliminated, or at least seen in a new perspective. Yet in his writings Michel Gauquelin is very careful not to call their work astrology. To avoid being ostracized within his profession, Gauquelin prefers to speak of "planetary heredity," "cosmic genetics," "astrobiology," or "cosmobiology." This is understandable, for there are still many orthodox scientists who would agree with French Academy member Jean Rostand's remark, "If statistics are used to prove astrology, then I no longer believe in statistics."

John Addey writes, "The specific importance of the Gauquelins is not in their direct contribution to the knowledge of astrological principles as such, though this has been valuable in some instances, but that, confronted by a mountain of prejudice against astrology in an age which demands secure empirical evidence, they have by dint of immense courage, tenacity, and intelligence, provided this on a massive scale and in a form which has never been refuted, despite repeated attempts by hostile critics in the scientific world."

Gemini (glyph ♊): The third sign of the zodiac, which the Sun transits during the last month of spring, from about May 21 to about June 20. The symbol for this sign is the twins. Its POLARITY is positive, its element is air (see ELEMENTS), its quality is mutable (see QUALITIES), its ruling planet is Mercury (see RULERSHIP), and its NATURAL HOUSE is the Third.

In Gemini the communicativeness of air and the changeability of mutability are combined with the rational influence of Mercury to produce a nature that is quintessentially human. Curious, restless, clever,

♊ Gemini

versatile, youthful, fun loving, and imitative, natives of this sign sometimes call to mind our chattering primate ancestors. As the first human sign of the zodiac, Gemini rules primitive man as well as those attributes that distinguish him from the primates—manual dexterity and language. Interested in everything they see around them, eager to learn and to communicate, Geminians—who include not only Sun-sign Geminis, but all in whose charts the sign is emphasized—are the eternal students and natural citizens of the planet Earth.

Intelligent, yet lacking in concentration; alert, yet easily distracted; mentally agile but physically nervous, they enthusiastically seek new ideas, information, and experiences to feed into the insatiable computer that is the Gemini mind. The glyph for Gemini is the Roman numeral two, and these natives are more aware than others of the duality of the human condition as mind and body, spirit and flesh. This awareness is a two-edged sword, giving them intellectual sophistication but also a tendency to emotional ambivalence.

Mercury, ruling planet of Gemini, forms more conjunctions than any other planet, oscillating back and forth on its orbit as if to be in on everything that is happening in the heavens. Mercury's nature is neither BENEFIC nor MALEFIC, but neutral, and there is a certain characteristic detachment to the Gemini personality—an interest in knowledge or experience for their own sake apart from emotions or values—which sometimes earns these natives a reputation for coldness.

Gemini babies are early and constant babblers and need to investigate everything with their fingers. At school Gemini children may tax their teachers' patience with their fidgeting, jabbering, and lack of concentration; yet these scatterbrains will learn readily if their attention can be held. True, they could grow up to be dilletantes who scatter themselves in so many directions that nothing is thoroughly mastered; but they might also turn into Renaissance men and women whose talents lie in several fields. They should not be pushed into specializing too early in life; they need time to explore their own versatility. Indeed, they seem to function best when doing two things at once. Typical Geminians have hobbies that may be just as important as their profession, or may even become their profession.

With their ready wit, enthusiasiam, and eternal youthful appearance, Geminis can be the charmers of the zodiac, and they need partners, if only to have someone to talk to and share ideas with. However, their love of freedom and variety often militate against lasting relationships. In the end, these restless spirits will be held only by someone who provides the intellectual stimulation that for many Geminis is even more important than physical love. They enjoy a literary buildup with notes and letters, and they may keep voluminous journals of their affairs. They might be happy with two lovers at the same time, or with another Gemini—which amounts to the same thing. Their most compatible signs are Libra, Aquarius, Aries, and Leo; Taurus, Cancer, Scorpio, and Capricorn are neutral; while Virgo and Pisces may be difficult. With Sagittarius, their polar opposite on the zodiac, there will be both attraction and tension; but in all cases, the success of the relationship will depend on how the two charts interact and not on the COMPATIBILITY of Sun signs alone.

Geminis need work that offers both variety and an opportunity to learn and will do best in fields where their gifts for communication can be used. The sign is associated with teaching, writing, translating, science, photography, journalism, and business. The Gemini gift for imitation can produce remarkable actors and impressionists, and their strong flexible hands are well adapted to both music and painting. Famous Sun-sign Geminis include Dante Alighieri, Albrecht Dürer, Bob Dylan, Ralph Waldo Emerson, Allen Ginsberg, Lillian Hellman, Christine Jörgensen, Thomas Mann, Marilyn Monroe, Sir Laurence Olivier, Alexander Pushkin, Marquis de Sade, Jean-Paul Sartre, Harriet Beecher Stowe, and William Butler Yeats. (See BIRTHSTONES; COLORS; DAYS OF THE WEEK; METALS.)

Gems: See BIRTHSTONES.

Genethliacal Astrology (from the Greek *genethlios,* of one's birth): The branch of astrology (now usually called *natal astrology*) that casts and interprets the birth charts of individuals with a view to understanding their character and experience. Genethliacal astrology is distinguished from *judicial astrology* (now usually called *mundane astrology*), which studies the motions of the planets in relation to world events, cultural trends, and the fate of nations. (See NATAL ASTROLOGY.)

Geniture: Archaic term for BIRTH CHART.

Geocentric Cosmography: See COSMOGRAPHY.

Geocentric Horizon: See HORIZON.

Geocentric Latitude: See TERRESTRIAL LATITUDE.

Geocentric Nodes: See NODES.

Geocentric System (from the Greek *gaia,* Earth, and *kentron* center): The conception, commonly held until modern times, that the Earth is the center of the universe, around which

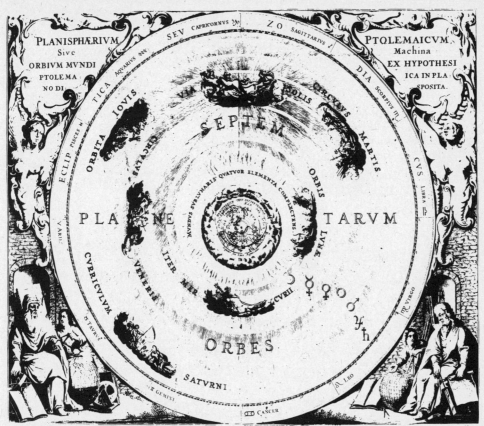

The Ptolemaic solar system; from *The Atlas of Astronomy*, published in the seventeenth century. (The Bettman Archive.)

the Sun, planets, and stars revolve. This system, known as the Ptolemaic system after Claudius PTOLEMY, who expounded it in the second century A.D., held sway until it was gradually displaced by the Copernican, or heliocentric, system in the sixteenth and seventeenth centuries. The fact that most astrologers continue to use a geocentric orientation is one of the main arguments used to discredit astrology. Copernicus himself seems to have seen no contradiction, since he gave his masterwork, *De Revolutionibus Orbium Coelestium*, to an astrologer, Joachim Rheticus, to publish.

Moreover, the advent of relativity physics in the twentieth century has vindicated the geocentric perspective as a reference system as valid as any other (see RELATIVITY, THEORY OF).

The geocentric birth chart focuses on the Earth as a planet not just with regard to its orbital revolution around the Sun (expressed by reference to the zodiac on the ECLIPTIC plane) but also with regard to its rotation on its own axis (which generates the CELESTIAL EQUATOR, the MIDHEAVEN, and the IMUM COELI). In addition, there is a special emphasis on the specific birthplace with its reference to the HORIZON plane, AS-CENDANT, DESCENDANT, EAST POINT, and VERTEX. Those astrologers who have adopted the HELIOCENTRIC SYS-TEM consider the two approaches complementary rather than mutually exclusive, and believe that the geocentric approach describes the down-to-earth, day-to-day personality of the native, the outward manifestation of the true inner self described by the heliocentric positions of the planets. (See COSMOGRAPHY; HELI-OCENTRIC ASTROLOGY.)

Geographic Latitude: See TERRES-TRIAL LATITUDE.

Geographic Longitude: See TERRES-TRIAL LONGITUDE.

Gleadow, Rupert: See SIDEREAL ZO-DIAC.

Glyph (from the Greek *glyphe,* carving): An ideographic symbol for a planet, or sign of the zodiac. Those for the planets are composed of various combinations of the circle, symbol of eternity or spirit; the half circle, symbol of soul; and the cross, symbol of the material world. Thus, in the glyph for Jupiter (♃), soul is elevated above matter, whereas in the glyph for Saturn (♄), the situation is reversed. Possible explanations for the zodiacal glyphs are as follows: Aries, ram's horns; Taurus, bull's horns; Gemini, Roman numeral two; Cancer, breasts; Leo, lion's tail; Virgo, virginal female genitalia; Libra, scales; Scorpio, erect male genitalia; Sagittarius, arrow; Capricorn, knee;

Aquarius, waves of water, light, or electricity; Pisces, two fishes.

The origin of the glyphs is obscure. Many astrologers, including Margaret Hone, believe that the glyphs as we know them today predate written language. Otto Neugebauer writes that in Roman times the glyphs were based on Egyptian hieroglyphs and do not resemble medieval glyphs, which are similar to those used today.

The glyphs for the signs and planets are as follows:

♈ Aries	☉ Sun
♉ Taurus	☽ Moon
♊ Gemini	☿ Mercury
♋ Cancer	♀ Venus
♌ Leo	⊕ Earth
♍ Virgo	♂ Mars
♎ Libra	♃ Jupiter
♏ Scorpio	♄ Saturn
♐ Sagittarius	♅ Uranus
♑ Capricorn	♆ Neptune
♒ Aquarius	♇ Pluto
♓ Pisces	

Goat: The eighth sign of the Chinese zodiac, including all persons born between

February 13, 1907, and February 2, 1908 (fire)
February 1, 1919, and February 20, 1920 (earth)
February 17, 1931, and February 6, 1932 (metal)
February 5, 1943, and January 25, 1944 (water)
January 24, 1955, and February 12, 1956 (wood)
February 9, 1967, and January 29, 1968 (fire)
January 28, 1979, and February 16, 1980 (earth)

Rarely satisfied with his fate, capricious, undisciplined, sometimes neurotic, the Goat is nevertheless one of the most engaging signs of the Buddhist zodiac, for these natives are

also endowed with great charm, elegance, and sweetness. And yet, it is rare for a Goat to reach a high position on the social scale. Lacking in motivation and the spirit of intiative, Goats prefer to remain in obscurity, willingly accepting this lack of recognition as long as their security is assured.

Intelligent and sensitive, Goats excel in the artistic professions, whereas the world of business, finance, and selling are totally alien to them.

This is a feminine sign, and its female natives are apt to have a more harmonious love life than are its males, who sometimes suffer from a certain lack of virility. They are definitely not the type to impose their will on their wives.

Compatible signs: Cat, Dragon, Horse, Monkey, Pig.

Neutral signs: Goat, Serpent, Tiger.

Incompatible signs: Cock, Dog, Ox, Rat.

Famous Goats include Honoré de Balzac, Alexander Graham Bell, Miguel de Cervantes, Lillian Hellman, Jesse James, Michelangelo Buonaroti, Benito Mussolini, Rudolph Valentino, Immanuel Velikovsky, Andy Warhol, and Orville Wright. (See CHINESE ASTROLOGY.)

Grand Cross: A MAJOR CONFIGURATION in which two OPPOSITIONS are in SQUARE to each other, forming a cross. Like the T-SQUARE, the grand cross tends to bring conflicting energies to the level of awareness and thus to act as a motivating force for growth. Unlike the T-square, it has no focal point; hence there is a greater tendency for these energies to become polarized. The configuration indicates a determined, dynamic, forceful personality with a strong sense of purpose or destiny— the "self-made" man or woman.

The tone of the grand cross varies according to whether it is CARDINAL, FIXED, or MUTABLE. The cardinal cross is associated with enormous energy and a need for control; the mutable cross with adaptability and service; the fixed cross with repetition and a concern for values.

An example of the fixed cross is the birth chart of Winston Churchill, in which an opposition of a Fifth-House Saturn in Aquarius to an Eleventh-House Uranus in Leo is crossed by an opposition of a Second-House Mercury in Scorpio to Pluto in Taurus in the Eight House. The configuration accurately describes the qualities of obsessive determination, charismatic leadership, and dramatic intensity that characterized this dynamic and legendary personality.

Grand Trine: A MAJOR CONFIGURATION in which three planets are all in TRINE to each other, forming an equilateral triangle. Since the grand trine tends to overemphasize one element (that is, FIRE, AIR, WATER, or EARTH), it is generally associated with imbalance, diffusion of energy, or unreality; but also with unusual sensitivity, intensity, and creativity. It lacks a focal point, but its energies may be effectively released by a planet in square or opposition to one of its members (see KITE). In the absence of such a hard aspect, the grand trine may indicate an individual who is locked into some kind of behavior pattern which may be either useful or detrimental.

The tone of the grand trine varies according to the element involved. The *grand earth trine* indicates sensuality, materialism, or a talent for business; the *grand water trine*, emotionalism, psychic ability, or artistic temperament; the *grand air trine*, abstraction, communicativeness, or literary ability, and the *grand fire trine*, energy, optimism, or a tendency to egotism.

An example of a grand water trine is the birth chart of the English poet and playwright Oscar Wilde, which features Venus in Scorpio, Saturn in Cancer, and Neptune in Pisces. The aesthetic hypersensitivity of this configuration, released by a close square to Neptune from Mars in extremist Sagittarius, suggests Wilde's affected, eccentric, and antisocial behavior, but it also describes his imagination, his wit, and his genius.

Graphic Ephemeris: A diagram in which the motions of the planets over a given period of time, usually a year, are represented as lines moving through space—usually measured on the vertical axis—and time—usually measured along the horizontal axis. The most popular version is designed on a 45° basis to display the hard aspects. By drawing in the radical chart positions as horizontal lines across the ephemeris, the astrologer can see at a glance all hard-aspect transits to radical positions for the year and study their ebb and flow. Figure 26 is a 45° graphic ephemeris for 1981.

Great Circle: Any circle on the inside or outside surface of a sphere, for example, the Earth or the heavens, whose plane passes through the center of the sphere. Great circles important in astrology are the Earth's Equator, meridians of TERRESTIAL LONGITUDE, the local MERIDIAN, the geocentric HORIZON, the ECLIPTIC, the PRIME VERTICAL, the CELESTIAL EQUATOR, meridians of RIGHT ASCENSION, and meridians of CELESTIAL LONGITUDE. (See COSMOGRAPHY.)

Greater Fortune (or **Greater Benefic**): See FORTUNES, THE.

Greater Infortune (or **Greater Malefic**): See INFORTUNES, THE.

Great Mutation Conjunction: See CYCLE.

Great Year: See PRECESSION OF THE EQUINOXES.

Greeks, Astrology among the: Modern scholars of antiquity tend to believe that the "rational" Greeks were "untainted" by astrology until after Alexander's Asian conquests (334–23 B.C.) opened the Hellenistic world to Chaldean influence. However, many

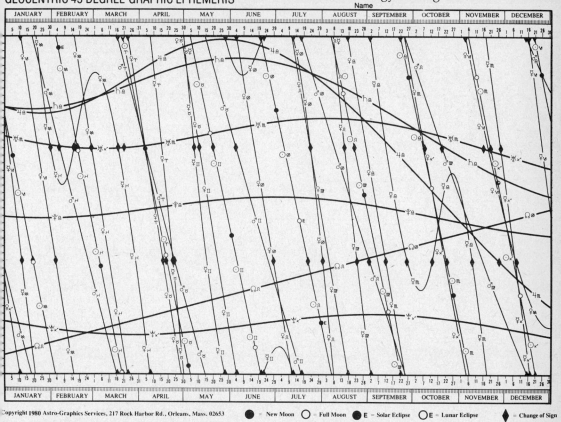

Figure 26. A 45° graphic ephemeris. (Reprinted by permission of Astro-Graphics Services.)

of the underlying ideas of traditional Western astrology are the legacy of classical Greek philosophy. The ancient Greeks were preoccupied with the beauty of number and form and how they relate to human nature. In the sixth century B.C. PYTHAGORAS envisioned the universe as a system of whole-number correspondences resembling musical intervals (see MU-SIC OF THE SPHERES). According to him, each human being was a *micro-cosm,* a miniature universe reflecting the *macrocosm,* the universe as a whole. This idea was echoed by Plato (?427–347 B.C.) in his *Timaeus,* where he places no limitation on the prac-

tice of astrology; later it was embodied into HERMETIC THEORY. It was Empedocles (fifth century B.C.), a follower of Pythagoras, who conceived the theories of the ELEMENTS and the HUMORS. Hippocrates (ca. 460–ca. 377 B.C.) applied these two theories to the practice of medicine; he emphasized the individual makeup of the patient as related to the positions of the planets at his birth.

It is true that Greek astrology after Alexander was heavily influenced by CHALDEAN ASTROLOGY. This was due in large measure to the teaching of Berosus, a Chaldean astrologer who conducted a school of astrology on the Greek island of Cos in about 280 B.C. and whose numerous disciples established centers of astrology in most of the Greek cities. Gradually the planets and stars took on the divinity the Chaldeans had attributed to them and became identified with the anthropomorphic Olympian gods. At the same time, astrology came to be regarded as an exact science based on such astronomical discoveries as those of Heraclides of Pontus (fourth century B.C.), who asserted that the Earth moves; Eratosthanes (third century B.C.), who estimated the Earth's circumference; Aristarchus of Samos (third century B.C.), who estimated the distance and size of the Moon, proposed the Sun as the center of the universe, and reckoned that the stars were extremely remote; and HIPPARCHUS of Rhodes (second century B.C.), who discovered the PRECESSION OF THE EQUINOXES. These and other advances enabled the Greeks to calculate accurate birth charts. The first known birthtime horoscope, utilizing the Ascendant, was cast in 70 B.C.

Later Greek astrology was influenced by Stoicism, a philosophy according to which all events are manifestations of divine will. Astrology was seen as a means of understanding that will. According to the Pythagorean idea of the microcosm and the macrocosm, all things in nature are related by *sympatheia* (sympathy): Whatever happens to a part of the universe affects the whole. The astrology of the Stoic Poseidonius (135–51 B.C.) was based on a comprehensive theory of nature in which God was the Life Force in a universe of perfect balance and harmony; only on the sublunary sphere—that is, on the Earth—could there be decay. Among Poseidonius' students were Pompey and Cicero, who later repudiated astrology (see ROMANS, ASTROLOGY AMONG THE). The astrologer-poet Manilius was so inspired by Poseidonius that he wrote a long poem, the *Astronomicon* (ca. A.D. 10), combining astrology with Stoic fatalistic philosophy, which influenced astrologers long after his time.

The person responsible for the transmission of ancient astrology to the modern world is Claudius PTOLEMY (second century A.D.), whose *Tetrabiblos* is a summation of the astrological knowledge of his day. Works more ancient than Ptolemy's did not survive the numerous destructions of the library at Alexandria.

Greenwich Mean Time (GMT): See TIME.

Greenwich Meridian: See TERRESTRIAL LONGITUDE.

Greenwich Sidereal Time (GST): See TIME.

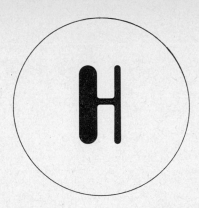

Half Sum: See MIDPOINT.

Haly, Albohazen: See ISLAM, ASTROLOGY IN.

Hamburg School: See URANIAN SYSTEM.

Hand of God: See DOUBLE QUINCUNX.

Hard Aspects: In modern astrology, the square, opposition, semisquare, and sesquisquare; the *soft aspects* are the trine and sextile. (See ASPECT; MIDPOINT; URANIAN SYSTEM.)

Harmonic Chart: A chart derived by multiplying all radical chart positions, expressed in absolute CELESTIAL LONGITUDE, by the harmonic number under consideration. The resulting longitudes are the positions in the harmonic chart. If a resulting longitude is more than 360°, then 360° is subtracted from it enough times to reduce it to less than 360°. For example, if in a chart the radical Sun is at 10°10′ Aries and the radical Moon at 20°10′ Taurus, then their ninth-harmonic chart positions (which are identical to the Hindu *navamsa* chart positions) are calculated as follows:

Sun's absolute longitude = 10°10′ × 9 = 91°30′ = 1°30′ Cancer

Moon's absolute longitude = 50°10′ × 9 = 451°30′ − 360° = 91°30′ = 1°30′ Cancer

After converting all radical positions in this way, the astrologer takes a chart form and either places the new Ascendant position in the normal place on the left and fills in the rest of the chart in equal houses, or places the new Midheaven in its normal position and fills in the rest of the chart in equal houses.

In judging a harmonic chart one must bear in mind the meaning of the harmonic number in question. Particular attention is paid to conjunctions. These reveal either that the factors were already in conjunction in the radical or that they were close to one harmonic wavelength apart or an exact number of wavelengths apart. Aspects within a harmonic chart can be interpreted, but strictly these imply a conjunction on a higher harmonic. Thus, oppositions in a harmonic chart will become conjunctions if the harmonic number is doubled. In judging a harmonic chart it is also of great importance to see if any of the harmonic chart positions are in conjunction with radical positions. If they are, this gives great emphasis to the factors involved.

It will be seen that cosmobiologists who use the 90° dial are actually examining the fourth harmonic of the chart, while those who use a 30° dial are working with the twelfth harmonic. (See CHART FORM; COSMOBIOLOGY; HARMONICS; INDIA, ASTROLOGY IN.)

Harmonics: Integral divisions of the circle; the study of such divisions, especially as they relate to astrology; the extension of the traditional concept of ASPECT to the division of the circle by any whole number. Thus, in traditional aspect terms, the second harmonic is $360°/2 = 180°$, the opposition; the third harmonic is $360°/3 = 120°$, the trine; the fourth harmonic is $360°/4 = 90°$, the square; and the sixth harmonic is $360°/6 = 60°$, the sextile; but the study of harmonics extends this sequence to much smaller divisions of the circle. Table 2 gives the first thirty harmonics:

The technique of harmonics has been in use for centuries in Indian astrology as a predictive device. In the West, the theory of harmonics was anticipated by PYTHAGORAS' ideas about the meaning of numbers and by KEPLER's theory of aspects and his introduction of the quintile series, which corresponds to the fifth harmonic. The concept as it is understood today was probably introduced in the 1930s by the Swiss astrologer Karl Krafft, who used the term *harmonics* to describe the wave patterns he observed in his statistical studies on longevity, illness, talent, and other effects. Interestingly enough, the term has been used independently by a number of researchers. Engineer John NELSON calls the clusters of planetary aspects he has observed in connection with radio interference "simultaneous multiple harmonics"; and Theodor Landscheidt uses the term *harmonics* to refer to the microaspects between the outer planets, which he has found to coincide with times of increased solar activity. But the term has come into its own, and the concept has been fully developed, through the work of the English astrologer John ADDEY.

Addey has extended the idea of harmonics beyond the theory of aspects and expanded it into the beginnings of a fundamental theory of the underlying principles of astrology. Addey's theory of the harmonic basis of astrology, which rests on the analysis of a vast range of statistical studies, suggests that all astrological effects—apart from the planets themselves—can best be understood in terms of the "harmonics of cosmic periods." By a "cosmic period" Addey means any one of the many cycles studied by astrologers, such as the zodiac, the houses, the aspect cycles, and so on. According to his theory, an understanding of the meaning of each number, in the Pythagorean sense, and an understanding of the meaning of each particular cycle will ultimately enable astrologers to reconstruct astrology from its first principles.

Addey's harmonics have had a profound impact on serious modern

Table 2. Harmonics.

Harmonic Number	Angular Interval	Aspect Name	Aspect Symbol
1	360° = 0°	conjunction	☌
2	180°	opposition	☍
3	120°	trine	△
4	90°	square, or quartile	□
5	72°	quintile	★
6	60°	sextile	✶
7	51°25.7′	septile	
8	45°	semisquare, or octile	∠
9	40°	novile	
10	36°	decile, or semiquintile	
11	32°43.6′	undecile	
12	30°	semisextile, or dodecile	⌄
13	27°41.5′		
14	25°42.8′		
15	24°		
16	22°30′		
17	21°10.6′		
18	20°		
19	18°56.8′		
20	18°	semidecile, or vigintile	
21	17°8.6′		
22	16°21.8′		
23	15°39.1′		
24	15°		
25	14°24′		
26	13°50.8′		
27	13°20′		
28	12°51.4′		
29	12°24.8′		
30	12°		

astrologers, especially in England. Charles Harvey, president of the Astrological Association, writes that the great achievement of the theory is that it "(1) provides a unified basis for understanding almost all existing astrological concepts in both Western and Eastern traditions; (2) provides a methodology for statistical research in all areas of astrology; and (3) allows the logical extension and articulation of existing astrological principles in a way that has not been possible before." Geoffrey Dean believes that the study of harmonics, along with a systematic investigation of the symbology of numbers, may at last yield a convincing scientific theory of astrology. (See HARMONIC CHART.)

Harmony of the Spheres: See MUSIC OF THE SPHERES.

Heart of the Sun: See CAZIMI.

Heavy Planets. The slower moving planets, which take more than 2 years to complete their orbits around the Sun: Jupiter, Saturn, Uranus, Neptune, and Pluto.

Hebrews, Astrology among the: The astrology practiced by the early Hebrews cannot be distinguished from that of the Chaldeans. Indeed, we must not forget that the Israelites are the descendants of the friends of Abraham, who formed a tribe related to the Babylonians.

Some astrologers have seen a correspondence between the twelve tribes of Israel, the twelve gates of the city of Jerusalem, the twelve angels in the Revelation of Saint John, and the twelve signs of the zodiac, but there is no historical evidence for the connection.

After the scattering of the Jews, which followed the destruction of the temple of Jerusalem, there arose two great schools of astrology. The first, which might be referred to as the Semitic school, flourished in the Middle East and differed very little from Arab astrology. The Jew Mash'allah, who opened a school of astrology in Baghdad at the time of the caliphs, had as many coreligionists as Moslems in his classes. The second of the Hebrew schools developed in medieval Spain, mainly among Cabalists. Abraham ben Ezra, Solomon ben Gabirol, and above all Abraham ben Reci (1089–1167) achieved reputations that spread well beyond the Jewish community.

According to the CABALA, the stars are Hebrew letters in the sky writing heavenly messages. For the Cabalists it was not just the days but the hours of the day that were subject to the influence of the stars. For example, it is written in the Sabbath Talmud that "he who is born at the hour of Venus will be rich and pleasure-loving, because this star rises with the light." This observation is astronomically correct, for the planet Venus, identified by the ancient Hebrews with Ishtar, the Chaldean goddess of fertility and pleasure, is always present at the rising and setting of the Sun.

Heliacal: Pertaining to the Sun. The *heliacal rising* of a star or planet is its first emergence from invisibility as it separates from a conjunction with the Sun; its *heliacal setting* is its disappearance from view as it approaches a conjunction with the Sun. Heliacal risings and settings can occur near either the rising or the setting of the Sun, depending on whether the body is faster or slower in motion than the Sun. The Moon heliacally rises after sunset and sets near dawn.

Heliocentric Astrology: Although heliocentric ephemerides have been available since 1767, heliocentric astrology has been neglected until quite recently. Yet one of the most convincing pieces of indirect evidence for the validity of astrology—John Nelson's demonstration of the influence of planetary relationships on sunspots and thus on the Earth's weather—uses the heliocentric system. (See NELSON, JOHN.)

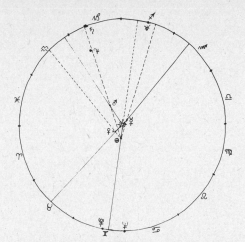

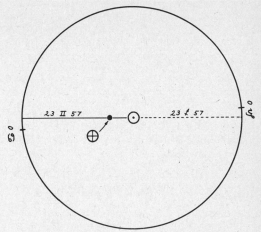

Figure 27. The solar system at the birth of Margaret Mead, showing the difference between the heliocentric and geocentric viewpoints. The unbroken lines represent lines of sight from the Sun; the broken lines represent lines of sight from the Earth. There is a vast difference in the zodiacal positions of the inner planets. For example, from the viewpoint of the Earth, Venus is in mid-Aquarius, but from the viewpoint of the Sun, Venus is in mid-Taurus. The diagram is proportional out to the orbit of Jupiter, but space limitations have made it necessary to show the positions of Saturn, Uranus, Neptune, and Pluto on the same circle, on which the signs of the zodiac are also displayed.

Figure 28. Sun-Earth system projected on the zodiac at the birth of Margaret Mead. The heliocentric (solid) line of sight to the Earth extends to a point on the ecliptic opposite that of the geocentric (dotted) line of sight to the Sun.

The difference between the heliocentric and geocentric positions of a planet increases the closer the planet is to the Earth. For example, heliocentric and geocentric positions for Pluto and Neptune can differ by no more than about 2° (called their *maximum phase angle*), but a heliocentric Mars may be as much as 47° from its corresponding geocentric position. Heliocentric and geocentric positions for Mercury and Venus can differ by as much as 180°. Figure 27 shows the difference between the positions of the planets for the two perspectives at the birth of Margaret Mead.

Heliocentric birth charts include the Earth (symbolized by the glyph ⊕), which is always directly opposite the Sun in the corresponding geocentric chart (see figure 28). On the other hand, a heliocentric chart lacks many of the familiar elements of a geocentric chart. There are no Ascendant, Descendant, Midheaven, or Imum Coeli—in fact, no houses at all, since these are specific to a location on the Earth's surface. The Sun and Moon are no longer significant elements. Actually, there is no Sun in a heliocentric chart; it is understood at the center, just as the Earth is understood at the center of the geocentric chart. And there is no Moon in a heliocentric chart, because from the viewpoint of the Sun, 93 million miles away from us, the mean distance of 239,000 miles between the Earth and the Moon is so slight as to be negligible. In effect the two bodies are in perpetual conjunction, making up the Earth-Moon system. There is no retrograde motion in heliocentric astrology, since retrogradation is an illusion peculiar to the geocentric orientation. Some heliocentric astrologers have even dispensed with the signs of the zodiac, since their starting point, the vernal point, is a geocentric phenomenon.

How can a chart be interpreted in the absence of Sun, Moon, Ascendant, or houses? Heliocentric astrologers maintain that the somewhat forbidding austerity of heliocentric charts is more than compensated by their greater simplicity, clarity, and profundity in laying bare the essence of the inner self divested of the accidents of personality and outward circumstance. Primary emphasis is on the planets, their archetypical meanings, and their aspects, especially such major configurations as the GRAND TRINE or T-SQUARE. Michael and Margaret Erlewine, who have done much to develop a systematic approach to heliocentric astrology, make an analogy with medicine, suggesting that a heliocentric chart bears somewhat the same relation to a geocentric chart that a holistic approach bears to the treatment of a single symptom. The two approaches are thus complementary rather than mutually exclusive. Interpretation of the geocentric positions of the planets as the significators of practical, down-to-earth problems is enriched rather than negated by interpretation of their heliocentric positions as the illuminators of the archetypal self.

For example, in Margaret Mead's

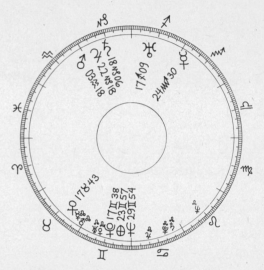

Figure 29. Heliocentric birth chart of Margaret Mead.

chart (see figure 29) the heliocentric position of the Earth is in Gemini, sign of learning, writing, and science. The heliocentric perspective shifts the emphasis of Mead's chart from teacher (Sagittarius) to student (Gemini). Gemini is also the sign of primitive man, a subject that is a primary concern of anthropology. The opposition of Earth and Uranus reveals that Mead's passionate interest in freedom, social change, and the future was an essential part of her being. The Earth is the focal point of a double quincunx involving Mercury, now in Scorpio, sign of research, and Jupiter, still in Capricorn, sign of organization, but now near Saturn's south node, a configuration describing a unique destiny in science involving the integration of objective information (Mercury) and humanitarian principles (Jupiter). No less than five planets are located within orb of planetary nodes; Venus, now in Taurus, is almost exactly conjunct the north node of Mercury, denoting Mead's profound understanding of human relationships and values. (See HELIOCENTRIC SYSTEM.)

Heliocentric Cosmography: See COSMOGRAPHY.

Heliocentric Nodes: See NODES.

Heliocentric System (from the Greek *helios*, Sun, and *kentron*, center): The conception of the universe, prevalent since the time of COPERNICUS (1473–1543), in which the Sun is at the center of our solar system. Astrology developed when the GEOCENTRIC, or Earth-centered, SYSTEM was still widely accepted, and since it is concerned with the impact of celestial events on the Earth and its inhabitants, most astrologers continue to work within the geocentric model. Most modern ephemerides list the positions of the planets in geocentric terms, even though these positions have been derived from heliocentric positions. A heliocentric ephemeris lists the planets' positions from the perspective of a hypothetical observer located at the center of the Sun. Heliocentric positions of the Sun's nine planets, including Earth, are given in the *American Ephemeris and Nautical Almanac*, published annually by the U.S. Government Printing Office. (See HELIOCENTRIC ASTROLOGY.)

Hemisphere: Half the houses in a horoscope, which is divided into upper and lower hemispheres by the HORIZON and eastern and western hemispheres by the MERIDIAN. A preponderance of planets above the horizon, or in the upper hemisphere, has traditionally been associated with extraversion; a preponderance of planets below the horizon, or in the lower hemisphere, with introversion. An eastern-hemisphere emphasis (which by definition means that planets are rising) is believed to indicate self-assertiveness; a western-hemisphere emphasis (which means that planets are setting) is believed to indicate other-directedness. Hemisphere emphasis is one of the most conspicuous features of a birth chart, and its consideration is thus one of the first steps in interpretation.

Hermetic Theory: A body of correspondences, which—according to modern scholars—was formulated at the beginning of the Christian era, based on the belief *"Omnia ab uno et in unam omnia"* ("One is in all and all is in one"), which is expressed in the astrological maxim "as above, so below" and also in the idea that the human being is a *microcosm* of the universe. The concept of the microcosm is developed in great detail in some of the earliest Hermetic writings, those attributed to the legendary Hermes Trismegistos. Everything in nature had its parallel in man; each sign of the zodiac governed a part of the body; there were seven types of people, corresponding to the seven known planets. The Greek concept of the four elements was readily incorporated into Hermetic theory. The theory, with its vast compendium of correspondences, became a vehicle for the perpetuation of Greek herbal medicine. (See BIRTHSTONES; COLORS; ELEMENTS; GREEKS, ASTROLOGY AMONG THE; HEBREWS, ASTROLOGY AMONG THE; HUMORS; MEDICAL ASTROLOGY; METALS; MIDDLE AGES, ASTROLOGY IN THE.)

Herodotus: See ASTROLOGY.

Herschel, Sir William: See URANUS.

Hindu Astrology: See INDIA, ASTROLOGY IN.

Hipparchus (190–120 B.C.): The greatest of the Greek astronomers, best known for discovering the PRECESSION OF THE EQUINOXES. Hipparchus catalogued over one thousand stars, developed trigonometry, and originated scientific geography by devising the method of locating positions on the Earth's surface by giving their terrestrial latitude and longitude. He was a student of Chaldean astronomy and a practicing astrologer.

History of Astrology: See BYZANTIUM, ASTROLOGY IN; CHALDEAN ASTROLOGY; CHINESE ASTROLOGY; CHRISTIANITY AND ASTROLOGY; EGYPT, ASTROLOGY IN; GREEKS, ASTROLOGY AMONG THE; HEBREWS, ASTROLOGY AMONG THE; INDIA, ASTROLOGY IN; ISLAM, ASTROLOGY IN; MIDDLE AGES, ASTROLOGY IN THE; MODERN ASTROLOGY; PRE-COLUMBIAN ASTROLOGY; RENAISSANCE, ASTROLOGY IN THE; ROMANS, ASTROLOGY AMONG THE.

Horary Astrology (from the Latin *hora,* hour): The branch of astrology in which questions are answered by casting horoscopes for the moment when they were asked. Horary astrology rests on the assumption that there is a sympathy between the cosmos and the human mind, so that a question is asked at the right time— that is, a time when the positions of the planets bear some relation to it and can thus shed light on its answer. The idea that everything that occurs at the same moment has a relationship of significance, if not of causality, underlies such divinatory techniques as the *I Ching* and the Tarot; JUNG called this idea synchronicity.

The rules for interpreting a *horary chart* differ somewhat from those governing natal charts. Less attention is paid to the intrinsic nature of the planets and more to their function as significators or promittors. The main *significators* are the ruler of the Ascendant, which usually represents the person asking the question, called the *querent,* and the ruler of the house that represents the subject of the question. The *promittors* are planets in aspect to the significators, which "promise" success or failure, help or hindrance, to the matter in hand. The Moon's next aspects before leaving the sign it is in are considered highly significant. If the Moon makes no aspects before leaving its sign, it is said to be VOID OF COURSE, and it is judged that nothing will come of the matter under consideration. The meaning of the houses is similar to that in natal astrology. All authorities stress the importance of clearly formulating the question before the chart is drawn up, in order to determine without prejudice which houses will be involved.

There is considerable literature on horary astrology, which was very popular in the Middle Ages. Its greatest exponent was William LILLY (1602–81). An excellent modern text is Barbara Watters, *Horary Astrology and the Judgment of Events*.

Horizon: A plane specific to a given locality on the Earth's surface that divides the visible hemisphere (what is above it) from the invisible hemisphere (what is below it). Astronomers think of the horizon as a plane passing through the eye of an observer and perpendicular to the vertical (plumb line) at any given place. A useful distinction is between the *apparent*, or *topocentric*, *horizon*, a plane tangent to the Earth's surface at the specific location, and the *geocentric horizon*, a plane, or great circle, parallel to the apparent horizon but passing through the center of the Earth (see CELESTIAL SPHERE; COSMOGRAPHY, TERRESTRIAL LATITUDE). It is the latter that is essential for establishing relationships with the other important reference planes or GREAT CIRCLES relevant to the calculation of a birth chart. The small amount of parallax introduced in the employment of the geocentric horizon is negligible when the relatively remote positions of the planets are considered (although it sometimes exceeds 1° for the Moon).

When the geocentric horizon is extended out into space to intersect other reference planes, it is called the *rational horizon*. The intersection of the horizon and the ECLIPTIC in the east is where the Sun rises (the As-CENDANT); the intersection of the horizon and the ecliptic in the west is where the Sun sets (the DESCENDANT). The two points where the horizon great circle intersects the MERIDIAN are the *North Point* and the *South Point*, true north and south. Distance along the horizon circle is measured in degrees and minutes of *azimuth*, beginning at the North Point; the entire horizon has 360° of azimuth. Distance above or below the horizon is measured in degrees and minutes of *altitude*; the altitude of the *zenith* is +90°; that of the *nadir* is −90°.

In a birth chart, in most systems of HOUSE DIVISION, the horizon is regarded as the line connecting the Ascendant and Descendant and dividing the first six HOUSES (below the horizon) from the second six (above the horizon). The horizon and the meridian are often referred to as the two *axes* of the chart. (See HEMISPHERE.)

According to tradition, a predominance of planets located above the horizon shows an extraverted personality, and a predominance of planets below the horizon indicates an introverted personality.

Horizontal System: See HOUSE DIVISION.

Horoscope (from the Greek *hora*, hour, and *skopos*, watcher): Originally, the degree of the zodiac rising at the eastern horizon at a given moment; in other words, the ASCENDANT. The term has come to mean the whole map of the sky as it appeared at the birth of an individual, or other significant moment, and even an astrologer's interpretation of this map. It is also used, even less accurately, to describe the predictions for the signs of the zodiac that appear in newspapers or magazines (one's "daily horoscope"). (See BIRTH CHART.)

Horoscopy: The art of casting and interpreting horoscopes; a synonym for astrology that is still found in old texts but has fallen out of popular use.

Horse: The seventh sign of the Chinese zodiac, including all persons born between

January 25, 1906, and February 13, 1907 (fire)
February 11, 1918, and February 1, 1919 (earth)
January 30, 1930, and February 17, 1931 (metal)
February 15, 1942, and February 5, 1943 (water)
February 3, 1954, and January 24, 1955 (wood)
January 21, 1966, and February 9, 1967 (fire)
February 7, 1978, and January 28, 1979 (earth)
January 27, 1990, and February 15, 1991 (metal)

Extraverted, gay, talkative, likable, with considerable personal magnetism, the Horse likes to shine in society. Natives of this sign charm people because they are very attractive, but they are more clever than intelligent. Ambitious, they can become ruthless when someone attempts to block their path. Money runs through their fingers; they have no conception of economy. It is in diplomacy that they are most successful. In love, they can be passionate, but sometimes their ardor is extinguished just as suddenly as it was kindled. As the head of the family, the Horse can be a petty tyrant.

Compatible signs: Cat, Cock, Goat, Horse, Serpent.

Neutral signs: Dog, Ox, Pig, Tiger.
Incompatible signs: Dragon, Monkey, Rat.

The fire Horse, which occurs every 60 years (1906, 1966, 2026, and so on) has traditionally been considered a highly unfavorable sign, portending defeats and catastrophes, and it was thought unwise to undertake anything important in the course of that year. In fact, through the centuries many Chinese have avoided having children in those years. As recently as 1966, though the Communist regime has outlawed what it considers to be superstitious practices, the number of abortions was extraordinarily high. Interestingly, the painful "reforms" of the Cultural Revolution undertaken in that year have been largely abandoned; and if we look further into the past, we find that the San Francisco earthquake and the great London fire both occurred in fire Horse years—1906 and 1666, respectively. However, close to a million people were killed in the Tanghsan earthquake of 1977, year of the fire Serpent, and not a single one of the six humiliating defeats China suffered in the nineteenth century occurred in a fire Horse year. Furthermore, there have been many highly successful fire Horses, including Rembrandt van Rijn, Pierre Corneille, Thomas Edison, Samuel Beckett, Margaret Bourke-White, and S. I. Hayakawa. Famous non-fire Horses include Cicero, Charlemagne, Isaac Newton, Theodore Roosevelt, Franklin Roosevelt, Nikita Khrushchev, Alexander Solzhenitsyn, Ingmar Bergman, and Neil Armstrong. (See CHINESE ASTROLOGY).

House Division: The dividing of the ECLIPTIC into twelve sections called HOUSES, usually of unequal size, according to one of several systems; the determination of house CUSPS; one of the two main operations involved in setting up a birth chart (see COSMOGRAPHY).

(Actually there is some argument for dividing the ecliptic into eight houses. Cyril FAGAN regards such a division, called the *oktotopos* as distinguished from the *dodekatopos*, or twelve-house system, as more ancient. He also claims that the eight houses were counted clockwise, not counterclockwise as in modern practice. The work of John ADDEY suggests that it may be possible to divide the mundane sphere into any number of sectors, each number having its own particular significance [see HARMONICS]. In the discussion that follows, however, we will consider only twelve-house systems.)

House division is probably the single most controversial question in all of modern astrology. At least twenty methods are currently in use, and although that of Placidus is probably still the most popular in the United States, there is no real agreement among astrologers as to which one is best. This state of confusion, which has led some astrologers (for example, the cosmobiologists) to abandon houses altogether, can be attributed in part to the 200-year gap in serious research that followed the rejection of astrology by science in the late seventeenth century and its banishment from the universities. On the other hand, the variety of systems that have been developed over the years reflects the increasing sophistication of man's conception of the universe and of his techniques of celestial measurement.

In recognition of the increasing popularity of the Koch system among professional astrologers, the editors have used Koch tables of houses for the sample calculation of a birth chart (see CHART CALCULATION). However, this does not constitute an endorsement of Koch as the one true system.

Astrologers may favor a system because of its simplicity (for example, Equal House) or because of its complexity (for example, Placidus). But ultimately a house system should be judged on the basis of the relevance of planets in each of its houses to matters associated with that house, the sensitivity of its cusps in the timing of events, and its adaptability to any birthplace in the world as well as its specific reference to that birthplace. Unfortunately there is little empirical evidence to support any system based on the first two criteria. Also, mainly because of the distortion involved in reducing a three-dimensional phenomenon to two dimensions, most systems do not work well in polar areas, and the Horizontal and Arcturan systems will not work at certain birthtimes in the tropics. Finally, only those systems that regard the Ascendant as the First-House cusp are specific to the birth-place (two exceptions to this rule are the Horizontal and Arcturan systems).

There are three main categories of house systems: (a) those that divide the ecliptic directly; (b) those that project divisions onto the ecliptic from direct divisions of some other GREAT CIRCLE; and (c) those that divide the arc of a moving point. There is one maverick system, the Topocentric, that cannot be included in these categories. (Other groupings are possible: *Quadrant systems* trisect each of the four quadrants defined by the HORIZON and the MERIDIAN; they are contrasted with systems that ignore one or both of these reference planes. *Spatial*, or *geometric*, *systems*, which divide space, are distinguished from *temporal systems*, which divide time taken to cover space, but the distinction is really a false one, since all systems divide lines in space and all can be expressed in terms of time.)

DIRECT DIVISION OF THE ECLIPTIC

These systems are very simple. The drawback with most of them is that one or both of the principal axes (horizon and meridian) are not represented.

Equal House, or Zenith, System. The ecliptic is divided into twelve segments of 30° each, beginning with the Ascendant, which is equivalent to the First-House cusp (see figure 30). The Midheaven rarely coincides with the Tenth-House cusp, usually falling somewhere in the Ninth or Tenth House. The Equal House system does not work for certain times of day on the Arctic or Antarctic circles. According to some authorities, this system was in use in India around 3000 B.C.; at any rate, it continues to be used there today. The British Faculty of Astrological Studies, in a study involving thousands of charts, compared the Equal House with the Placidus system and concluded that the former was more reliable, though not denying the value of quadrant systems as such. Equal House is the most popular system in Great Britain today. (The Placidean system was already unpopular there because it resulted in such distorted houses at Britain's northern latitudes.) Though not specifically referred to by him,

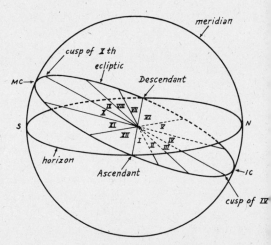

Figure 30. The Equal House system.

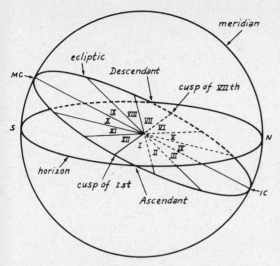

Figure 31. The Midheaven House system.

the Equal House is very likely the system used by PTOLEMY.

Midheaven House System. The ecliptic is divided into twelve segments of 30° each, beginning with the Midheaven, which is equivalent to the Tenth-House cusp (see figure 31). This system is not specific to the birthplace; the Ascendant rarely coincides with the First-House cusp and usually falls somewhere in either the First or the Twelfth House. The Midheaven House System was propagated in 1951 by Brigadier R. C. Firebrace, Jeff Mayo, and others at the British Faculty of Astrological Studies as a result of investigating the question of Equal House division from the Ascendant. It was concluded that equal houses from the Ascendant "show the tendencies of character . . . and events which arise from character," while equal houses from the Midheaven "represent the Earth's impress on our lives." The system has been taught to all stu-

dents at the Faculty since 1952. The Uranian Hamburg School promoted a theoretically more correct variation in which the cusps are calculated in terms of RIGHT ASCENSION. By this method the Midheaven First-House cusp coincides with the EAST POINT.

Porphyry System. This is a quadrant system: The Midheaven is the Tenth-House cusp and the Ascendant is the First-House cusp. Intermediate houses are equal divisions of each quadrant, measured on the ecliptic (see figure 32). The system breaks down at certain places in polar regions. Many astrologers are disturbed by the "unnatural" juxtaposition of three equally small houses in one quadrant to three equally large houses in the next (see figure 33). The system dates from the third century A.D. and is attributed to the Neoplatonist Porphyry (ca. 233–303).

Natural Graduation System. This is a twentieth-century "improvement" on the Porphyry quadrant system, in

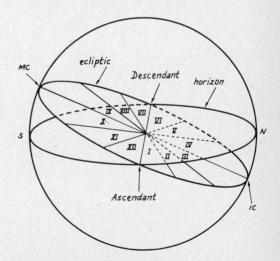

Figure 32. The Porphyry system.

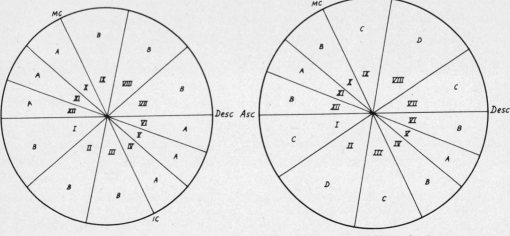

Figure 33. The Porphyry system's "unnatural" distribution of houses. In this example the first and third quadrants (**B** houses) are large, whereas the second and fourth quadrants (**A** houses) are small. At each angle there is a sudden discontinuity in the size of the houses.

Figure 34. The Natural Graduation system. This drawing represents the same chart as in figure 33, but the increase or decrease in house size has been made continuous. The two **A** houses are the smallest, the four **B** houses are slightly larger, the four **C** houses larger still, and the two **D** houses are the largest.

which the sizes of the intermediate houses are graduated. Thus, in a quadrant of equally small Porphyry houses the middle house of the quadrant is made smaller and the two on either side of it made larger; in its neighboring quadrant, where there are equally large Porphyry houses, the middle house is made larger and the two on either side smaller. (See figure 34, which depicts the same chart as in figure 33.) The system has been criticized because the basis for the graduation is arbitrary. It also breaks down in certain places in polar regions.

Solar House System. The CELESTIAL LONGITUDE of the Sun is the First-House cusp, and each successive house is advanced 30°. This system is not specific to the birthplace.

Uranian Direct-Division House Sys-

tems. These are used in Uranian astrology and include (a) the *Earth House system,* in which the First-House cusp is 0° Libra and each successive house is advanced 30°; (b) the *Moon House system,* in which the Fourth-House cusp is the celestial longitude of the Moon and each successive house is advanced 30°; (c) the *Sun House system,* in which the Fourth-House cusp is the celestial longitude of the Sun and each successive house is advanced 30°; (d) the *Nodal House system,* in which the First-House cusp is the celestial longitude of the north lunar node and each successive house is advanced 30°; and (e) the *Ascendant House system,* which is identical to the Equal House system (see page 138). None of these systems is specific to the birthplace.

PROJECTED DIVISION OF THE ECLIPTIC

In any of the systems in this category one out of three of the five great circles shown on page 84—PRIME VERTICAL, CELESTIAL EQUATOR, and horizon—is divided into twelve equal segments. Lines perpendicular to that circle or to one of the other two circles are passed through the points where the division is made. The points where these lines intersect the ecliptic are the projected house cusps. (Though it is theoretically possible to divide the meridian too and project the divisions onto the ecliptic, the resulting houses are so distorted at any terrestrial latitude that such systems are not in use.)

Campanus System. A quadrant system. The prime vertical is divided into twelve equal segments, beginning at the East Point, and lines perpendicular to the prime vertical (called *house circles*) are drawn through the points of division and projected onto the ecliptic as the house cusps (see figure 35). At terrestrial latitudes remote from the Equator, houses can become quite unequal in size. In polar regions there is extreme distortion, and at certain birthtimes and birthplaces planets may "disappear," the absorption taking place in the First and Seventh Houses. This system may date from the thirteenth century, since it is often attributed to Giovanni Campanella (d. 1297), but some astrologers believe it was invented by two brothers, Joseph and Matthew Campanus, who lived in the late fifteenth century. It is still

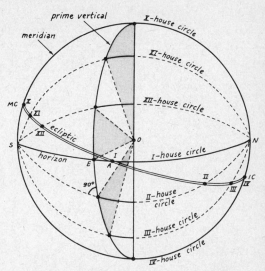

Figure 35. The Campanus system. **O** = birthplace, **E** = East Point, and **A** = Ascendant.

preferred today by many astrologers, including Dane RUDHYAR and Charles JAYNE.

Regiomontanus System. A quadrant system. The celestial equator is divided into twelve equal segments, beginning at the East Point, and lines perpendicular to the prime vertical are drawn through the points of division and projected onto the ecliptic as the house cusps (see figure 36). The Regiomontanus system is identical to the Campanus system for birthplaces on the Equator. As with the Campanus system, at locations far from the Equator, Regiomontanus houses can become quite unequal in size. In polar regions there are birthtimes and birthplaces where the planets "disappear," and at the exact North or South Pole it is mathematically impossible to erect a Regiomontanus chart. The system was invented in the fifteenth century by

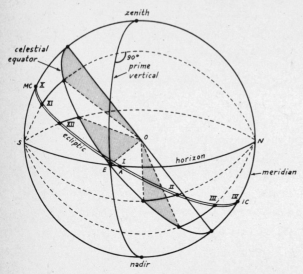

Figure 36. The Regiomontanus system. **O** = birthplace, **E** = East Point, and **A** = Ascendant.

the German astronomer REGIOMON-TANUS.

Morinus System. The celestial equator is divided into twelve equal segments, beginning at the East Point, and lines perpendicular to the ecliptic (that is, circles of celestial longitude) are drawn through the points of division and projected onto the ecliptic as the house cusps (see figure 37). This system does not fail in polar regions, but it is not specific to the birthplace. The First-House cusp is not the Ascendant, and—except for birthplaces on the Equator—the Tenth-House cusp is not the Midheaven. The Morinus system was invented in the seventeenth century by the French astrologer Jean-Baptiste MORIN, also known as Morin de Villefranche.

Meridian, or Zariel, System. The celestial equator is divided into twelve equal segments, beginning at the

meridian, and lines perpendicular to the celestial equator (that is, right-ascension meridians) are drawn through the points of division and projected onto the ecliptic as the house cusps (see figure 38). Like the Morinus system, this system is quite applicable to polar regions, but it is not specific to the birthplace. The Tenth-House cusp is the Midheaven, but the First-House cusp is not the Ascendant. The origin of this system is unknown, but it was rediscovered in the nineteenth century by the Australian astrologer Zariel and is widely used by Uranian astrologers.

Horizontal System. The horizon is divided into twelve equal segments, beginning at the East Point, and lines perpendicular to the horizon (that is, prime vertical, meridian, and intermediate great circles connecting ZENITH and NADIR) are drawn through the points of division and projected onto the ecliptic as the house cusps

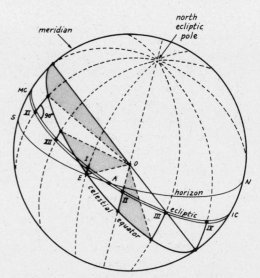

Figure 37. The Morinus system. **O** = birthplace, **E** = East Point, and **A** = Ascendant.

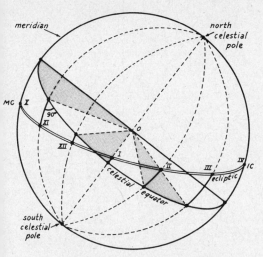

Figure 38. The Meridian system. **O** = birthplace.

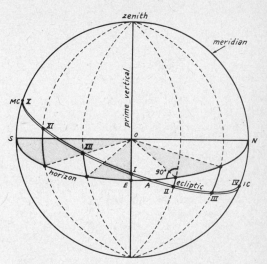

Figure 39. The Horizontal system. **O** = birthplace, **E** = East Point, and **A** = Ascendant.

(see figure 39). This system *is* specific to the birthplace, and the Tenth-House cusp is the Midheaven, but the First-House cusp is not the Ascendant. The system works quite well in polar regions, but it may fail at certain locations and birthtimes in the tropics. The origin of the Horizontal system is unknown.

Arcturan System. The horizon is divided into twelve equal segments, beginning at the East Point, and lines perpendicular to the ecliptic (that is, circles of celestial longitude) are drawn through the points of division and projected onto the ecliptic as the house cusps (see figure 40). As with the Horizontal system, the Tenth-House cusp is the Midheaven, but the First-House cusp is not the Ascendant. The system works quite well in polar regions, but it may fail at certain locations and birthtimes in the tropics. This system was invented by Michael Munkasey.

DIVISION OF THE ARC OF A MOVING POINT

The apparent daily motion, due to the Earth's rotation, of any celestial object or point, from the eastern ho-

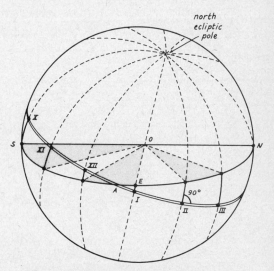

Figure 40. The Arcturan system. **O** = birthplace, **E** = East Point, and **A** = Ascendant.

rizon to culmination on the meridian to the western horizon and then under the Earth's surface to the eastern horizon again, follows a path called a parallel of DECLINATION. It should be noted that each such object or point has its *own* Ascendant, Midheaven, Descendant, and Imum Coeli, specific to its declination. The portion of the declination parallel that is above the horizon is called the *diurnal arc*; the portion below is known as the *nocturnal arc*. Each of these arcs is bisected by the meridian into *semiarcs* (see figures 41 and 42). The following three systems determine the intermediate house cusps by trisecting a particular semiarc.

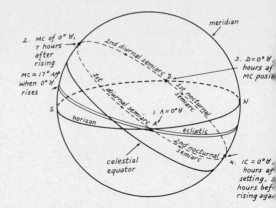

Figure 42. The arc of a specific degree on the celestial sphere. Here **A** is taken as 0° Taurus, a specific degree of celestial longitude. When **A** is at the Ascendant in position **1**, the Midheaven is 17° Capricorn. After its first diurnal semiarc, which takes about 7 hours, point **A** is the degree on its own Midheaven (position **2**), which happens to be a more elevated position on the meridian than the Midheaven for position **1**. After its second diurnal semiarc (about 6½ hours), point **A** is at its Descendant (**D**), position **3**. It takes point **A** another 5¼ hours to complete its first nocturnal semiarc and arrive at position **4**, its IC. After another 5¼ hours (the second nocturnal semiarc), point **A** will again be at the Ascendant. The entire arc takes 24 sidereal hours (23 hours and 56 minutes of solar time). The actual duration of any particular point's semiarc depends on the point's degree of celestial longitude and the terrestrial latitude of the birthplace.

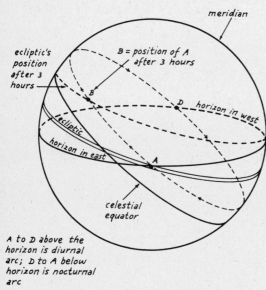

A to D above the horizon is diurnal arc; D to A below horizon is nocturnal arc

Figure 41. The arc of a moving point on the celestial sphere. The original position of the Ascendant is point **A**, expressed as some degree of celestial longitude. **B** is the position of the degree of **A** (no longer the Ascendant) 3 hours later. The ecliptic has also moved relative to the horizon. Point **A**'s diurnal arc is its path above the horizon; its nocturnal arc is its path below the horizon.

Alcabitius System. A quadrant system. The Ascendant is the First-House cusp. The degree that will be on the Midheaven when the present Ascendant degree has traveled one-third of its diurnal semiarc between its present position and its own Midheaven is the degree on the cusp of the present Eleventh House. The degree that will be on the Midheaven when the present Ascendant degree has traveled two-thirds of its diurnal semiarc is the degree on the cusp of the present Twelfth House. The Eighth and Ninth House cusps are

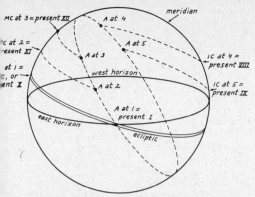

Figure 43. The Alcabitius system. Position 1 is the present.

determined by a similar trisection of the other diurnal semiarc—that is, from Midheaven to Descendant—but the degree on the Imum Coeli is used (see figure 43). One virtue of this system is that it does not fail in polar regions. On the other hand, at certain birthtimes there may be great variation in house size, no matter what the terrestrial latitude. The Alcabitius system dates at least from the first century A.D. and is the one used in the few surviving examples of Greek horoscopes.

Placidus System. A quadrant system. The Ascendant is the First-House cusp, and the Midheaven is the Tenth-House cusp. The Twelfth-House cusp is that degree of the ecliptic that has completed one-third of its diurnal semiarc from its own Ascendant to its own Midheaven; the Eleventh-House cusp is that degree that has completed two-thirds of its diurnal semiarc. The Ninth- and Eighth-House cusps are determined similarly—the degrees of the ecliptic that have completed one-third and two-thirds, respectively, of their diurnal semiarcs from their own Mid-

heaven to their own Descendant. Since each cusp is determined by the diurnal semiarc of a particular degree, several arcs are involved (see figure 44). The individual house cusps are found by a laborious procedure involving repeated trial and error. Although most astrologers using the Placidus system determine the house positions of planets by their ecliptic longitudes, these positions are not consistent with the theory upon which the system is based. The house positions should properly be derived from the planets' own semiarcs—an extremely rigorous procedure.

The Placidus system is an outrageous failure in polar regions. Over half the zodiac may be unrepresented in the chart, and it is possible for a single house cusp to have three different zodiac degrees.

The Placidus system was invented in the seventeenth century by the Italian monk PLACIDUS DE TITUS. It became very popular in English-speaking countries through the annual publication, beginning in 1820,

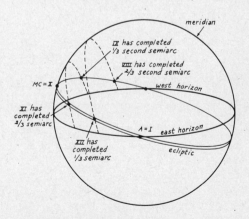

Figure 44. The Placidus system.

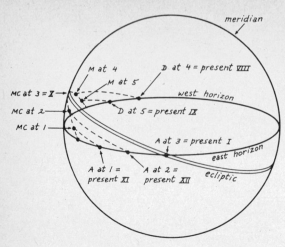

Figure 45. The Koch system. Position **3** is the present.

of *Raphael's Almanac*, which included tables based on this method. In fact, for the last two centuries Placidean tables have been the only ones available to most astrologers; when the particular house system being used is not specified, it is almost always Placidus. It is still the most popular system in the United States. The Church of Light, after three decades of study, claims to have validated the Placidus system by the usefulness of its cusps in timing events. However, the methods of research used have been severely criticized, and many astrologers have accumulated evidence that they claim invalidates the system.

Koch, or Birthplace, System. A quadrant system. The degree that was on the Ascendant when the present Midheaven degree had traveled one-third of its diurnal semiarc from its own Ascendant to its present position is the degree of the present Eleventh House. The degree that was on the Ascendant when the present Midheaven degree had traveled two-thirds of its diurnal semiarc is the degree of the present Twelfth House. The Eighth- and Ninth-House cusps

are determined by a similar trisection of the other diurnal semiarc—that is, from Midheaven to Descendant—but the degree on the Descendant is used (see figure 45).

Walter Koch (1895–1970), the inventor of this system, claimed that it is the only system determined from the exact birthplace, since (a) dividing the ecliptic directly or through projection inevitably fixes house cusps at other terrestrial latitudes than that of the birthplace; and (b) in both the Placidus and Alcabitius systems, only the First and Seventh Houses involve the declination corresponding to the birthplace latitude. As with the Placidus system, there are certain birthtimes and birthplaces in polar regions where much of the zodiac cannot be represented in the chart.

THE TOPOCENTRIC SYSTEM

All previously mentioned systems were derived theoretically; the topocentric system was derived empirically: Its theoretical basis was formulated only after empirical evidence (primary directions to certain zodiac degrees, see PROGRESSION AND DIRECTION) had indicated the house cusps. The cosmography for this system is *topocentric*, not *geocentric*—that is, the birthplace remains on the surface of the Earth, rather than being projected to the center of the Earth in order to take advantage of great circles of the celestial sphere from which to derive cusps (see COSMOGRAPHY). Nonetheless, the geocentric horizon is used; it rotates around the Earth's axis projected from the to-

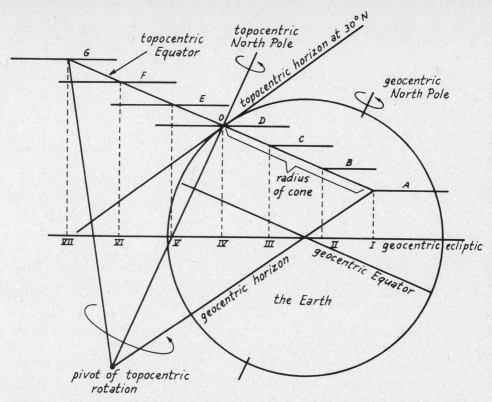

Figure 46. The Topocentric system. **O** = birthplace. **A** through **G** = the topocentric ecliptic at its intersection with the trisection points of the cone radius. Cusps are designated on the geocentric ecliptic. For Southern Hemisphere birthplaces the rotation would be in the opposite direction, around the topocentric South Pole.

pocentric horizon, which produces a cone. The radius of the cone, drawn along the topocentric Equator, is trisected; the house cusps are where the lines of trisection intersect the ecliptic (see figure 46). A *polar variant,* derived arbitrarily, makes it possible to use the Topocentric system in polar regions. Critics of the system claim that the empirical evidence supporting it is not statistically sound, that the events corresponding to transits or directions to its cusps are "petty and trivial," and that the exposition of the system is muddled. The Topocentric system was intro-

duced in the twentieth century by the Argentine astrologers Vendal Polich and Anthony Page. Interestingly, although its mathematical basis is entirely different, it produces cusps that are within 1° of the Placidus cusps up to about 56° north or south latitude.

NO SYSTEM AT ALL

Johannes KEPLER (1571–1630) considered the houses "rather superstitious, a sort of fortune telling, and a kind of Arabian sortilege, where one can get an answer 'yes' or 'no' to any question that may occur to anyone at any time without knowing the person's hour of birth, thereby making of astrology an oracle, and consequently depending on the inspiration of heavenly (or rather devilish) spirits." Of course, he was referring to HORARY ASTROLOGY; he felt houses had no place in natal astrology and did not wish to insert them in the chart he erected for Wallenstein.

Today, too, it is difficult for astrologers to justify their use of houses—beyond the unanswerable "they work." Unlike the planets and even the signs, the houses seem an arbitrary slicing up of imaginary lines in space and time. Which lines and how many slices are issues that continue to elude consensus, and as yet there is no irrefutable evidence for any of the systems of division. However, some traditionalist astrologers continue to make extraordinarily precise delineations and predictions based on the house cusps of one or another system. It is also interesting to note that the results of Michel and Françoise GAUQUELIN and John ADDEY imply that the mundane circle is nonetheless extremely important. That the Gauquelins' thirty-six sectors approximate very closely the Placidean and Topocentric divisions suggest that these two systems may be on approximately the right lines. Statistical studies should make it possible to demonstrate which system of house division gives the most significant results.

Due to the present lack of evidence supporting any specific house system and the absurdities of interpretation to which reliance on unproven systems can lead, a number of astrologers have abandoned house systems altogether. In his explanation of COSMOBIOLOGY, Reinhold Ebertin concludes that by using midpoints "excellent results in interpretation can be achieved without having recourse to [any] traditional system of houses."

Houses: In a horoscope, twelve pie-shaped sections, usually unequal in size, into which the circle representing the CELESTIAL SPHERE is divided, and whose boundaries intersect the ECLIPTIC at points called *cusps*. In most systems of house division, the houses are regarded as fixed with respect to the horizon and are numbered from I to XII, starting at the eastern horizon, or ASCENDANT, and proceeding downward and counterclockwise, in the direction of the Earth's rotation, the planets passing through them in clockwise direction every 24 hours. Thus the houses are divisions of a daily cycle resulting from the Earth's rotation on its axis, whereas the signs are divisions of a yearly cycle resulting from the Earth's revolution around the Sun (or the Sun's apparent revolution around the Earth along the ecliptic).

The cusps of the First and Seventh Houses, also known as the Ascendant-Descendant axis, form the horizon, which divides the houses into two groups of six each, houses I–VI being below the horizon and houses VII–XII being above it. In most systems of house division the size of each house is approximately determined by the number of degrees of celestial longitude that rise above the horizon in 2 hours (one-twelfth of a 24-hour day) at a given point on the

Earth's surface. (The actual basis for determination varies with the house system used; see HOUSE DIVISION.) The inequality in the size of houses results from the inclination of the Earth's axis in relation to the ecliptic, which causes the number of degrees passing over the horizon in 2 hours, or the rate of ascension, to vary according to the time of year and the latitude of the birthplace. Because of this variation in the size of houses (from 15° to 60° in the temperate zone), it is possible for one house to contain portions of two or even three 30° signs and thus for a sign to be completely contained within a house without appearing on any house cusp. Such a sign is said to be INTERCEPTED, and its strength in the chart—as well as that of any planet placed in it—is considered to be diminished. For an explanation of the operations involved in finding the Ascendant, MIDHEAVEN, and other house cusps, see CHART CALCULATION.

The irregularity in the size of houses increases as one approaches the North Pole, until in the farthest northern latitudes it is impossible to erect a chart at all by most known systems of house division. This phenomenon is one of the arguments most often cited by opponents of astrology. For example, Paul Couderc, director of the Paris Observatory, points out that at certain times of the day on the polar circle the ecliptic coincides with the horizon, and thus "the poor wretches born at these moments can have no horoscopes at all!"

Astrologers have been aware of this objection for some time. Some would reply that the living conditions of peoples born in the polar regions are accurately reflected in their unbalanced birth charts.

In chart interpretation, the houses represent areas of experience where the energies symbolized by the signs and planets are expressed. The following indications will give a preliminary idea of the meanings of the houses and the kinds of activities with which each is associated:

First House: The self. Personality, physical appearance, body type, mannerisms, general health and vitality, temperament, unconscious attitudes, approach to life, the first impression the native makes on people.

Second House: Resources. Material possessions, including money; talents and values; the five senses; sense of self-worth.

Third House: Communication and relationship. The early environment and learning experiences, brothers and sisters, neighbors, acquisition of motor skills and language, education, movement within the immediate environment, psychological adjustment.

Fourth House: Home and mother (sometimes father). Emotional foundations, parents, the unconscious, heredity, inheritance, real estate, conditions at the end of life, the grave.

Fifth House: Creative self-expression. Love, romance, children, art, pleasure, recreation, entertainment, theater, games, parties, gifts, gambling, speculation.

Sixth House: Health and service. Work, diet, short illnesses, jobs, servants, employees, tools, operating expenses, overhead, maintenance, landlords, pets, utilities, involuntary labor.

Seventh House: The other. One-to-one relationships, close friends, lovers, marriage or business partners, open enemies, other people in general, contracts, marriage, divorce, quarrels, lawsuits.

Eighth House: Crisis. Sex, birth, death, rebirth, reincarnation, healing, the occult, other people's resources, wills, insurance, taxes, unearned money, recycling, losses, renunciation, letting go.

Ninth House: Higher education. Travel, the professions (especially religion, philosophy, science, and law), graduate school, the search for meaning, wisdom, the spiritual path, one's *Weltanschauung*, or view of the universe.

Tenth House: Honors. Profession, career, fame, success, public image, ambition, reputation, social position, the father (sometimes mother), authority figures, employers; the sign on the cusp of the Tenth House indicates the qualities the native aspires to and for which he or she will be remembered.

Eleventh House: Friends and future. Hopes, wishes, plans, ideals, groups, professional contacts, clubs, organizations, political parties, trade or labor unions, communes.

Twelfth House: Limitation; once called the house of "self-undoing," the "hell of the zodiac," and the "house of the evil demon" (Ptolemy). Hidden enemies, long or chronic illnesses, hospitalization, imprisonment, retreats, solitude, debts, punishments, old karma, mourning, convalescence, self-sacrifice, charity, meditation, research, activities behind the scenes.

It will have been remarked that the meanings of the twelve houses are closely related to the meanings of the twelve signs of the zodiac from which, indeed, they have been derived. Ptolemy used the word *house* as a synonym for *sign*; the term *domicile* for a sign where a planet is "at home" is a vestige of this old connection.

In a birth chart, the nature of the activities and experiences represented by the twelve houses are indicated by the condition of the planets that occupy them. An empty house does not, however, indicate a lack of experiences in the matters of that house. In the absence of planets in a house, the nature of its activities is indicated by the sign on the cusp and the condition of the planet that rules that sign (see RULERSHIP). Brief suggestions as to the meaning of the planets in the twelve houses will be found under the entries for the planets.

Humanistic Astrology: An approach to astrology developed primarily by Dane RUDHYAR. Humanistic astrology represents a reaction to the emphasis on prediction of specific events that characterizes both traditional astrology, with its tendency to degenerate into fortune-telling, and the modern scientific or statistical school. Whereas both of these approaches are event-oriented, humanistic astrology is person-oriented. Rudhyar used the word *humanistic* not in the sense used to describe the neoclassical philosophy of the Renaissance, which was rationalistic and even atheistic, but in the sense of Abraham Maslow, founder of the humanistic school of modern psychology. Humanistic astrology reflects the influence of depth psychology, especially the work of JUNG, and of holistic philosophy. The original subtitle of Rudhyar's best-known work, *The Astrology of Personality* (1936), is *A Reformulation of Astrological Concepts and Ideals in Terms of Contemporary Psychology and Philosophy.* Humanistic astrologers, like the members of the French symbolist school, see astrology primarily as a symbolic language that can serve as a guide to the integration of personality. The birth chart is regarded as a representation of an individual's total potential, in which no planet or aspect is "good" or "bad," but each element is part of an organic whole. Emphasis is less on isolated events than on phases of developmental cycles; destiny is a process of self-realization.

Humors: In old physiology, the four fluids—blood, phlegm, choler (yellow bile), and melancholy (black bile)—present in the human body, whose relative proportions determined the health and temperament of an individual. The theory of the humors, known also as humoralism, was the application to medicine of the theory of the four ELEMENTS. According to Galen, all diseases were the result of an imbalance of the humors in the human organism. This theory was accepted by most physiologists until the late seventeenth century.

In astrology the theory of the humors has been used since PTOLEMY to delineate temperament in a birth chart. Yellow bile corresponds to fire (Aries, Leo, Sagittarius), black bile to earth (Taurus, Virgo, Capricorn), blood to air (Gemini, Libra, Aquarius), and phlegm to water (Cancer, Scorpio, Pisces). (See MEDICAL ASTROLOGY.)

Hyleg (from the Persian *haylaj*, the material body): An Arabic term for the significator of longevity in a horoscope, also known as the *apheta* (from the Greek *aphetes*, one who starts an engine), the giver of life or the *prorogator* (from the Latin *prorogare*, to prolong). All three terms have fallen into disuse, partly because the rules for determining hylegiacal, or aphetic, places were extremely complex, and partly because the prognostication of death is now considered unethical.

IC: See IMUM COELI.

Imum Coeli (Latin for "bottom of the sky"; usually abbreviated **IC**): In a horoscope, the point at which the lower MERIDIAN intersects the ECLIPTIC; the position of the Sun at local apparent midnight (see TIME). The Imum Coeli is always directly opposite the MIDHEAVEN and forms the northern angle (southern angle for birthplaces in the Southern Hemisphere) and, in most systems of HOUSE DIVISION, the cusp of the Fourth House. It should not be confused with the *nadir*, or lowest point below the horizon, which is opposite the *zenith*. (See COSMOGRAPHY.)

In chart interpretation, the Imum Coeli represents the ground of the native's being: family background, parents, unconscious, private self. A planet on the IC represents qualities not conspicuous on the surface that are nevertheless a profound part of the native's psyche and may eventually find expression in his or her work.

Inceptional Figure: See ELECTIONAL FIGURE.

Inconjunct: See QUINCUNX.

India, Astrology in: Although there is little evidence that Hindu astrology predated the invasion of Alexander the Great in 327 B.C., there is a long-standing tradition that it is thousands of years old. Nonetheless, it was not until the sixth century A.D. that the principles of Hindu astrology, by then heavily influenced by Chaldean and Greek concepts, were outlined in the *Brihat Jataka* of Vahara Mihara.

For centuries Indian astrologers made no distinction between astrology and magic. But after the Turks invaded the Punjab in the tenth century, Arab travelers reformed Indian astrology and purged it of charlatanism. Their teaching is the basis for astrology as it is practiced from the Indus River to Ceylon.

The ancient Indians adopted the luni-solar calendar, which is still used today by the Catholic church to determine the dates of such movable feasts as Easter and Pentecost (see LUNAR YEAR). The year had approximately twelve lunations and consisted of 354 days, so that it was necessary to add a thirteenth lunation from time to time to make the calendar agree with the Earth's period of revolution around the Sun. In the beginning, astrologers divided the

Observatory at Delhi. (Photo by Lauros.)

luni-solar year into twenty-eight periods, or *lunar mansions*, called *nakshatras*, as many as there are days in a lunation cycle: This was the first zodiac used in India. However, this zodiac did not correspond exactly enough to the motions of the planets, and over the centuries the number of *nakshatras* was reduced to twenty-seven. The discarded *nakshatra*, Abhijit, continued to be used in horary astrology.

Later, a new solar zodiac of twelve constellations, or *rasi*, like our Western SIDEREAL ZODIAC, made its appearance: Mesha (Aries), Vrishabha (Taurus), Mithuna (Gemini), Kataka (Cancer), Simha (Leo), Kanya (Virgo), Thula (Libra), Vrischika (Scorpio), Dhanus (Sagittarius), Makara (Capricorn), Kumbha (Aquarius), and Meena (Pisces.). The difference in CELESTIAL LONGITUDE between the Indian sidereal constellation and its corresponding Western tropical sign is called the AYANAMSA.

Since twenty-seven is not divisible by twelve, there was no exact correspondence between a *rasi* and a *nakshatra*, so the latter were subdivided into four *pada* (quarters), nine of which were assigned to each *rasi*. Thus the *rasi* of Mesha (Aries) contains the four *pada* of the *nakshatra* of Aswini, the four *pada* of Bharani, and one of Krithika. The three remaining *pada* of Krithika are assigned to the second sign of the Indian zodiac, Vrishabha (Taurus), along with the four *pada* of Rohini and two of Mrigasira. It is on this new zodiac—somewhat more complex, perhaps, but also more precise than the old one—that modern Indian astrology is based.

The essential characteristic that distinguishes Indian astrology from Western astrology is that it is not tropical—that is, its zodiac is not aligned with the seasons. Another great difference is its preoccupation with REINCARNATION and KARMA accumulated over many lifetimes, a feature that had a profound impact on Western ESOTERIC ASTROLOGY in the early twentieth century. Hindu astrologers are concerned with the steps necessary for the attainment of wisdom or the emancipation from karma (*mookshu*).

A planet's importance in a horoscope is evaluated according to a system known as the *shad bala* ("six strengths"), which takes into account many more than six factors, including the planet's sign position, direction, speed, exaltation, declination, brightness, and position in relation to the Moon, as well as its position in subdivisions of signs known as *shodasavargas*, which are directly related to harmonics. Indian astrologers concern themselves with planetary periods of life (*dasas*, subdivided into *bhuktis*) whose order is not fixed, but varies for each individual according to the position of the Moon at birth. Indian astrologers tend to spell out their interpretations in great detail, including precise predictions of longevity (*ayurdaya*), a practice that is considered unethical by most modern Western astrologers.

As in the West, it would perhaps be more accurate to speak of astrologies; for although the broad outlines are the same, there are various schools of astrology that disagree on minor matters. Generally speaking, these schools correspond to the principal religions of India. Members of certain sects, especially those devoted to the worship of Shiva, are more inclined to practice astrology than are members of the sects devoted to the worship of Vishnu. Shiva is one of the two great divinities of Hinduism and is identified with Death and with Time, regarded as the destroyer of the present. The identification is not macabre; Shiva also presides over sexual activity and procreation, since each generation causes the destruction of the one that went before. But whatever their sect, Indians accord great importance to astrology and never make an important decision without consulting their horoscopes. Until the old maharajas were banished following World War II, they had their official astrologers to back up their decisions. In the kingdoms of the north, such as Nepal or Sikkim, these posts still exist, in spite of the advance of rationalism. In 1963 in Sikkim, the crown prince had to postpone the date of his wed-

ding because of the opposition of the court astrologers, which demonstrates the extraordinary vitality of Indian astrology.

Indian astrology still awaits a real analysis and exploration by Western astrologers. Its traditions preserve much that is lost in Western astrology. Most remarkably, harmonic concepts (see HARMONICS) are an integral part of the Hindu method. Thus the *navamsa* chart, used by all Indian astrologers, is identical to the independently postulated ninth-harmonic chart. (See NADI ASTROLOGY.)

Indirect Midpoint: See MIDPOINT.

Inferior Conjunction: A CONJUNCTION of the Sun and an inferior planet (Mercury or Venus) in which the planet is between the Earth and the Sun; as distinguished from a *superior conjunction*, in which the planet is on the opposite side of the Sun from the Earth. (See ELONGATION.)

Inferior Planet: A planet whose orbit lies inside the Earth's orbit; the inferior planets are Mercury and Venus.

Infortunes, the (also called **the Two Infortunes** or **the Malefics**): In classical astrology, Mars and Saturn, known as the *Lesser Infortune* and the *Greater Infortune*, respectively. Both were believed to have harmful effects, especially if ANGULAR and afflicting the luminaries. Modern astrologers tend to regard them as energies that can be used either creatively or destructively, depending on the individual's degree of self-awareness and self-control. (See MALEFIC.)

Ingress: The entrance of the Sun, the Moon, or a planet into a sign of the zodiac. Many EPHEMERIDES give the exact time of the ingresses, and some give the positions of the planets at the time of the twelve solar ingresses. Times for lunar ingresses are given on the sample page from an ephemeris, page 48. The configuration of the heavens at the time of solar ingresses, especially the Aries ingress, is of particular importance in MUNDANE ASTROLOGY.

Initiating Signs: See CARDINAL.

Intercepted: A term used to describe a sign of the zodiac that is wholly contained in one of the houses of a birth chart, without appearing on any house CUSP. When a sign is intercepted, the sign opposite it on the zodiac will be intercepted as well. In Margaret Mead's chart (see page 61), Pisces is intercepted in the Second House and Virgo in the Eighth House. In chart interpretation, the influence of an intercepted sign is regarded as less conspicuous and slower to manifest than that of a sign that does occupy a house cusp.

In most systems of HOUSE DIVISION, the frequency of interception is directly proportional to the distance of the birthplace from the Equator. (See HOUSES.)

Interpretation: See CHART INTERPRETATION; DELINEATION; SYNTHESIS.

Inverse Midpoint: See MIDPOINT.

Islam, Astrology in: The first tribes to inhabit the Arabian peninsula seem not to have known astrology, although they did practice magic. It was the Chaldean merchants who introduced astrology to these regions. Later, Arab astrologers adopted the Greek astrology of PTOLEMY and continued to practice it after Muhammad, since its underlying Neoplatonism did not seem contradictory to the teachings of the Qur'an. They soon became proficient, and it was through the two great expansions of Islam (632–732 and 1326–1687) that the astrology of the ancients was carried to Spain through North Africa and to the Balkans by way of Turkey.

The Arabs saw astrology as part of a larger whole—not merely as a tool for predicting events, but as a key for understanding life by contemplating the marriage of Heaven and Earth, for everything in one had its counterpart in the other. Each planet was seen as a spiritual channel and had a symbolic role that incorporated elements of the Bible and the Qur'an: Saturn was associated with Ibrahim (Abraham), Jupiter with Musa (Moses), Mars with Harun (Aaron), Venus with Yusuf (Joseph), and Mercury with Isa (Jesus).

The Arabs are famous for devloping the ancient theory of "Parts" (possibly borrowed from the Hebrews); these are mathematical combinations of three positions in a birth chart. For example, the PART OF FORTUNE is found by adding the longitude of the Ascendant to the longitude of the Moon and then subtracting the longitude of the Sun. The Arab's use of parts is one of the earliest attempts to view the chart as a whole and anticipates the modern technique of SYNTHESIS.

Arab astrologers calculating an angle. (Macrobius, *In Somnium Scipionis*, Venice, 1513.)

In the golden age of Islam (ninth, tenth, and eleventh centuries) there were great advances in astrology and in astronomy, which latter was then considered as a means of refining astrological measurement. The Arabs invented the ASTROLABE, possibly as an aid for determining the direction of Mecca for noontime prayers. Al-Munsur established a library and observatory in Baghdad. ALBUMAZAR (805–86) originated the theory of cycles and is said to have predicted the French Revolution. Thâbit ibn Qarra (d. 901) wrote a treatise on the art of making astrological talismans and amulets. Albohali (Latinized

name of Aby Ali Yakub ibn al-Kayer) specialized in genethliacal astrology. Rhazes (Latinized name of al-Razi, late tenth century), later known as the Paracelsus of the Arabs, practiced an early form of medical astrology. Albohazen Haly (Latinized name of Ibn Aby Ridschal, eleventh century), known in the West as Summus Astrologicus (the greatest astrologer), wrote a treatise in eight volumes that may be regarded as a compendium of the astrological knowledge of Islam. Al-Biruni (Abu al-Rayhan Muhammad ibn Ahmad al-Biruni, 973–1048) wrote the *Elements of Astrology*, which was the standard astrological text for centuries; to him modern astrology owes such concepts as the Moon's signifying the feminine principle and the collective memory.

Like the Hindus and Chinese, the Arabs conceived of twenty-eight lunar mansions, which they called *manzils*. Each *manzil* represented 1 day in the Moon's cycle and was associated with both a meteorological and a magical influence. For example, the *manzil* beginning with the star Aldebaran was auspicious for marriage or travel when transited by the Moon, was associated with dry weather, and was used in magical incantations to wreak revenge and promulgate ill will.

Arab astrology is unique in the way it combines the interpretation of a chart with divinatory practices such as geomancy and in the importance it accords to pentacles and talismans.

Jayne, Charles (October 9, 1911, 10:39:12 P.M. EST, Jenkintown, Pa.–): American astrologer, author, and teacher. Jayne came to astrology in 1931, at the age of twenty. He published his first article in 1940 and began practicing in 1949. He contributed substantially to Nicholas de Vore's *Encyclopedia of Astrology* (1947), now a classic. He was president of the Astrologers Guild of America from 1958 to 1960. In 1958 he founded Astrological Research Associates, which, under the editorship of himself and his wife, Vivia Jayne, published *In Search* (1958–62), the first international journal of astrology. In 1970 he founded the Association for Research in Cosmecology, a private organization made up of astrologers and academics in many fields and devoted to the reintegration of astrology and science. Since 1975 the Jaynes have published *Cosmecology Bulletin,* a biannual journal that focuses on scientific inquiry into astrology. In 1979 Jayne received the annual Johndro Award for his contributions to the technical side of astrology.

Jayne has emphasized the importance of the third dimension in both the ecliptic and the equatorial systems of CELESTIAL COORDINATES, and has helped to make modern astrologers more conscious of DECLINATION (see his *Parallels, Their Hidden Meaning,* 1978) and CELESTIAL LATITUDE (see his *A New Dimension in Astrology,* 1975). His work on eclipses, which he views as conjunctions or oppositions in latitude as well as longitude, is typical of the three-dimensional approach that led him to the discovery—independently of the late L. E. JOHNDRO—of the VERTEX (see ECLIPSE).

Much of Jayne's early work was devoted to the study of long-term

Charles Jayne.

planetary cycles (see CYCLE). He found that the major recurrence cycles of the five outermost planets corresponded to half a dozen major cycles discovered by such historians and sociologists as Arnold Toynbee, Oswald Spengler, Karl Lamprecht, Dr. J. S. Lee, and others. For example, the 794-year Jupiter-Saturn cycle corresponds to Toynbee's and Lee's cycle of the breakdown and reintegration of civilizations; the 1,089-year Saturn-Uranus cycle to Lee's cycle in the shifts of China's capital; the 248-year Pluto cycle to Lamprecht's and Spengler's cycle of phase changes in collective consciousness; and a 600-year compound cycle involving Sun, Moon, Mars, Jupiter, Saturn, Uranus, and Neptune to Toynbee's cycle of migration.

Jayne's most innovative work has been the discovery of prenatal and postnatal epochs and the laws governing their charts, which he arrived at through long experience in the techniques of RECTIFICATION. A critic of most so-called ESOTERIC ASTROLOGY, Jayne believes that these charts, which are correlated to cosmic centers beyond our planetary system, form the basis for a genuine arcane astrology (see his *Preface to Prenatal Charts*, 1975).

Other publications include *The Technique of Rectification* (1970), *Progressions and Directions* (1972), and *The Unknown Planets* (1976). Vivia Jayne is a practicing astrologer and author of *Aspects to Horoscope Angles* (1975). (See CHIRON, CONCEPTION CHART, LOCATIONAL ASTROLOGY, PROGRESSION AND DIRECTION.)

Jewels: See BIRTHSTONES.

Johndro, L. Edward (January 30, 1882, 12:53 A.M. EST, 80W22 and 44N58–November 1951): American astrologer, mathematician, and radio engineer. Between 1936 and 1951 Johndro acted as silent partner to W. Kenneth Brown, another astrologer whom he never actually met. The two men carried on a highly paid consulting service that advised prominent businessmen about their investments. Johndro and Brown used both natal and conception charts in their professional work (see CONCEPTION CHART).

Johndro was codiscoverer, with the author of this article, of the VERTEX, which he called the *Electrical Ascendant*. This was not just a fanciful name, as Johndro had an electrodynamic field theory that he advanced as the scientific basis for astrology. In his *The Stars, How and Where They Influence* (1929), he uses this field theory and very narrow orbs to relate stellar influence to various terrestrial latitudes. Oddly enough, the so-called siderealists have paid no attention to this work. In his *A New Conception of Sign Rulerships*, he presents a radically different theory of RULERSHIP that in spite of its merits has been generally ignored. He is best known for *The Earth in the Heavens* (1929), in which he presents his system of projecting the zodiac on the Earth via a moving baseline (see LOCATIONAL ASTROLOGY). In 1950 Johndro rejected his moving baseline in favor of a fixed one that equated the Greenwich Meridian to 0° Aries; yet many astrologers continue to use his earlier baseline. Johndro's system is the basis of the *birthday locality chart*, whose angles may be used for timing events even when the BIRTHTIME is unknown.

Johndro also developed an unpublished method of locality shifting in which natal bodies are shifted to any other locality via equator, prime vertical, and horizon and then brought back to the ecliptic, where they can be aspected to natal positions. After extensive testing, the author has found this method—which, again, is largely unaffected by inaccurate birthtimes—to be the most important contribution ever made to locality astrology.

Johndro's last published articles, on his revised baseline for locality charts and the Vertex, appeared in 1950 and 1951 in Margaret Morrell's *Modern Astrology*. But much of his later work, including his brilliant work on stocks and commodities, was never published. Shy, reclusive, and sometimes uncommunicative, Johndro was nevertheless a powerful force in modern astrology and is now generally regarded as the greatest technical astrologer of the United States. In 1978 the annual Johndro Award for outstanding achievement in technical astrology was created by the Association for Research in Cosmecology in his honor.

—CHARLES JAYNE

Jones, Marc Edmund (October 1, 1888, 8:37 A.M., St. Louis, Mo.– March 5, 1980, 2 A.M., Stanwood, Wash.): American astrologer,

Marc Edmund Jones.

teacher, and author. One of the few real scholars to devote themselves to astrology in the twentieth century, Jones was a major influence in raising the standards of astrology in the United States. Like Dane RUDHYAR, he was a man of talent and education; in a long and distinguished career, he served in such varied capacities as motion picture scenarist, editorial consultant, and Protestant minister.

Jones came to astrology in 1913. In 1923 he founded the Sabian Assembly, an association devoted to research and instruction in occult psychology and philosophy. He taught widely, both in his classes and through his numerous books on astrology and other occult subjects. Like England's Alan LEO, Jones was an indefatigable lecturer.

Jones is best known for his unique approach to horoscope interpretation, which laid primary emphasis on the chart as a whole rather than on the delineation of its separate pieces.

His "piano key" technique for representing the planets (see his *How to Learn Astrology,* 1941) is particularly useful to beginners, who are apt to be so overwhelmed by the many factors to be considered in a chart that they cannot see the forest for the trees. In his *Guide to Horoscope Interpretation* (1941), Jones classifies horoscopes into seven different types—*splash, bundle, locomotive, bowl, bucket, seesaw,* and *splay*—which have become part of the working vocabulary of many American astrologers. A major advantage of such techniques is that they may be used in the absence of an exact BIRTHTIME; for Jones appears to have realized that few birthtimes are really accurate.

Marc Edmund Jones was the best teacher of astrology this country ever produced. His understanding of astrology was combined with a profound intellectual grasp of occult philosophy and deepened by many decades of experience as a consultant astrologer—a vital offset to his theoretical tendencies. There is no doubt that he was easier to listen to than to read, but anyone who really studies his work will become a better astrologer. Astrologers tend to be a fuzzy lot, but those who follow his methods have been compelled to bring discipline into their thinking. Fortunately, he is survived by many fine teachers who are carrying on his methods. In 1976 the annual Marc Edmund Jones Award for outstanding achievement in technical astrology was created by Astrology Services International in his honor.

—CHARLES JAYNE

Judicial Astrology: Traditionally, the branch of astrology that judged the motions of the planets as they related to world events, war and peace, and the fate of nations. Judicial astrology is now known as MUNDANE ASTROLOGY.

Jung, Carl Gustav (July 26, 1875, 7:32 P.M., Kesswil, Basel, Switzerland–June 6, 1961, Küsnacht, Zurich): Swiss psychologist and psychiatrist, founder of analytic psychology. After studying medicine, Jung turned to psychiatry. A convert to psychoanalysis in 1907, he became the disciple and friend of Freud, but after a collaboration of several years he broke with Freud and founded his own school. Jung developed the idea of the collective unconscious, a reservoir of racial memories, dreams, and myths functionally potential within each individual, and peopled with images called archetypes. The search for these archetypes led him to an original meditation on aesthetics, primitive and oriental religions, alchemy, and astrology.

Jung had considerable respect for astrology, which he said was "knocking at the doors of the universities from which it was banished three hundred years ago." He cast horoscopes of his patients and used them to help diagnose their problems. He made a statistical study of the relationships between the horoscopes of marriage partners, which he describes in *Synchronicity: An Acausal Connecting Principle* (1955). Synchronicity was a theory Jung developed in the 1940s according to which certain

Carl Gustav Jung. (The Bettman Archive.)

categories of events are connected by meaning rather than by causality. At times he used the principle of synchronicity to explain astrology; at other times his theoretical approach came closer to an acceptance of planetary influence.

In an interview in 1954 he said, "There are many analogies which can be made between the horosocope and the character disposition. There is even the possibility of certain predictive powers . . . . The horoscope seems to correspond to psychic archetypes." And in *Modern Man in Search of a Soul* he wrote, "We are born at a given moment, in a given place, and we have, like the best wines, the quality of the year and the season which witness our birth. Astrology claims no more than this."

Jung's ideas have had a profound impact on modern astrology, especially the humanistic approach to astrology, which is interested in inte- grating astrology with depth psychology. Jung's daughter, Frau Gret Baumann-Jung, is also a psychologist. Astrology is completely integrated into her work, both in counseling and in the training of Jungian analyists. (See HUMANISTIC ASTROLOGY.)

Juno (glyph ⚵): The fourth largest of the ASTEROIDS, discovered in 1804. Both Zipporah Dobyns and Eleanor Bach associate it with marriage, and the problem of equality between the sexes.

Jupiter (glyph ♃): The largest planet in our solar system, with a mean diameter of 87,000 miles and a brilliance second only to that of Venus. Its mean distance from the Sun is 483.3 million miles, and its SIDEREAL PERIOD is 11.86 tropical years. It has four large satellites, which were discovered by Galileo in 1610, the first celestial objects to be seen with a telescope. In addition there are nine known smaller moons.

In astrology, Jupiter is traditionally known as the Greater Fortune, the Lesser Fortune being Venus; thus its nature was regarded as BENEFIC. The planet was named after the ancient Italian god of the heavens who corresponded to the Greek Zeus and who also became the official guardian of the Roman state and of law itself.

Jupiter rules the sign of Sagittarius and is traditional ruler of the sign of Pisces, which most modern astrologers now assign to Neptune (see RULERSHIP). Thus it is in DETRIMENT in the opposite, Mercury-ruled signs of

Gemini and Virgo. Jupiter is exalted in Cancer (see EXALTATION) and in FALL in Capricorn.

In chart interpretation, Jupiter stands for growth and expansion on every level, from material wealth through humanitarian feelings and breadth of outlook to spiritual evolution and wisdom. Its qualities are optimism, faith, good fortune, generosity, geniality, joviality, humor, idealism, judgment, benevolence, philanthropy, sociability, respectability. It rules higher education, especially religion, philosophy, and law. When afflicted, Jupiter is associated with overconfidence, overindulgence, and extravagance.

The following delineations are offered to show some of the ways Jupiter may operate in the signs and houses. It should be remembered that they are merely suggestions and that their accuracy in any given case depends on the overall strength and condition of Jupiter in relation to the chart as a whole, especially the aspects it forms with other planets and important points.

JUPITER IN THE SIGNS

Jupiter in Aries: enthusiasm, independence, self-confidence, impulsiveness, arrogance, prodigality.

Jupiter in Taurus: sensuality, understanding of business and finance, conservatism, materialism, overindulgence.

Jupiter in Gemini: intellectual and literary ability, loquacity, universal curiosity, versatility, faith in reason.

Jupiter in Cancer: strong sense of family, sensitivity, generosity, idealism, self-righteousness.

Jupiter in Leo: leadership, nobility, love of pleasure, taste for display, pride.

Jupiter in Virgo: judgment, discrimination, critical faculty, love of detail, perfectionism, overwork.

Jupiter in Libra: tact, sociability, sense of fair play, altruism, aesthetic sense.

Jupiter in Scorpio: resourcefulness, penetrating insight, sense of irony.

Jupiter in Sagittarius: desire for knowledge and travel, spirituality, self-confidence, sense of humor, generosity, self-righteousness.

Jupiter in Capricorn: ambition, conservatism, respect for established institutions, law and order.

Jupiter in Aquarius: humanitarianism, philanthropy, sociability, socialism, publishing.

Jupiter in Pisces: sympathy, social consciousness, spirituality, universality, self-sacrifice.

JUPITER IN THE HOUSES

Jupiter in the First House: self-confidence, optimism, generosity, expansiveness, opportunities, overweight.

Jupiter in the Second House: talent for handling money, prosperity, financial success.

Jupiter in the Third House: good education, love of study, sociability, interest in communication.

Jupiter in the Fourth House: domesticity, chance of inheritance, happy old age.

Jupiter in the Fifth House: urge to

create, love of pleasure, many love affairs, love and understanding of children.

Jupiter in the Sixth House: strong desire for service, possibility of overwork, medical or charitable work.

Jupiter in the Seventh House: outgoing personality, many relationships, fortunate marriage.

Jupiter in the Eighth House: possibility of inheritance or wealthy marriage partner, philosophical acceptance of death, many sexual contacts.

Jupiter in the Ninth House: love of learning (especially religion, philos-ophy, law), love of travel, self-improvement, spiritual growth.

Jupiter in the Tenth House: professional success, honors, comfortable circumstances.

Jupiter in the Eleventh House: many friends, professional contacts, high ideals.

Jupiter in the Twelfth House: activity behind the scenes, social work, psychic or spiritual experiences.

Juvenal: See ROMANS, ASTROLOGY AMONG THE.

Kabala (also **Kabbala** or **Kabbalah**): See CABALA.

Karma (from the Sanskrit *karman,* deed): The concept, in Hindu and Buddhist philosophy, that a person's deeds determine his future destiny, not merely within a single lifetime but throughout as many lifetimes as are necessary to obtain freedom from the "wheel" of karma; the Hindu and Buddhist principle of causality. Since it refers to the ethical consequences of one's actions, and hence to moral responsibility, the concept is related in Western astrology to the planet Saturn, sometimes called the Lord of Karma. The term is used frequently in ESOTERIC ASTROLOGY.

Kepler, Johann (January 6, 1571, Weil, Württemberg, Germany–November 15, 1630, Regensburg, Germany): German astronomer, mathematician, and astrologer, regarded as the father of modern astronomy. Kepler discovered the three great laws of planetary motion governing the elliptical orbits of the planets around the Sun, which later led to Newton's law of universal gravitation. The son of poor peasants, in 1600 Kepler became assistant to the

Danish astronomer Tycho BRAHE at Prague, succeeding him a year later as court astronomer to Emperor Rudolf II. Kepler was an intensely religious man with mystical and Neoplatonist ideas, and his astronomical discoveries were motivated by his desire to prove the Pythagorean theory of the MUSIC OF THE SPHERES.

Despite his rank as imperial astronomer, Kepler lived on the edge of poverty, and he cast horoscopes and published astrological almanacs predicting events for the coming year in order to supplement his meager income. Although he practiced astrology all his life, in his early years this was more by financial necessity than personal choice. He even disparaged astrology as "the foolish and disreputable daughter of astronomy, without whom the wise old mother would starve," a remark frequently quoted by astronomers anxious to underplay Kepler's allegiance to astrology. However, with time and experience, Kepler's attitude toward astrology changed, and later in life he wrote, "A most unfailing experience (as far as can be expected in nature) of the excitement of sublunary [that is, human] natures by the conjunctions and aspects of the

Johannes Kepler. (The Bettman Archive.)

planets has instructed and compelled my unwilling belief." He also declared that "the belief in the effect of the constellations derives in the first place from experience, which is so convincing that it can be denied only by those who have not examined it.".

As his initial skepticism was overcome by experience, Kepler became intrigued with astrology and wrote friends repeatedly of his desire to separate the "gems from the slag." He warned "certain theologians, physicians, and philosophers who rightly reject the superstitions of the astrologers, not to throw out the baby with the bathwater."' Like Saint Thomas AQUINAS, Kepler believed that human destiny is not altogether determined by the stars but that there is something in human nature that can rise above their influence. Thus his predictions were limited to tendencies and probabilities, in which he anticipated modern astrology. Kepler was the first to formulate a general theory of aspects, and his work in that area anticipates ADDEY'S

HARMONICS. In an address given at the University of Copenhagen, he said, "We cannot deny the influence of the stars, without disbelieving in the wisdom of God." (See also HOUSE DIVISION.)

Kite: A MAJOR CONFIGURATION in which three planets are in TRINE, forming a GRAND TRINE, with a fourth planet at the MIDPOINT of one of the trines, forming SEXTILES to two of the members of the trine and an OPPOSITION to the third. This formation is considered highly desirable, since it combines the sensitivity of the grand trine, the awareness of the opposition, and the productivity of the sextile. A good example is the chart of the actress Mia Farrow, in which a grand air trine consisting of Mercury in Aquarius in the Tenth House, Uranus in Gemini in the First House, and Neptune in Libra in the Sixth House is energized by Venus in Aries in the Twelfth House. The slightly androgynous Arian Venus opposes Neptune, giving an ethereal glamor, and sextiles Uranus, adding originality and unconventionality, and Mercury, indicating intelligence and a gift for self-expression. With a total of three planets in the Tenth House, Farrow has received considerable attention and several important awards for her performances.

Koch Birthplace System: See HOUSE DIVISION.

Kowal, Charles: See CHIRON.

Krafft, Karl: See HARMONICS; OFFICIAL ASTROLOGERS; STATISTICS AND ASTROLOGY.

Landscheidt, Theodor: See GALAC-TIC CENTER; GALAXY.

Latitude: See CELESTIAL LATITUDE; TERRESTRIAL LATITUDE.

Law, Astrology and the: See ASTROL-OGY AND THE LAW.

Leo (glyph ♌): The fifth sign of the zodiac, which the Sun transits during the height of summer, from about July 23 to about August 22. The symbol for Leo is the lion. Its POLARITY is positive, its element is fire (see ELE-MENTS), its quality is fixed (see QUAL-ITIES), its ruling planet is the Sun (see RULERSHIP), and its NATURAL HOUSE is the Fifth.

Like the Sun, which is their plan-etary ruler, natives of this sign be-long at the center of their world, ra-diating the energy of fire and exerting the magnetism of fixity. Leos—who include not only Sun-sign Leos, but all in whose charts the sign is emphasized—do not need to sally forth to assert their powerful in-dividuality; their business is simply to be and by their very existence to influence the lives of those around them. There is a natural assumption of authority in Leo that is different from the driving ambition of Capri-corn. While Capricorn seeks to climb to a position of power, Leo already possesses that power by divine right. Like the infant who rules the house-hold from his crib, the king sur-rounded by loyal subjects, or the art-ist in his studio, Leo is in total control of his universe.

Although they seem self-con-tained, Leos actually need other peo-ple to give to, and they need to feel that their gifts are appreciated. Gen-

erous and noble of spirit, they are also victims of pride, and they can become isolated from the love and support they need because they are too proud to ask for it. If in their insecurity they imagine that their power is of their own making, they can fall into the trap of tyranny and take some spectacular falls.

Hence Leo can be the most charming or the most obnoxious of signs, depending on early education and other factors in the chart. There is no use telling the Leo child, "The world does not revolve around you!" She knows otherwise, and parents must find ways to curb the annoying Leo egocentricity without nipping the joyous Leo creativity in the bud. These children love to please and to perform; but if the focus is temporarily away from them, they may stage loud dramatic scenes in order to regain center stage. In dealing with the sensitive young Leo ego, the use of parental authority will probably just encourage resistance, but genuine affection and an appeal to their "better nature" works wonders. For Leo is, or should be, essentially a sign of joy: innocent, fun-loving, eternally childlike, living in the moment, discovering the infinite richness of the creation, the true child of God, like Adam in the garden before the fall. In modern psychology Leo corresponds to the pleasure principle.

The Leo dramatic sense and tendency to dominate, while great assets on stage, can create problems in an intimate relationship. The need to give can also be a need to control the person to whom one is giving, and the very intensity of Leo's giving can be hard to take and can cause an affair to "burn out" before its time. On the other hand, an evolved Leo who is conscious of his or her own ego games can be a wonderful lover: generous, imaginative, witty, loyal, romantic, and totally committed to giving his or her partner the best of everything. Leo exhibitionism may not be everyone's cup of tea, but those who can respond to it will be royally entertained. Although Leo rules children, it is not a particularly fertile sign, and many Leos will produce no offspring, preferring to remain the child themselves or to produce works of art—which won't compete with them for attention—instead of children.

Their most compatible signs are Aries, Sagittarius, Gemini, and Libra; Cancer, Virgo, Capricorn, and Pisces are neutral; and Taurus and Scorpio are likely to be difficult. With another Leo, there may be competition for attention and control. With Aquarius, their polar opposite on the zodiac, there will be both tension and attraction, the outcome depending, as with all combinations, on how the two charts interact as a whole and not on the COMPATIBILITY of Sun signs alone.

With their faith in their own abilities, will power, and flair for attracting attention, Leos are born leaders and almost always succeed, sometimes even in the absence of any real talent or particular expenditure of effort on their part. Their ruling planet is a star, and Leos are particularly apt to shine in the entertainment world, the theater, the arts, the world of fashion, and the arena of politics. But they will naturally rise to the top of any field. Famous Sun-sign Leos include Napoleon Bonaparte, Clara Bow, Emily Brontë, Fidel Castro, Coco Chanel, Julia Child, Cecil B. DeMille, Amelia Earhart, Henry Ford, Alfred Hitchcock, Aldous Huxley, Mick Jagger, Carl Jung, Bert Lahr, Benito Mussolini, Jacqueline Kennedy Onassis, Jean Piaget, Yves Saint Laurent, Haile Selassie, George Bernard Shaw, Percy Bysshe Shelley, Andy Warhol, and Mae West. (See BIRTHSTONES; COLORS; DAYS OF THE WEEK; METALS.)

Leo, Alan (born William Frederick Allan; August 7, 1860, 5:49 A.M., London–August 30, 1917, 10:00 A.M., Bude, Cornwall): Anglo-Scottish astrologer, generally acknowledged to be the father of modern astrology.

At the end of the nineteenth century in Britain and Europe astrology was still essentially an uncoordinated and unapproachable hodgepodge of unsifted tradition whose students were scattered and isolated. A natural leader and organizer, Alan Leo took every opportunity offered by his work as a commercial traveler to meet and lecture to students around the country.

In May 1890 Leo joined the Theosophical Society, and in August 1890, together with F. W. Lacey, he launched the monthly *Astrologer's Magazine,* which in 1895 was renamed *Modern Astrology.* With this magazine he succeeded in drawing together serious students in Britain and from around the world, and in propagating a philosophically sound

Alan Leo. (Photo by Alvin Langdon Coburn.)

and spiritually oriented astrology that could be used for psychological analysis of character rather than simply as a means of forecasting (its main use until that time).

Leo also wanted to educate the larger public as to the value of the art. This he did with a series of "shilling" horoscopes. Through one of these he met the future Bessie Leo, whom he married in 1895. Over the next twenty or so years he produced, either in whole or in part, some thirty books, including *How to Judge a Nativity, Astrology for All, The Key to Your Own Nativity, The Progressed Horoscope,* and *Esoteric Astrology.* At the same time he employed specialists to prepare works on every aspect of the tradition, from medical and mundane astrology to weather predicting, so that these could be made accessible to all. It was mainly through the translation of this comprehensive literature and *Modern Astrology* that the astrological "renaissance" spread into Europe and around the world.

Thus Leo can be seen not only as the forerunner of such contemporary movements as the humanist astrology of Dane RUDHYAR and Marc Edmund JONES but also as the natural progenitor of such special schools as the URANIAN SYSTEM and COSMOBIOLOGY in Germany and the Ram School in Holland.

On October 15, 1915, Leo founded the Astrological Lodge of the Theosophical Society, with Bessie Leo as its first president. The Lodge not only served as the base for Charles CARTER's fine work, but also produced the Faculty of Astrological Studies in 1948 and the Astrological Association in 1958. Though independent bodies, they nonetheless still regard themselves as rooted in Leo's larger vision of the astrology that is yet to come.

—CHARLES HARVEY

Lesser Fortune (or **Lesser Benefic**): See FORTUNES, THE.

Lesser Infortune (or **Lesser Malefic**): See INFORTUNES, THE.

Leverrier, Urbain: See NEPTUNE.

Libra (glyph ♎): The seventh sign of the zodiac, which the Sun transits during the first month of autumn, from about September 23 to about October 22. The symbol for this sign is the scales or balance. Its POLARITY is positive, its element is air (see ELEMENTS), its quality is cardinal (see QUALITIES), its ruling planet is Venus (see RULERSHIP), and its NATURAL HOUSE is the Seventh.

The communicativeness of air combined with the activity of cardinality and the charm of Venus conspire to give the Libra native an engaging, sociable, outgoing personality. The symbol for Libra is the balance, and natives of this sign feel incomplete without a partner. A psychologist would call them "other-directed"; ordinary people would say they are unselfish. It is their blessing and their curse to see both sides of every question, and though this makes them valuable as peacemakers, it often means that they are painfully slow in coming to personal decisions.

Librans—who include not only Sun-sign Libras, but all in whose charts the sign is emphasized—crave peace and harmony above all else. They will often stifle their own feelings and opinions (if, indeed, they know what they are) in order to avoid an unpleasant scene. They hate ugliness and disorder and can be-

♎ Libra

come physically ill if their surroundings do not meet their high standard of aesthetic refinement. They may be obsessively concerned with what other people think of them and go to great lengths to make a good, even a false, impression.

Libra babies are famous for their winning smiles from a remarkably early age, but the demand beneath their overflowing congeniality is constant interaction. As children, Libras learn good manners and sharing more easily than other children because of their instinctive sense of fair play, their horror of fighting, and their need to be liked. If they have a behavior problem, it is that they are too good, too nice, too willing to please. In later years they may find that they have given in to others so often that they have forgotten what they want themselves or even who they are. They may have to learn the courage and self-assertiveness that come so naturally to Aries, the sign opposite them in the zodiac.

The element of air combined with the influence of Venus often gives the Libra native a somewhat androgynous appeal that can be devastating. Although they need and attract partners, they are not particularly sexual people, nor are they given to grand passions. They often marry young and usually more than once. Surprisingly often, this will be to another Libra, as if only in the sign of the scales could they find the delicate balance they need, and only in someone just like them could they learn to love themselves. Other compatible signs are Gemini, Aquarius, Leo, and Sagittarius; Virgo, Scorpio, Pisces,

and Taurus are neutral, although the last two are potentially better through the shared influence of Venus; Cancer and Capricorn may well be difficult. With Aries, there is both attraction and tension; in all cases, however, the success of the relationship will depend on the relationship between two whole charts—and the natives' willingness to compromise, which in Libra is strong (see COMPATIBILITY).

As the sign of justice, Libra has a natural affinity for the law; but Librans' ability to anticipate others' reactions makes them excel in the military as well. Their feeling for balance and beauty, the gift of Venus, combined with their understanding of form and structure, the legacy of Saturn, give them a natural bent for literature and the visual arts. The sign is especially associated with architecture, sculpture, drawing, design, and interior decoration; crafts such as dressmaking, jewelry, and weaving; and all fields concerned with the beautification of people and their surroundings. The Libra love of justice and interest in the law may draw them into politics, despite their tender sensibilities, if other indications in the chart point in that direction. Famous Librans include Hannah Arendt, Sarah Bernhardt, Lenny Bruce, Michelangelo Caravaggio, Miguel de Cervantes, John Dewey, William O. Douglas, Dwight Eisenhower, T. S. Eliot, F. Scott Fitzgerald, Mohandas Gandhi, Timothy Leary, Le Corbusier, John Lennon, Admiral Horatio Nelson, Giovanni Piranese, Emily Post, Eleanor Roosevelt, and Oscar Wilde. (See BIRTH-

STONES; COLORS; DAYS OF THE WEEK; METALS.)

Lights, the: See LUMINARIES.

Lilly, William (May 1, 1602, Leicestershire—June 9, 1681, London): English astrologer, author of one of the first prophetic almanacs and of *Christian Astrology* (1647). Lilly is best known as a practitioner of HORARY ASTROLOGY and for accurately predicting the Great Plague of London of 1665 and the Great Fire of London of the following year.

LMT Method: See CHART CALCULATION.

Local Mean Time (LMT): See CHART CALCULATION; TIME.

Local Sidereal Day: See TIME.

Local Sidereal Time (LST): See CHART CALCULATION; TIME.

Local Space Chart: See LOCATIONAL ASTROLOGY.

Local Time: See TIME.

Locational Astrology: The use of astrological principles in choosing a suitable place to live—a place where, as L. E. JOHNDRO put it, "the best promise of the nativity is the most intensified and the detrimental qualities are the most minimized." Various techniques have been used. For example, one can compare the chart of an individual with the chart of the city, county, or nation where he or she is considering relocating, if available (see CHART COMPARISON). The most usual form of locational astrology is to set up the natal chart for the same Universal Time (see TIME) but to use the latitude and longitude of the new locality. In the event that this is some distance from the birthplace, the planets will move into different houses. This is a simple and useful locality shift.

In addition, a number of astrologers—including Sepharial, Doane, RUDHYAR, and Johndro—have sought to project the zodiac on Earth. According to Johndro's system, described in *The Earth in the Heavens,* the degree on the MIDHEAVEN of a given locality at the time of the Aries INGRESS changes gradually over a period of 28,174 years, which is the precessional year as measured on the celestial equator rather than on the ecliptic (see PRECESSION OF THE EQUINOXES). Thus all cities and nations pass successively through all twelve signs. At some time shortly before the birth of Christ, the degree on the Midheaven at Greenwich had been 0° tropical Aries, but the VERNAL POINT had shifted gradually westward so that by January 1, 1930, the degree on the Midheaven at Greenwich was 1°10′ Taurus. The Johndro *birthday locality chart* is made up of the native's planetary positions and the Johndro locality angles, corrected to account for the amount of precession for the day of birth. The exact time of birth does not enter into the calculations; thus a Johndro locality chart can be cast for the birthplace— or any other location—when the birthtime is unknown.

Alfred Witte's partner, Friedrich

Sieggruen (see URANIAN SYSTEM), introduced the *zenith horoscope,* in which the planets are projected on the HORIZON in AZIMUTH, a system used in Michael Erlewine's *local space chart.* Cyril FAGAN's *mundoscope* is the projection of the planets on the PRIME VERTICAL in Campanus houses (see HOUSE DIVISION). The latest technique in locational astrology is *Astrocartography,* a computerized system developed by Jim Lewis in which personal planetary data are superimposed on a map of the world. Such a map reveals geographic locations that shift the emphasis of the natal chart by placing different planets on the angles.

Long Ascension, Sign of: See ASCENSION, LONG OR SHORT.

Longitude: See CELESTIAL LONGITUDE; TERRESTRIAL LONGITUDE.

Longitude Acceleration: In the so-called LMT method of CHART CALCULATION, a correction to account for the TERRESTRIAL LONGITUDE of the birthplace—that is, its position east or west of the Greenwich Meridian (0° longitude), which is the location of the daily sidereal time listed in ephemerides. Longitude acceleration is one of the adjustments necessary to convert the Greenwich sidereal time (GST) listed in the ephemeris to local sidereal time (LST). It amounts to 2/3 second of time for each degree of terrestrial longitude east or west of Greenwich. The correction is added for birthplaces with west longitude and subtracted for birthplaces with east longitude. Thus the longitude acceleration for Denver, Colorado (105W), is 105 × 2/3 = 70 seconds, which is added to the other factors in the calculation.

The reason for longitude acceleration is as follows: There are 360° of longitude all around the Earth—180° west and 180° east. In the 24 hours of mean solar time elapsed from one given GST in the ephemeris to the next, 24 hours 4 minutes of sidereal time have elapsed (see TIME). In 24 hours of sidereal time all 360° of longitude have passed under any given star (excluding the Sun) once and only once. In the extra 4 minutes, however, 1 longitude degree has passed under the star in question a second time. To account for this discrepancy, which becomes greater the farther one is from Greenwich, the 4 minutes (240 seconds) must be divided by the 360°, which yields 2/3 second per degree.

Longitude Circle: See CELESTIAL LONGITUDE.

Long Sextile: See MUNDANE ASTROLOGY.

Lord: An archaic term for ruling planet. Thus Mars, for example, was said to be the lord of Aries. A planet could also be the lord of a house if it ruled the sign on the cusp or the lord of a nativity if it ruled the sign on the Ascendant. In the case of the Moon, the term *lady* was used. (See RULERSHIP.)

Lowell, Dr. Percival: See PLUTO.

Lower Culmination: See MERIDIAN.

Lower Meridian: See MERIDIAN.

Lucretius: See ROMANS, ASTROLOGY AMONG THE.

Luminaries: In classical astrology, the Sun and the Moon, which were also known as the two *lights,* thus distinguishing them from the planets by their property of illuminating the Earth. Strictly speaking, the term is inaccurate, since the Sun is the only direct source of light; the light of the Moon, like that of the planets, is reflected from the Sun. However, the greater relative importance of the Sun and the Moon in chart interpretation justifies their being set apart from the planets, and the archaic language continues to be used by modern astrologers.

Lunar Ascendant: See PART OF FORTUNE.

Lunar Eclipse: See ECLIPSE.

Lunar Mansions: Divisions of the Moon's orbit, each approximately equivalent to the Moon's DAILY MOTION. Mansions are probably older than the signs or constellations of the zodiac. They were developed by the Arabs, the Chinese, and the Hindus into a comprehensive system of interpretation in which they were used more or less like signs. Since the Moon takes 27.32166 days to complete its orbit (the *sidereal month*), there are either twenty-seven or twenty-eight lunar mansions. All three cultures originally employed twenty-eight mansions, but the Hindus eventually dropped one. The boundaries between mansions were originally marked by certain stars; according to Vivian Robson, the star Alcyone in the Pleiades, which marked the VERNAL POINT in 2337 B.C., was originally the beginning of the first mansion. Modern astrologers who use mansions usually consider them as equal in length—12°51'25.2" of CELESTIAL LONGITUDE—and mark the beginning of the first mansion at 0° sidereal Aries (which is about 24° tropical Aries; see SIDEREAL ZODIAC). Since the starting point of sidereal Aries is in dispute, extreme precision regarding the length of a mansion is somewhat academic; many astrologers round it off to 13°. (See CHINESE ASTROLOGY; INDIA, ASTROLOGY IN; ISLAM, ASTROLOGY IN.)

Lunar Nodes: See NODES.

Lunar Return: See SOLAR RETURN.

Lunar Year: A 354.367-day period of 12 lunar months that are usually based on the SYNODIC PERIOD of the Moon, or 29 days 12 hours 44 minutes 2.7 seconds. There are 34 lunar years for every 33 tropical (solar) years. The most widely used lunar calendar in modern times is that of the Muslims, in which the 12 lunar months consist alternately of 29 and 30 days apiece, with an extra day added to one of the months during lunar leap years. In one 30-year lunar cycle there are 19 lunar common years of 354 days each and 11 lunar leap years of 355 days each. Many cultures, including the Hindus, Hebrews, and Chinese, adopted a *soli-*

lunar year, with 12 months based on the Moon's synodic cycle and 1 extra, intercalary month making up the difference.

Lunation: The period of time, averaging 29 days 12 hours 44 minutes and 2.7 seconds, between two successive New Moons; the *synodic month.* The term is also popularly used by astrologers as a synonym for the New Moon—that is, the exact moment of the Moon's conjunction with the Sun.

Since the New Moon represents the beginning of a new cycle, a lunation in a certain house of a birth chart will mark the beginning of a cycle involving the activities of that house. For example, a lunation in the Seventh House could indicate a new relationship; a lunation in the Sixth House, a new job, and so on. The significance of the soli-lunar relationship as a guide to personality in the interpretation of birth charts is analyzed extensively by Dane RUDHYAR in *The Lunation Cycle.* Lunations are also of particular importance in MUNDANE ASTROLOGY. (See CYCLE; ECLIPSE; MOON.)

Lunation Cycle: See LUNATION; MOON.

Luther, Martin: See RENAISSANCE, ASTROLOGY IN THE.

Macrocosm (from the Greek *makros,* great, and *kosmos,* world): The universe; as distinguished from the MICROCOSM, or the human being as a miniature of the universe. (See HERMETIC THEORY.)

Major Aspect: See ASPECT.

Major Configuration: In a birth chart, a symmetrical pattern of three or more planets in mutual aspect that provides a focus for the energies in the chart and responds as a unit when activated by transit. Major configurations include the T-SQUARE, the GRAND CROSS, the GRAND TRINE, the KITE, the MYSTIC RECTANGLE, the DOUBLE QUINCUNX, and the DOUBLE BIQUINTILE. (See ASPECT.)

Major Progression: See PROGRESSION AND DIRECTION.

Malefic: Literally, "doing ill"; a term applied by ancient and classical astrologers to planets or aspects regarded as having an evil influence; the opposite of BENEFIC. PTOLEMY classifies Mars and Saturn as malefic planets and the square and the opposition as inharmonious aspects.

Modern astrologers are moving away from the categorization of planets and aspects as good or bad and the outmoded determinism this implies. They tend to regard the planets as energies that can operate for either good or ill, depending on how they are used. Thus Mars is a principle of desire, and Saturn is a principle of discipline, both of which are necessary elements in human nature. Similarly, in referring to aspects, the words *benefic* and *malefic* and being replaced with such terms as *helpful* and *stressful,* or *soft* and *hard.*

Manetho: See EGYPT, ASTROLOGY IN.

Map: See BIRTH CHART.

Mars (glyph ♂ or ♂): The planet in our solar system that is fourth in order from the Sun—mean distance about 141.5 million miles—and conspicuous for the red color of its light. Mars has a diameter of about 4,200 miles, a SIDEREAL PERIOD of 687 days, and two small satellites, Deimos and Phobos.

In astrology, Mars was traditionally known as the "Lesser Infortune," the "Greater Infortune" being

Saturn; thus its nature was regarded as MALEFIC. The planet was named after the Roman god of war, counterpart of the Greek Ares.

Mars rules the sign of Aries and is traditional ruler of the sign of Scorpio, which most modern astrologers now assign to Pluto (see RULERSHIP). Thus it is in DETRIMENT in the opposite, Venus-ruled signs of Libra and Taurus. Mars is exalted in Capricorn (see EXALTATION) and in FALL in Cancer.

In chart interpretation Mars stands for desire, or goal-directed energy, which includes both sexuality and aggression. Its qualities are energy, strength, courage, action, passion, competition, and the fighting spirit. It rules the sex drive, the muscles, the appetite, the sense of smell, the voice, the breath, the prana or vital energy, as well as steel, knives, weapons, and fire. When afflicted, Mars is associated with anger, irritability, impatience, haste, and accidents.

The following delineations are offered to show some of the ways Mars may operate in the signs and houses. It should be remembered that they are merely suggestions and that their accuracy in any given case depends on the overall strength and condition of Mars in relation to the chart as a whole, especially the aspects it forms with other planets and important points.

Mars in Taurus: sensuality, appetite, acquisitiveness, perseverence, stamina.

Mars in Gemini: insatiable curiosity, passion for reading, sexual promiscuity, diffusion of energy, loquacity, literary ability.

Mars in Cancer: imagination, intuition, unexpressed passion, Oedipus complex, hypersensitivity, repressed anger.

Mars in Leo: leadership ability, love of pleasure, dominant personality, pride, prodigality.

Mars in Virgo: industriousness, passion for detail, fault finding, anal eroticism, difficulty expressing anger, nervous energy.

Mars in Libra: passion for justice, strong social conscience, sublimated sexuality, sociability, artistic ability.

Mars in Scorpio: strong sexuality, resourcefulness, good recuperative powers, power drive, jealousy, seductiveness.

Mars in Sagittarius: love of the outdoors and exercise, self-confidence, enthusiasm, love of travel, lusty appetites, tendency to overindulge.

Mars in Capricorn: drive to succeed, ambition, sense of timing, self-control, executive ability, desire to build.

Mars in Aquarius: revolutionary zeal, political activism, sociability, inventiveness, offbeat sexuality.

Mars in Pisces: crusading spirit, self-sacrifice, compassion, susceptibility, dissipation of energy.

MARS IN THE SIGNS

Mars in Aries: impulsiveness, decisiveness, courage, physical strength, energy, self-assertion.

MARS IN THE HOUSES

Mars in the First House: courage, physical strength, energy, action, aggression.

Mars in the Second House: ability to earn money, inability to save money, energy in reserve, good health.

Mars in the Third House: activity in immediate environment, communicativeness, desire for education, belligerent manner.

Mars in the Fourth House: strong attachment to home, interest in psychology or architecture, sexual bond with mother, unconscious anger.

Mars in the Fifth House: creative energy, love of pleasure, desire for children, romantic passion.

Mars in the Sixth House: love of work, desire to serve, health problems, danger of overeating.

Mars in the Seventh House: much energy devoted to relationships, active partner, quarrels with partners, possibility of lawsuits.

Mars in the Eighth House: strong sex drive, possibility of accidents, interest in occult, desire for offspring.

Mars in the Ninth House: love of travel, continuing education, self-improvement, professional ambition.

Mars in the Tenth House: ambition, vitality, career as athlete, soldier, surgeon, butcher, and so on.

Mars in the Eleventh House: many friends, social or political work, quarrels with friends.

Mars in the Twelfth House: activity behind the scenes, secret love affairs, difficulty expressing anger, possibility of chronic health problems.

Marsden, Dr. Brian: See CHIRON.

Masculine Planets: According to PTOLEMY, Sun, Mars, Jupiter, and Saturn; modern authorities often include Uranus and Pluto.

Masculine Signs (also called **Positive**, **Diurnal**, or **Fortunate Signs**): The signs of the fire and air triplicities, namely, Aries, Gemini, Leo, Libra, Sagittarius, and Aquarius. The *feminine signs* belong to the earth and water triplicities. (See POLARITY.)

Mash'allah: See HEBREWS, ASTROLOGY AMONG THE.

Matutine (or **Matutinal**): A term used to describe a star or planet that rises before the Sun in the morning.

Maximum Phase Angle: See HELIOCENTRIC ASTROLOGY.

MC: See MIDHEAVEN.

Mead, Margaret: See CHART INTERPRETATION; HELIOCENTRIC ASTROLOGY; PROGRESSION AND DIRECTION; SOLAR RETURN.

Mean Nodes: See NODES.

Mean Solar Day: See TIME.

Mean Solar Time: See TIME.

Medical Astrology: Ever since the birth of astrology, astrologers have associated the different parts of the body and the illnesses connected with them with the signs of the zodiac and their ruling planets. Hippocrates (460–337 B.C.), the Greek physician who is regarded as the father of medicine, insisted that his students study astrology, saying, "He who does not understand astrology is not a doctor but a fool." Later, Arabian astrologers codified these anatomical correspondences in

The correspondences between the signs of the zodiac and the parts of the human body; from *Les Très Riches Heures du Duc de Berry*, 1485. (Musée Condé, Chantilly; photo by Giraudon.)

a form that was accepted by most doctors until the seventeenth century.

Modern astrologers continue to work with these correspondences, which are useful not only for locating potential health problems in a birth chart but also for rectifying an uncertain time of birth. For example, let us suppose that someone's Ascendant seems to fall on the Aries-Taurus cusp. If she is subject to headaches, eyestrain, or congested sinuses, chances are she really has Aries rising; if she is particularly susceptible to sore throats and stiff necks, the Ascendant is more likely to be Taurus.

Modern medical astrology tends to employ the *principle of polarity*, that is, to use the signs not so much individually as in pairs. Thus someone

with an afflicted Sixth-House Moon in Leo would be subject to problems not only with the heart (ruled by Leo) but also with the circulation in general (ruled by the opposite sign of Aquarius). The following list of anatomical correspondences suggests sensitive areas for natives of each of the twelve signs; that is, people in whose charts the sign is emphasized, whether by Sun, Moon, Ascendant, or planet. The indications become particularly significant if the Sixth and/or Twelfth Houses are involved:

Aries rules the head and face, which are sensitive areas for natives of this sign. Arians are subject to colds, congestion of the brain, sinusitis, headaches, neuralgia, cutaneous eruptions on the face, and problems with the eyes. They usually have strong muscles and good muscle tone.

Taurus rules the neck, throat, pharynx, larynx, vocal cords, and thyroid gland. Natives of this sign are thus subject to sore throats, stiff necks, laryngitis, polyps, goiters, and cancer of the throat. They are usually endowed with a strong constitution and great stamina.

Gemini rules the hands, arms, shoulders, lungs, and upper rib cage, whence the predisposition of natives of this sign to arthritis, bursitis, upper back pain, and intercostal pain. Mercury, the ruling planet, governs the respiratory and nervous systems, so that these are also sensitive areas. Geminis usually have strong hands and arms, and good wind—if they don't smoke.

Cancer rules the breasts, stomach, thorax, liver, digestive system, and general metabolism. Since Cancer is the most sensitive of the signs, its natives are extremely susceptible to disease, especially colds, depression, and alcoholism. They are also gifted with amazing recuperative powers.

Leo rules the heart, the spinal column, and the lower back. The Leo native is more susceptible than natives of other signs to lower back pain, coronary disease, and heart attacks and should therefore avoid leading too sedentary an existence. However, unless the chart is afflicted, he or she probably enjoys excellent health.

Virgo rules the abdomen and the organs it contains, especially the digestive tract, the spleen, and the duodenum. Virgo natives are particularly susceptible to intestinal and eliminatory problems, such as diarrhea, colitis, peritonitis, and hemorrhoids. Virgo's sensitivity to impurities in the environment and Mercury's rulership of the respiratory and nervous systems may account for these natives' greater tendency to be afflicted with allergies. But their greatest enemy is worry.

Libra rules the kidneys, adrenal glands, lumbar region, ovaries, and skin. Afflictions in this sign, combined with dietary overindulgence, may eventually lead to such diseases as cystitis, renal colic, kidney stone, diabetes, and Bright's disease. Libra people should drink plenty of fluids in order to promote the proper functioning of the kidneys.

Scorpio rules the reproductive system, the excretory system (especially the large intestine and the bladder), and psychic healing. Natives of this sign are famous for their recuperative powers. They are also those most susceptible to venereal disease.

Sagittarius rules the hips, thighs, sciatic nerve, sacrum, and coccyx. Sagittarians must guard against rheumatism, sciatica, fractures of the hips or femur, and overdoing it in general. They love outdoor exercise and, like the other fire signs, have plenty of energy.

Capricorn rules the knees, the joints, the connective tissue, and, through Saturn's rulership, the body's defenses—the skin, bones, hair, and nails. These people are particularly susceptible to colds, skin problems, anxiety, and chronic disease. They must learn to relax and enjoy themselves.

Aquarius rules the calves, ankles, and the circulation of the blood. Aquarians tend to be absentminded and to suffer from poor muscular coordination. Through the influence of Uranus, they may be prone to accidents, especially those involving the feet and ankles.

Pisces rules the feet, the lymphatic system, and the glands, especially the lachrymal glands. Afflictions in this sign are associated with water retention, low vitality, and a predisposition to melancholy, fantasy, and the abuse of drugs.

It will have been noted that these anatomical correspondences of the signs of the zodiac work their way down the human body from head to foot. The ancient astrologers believed that the human being is a microcosm of the universe and that the whole zodiac must therefore be contained in our body.

In addition to these anatomical correspondences with the signs of the zodiac, and related to them by rulership, there are correspondences with the planets. The following list of planetary significations is suggestive rather than definitive; for more complete information, the reader is referred to H. L. Cornell's *Encyclopaedia of Medical Astrology.*

Sun: heart, spine, and general vitality.

Moon: stomach, digestive system, female organs, lymphatic system, sympathetic nervous system.

Mercury: brain, central nervous system, thyroid gland, five senses (especially sight), hands.

Venus: throat, kidneys, thymus gland, sense of touch.

Mars: muscles, head, senses of smell and taste, adrenal glands.

Jupiter: liver, thighs, pituitary gland, growth.

Saturn: skin, hair, teeth, bones (in other words, the body's defenses); sense of hearing; spleen.

Uranus: parathyroid gland, aura.

Neptune: pineal gland, psychic healing.

Pluto: pancreas, metabolism, elimination.

The foregoing rulerships isolate sensitive areas of the body for certain signs or planets, but in no way do they suggest that diseases of those areas are inevitable. The emphasis of certain signs in a birth chart indicates predisposition only. Disease is an abnormal state of affairs and will manifest only if planets in those signs are afflicted or planetary energies are misused. Even then disease can be avoided through appropriate exercise, good nutrition, and a positive attitude.

Medium Coeli: See MIDHEAVEN.

Mercury (glyph ☿): The smallest known planet in our solar system (with the possible exception of the "planetoid" Chiron) and the closest known planet to the Sun. Its diameter is about 3,000 miles, its mean distance from the Sun is 36 million miles, and its SIDEREAL PERIOD is about 88 days.

In astrology, Mercury has traditionally been regarded as neutral—that is, neither BENEFIC nor MALEFIC, but changeable, taking on the qualities of the sign it is in and the planets with which it forms aspects. The planet was named after the Roman god of commerce and gain who, as the counterpart of the Greek Hermes, inherited his attributes of messenger of the gods, conductor of souls to the underworld, and god of eloquence.

Mercury rules the signs of Gemini and Virgo (see RULERSHIP); thus it is in DETRIMENT in the opposite, Jupiter-ruled signs of Sagittarius and Pisces. It is exalted in Aquarius (see EXALTATION) and in FALL in Leo.

In chart interpretation Mercury stands for the mind, learning, language, memory, and perception. Its qualities are rationality, intelligence, wit, facility, cleverness, cunning, skill, and dexterity. Its rules thought, reason, intellect; education, reading, writing, speech, information; communication and transportation; business, commerce, selling; adaptation for survival, the nervous system, and the brain. When afflicted, Mercury is associated with emotional coldness, detachment, amorality, expediency, overintellectualization, and difficulty thinking or communicating.

The following delineations are offered to show some of the ways Mercury may operate in the signs and houses. It should be remembered that they are merely suggestions and that their accuracy in any given case depends on the overall strength and condition of Mercury in relation to the chart as a whole, especially the aspects it forms with other planets and important points.

MERCURY IN THE SIGNS

Mercury in Aries: impulsive speech, spontaneous expression, quick thinking, quick study, primitive mentality, sharp tongue, short memory.

Mercury in Taurus: good memory, slow speech, slow learning but good retention, conservative thinking, business sense, keen senses.

Mercury in Gemini: keen intelligence, gift for languages, literary ability, nose for news, flexible mind, high-strung nervous system, flair for business, lack of concentration.

Mercury in Cancer: intuitive mind, telepathic and psychic ability, imagination, empathy, perceptions clouded by emotional reactions.

Mercury in Leo: enthusiastic and dramatic expression, speaking and acting ability, teaching skill, generosity, egocentrism, monologues.

Mercury in Virgo: logical and critical mind, manual dexterity, conscientious scholarship, practical intelligence, good memory, overattention to details.

Mercury in Libra: diplomatic manner, understanding of law, balanced phrases, social skills, altruistic ideas, debating ability, mental equilibrium, difficulty making decisions.

Mercury in Scorpio: investigative mind, gift for research, penetrating insight, interest in occult, sexual awareness, sarcasm.

Mercury in Sagittarius: gift for gab, super salesman, theoretical mind, sense of humor, broadmindedness, tendency to dogmatism.

Mercury in Capricorn: orderly, methodical mind, careful student, desire to learn, love of science, interest in grammar, good memory, business sense, patience, tendency to depression.

Mercury in Aquarius: independent, inventive mind, interest in technology, insightful intelligence, original expression, creative ability, perhaps genius; fixed ideas.

Mercury in Pisces: poetic imagination, mathematical or musical gifts, impressionability, mimicry, mediumistic tendencies, vagueness, poor memory for dates or details.

MERCURY IN THE HOUSES

Mercury in the First House: urge to communicate, intellectual or literary ability, salesmanship, good speaker or teacher, dexterity.

Mercury in the Second House: business sense, interest in money or possessions, intellectual profession, lives by wits.

Mercury in the Third House: gift for communication, good student, writing or teaching ability, much moving around in local environment.

Mercury in the Fourth House: interest in home, history, or politics, psychological insight, intellectual family.

Mercury in the Fifth House: artistic or dramatic ability, good communication with children, speculative investments, intellectual pleasures.

Mercury in the Sixth House: interest in health, self-employment, literary or intellectual profession.

Mercury in the Seventh House: young, intellectual, or literary partner, considerable communication with other people, business partnership.

Mercury in the Eighth House: consciousness of death or sex, skill in handling others' resources, interest in occult.

Mercury in the Ninth House: eternal student, avid traveler, evangelical streak, professional status.

Mercury in the Tenth House: writer or businessman, need to communicate with a wide audience, intellectual profession, financial success.

Mercury in the Eleventh House: young friends, intellectual friends, political interests, gregariousness, interest in future.

Mercury in the Twelfth House: interest in dreams and the unconscious, health or service profession, dealings behind the scenes.

Meridian (or **Local Meridian**; from the Latin *medius*, middle, and *dies*, day): **1.** The GREAT CIRCLE specific to a given locality on the Earth's surface that is perpendicular to the HORIZON, intersecting it at its North and South Points, and passes through the ZENITH and NADIR (see CELESTIAL SPHERE; COSMOGRAPHY). The half of this circle that is above the horizon is the *upper meridian*; the half below is the *lower meridian*. As the Earth rotates, each heavenly body appears to rise in the east, reach its uppermost point in the sky (that is, *culminate*), and set in the west. By definition *culmination* always takes place on the upper meridian. A corresponding *lower culmination* occurs when an object reaches its lowest point below the horizon—that is, when it crosses the lower meridian.

The local meridian is also perpendicular to the CELESTIAL EQUATOR and passes through the celestial north and south poles (see COSMOGRAPHY). It should be distinguished from meridians of TERRESTRIAL LONGITUDE and meridians of RIGHT ASCENSION, both of which are also perpendicular to the celestial equator. The local meridian—or *the* meridian—is the local meridian of terrestrial longitude projected onto the celestial sphere. It can be considered stationary while meridians of right ascension rise in the east, coincide with it at culmination, and set in the west; or—taking the whole-Earth viewpoint—the meridian can be considered to move as the Earth spins from west to east, momentarily coinciding with a right-ascension meridian and going on to the next right-ascension meridian. Either way, the right-ascension meridian (expressed in hours, minutes, and seconds) that coincides with the local meridian is the local sidereal time (see TIME); when expressed in degrees, minutes, and seconds, it is the *RAMC*.

The point where the upper meridian intersects the ECLIPTIC is the MIDHEAVEN; the point where the lower meridian intersects the ecliptic is the IMUM COELI. In *quadrant* systems of HOUSE DIVISION, the meridian is one of the two axes of the birth chart, the other being the horizon; the meridian axis connects the cusps of the Fourth and Tenth Houses. The term *meridian* is sometimes improperly used to refer to the Midheaven or even to the whole of the Tenth House.

    2. The local terrestrial meridian (see TERRESTRIAL LONGITUDE).

Meridian Distance: The difference between the RIGHT ASCENSION of a planet and that of the MIDHEAVEN (the *RAMC*; see MERIDIAN).

Meridian System: See HOUSE DIVISION.

Metals: According to HERMETIC THEORY, every sign of the zodiac is traditionally associated with one or more metals, which are regarded as having an affinity with natives of that sign. Although there is some disagreement in the case of the signs ruled by the modern planets, the following list of correspondences is generally accepted:

Aries	iron, steel
Taurus	copper, brass, bronze
Gemini	mercury
Cancer	silver
Leo	gold
Virgo	mercury
Libra	copper
Scorpio	iron, steel, plutonium
Sagittarius	tin
Capricorn	lead
Aquarius	lead, uranium
Pisces	tin, platinum

Meteorological Astrology: See ASTROMETEOROLOGY.

Microcosm (from the Greek *mikros,* little, and *kosmos,* world): A little world; a miniature universe; hence, man or woman. The idea that human beings are a microcosm, or miniature version of the universe around them (the *macrocosm*), dates from the dawn of speculative thought in Greece. It can be traced from Heraclitus and Empedocles through Pythagoras, Plato, Aristotle, and the scholastic philosophers, to thinkers of the Renaissance and modern times. It is expressed in the Hermetic axiom "as above, so below." It is implicit in classical astrology, which teaches that the entire zodiac is mirrored in the human body, as well as in much of modern astrology, which shares its underlying assumption of the fundamental unity of the universe. (See HERMETIC THEORY.)

Middle Ages, Astrology in the: The end of Roman civilization saw a decline in astrology. The Church officially condemned it: the Council of Laodicea forbade priests to practice it, and the Council of Toledo threatened anyone who believed in astrology or divination with a curse. This position was confirmed by the councils of Braga, Agda, Orleans, Auxerre, Narbonne, and Reims.

    Legislation enacted by lay authorities was no less severe. Salic law, attributed to Pharamond, condemned astrologers along with fortune-tellers and casters of spells. Charlemagne also passed edicts against them, as did the last Carolingian kings. Nevertheless, astrology continued to flourish in Europe, thanks especially to Arab philosophers and to the Jewish Cabalists of Spain, who maintained the tradition of PTOLEMY. The harsh laws were rarely applied, at least in the case of astrologers, and over the years it became fashionable for every great lord to have his official caster of horoscopes. Gerbert of Auvergne, who became Pope Sylvester II on the eve of the year 1000, practiced astrology and other Hermetic sciences in which he was initiated in Cordova (see HERMETIC THEORY). His accession to the papacy coincided with a revival of astrology throughout the medieval West.

Among the great figures of this age were Michael Scot (1175–1234), translator of Aristotle from Arabic to Latin and astrologer to Emperor Frederick II; Guido Bonati (d. ca. 1300), adviser to the Ghibelline condottiere Guido de Montefeltro, who never fought a battle without consulting the stars; Cecco d'Ascoli, Italian poet and philosopher and favorite at the court of Florence before being burned for heresy in 1327; Lutbert Hautschild (1347–1417), abbot of Saint Bartholemew of Eeckhout and protegé of the duc de Berry, whose celebrated *Très Riches Heures* are decorated with astrological symbols; Jacques Coeur (1395–1456), who practiced astrology and alchemy; and Arnaud de Villeneuve (1235–1313), an authority on the Hermetic sciences who became rector of the University of Montpellier before running afoul of the ecclesiastical authorities. But the astrological thought of the Middle Ages is best exemplified by two great thinkers, Saint Thomas AQUINAS (1225–74) and Roger Bacon (1212–94).

The great scholastic philospher and theologian acknowledged the influence of the planets upon human destiny, but Aquinas' attempt to reconcile Aristotelian thought with Christianity led him to preserve the role of grace. Opposing a rigidly deterministic interpretation of astrology as inconsistent with the Christian doctrine of free will, he argued in *Summa theologica* that the stars exert a direct and essential influence on men's bodies but an indirect and accidental influence on their souls. This position would long be that of the many Dominicans who practiced astrology. (Many Franciscans, on the other hand, more influenced by Augustine than by Aristotle, openly admired the theories of Ptolemy, although Saint Augustine himself had fiercely opposed them.)

Roger Bacon, the English philosopher, scientist and writer whose encyclopedic knowledge embraced theology, mathematics, geography, astronomy, perspective, physics, alchemy, and the experimental method, was convinced that the movements of the planets influenced human behavior. At least two of his works, *De Secretis Operibus Naturae* and *De Notitia Coelestium*, contain astrological predictions. Bacon contributed original research on MUNDANE ASTROLOGY and developed the *theory of elections*, a method for determining a propitious moment to begin an enterprise by observing the configurations of the planets. Bacon made a distinction between two kinds of astrology, one legitimate, which is limited to studying the influence of the stars, and the other illegitimate, which he associated with witchcraft and magic.

Another astrologer, the Franciscan Giovanni di Fidanza (1221–74), who ranked Plato well above Aristotle, was beatified under the name of Bonaventura, which was given to him by Saint Francis himself. A leading medieval writer and mystic, Bonaventura was venerated during his lifetime and canonized after his death. Henceforth the legitimacy of astrology was no longer in question, even though the condemnations of the early Church councils were never repealed.

Midheaven (also **Medium Coeli**, Latin for "middle of the sky"; often abbreviated **MC**): In a horoscope, the point at which the upper MERIDIAN intersects the ECLIPTIC; the position of the Sun at local apparent noon (see TIME). The Midheaven is always directly opposite the IMUM COELI ("bottom of the sky") and forms the southern angle (northern angle for birthplaces in the Southern Hemisphere) and, in most systems of HOUSE DIVISION, the cusp of the Tenth House. It should not be confused with the *zenith*, the point directly overhead at a given location. Most tables of houses give the CELESTIAL LONGITUDE of the Midheaven either for every 4 minutes of local sidereal time or for even degrees at approximate 4-minute intervals. (See COSMOGRAPHY.)

In chart interpretation, the Midheaven represents the native's aspirations, ideals, and public image. The Midheaven–Imum Coeli axis is traditionally associated with the parents, the Midheaven relating to the parent who has the strongest influence on the native's values. The sign on the Midheaven, close aspects to the Midheaven, and the condition of the ruling planet of that sign all provide clues to possible choice of career or profession. Planets conjunct the Midheaven are considered to be of paramount importance both for career and for personality, a theory which has been borne out by the statistical work of Michel and Françoise GAUQUELIN. Transits to the Midheaven are associated with promotions, honors, changes of job, changes of residence, and other public events in the life of the native.

Midheaven House System: See HOUSE DIVISION.

Midpoint (also called **Half Sum**): In modern astrology, a point on the zodiac located halfway between two *primary points*, such as planets or angles, and obtained by finding the average of their celestial longitudes, that is, the sum of their longitudes divided by 2. For example, if Venus is at 10° Gemini and Mars is at 20° Leo, their midpoint is 15° Cancer. (They also have an *inverse*, or *opposition*, *midpoint* at 15° Capricorn.) The midpoint between Venus and Mars is written ♀/♂. If a planet *x* is located at the midpoint between Venus and Mars (*direct midpoint*) or in hard aspect to it (*indirect midpoint*), this information is written *x* = ♀/♂.

Astrologers who work with midpoints have found that they are sensitive points in a birth chart, and that patterns formed by midpoints and primary points reveal personality traits that may not be clear by the use of classical astrology alone. An example is the chart of Adolf Hitler, which (with Libra rising and Sun in Taurus) does not seem to furnish sufficient indication of his psychopathic and megalomaniac character. The sesquisquare between Uranus and Pluto accurately describes a violent temperament and a drive for power, but this aspect would ordinarily be overlooked, since it is common to an entire generation. However, as Geoffrey Dean points out, "in this case both planets are at the Sun/Moon midpoint and thus become central to the whole chart." Conjunctions or hard aspects formed to midpoints by transiting planets are believed to trigger events; German astrologers have developed this theory into a precise method of prediction.

The use of midpoints in astrology is not without historical precedent. They were used in the thirteenth century, especially by the school of Guido Bonati, and probably even earlier. Largely abandoned until the twentieth century, they were revived by the German astrologer Alfred Witte (1878–1943), founder of the UR-ANIAN SYSTEM, or Hamburg school, of astrology. Witte's techniques were further developed and refined by another German astrologer, Reinhold Ebertin (1901—), founder of the system known as COSMOBIOLOGY, into a sophisticated method of planetary interpretation.

Minor Aspect: See ASPECT.

Minor Planets: See ASTEROIDS.

Minor Progression: See PROGRESSION AND DIRECTION.

Modern Astrology: The body of current astrological doctrine does not form a coherent whole. This is another way of saying that astrology is not yet a science, in the modern sense of the word. If science is defined as a body of assumptions about the nature of the universe that are supported by evidence and on which there is general agreement, then astrology falls short of the mark. Ancient and venerable as it is as a human activity, it is still immature and undisciplined when judged by the rigorous standard of the scientific method.

Since the Renaissance, science has concentrated on data capable of measurement and has relegated questions of value, including speculations about human destiny, to theologians and philosophers. The rise of rationalism and materialism, the split between astronomy and astrology, and the banishment of astrology from the universities all helped to bring about a period of stagnation and demoralization for astrology from which it is only beginning to recover. For almost three centuries, few first-rate minds devoted themselves to a discipline that was discredited by the scientific and intellectual establishment. Few serious books were written, little or no research was undertaken, and astrologers worked in isolation and obscurity, their status reduced to that of fortune-tellers. Cut off from the mainstream of science, astrological doctrine tended to become fixed in a traditional mold. However, the incredible twentieth-century resurgence, which may be attributed partly to the rise of the social sciences, especially psychology, which has reinstated the study of human beings as a proper subject of scientific inquiry, has forced astrology out of its defensive conservatism. The current state of the art is chaotic and confusing, but it is also exciting and alive. At present writing, several schools of astrology dominate the scene.

The *traditionalist school* adheres rather closely to the principles of astrology as expounded by PTOLEMY in the second century and as developed until the decline of astrology in the late seventeenth and early eighteenth centuries. (It is the astrology of this 1,500-year period that is referred to in this book as classical, or traditional, astrology.) Traditionalist astrologers may recognize the necessity of redefining astrological terms to accommodate new cultural phenomena, but generally speaking they do not deviate significantly from the structure of classical astrology. For example, they may expand or refine the meanings of the signs, but they do not question the validity of the zodiac. At their best, traditionalist astrologers have helped to correct the gloomy determinism of much of medieval astrology that persists in such terms as *malefic, evil aspect, destroyer of life, hell of the zodiac*, and so on, and to shift the focus of astrology away from the prediction of events and

onto the description of character. In this they laid the groundwork for the work of the humanist and symbolist schools. The British are famous for producing competent astrologers with a solid grounding in tradition; distinguished examples of these British traditionalists are Alan LEO and Charles CARTER.

The French *symbolist school* came out of Freud's work on the unconscious and Jung's depth psychology. Jung wrote, ''It is clear that astrology has a great deal to contribute to psychology. But it would also be well for astrology to become aware of the existence of psychology, especially insofar as it deals with personality and the unconscious. I am almost certain that we have something to learn from astrology's language of symbols.''

In France the symbolists are helping to purify astrology of its mechanistic aspect, the rigid application of traditional formulas. The formal description of character is gradually giving way to a study of the unconscious that uses symbols in their modern psychoanalytic sense. According to this approach, a symbol is the only available means of expressing a complex emotional reality that cannot be clearly conceptualized. This school has enriched the traditional interpretation of the zodiac with new relationships between the signs and the complexes.

The American counterpart of the symbolist school is the *humanistic astrology* developed by Dane RUDHYAR. Like the French symbolists, humanistic astrologers see astrology primarily as a symbolic language that, if properly interpreted by a responsible astrologer, can provide insight into the human psyche. Also like the French symbolists, the humanists have been profoundly influenced by contemporary psychology, especially the ideas of Jung. For Dane Rudhyar, astrology is not a science but a "technique in human understanding." The humanistic approach to astrology is person oriented rather than event oriented. Humanistic astrologers see the planets as symbols of human functions rather than transmitters of physical influence and are not involved in the current movement to make astrology scientific.

The *scientific school* grew out of the work of Paul CHOISNARD and others who came to astrology from scientific backgrounds and resolved to rid it of imprecision and restore it to the level of a science. Known as COSMOBIOLOGY in Germany and Switzerland, where it is very popular, the scientific school assumes that there is a measurable physical relationship between the cycles of the celestial bodies and human behavior. It tries to incorporate the results of astronomical research into astrology and studies the influence of such celestial phenomena as solar flares, sunspots, lunations, or meteor showers on terrestrial phenomena.

The movement to reinstate astrology as a science has enlisted the aid of statistics. Early examples of the *statistical approach* are due to Paul Choisnard in the 1920s and Karl Krafft in the 1930s, but the first work that met the standards of orthodox research was that of the French statisticians Michel and Françoise GAUQUELIN, starting in the 1950s. While statistical studies have failed to confirm certain aspects of traditional astrology, they have provided experimental support for others and have opened up fruitful new areas for investigation, such as the HARMONICS of John ADDEY.

Both the symbolist (or humanistic) approach and the scientific movement represent reactions to traditional astrology: the symbolist school to its mechanical determinism and its overemphasis on prediction of events, and the scientific school to its imprecision, high level of disagreement on basic principles, and cavalier disregard for evidence. These two reactions have taken very different forms and tend to become polarized into two opposing camps.

Thus Rudhyar maintains that the truths of astrology are not empirical and rejects the scientific approach because "modern science is obliged to ignore the individualness of every living entity," whereas astrology "deals essentially with the individual." He argues that objective tests of astrology are meaningless; the real test of astrology is whether it helps to make people's lives more meaningful. Geoffrey Dean, the compiler of *Recent Advances in Natal Astrology: A Critical Review 1900–1976*, a monumental survey that attempts to introduce some order into the confusion of modern astrology, sees the matter differently. Dean points out that subjective benefit does not necessarily imply objective validity and concludes that "the current chaos in astrology is largely the result of a chronic infatuation with symbolism at the expense of reason. . . . This is because the majority of astrologers reject a scientific approach in favor of symbolism (based on dubious tradition), intuition, and holistic understanding."

While a certain amount of controversy is no doubt a sign of vitality, the tendency to polarization between these two groups shows that the 200-year-old rift between astrology and science is far from being healed. There is, however, a growing number of influential astrologers who see no reason why astrology should not be both humanistic *and* scientific, as it was before the split that took place in the Renaissance. Speaking at a recent conference of the National Council for Geocosmic Research, in Chicago, American astrologer Robert Hand acknowledged that he found himself in both camps and called for "a synthesis of the single point of view which ought to be the *only* point of view in astrology; and that single point of view is both humanistic and scientific." (See SIDEREAL ZODIAC; STATISTICS AND ASTROLOGY; URANIAN SYSTEM.)

Modern Planets (also called **Extra-Saturnian Planets** or **Trans-Saturnian Planets**): Uranus, Neptune, and Pluto, so called because of their comparatively recent discovery—1781, 1846, and 1930, respectively—in relation to the planets considered by classical astrology. (See EXALTATION; MODERN RULERS; NEPTUNE; PLUTO; RULERSHIP; URANUS.)

Modern Rulers: Uranus, Neptune, and Pluto are now generally considered to be the modern rulers of the zodiacal signs Aquarius, Pisces, and Scorpio, respectively (see RULERSHIP). Before the discovery of Uranus in 1781, rulership of Aquarius was assigned to Saturn; before the discovery of Neptune in 1846, rulership of Pisces was assigned to Jupiter; and before the discovery of Pluto in 1930, rulership of Scorpio was assigned to Mars. Thus Saturn, Jupiter, and Mars are now often referred to as the *traditional rulers,* or *corulers,* of those signs. The traditional rulerships were assigned by PTOLEMY on the basis of observed affinities between the signs and the planets. Modern rulerships have been assigned gradually over the years since the discoveries of the modern planets on the basis of accumulated evidence of their nature and influence. Some astrologers feel that the traditional and modern rulers "share" rulership of those particular signs. Others believe that since the modern planets have impinged on human consciousness, their influence has accelerated and that their rulership is therefore stronger and more relevant to our age. Still others feel that the whole rulership system, traditional and modern, lacks experimental support and is open to question. (See URANUS; NEPTUNE; PLUTO.)

Modes: See QUALITIES.

Monkey: The ninth sign of the Chinese zodiac, including all persons born between

February 2, 1908, and January 22, 1909 (earth)
February 20, 1920, and February 8, 1921 (metal)
February 6, 1932, and January 26, 1933 (water)
January 25, 1944, and February 13, 1945 (wood)

February 12, 1956, and January 31, 1957 (fire)
January 29, 1968, and February 17, 1969 (earth)
February 16, 1980, and February 5, 1981 (metal)

The messenger of Okuni-Nushi-No-Mikoto, Shinto god of sailors, the Monkey is a pleasant companion: vivacious, gay, witty, one of the most whimsical signs of the Chinese zodiac. Natives of the sign are also actors who excel at covering up their feelings. Their sincerity is often questionable; they are capable of bad faith and even of dishonesty when they think this is the only way they can achieve their ends. Endowed with an insatiable curiosity and a remarkable memory, they are a veritable storehouse of information, a quality that is a powerful advantage in their professional life. They are shrewd businesspeople and clever investors.

In love Monkeys are changeable, and as a result their romantic life is seldom happy. They often fall in love at first sight, but quickly tire of their conquests, for their critical sense cools their ardor. They are ambitious and may marry for money, breaking off the match when there is nothing more in it for them. However, when they succeed in controlling their negative tendencies, they can be charming people.

Compatible signs: Cat, Dragon, Monkey, Ox, Pig, Rat, Tiger.

Neutral signs: Dog, Serpent.

Incompatible signs: Cock, Horse.

Famous Monkeys include Simone de Beauvoir, Lord Byron, Bette Davis, René Descartes, Paul Gauguin, Mick Jagger, Timothy Leary, Amedeo Modigliani, John Milton, Grandma Moses, Charlie Parker,

Ezra Pound, Eleanor Roosevelt, Bertrand Russell, Baruch Spinoza, Elizabeth Taylor, Harry Truman, the United States of America, and Leonardo da Vinci. (See CHINESE ASTROLOGY.)

Moon (glyph ☽): The brightest celestial body after the Sun; the Earth's satellite, revolving around it in a little less than a calendar month (27 days 7 hours 43 minutes 11.5 seconds, called the *sidereal month*) and accompanying it in its annual revolution around the Sun. The Moon's diameter is 2,160 miles—a little over a quarter of the Earth's—and its mean distance from the Earth is 239,000 miles.

The Moon has no light of its own and shines only because it is illuminated by the Sun. Its changes in position in the course of its orbit around the Earth are accompanied by changes in appearance, which constitute the familiar phases of the Moon (see figure 47). The Moon is New when in conjunction with the Sun; at First Quarter when in first square to (or 90° east of) the Sun, when half its disk is illuminated; Full when in opposition to the Sun, when the Earth is between it and the Sun; and at Third, or Last, Quarter when in second square to (or 90° west of) the Sun, when half its disk still remains visible. The entire cycle from one New Moon to the next is called the *synodic month* and takes 29 days 12 hours 44 minutes 2.8 seconds (see CYCLE; LUNATION). Times for the quarter phases of the Moon are given on the sample page from an ephemeris, page 48.

Two other periods are associated with the Moon, the *draconic month* (27 days 5 hours 5 minutes 35.8 seconds), the interval between one conjunction of the Moon with its north node and the next; and the *anomalistic month* (27 days 13 hours 18 minutes 37.5 seconds), the interval between one *perigee* (closest approach to the Earth) and the next. Technically, the Moon does not revolve around the Earth; both Moon and Earth revolve around a common center of gravity 1,000 miles beneath the Earth's surface and 3,000 miles from its center.

In astrology, the Moon is regarded as neither BENEFIC nor MALEFIC, al-

though PTOLEMY classified it as benefic. It rules the sign of Cancer (see RULERSHIP) and is therefore in DETRIMENT in the opposite, Saturn-ruled sign of Capricorn. It is exalted in Taurus (see EXALTATION) and in FALL in Scorpio.

In chart interpretation the Moon stands for the emotions, the instincts, the unconscious, the mother, and women in general. Its qualities are receptivity, sensitivity, moodiness, instability, and change. It rules our animal nature and gut reactions; childbirth, infancy, and childhood; dreams, imagination, memory, conditioning, habits, the past; liquids, glands, secretions, the stomach; the anima, yin energy (yang energy is ruled by the Sun); private, daily, and domestic life; and the moods and tastes of the public. When afflicted, the Moon is associated with hypersensitivity and overreaction or difficulty getting in touch with one's feelings and inability to respond.

The following delineations are offered to show some of the ways the Moon may operate in the signs and houses. It should be remembered that they are merely suggestions and that their accuracy in any given case depends on the overall strength and condition of the Moon in relation to the chart as a whole, especially the aspects it forms with other planets and important points.

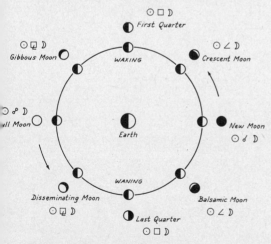

Figure 47. The phases of the Moon.

MOON IN THE SIGNS

Moon in Aries: impulsiveness, erratic emotions, independence, changeability, love of adventure, need for physical freedom.

Moon in Taurus: sensuality, possessiveness, loyalty, determination, obstinacy, need for security.

Moon in Gemini: curiosity, restlessness, literary ability, emotional instability, need for variety.

Moon in Cancer: sensitivity, psychic ability, sense of family, defensiveness, need for intimacy.

Moon in Leo: dramatic ability, creativity, love of pleasure, desire for control, need for attention.

Moon in Virgo: love of work, skepticism, perfectionism, orderliness, low self-esteem, need to be useful.

Moon in Libra: desire to please, love of beauty, self-effacement, indecisiveness, need to relate.

Moon in Scorpio: psychological insight, resourcefulness, reserve, desire for power, need to understand.

Moon in Sagittarius: salesmanship, idealism, broad perspective, love of travel, tendency to excess, need to be right.

Moon in Capricorn: high standards, sense of form, seriousness, economy, anxiety, need for approval.

Moon in Aquarius: originality, insight, inventiveness, eccentricity, need for community.

Moon in Pisces: dreaminess, impressionability, mysticism, gullibility, escapism, need to serve humanity.

MOON IN THE HOUSES

Moon in the First House: extreme receptivity, changeability, imagination, appetite, attachment to mother, emotional instability.

Moon in the Second House: unstable finances, artistic ability, psychological insight, need for financial security.

Moon in the Third House: emotional thinking, imagination, restlessness, literary ability, need for variety.

Moon in the Fourth House: strong attachment to home and mother, rich inner life, reclusive tendencies, changes of residence.

Moon in the Fifth House: romantic, dramatic personality, love of pleasure, love of children, many love affairs.

Moon in the Sixth House: concern with health and diet, frequent changes of employment, need to serve.

Moon in the Seventh House: emotional attachments to other people, changes of partner, psychic ability, need for relationships.

Moon in the Eighth House: intense emotional life, critical experiences, strong sexuality, consciousness of death, interest in the occult.

Moon in the Ninth House: strong religious convictions, desire for continuing education, love of travel.

Moon in the Tenth House: need for recognition, emotional attachment to the father, interest in art, changes of profession.

Moon in the Eleventh House: many friends, attraction to politics, turnover of friends, need for group activities.

Moon in the Twelfth House: love of solitude, sensitivity, mysticism, psychic ability, rich dream life.

Moon House System: See HOUSE DI-VISION.

Moon's Nodes: See NODES.

Morin, Jean-Baptiste (also known as **Morin de Villefranche** or **Morinus**; February 23, 1583, Villefranche, France–November 6, 1656, Paris): French physician, mathematician, and astrologer. After earning the degree of doctor of medicine at Avignon in 1613, he stopped practicing medicine to become astrologer to the duke of Luxembourg and then to the duc d'Effiat. In 1630 the king offered him the chair in mathematics at the Collège de France. He wrote many books, the most important of which is *Astrologia Gallica*, published in 1661. Considered the greatest astrologer of his time, Morin was astrologer to Cardinal Richelieu, whose death he predicted within 10 hours. He also predicted the exact dates of death of Louis XIII, Wallenstein, and Gustavus Adolphus. His major contribution was to modernize Ptolemaic astrology in the light of discoveries made in the seventeenth century. (See RENAISSANCE, ASTROLOGY IN THE.)

Morinus System: See HOUSE DIVISION.

Morrison, Al: See CHIRON; VOID OF COURSE.

Movable Signs (also called **Moving** or **Leading Signs**): An outmoded and confusing term for the CARDINAL signs, so called because they cause movement and initiate change.

Moving Signs: See CARDINAL.

Müller, Johann: See REGIOMONTANUS.

Mundane Aspect: An aspect measured along the celestial equator, in RIGHT ASCENSION; as distinguished from a zodiacal aspect, which is measured along the ecliptic, in CELESTIAL LONGITUDE. Mundane aspects are sometimes referred to as aspects *in mundo* (in the world) and zodiacal aspects as aspects *in zodiaco* (in the zodiac). Since the meridian is by definition at right angles to the horizon, a planet conjunct the Midheaven is in mundane square to a planet conjunct the Ascendant, even though the same two planets may be in zodiacal trine—that is, separated by 120° of celestial longitude. Mundane aspects are based on subdivisions of the earth's diurnal rotation on its axis and can only be computed on a horoscope cast for a given time and place, whereas zodiacal aspects are based on subdivisions of the planets' orbits along the ecliptic and can thus be computed without reference to a horoscope. Mundane aspects are ignored by most modern astrologers.

Mundane Astrology (from the Latin *mundus*, the world; also called **Judicial**, or **Political**, **Astrology**): The branch of astrology devoted to the study of planetary cycles and patterns as reflected in world events, cultural trends, and collective phenomena generally; as distinguished from *natal*, or *genethliacal*, *astrology*, which studies the birth charts of individuals. Undoubtedly one of the earliest forms of astrology, mundane astrology was practiced extensively in the days when princes consulted their soothsayers on the progress of their affairs.

Modern mundane astrologers seek to predict the future of states, nations, and societies from the movements of the planets, using various techniques. Some treat a state or a historical event such as a war as if it were a human being and cast a chart for it, using the adoption of a constitution, a declaration of hostilities, and so on, as its date of birth. Others try to predict the course of events from the birth charts of political leaders and monarchs, which are considered of great importance in judging the prevailing trends and developments for a nation. But mundane astrology properly speaking tends to relate the course of history to the motions of the planets without reference to the chart of an individual. Mundane astrologers study the planets' positions at the time of LUNATIONS, EQUINOXES, SOLSTICES, CONJUNCTIONS of the heavy planets, and phenomena such as ECLIPSES and COMETS.

In interpreting a mundane chart, the meanings of the planets and houses are somewhat different from those in a natal chart. To select only the most important delineations, the Sun may refer to heads of state, the

Moon to the people, Mercury to the intelligentsia and the press, Venus to diplomats and artists, Mars to military leaders, wars, and epidemics, Jupiter to the courts and the clergy, Saturn to law enforcement or scarcity, Uranus to the media, Neptune to charity, and Pluto to organized labor or crime. Similarly, the First House may refer to the body politic, the Second House to national wealth or resources, the Third House to domestic transportation and communication, the Fourth House to real estate and farming, the Fifth House to children and entertainment, the Sixth House to public health and the working class, the Seventh House to foreign policy, the Eighth House to the national debt, the Ninth House to overseas transportation and communication, the Tenth House to the chief executive, the Eleventh House to the legislative branch of government, and the Twelfth House to prisons or hospitals.

Mundane astrology also includes the analysis of broad cultural movements and religious ideas in relation to such slow cycles as the great astrological ages associated with the PRECESSION OF THE EQUINOXES and the cycles of the outer planets. Now, for example, the human race is in the throes of transition between the Age of Pisces, which was marked by the rise of Christianity, a religion of salvation, and the Age of Aquarius, which is thus far marked by the rise of technology but may indeed see the birth of a new religion more oriented toward the realization of the human potential (see AQUARIAN AGE; PRECESSIONAL AGE).

The planetary patterns accompanying this transition are dominated by the movement of Pluto, which is approaching its 1989 PERIHELION while accelerating in speed, having moved inside the orbit of Neptune in late 1978. According to Dane RUDHYAR, the entire solar system is now being "fertilized" by Pluto's galactic consciousness, a process whose fruits will begin to be evident during the next few decades.

Since 1940 Pluto has been receiving a sextile from Neptune, an aspect that will continue until 2030, moving from the signs of Leo and Libra to the signs of Aquarius and Aries. This 90-year aspect, the first part of the 492-year Neptune-Pluto synodic cycle, has been termed the *Long Sextile*. The last Long Sextile occurred during the European Renaissance and the beginning of the Protestant Reformation, a time characterized by the final collapse of the (Eastern) Roman Empire, the revival of classical culture, the discovery of the New World, and the invention of the printing press; in other words, a time of accelerated social change and vast broadening of consciousness. The period closed as the Reformation, by then irreversibly under way, brought the Renaissance to the masses with its message of the supremacy of the individual conscience.

The current Long Sextile, which began just before World War II, is characterized by the collapse of colonial empires, the emergence of the Third World and the renaissance of cultures long suppressed, the exploration of space, the proliferation of the media, the development of nuclear power, and the threat of nuclear or ecological extinction. Many astrologers predict that after a period of intense, painful trial during the 1980s, there will be a spiritual reawakening comparable to the Reformation. (See CYCLE.)

Mundoscope: See LOCATIONAL ASTROLOGY.

Music of the Spheres: According to the followers of the Greek mathematician and philosopher PYTHAGORAS (sixth century B.C.), an ethereal harmony produced by the movements of the planets along their orbits. The Pythagoreans believed that the intervals between these orbits, then thought to be concentric spheres, had a mathematical relationship that corresponded to the frequencies of the tones of the musical scale and that it was this relationship that accounted for the "music." The concept was developed by Johannes KEPLER (1571–1630) in his *Harmonices Mundi*, where he advanced the idea that each planet had its own specific rhythm. He asserted that microcosmic humans had an "instinct to perceive the harmonies of the celestial spheres, for a harmony exists only to be perceived. Light is not only emitted from the Sun but from the harmony of the whole."

Mutable: One of the three *qualities,* or modes, that characterize the signs of the zodiac, the other two being CARDINAL and FIXED. The mutable quality has been compared to wave motion in physics, or to information. The mutable signs of the zodiac (also called *common signs*) are the four signs that follow the fixed signs and precede the cardinal signs, namely, Gemini, Virgo, Sagittarius, and Pisces. The Sun transits these signs during the last month of a season, or the period of transition between one season and the next. Mutable signs are characterized by changeability, adaptability, and service; on the negative side, they are associated with instability and diffusion.

In classical astrology, the mutable signs were known collectively as the *mutable quadruplicity,* since there are four of them. They are also sometimes referred to as the *mutable cross,* since if planets in them are connected by straight lines, they form a cross. A *grand mutable cross* is a major configuration in which two pairs of opposing planets, all in mutable signs, are in square aspect to each other, forming a cross (see GRAND CROSS).

Mutual Aspect: An aspect between two transiting bodies, as distinguished from an aspect between a transiting body and a natal point; also, sometimes, an aspect between two planets, or between a planet and Sun or Moon, as distinguished from an aspect formed by a planet to a point such as Ascendant, Mid-heaven, Part of Fortune, node, and so forth.

Mutual Reception: A relationship between two planets each of which occupies the other's sign of election or EXALTATION (see ELECTION, SIGN OF). For example, if Mercury is in Pisces (ruled by Neptune) and Neptune is in Virgo (ruled by Mercury), Mercury and Neptune are said to be in mutual reception. If in this case Mercury and Neptune are also within ORB of opposition, their condition of mutual reception will both strengthen the aspect and help to offset its negative effects.

Mystic Rectangle: A MAJOR CONFIGURATION involving at least four planets in which a pair of TRINES is connected by a pair of SEXTILES, with OPPOSITIONS connecting all four corners. The configuration does not necessarily indicate mystical tendencies, though it sometimes does. Michael Meyer associates it with "an incredible capacity for sustained productivity" and "synthetic and integrative ability," since it combines the awareness of the opposition, the understanding of the trine, and the productivity of the sextile. An example is the birth chart of Madame Blavatsky, in which a conjunction of Moon and Venus in Libra trines a conjunction of Uranus and Jupiter in Aquarius, opposes Pluto in Aries, and sextiles the Sun in Leo, while Jupiter and Uranus are also opposing the Sun and in sextile to Pluto, and the

Sun and Pluto are in trine. The energy, ambition, will power, and volubility of the founder of the Theosophical Society can be seen in this powerful formation of six planets including both Sun and Moon and a Tenth-House Pluto. At her death, Blavatsky was acknowledged leader of a community numbering almost 100,000.

Nadi Astrology: A type of Indian astrology in which astrologers have vast collections of horoscopes, called *nadis,* which are erected and delineated in detail before—sometimes centuries before—the appearance of their clients. In other words, when the client locates a nadi astrologer, the astrologer has a large number of charts, one of which may be his. For reasons not as yet understood, these charts are said to be surprisingly accurate. (See INDIA, ASTROLOGY IN.)

Nadir: The point of the CELESTIAL SPHERE directly underneath any location on the Earth's surface, where the lower MERIDIAN intersects the PRIME VERTICAL; the opposite of *zenith.* The nadir should not be confused with the *Imum Coeli,* which is the point where the lower meridian intersects the ECLIPTIC. (See COSMOGRAPHY.)

Naibod Arc: See PROGRESSION AND DIRECTION.

Natal Astrology (from the Latin *natus,* born): The branch of astrology that studies the birth charts of individuals, traditionally referred to as *natives.* Natal astrology is based on the ancient belief that the positions of the planets at the birth of an infant provide information regarding his or her personality, character, and destiny. (See ASTROLOGY.)

Natal Chart: See BIRTH CHART.

Native: Literally, "one who is born"; in astrology, the subject of a nativity, or BIRTH CHART; also, one who was born "under" a particular sign—that is, one at whose birth the Sun, Moon, or Ascendant was in that sign—as, a "native of Aries."

Nativity: A horoscope cast for the time and place of a birth, as distinguished from an electional or horary chart; a BIRTH CHART.

Natural Astrology: Traditionally, the branch of astrology that studied (a) the motions of the heavenly bodies; and (b) their physical effects on the Earth as related to agriculture, weather conditions, earthquakes, and so forth. These two activities are now known as (a) ASTRONOMY; and (b) ASTROMETEOROLOGY. (See NELSON, JOHN.)

Natural Graduation System: See HOUSE DIVISION.

Natural House: The house that corresponds to a given sign of the zodiac, or to the planet that rules that sign. Since the twelve houses are subdivisions of a daily cycle that have their origin in the subdivisions of a yearly cycle, that is, the signs of the zodiac, each house corresponds to a sign in terms of its meaning, although it does not usually coincide with that sign in a given horoscope. Thus, the natural house of Aries, the first sign, or of Mars, its ruler, is the First; the natural house of Taurus, the second sign, or of Venus, its ruler, is the Second; and so on through the zodiac. Note that Mars has another natural house, the Eighth, since Mars is traditional ruler of Scorpio; Venus has another natural house, the Seventh, since Venus rules Libra as well as Taurus; and so on. Mars is said to be the "natural ruler" of the First and Eighth Houses; Venus the "natural ruler" of the Second and Seventh Houses, and so on.

A sign that appears on the cusp of its natural house is one indication of smooth functioning of the matters relating to that house. A planet occupying its natural house is thereby strengthened; such a planet is said to be accidentally dignified. (See DIGNITY.)

Natural Ruler: See NATURAL HOUSE.

Natural Year: See TROPICAL YEAR.

Navamsa: In Hindu astrology, the ninth harmonic (see HARMONICS). For centuries Hindu astrologers have used a technique of subdividing the natal chart into a number of subcharts, or *shodasavargas,* calculated by dividing each sign into segments. These subcharts correspond to the modern harmonic charts of ADDEY and others, but their interpretation usually involves complex RULERSHIP systems rather than aspects.

Negative Signs (also called **Feminine**, **Nocturnal**, or **Unfortunate Signs**): The signs of the earth and water triplicities, namely, Taurus, Cancer, Virgo, Scorpio, Capricorn, and Pisces. (See POLARITY.)

Nelson, John (b. 1903): American radio engineer, specializing in shortwave radio propagation analysis. From 1949 to 1971, as an employee of RCA Communications, Nelson systematically investigated the connection between shortwave radio disturbances and the heliocentric configurations of the planets. His discoveries ultimately enabled him to forecast such disturbances, sometimes months in advance, with an accuracy of over 93 percent. For example, he found that HARD ASPECTS linked with other aspects caused heavy static, but if a TRINE unconnected to this configuration came exact during the disturbance, the static died down with amazing rapidity. He also found that although an underlying pattern for radio signal degradation might be established by aspects and mid-point combinations between slower planets (Jupiter, Saturn, Uranus, Neptune, and Pluto), the static would be triggered by a faster planet (Mercury, Venus, Earth, or Mars) joining the configuration.

Although Nelson does not consider himself an astrologer, the implications of his findings for astrology—especially the traditional theory of aspects—are enormous. One of the principal arguments against the scientific validity of astrology has been that the gravitational effect of other planets on the Earth was small and that any other "action at a distance" was unsupported by evidence. Although Nelson has carefully noted that there is no proof that planetary aspects *cause* radio disturbance, he has shown a definite correlation between certain aspects and solar atmospheric behavior resulting in magnetic storms in the Earth's ionosphere. He feels that it is reasonable to assume that phenomena other than radio signal propagation—such as weather, or events in the biosphere—might also have fluctuations that can be traced to planetary patterns, but he leaves that question to future investigators. (See RELATIVITY, THEORY OF.)

Neptune (glyph ♆): The third largest planet in our solar system, discovered in 1846 as the result of the computations of the French astronomer Urbain Leverrier (1811–77) following observation of irregularities in the orbit of Uranus. Its diameter is 31,500 miles, its mean distance from the Sun is 2,797 million miles, and its SIDEREAL PERIOD is 164.79 tropical years. It has two known satellites.

In astrology, Neptune is not generally classified as either BENEFIC or MALEFIC. As with the other modern planets, there is no weight of tradition one way or the other. In any case, modern astrologers are moving away from these categories and coming to believe that the positive or negative value of planetary energies depends on the way in which they are used. Neptune was named after the Roman god who had dominion over springs and streams and who was later identified with the Greek Poseidon, god of the sea.

Regarded as a "higher octave" of Venus, Neptune has been assigned RULERSHIP of the sign of Pisces, whose traditional ruler was Jupiter. Hence it is in DOMICILE in Pisces and in DETRIMENT in the opposite, Mercury-ruled sign of Virgo. Opinion as to Neptune's sign of EXALTATION is divided. Some astrologers believe the planet to be exalted in Leo and therefore in FALL in Aquarius; others consider Cancer the exaltation and Capricorn the fall.

The attributes of the modern planets have been deduced by careful observation, over a period of time, of cultural trends that appeared around the time of their discovery. The late nineteenth and early twentieth centuries saw the development of anesthesia and chemotherapy; the birth of hypnotism and psychoanalysis; Freud's exploration of the unconscious and Jung's search for the collective unconscious; renewed interest in the occult and Oriental philosophy and the rise of spiritualism; the abolition of slavery, the end of serfdom in central Europe, and the rise of communism, internationalism, and pacifism; the publication of Einstein's theory of relativity and Max Planck's quantum theory, breaking down Newtonian concepts of space, time, and matter; the stream-of-consciousness movement in literature, cubism in art, and the birth of the cinema.

Neptune has come to be associated with those subtle forces that tend to undermine and dissolve the artificial barriers of time, space, egos, and nations. Its qualities are universality, impressionability, idealism, compassion, spirituality, self-sacrifice; nebulousness, formlessness, elusiveness, vagueness, invisibility, subtlety, secrecy, mystery, unreality, fantasy, illusion, and delusion. It rules international languages, mathematics, music, dance, poetry; imagination, inspiration, mysticism, meditation; loss, clouds, veils, film, movies, glamor, propaganda, subversion; liquids, poisons, chemicals, drugs; the unconscious, hypnosis, suggestion, dream states, trance, visions, mediumship, psychic phenomena, out-of-body states, the astral plane; hallucination, paranoia, obsession, and all states in which ordinary categories of perception break down, conditioning is transcended, and there is receptivity—for good or for ill—to other levels of reality. When afflicted, Neptune is associated with confusion, escapism, addiction, deception, masochism, neurosis, psychosis, and possession.

The following delineations are offered to show some of the ways Neptune may operate in the signs and houses. It should be remembered that they are merely suggestions and that their accuracy in any given case depends on the overall strength and condition of Neptune in relation to the chart as a whole, especially the aspects it forms with other planets and important points.

Since Neptune remains in a sign for approximately 13 years, its influence is more obvious on an entire generation than on a single individual. However, individuals in whose birth charts Neptune is angular or closely aspected by Sun, Moon, or Ascendant may be more closely attuned to its energy in that particular sign and may express it in a more conspicuous way. Bear in mind that the planet is simultaneously influencing the present, through cultural patterns and world events, and the future, through the children born during those years.[1] (See MUNDANE ASTROLOGY.)

NEPTUNE IN THE SIGNS

Neptune in Capricorn (1820–34): Metternich conservatism, political reaction; Mormonism; Hegel's glorification of the state. *Contributions of this generation*: Herbert Spencer's social Darwinism; belief in authority and tradition.

Neptune in Aquarius (1834–47/48): discovery of anesthesia; spread of hypnotism; first scientific attempt to understand the aura; beginnings of socialism and communism; antislavery movement; first electric telegraph. *Contributions of this generation*: William James's pragmatism; Émile Zola's humanitarianism; Paul Verlaine's revolution in poetic expression.

Neptune in Pisces (1847/48–1861/62): end of serfdom in central Europe, abolitionist movement in America; first undersea cable; rise of spiritualism (first séances at Fox farm in 1848); literary transcendentalism. *Contributions of this generation*: Henri Bergson and the *élan vital*, an antimaterialistic philosophy; the impressionists.

Neptune in Aries: (1861/62–1874/75): the Red Cross; the Geneva Convention; the Salvation Army; the founding of the Theosophical Society. *Contributions of this generation*: religious leaders and mystics, such as Sri Aurobindo, Mohandas Ghandi, Swami Vivekananda.

Neptune in Taurus: (1874/75–1887/89): idealism about the distribution of wealth: rise of philanthropy, socialism, syndicalism; Christian Science; founding of the English Society for Psychical Research (1882). *Contributions of this generation*: Albert Einstein, Harlow Shapley, Arthur S. Eddington, and the physical understanding of space, time, and the heavens; Keynesian economics.

Neptune in Gemini (1887/89–1901/02): imaginative leaps in science: quantum theory, relativity; experiments in telepathy; symbolist poetry with its emphasis on suggestion, imagination, and free verse. *Contributions of this generation*: Hitler and the use of propaganda; William Faulkner's elliptical style.

Neptune in Cancer (1901/02–1914/16): Freud's exploration of the unconscious, Jung's search for the collective unconscious; the revival of popular astrology; the work of Edgar Cayce. *Contributions of this generation*: idealization of home and tradition, ultranationalism.

Neptune in Leo (1914/15–1928/29):

the roaring twenties, wild speculation; exploration of the unconscious in art: Proust, Joyce, and stream of consciousness; rise of cinema, jazz, radio; invention of TV. *Contributions of this generation*: idealization of individualism; Norman Mailer, Timothy Leary, and Henry Kissinger.

Neptune in Virgo (1928/29–1942/43): Great Depression; rise of communism ("the religion of the working class"); discovery of penicillin, rise of chemotherapy and chemical adulteration of foods. *Contributions of this generation*: materialism, skepticism, idealization of work and duty, obsession with cleanliness; Martin Luther King, Jr. (breakdown of racial discrimination), Andy Warhol (pop art), Ralph Nader (consumer protection), Elvis Presley, Bob Dylan, and the Beatles (integration of folk music and rhythm and blues).

Neptune in Libra (1942/43–1955/57): establishment of the United Nations; decline of marriage and the rise of divorce; interest in Zen Buddhism; birth of rock 'n' roll. *Contributions of this generation*: "flower children," internationalism, belief in racial and sexual equality.

Neptune in Scorpio (1955/57–1970): emergence of the Beat Generation with the publication of *On the Road* (1957); breakdown of sexual taboos, explicit sex in films; widespread use of hallucinogenic drugs; renewed interest in the occult, spiritual teachings, reincarnation; hard rock and hippies; sex changes. This generation has not been heard from yet, but many of its members seem to lack the traditional attitudes toward sex and death and are drawn to the investigation of mysterious and psychic phenomena.

Neptune in Sagittarius (1970–84): breakdown of national boundaries by increased foreign travel; spread of Oriental religions in the West, rise of religious cults and gurus; teaching of meditation, astrology, and parapsychology in universities; social reform.

NEPTUNE IN THE HOUSES

Neptune in the First House: extreme impressionability, charm, glamor, charisma; acting ability, musical or mathematical talent; inspiration, idealism, otherworldliness; confusion, disorientation, poor sense of time.

Neptune in the Second House: talent for music, dancing, poetry, or mathematics; confusion regarding finances; tendency to dissipate one's resources.

Neptune in the Third House: dreamy, reclusive nature; mediumistic gifts; poetic imagination; idealization of childhood.

Neptune in the Fourth House: musical home; rich dream life; emotional instability; possibility of broken home.

Neptune in the Fifth House: artistic ability, love of the theater, romanticism, creative inspiration.

Neptune in the Sixth House: desire to serve humanity; lack of ego gratification in work; mysterious and undiagnosable health problems.

Neptune in the Seventh House: musical, poetic, or mathematical partner; ill or alcoholic partner; dissolving relationships; confusion, deception, or self-sacrifice in relationships.

Neptune in the Eighth House: interest in the occult, strange sexual patterns, possible celibacy or renunciation of sex.

Neptune in the Ninth House: interest in mysticism, idealism, spirituality, evangelism, fanaticism.

Neptune in the Tenth House: unusual profession; psychology, music, acting, or the arts; spiritual leadership; possibility of public disgrace or ruin, or martyrdom.

Neptune in the Eleventh House: unusual friendships, humanitarian causes, idealism, possibility of loss of friends.

Neptune in the Twelfth House: reclusive tendencies, sensitivity to other planes, rich inner life, active dream life, tendency to escapism, possibly through drugs.

New Moon: See LUNATION; MOON.

Newton, Sir Isaac (January 5, 1642, Woolsthorpe, Lincolnshire, England–March 31, 1727, Kensington, England): English scientist and mathematician, discoverer of the law of universal gravitation. According to Voltaire, Newton first conceived the idea in 1665 after seeing an apple fall in his garden. Study of KEPLER's third law of motion led him to the theory that the force between the Earth and the Moon must be inversely proportional to the square of the distance between them. The law

[1] For some of the delineations of Neptune in the signs we are indebted to the following: Robert Hand, *Planets in Youth* (Rockport, Mass.: Para Research, 1977); Marcia Moore and Mark Douglas, *Astrology, The Divine Science* (York Harbor, Me.: Arcane Publications, 1971); Frances Sakoian and Louis Acker, *The Astrologer's Handbook* (New York: Harper & Row, 1973).

Sir Isaac Newton. (The Bettman Archive.)

of universal gravitation is set forth in his *Principia Mathematica*, first published by the astronomer Edmund Halley in 1687. Its thesis is that every particle of matter in the universe attracts every other particle with a force that varies inversely as the square of the distance between them and directly as the product of their masses. This led him to the explanation of the flattening of the poles, the tilting of the Earth, and hence the PRECESSION OF THE EQUINOXES, the phenomenon first discovered by Hipparchus in the second century B.C. Newton is said to have invented both differential and integral calculus. He originated the emission theory of light; constructed a reflecting telescope; was warden of the mint and president of the Royal Society (1703–27).

As a young student of mathematics, Newton studied astrology. There is a famous anecdote, possibly apocryphal, that Halley once chided Newton for his interest in astrology, whereupon Newton is said to have replied, "I have studied the subject, Mr. Halley, and you have not." Although Newton's interest in astrology may have waned, he never repudiated it or intimated that any of the new scientific discoveries, including his own, had rendered it invalid.

90° Dial: See CHART FORM; HARMONICS; URANIAN SYSTEM.

Nocturnal Arc: See HOUSE DIVISION.

Nocturnal Planets (from the Latin *nox,* night): According to PTOLEMY, Moon, Venus, and Mars. The Moon and Venus were classified as nocturnal because they were FEMININE PLANETS, and the night was "more feminine because of its moisture and its gift of rest." Mars was classified as nocturnal by the principle not of affinity but of complementarity, so that its dryness would offset the moisture of the night. Later the term was extended to include those planets in a birth chart that were placed below the HORIZON. The term is seldom used in modern astrology.

Nocturnal Signs: In classical astrology, the FEMININE SIGNS: Taurus, Cancer, Virgo, Scorpio, Capricorn, and Pisces.

Nodal House System: See HOUSE DIVISION.

Nodal Line: See NODES.

Nodes (symbols ☊ ☋): Any pair of points marking the intersection of two planetary orbits, especially the orbit of the Earth (that is, the ECLIPTIC) and that of another planet or the Moon. Nodes are four-dimensional aspects: They express the range of all possible positions of two planets over

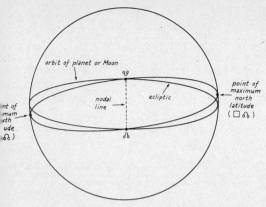

Figure 48. The celestial sphere, showing the intersection of a planetary orbit with the ecliptic.

time rather than relating their momentary position, as do ordinary aspects.

The *north*, or *ascending*, *node* of a planet or the Moon is the point where it crosses the ecliptic moving north (in the general direction of the north celestial pole—see COSMOGRAPHY); the *south*, or *descending*, *node* is the point where the body crosses the ecliptic moving south. The north node is directly opposite the south node, except in the case of geocentric planetary nodes (see "Planetary Nodes," page 206). The line joining the two nodes is called the *nodal line*; it represents the intersection of the two orbital planes (see figure 48).

At its node with the ecliptic, a planet (or the Moon) has a *celestial latitude* of 0°. It attains its greatest latitude when it is square to its node. Greatest north latitude occurs when the planet has moved 90° of CELESTIAL LONGITUDE beyond its north node; greatest south latitude occurs when it has moved 90° of celestial longitude beyond its south node.

Because of variations in the orbital

planes themselves, the actual positions of the nodes—the *true nodes*—move with some irregularity. Most astrologers rely on the positions averaged out over time—that is, the *mean nodes.*

LUNAR NODES

The points where the Moon's orbit intersects the Earth's orbit (the ecliptic) are known as the *lunar nodes.* The mean lunar nodes move backward through the zodiac at a rate of about 3' of celestial longitude per day; the complete RETROGRADE cycle of the nodes takes about 18.6 years. The true lunar nodes can move faster or slower than the mean rate; and they can move forward or backward. Since the south lunar node is always directly opposite the north lunar node, ephemerides give only the position of the north node, often at 3-day intervals. The sample page from the *American Ephemeris* on page 48 shows the daily positions of both the mean lunar node and the true lunar node.

When a New Moon occurs near either the north node or the south node, there is a solar eclipse; when the Full Moon occurs near the nodes (the Sun at one node, the Moon at the other), there is a lunar eclipse. The ancient names for the north and south nodes—*Caput Draconis* ("Dragon's Head") and *Cauda Draconis* ("Dragon's Tail"), respectively —refer to the notion that a gigantic celestial dragon was swallowing the Sun or the Moon at their respective eclipses.

The meaning of the nodes in astrology is a controversial subject on which comparatively little has been written, and almost all the existing literature focuses on the nodes of the Moon. The traditional view in both Western and Oriental astrology is that the north node is BENEFIC and the south node MALEFIC, although in modern Hindu astrology the tendency is to regard both nodes as malefic. (Indian astrologers treat the lunar nodes as actual planets by the names of Rahu [north node] and Ketu [south node].) In the West the ancients believed that the north node of the Moon partook of the nature of Venus and Jupiter and the south node partook of the nature of Mars and Saturn. Since the nodes are points rather than planets, they were not thought to have any true influence of their own, but to be significant when aspected by a planet. Thus a planet in close conjunction with the north node was believed to bring honors or wealth, whereas a planet at the south node would bring afflictions or poverty, according to the nature of the planet.

The German astrologers Alfred Witte, founder of the URANIAN SYSTEM, and Reinhold Ebertin, founder of COSMOBIOLOGY, have broken with Western tradition in minimizing the distinction between the north and south nodes and treating the two as a unit. The German school regards the nodes as the axis of associations, connections, and relationships. American astrologer Robert Hand agrees that the nodes are important in relationships, but maintains the distinction between north and south, finding that the north node is involved in forming relationships and the south node in dissolving them.

Some contemporary esoteric astrologers regard the nodes as clues to karmic relationships, past lifetimes, and the overall direction and purpose of the incarnation represented by the birth chart. Thus the sign on the south node is believed to represent qualities brought over from previous lifetimes, which may be valuable in themselves, but whose negative aspects need to be eliminated. The sign on the north node, on the other hand, is believed to represent qualities that need to be developed in the present lifetime, with the help of karmic friends and teachers who have that sign emphasized in their chart. According to this approach, the house in which the north node falls stands for the areas of experience in which the native will learn the important lessons of this lifetime, and the house in which the south node falls represents areas of experience he may have overemphasized and needs to put behind him. This view seems to accord with the ancient image of the dragon's head and tail, the north node corresponding to the mouth, or a point of openness and receptivity, and the south node to the anus, or a point of elimination and release.

PLANETARY NODES

The *heliocentric planetary nodes* are the points where two planetary orbits intersect, considered from the view-

Table 3. Positions of Mean Planetary Nodes (January 1, 1980).

| | Heliocentric | | Geocentric | |
	☊	☋	☊	☋
Mercury	17♉59	17♏59	27♑01	23♐59
Venus	16♊30	16♐30	21♒10	29♐49
Mars	19♉24	19♏24	7♈28	8♐29
Jupiter	10♋15	10♑15	10♋16	10♑05
Saturn	23♋30	23♑30	25♋04	22♑11
Uranus	14♊01	14♐01	12♊31	15♐12
Neptune	11♌33	11♒33	12♌29	10♒30
Pluto	19♋54	19♑54	20♋08	19♑35

point of the Sun. The heliocentric north node of a planet is always opposite its heliocentric south node. Heliocentric planetary nodes move forward through the zodiac at an extremely slow rate—about 1° per century.

The *geocentric planetary nodes* are the points where a planet's orbit intersects the ecliptic, considered from the viewpoint of the Earth. The geocentric north node and its corresponding south node are rarely exactly opposite each other, although the nodes of Saturn, Uranus, Neptune, and Pluto range close to opposition. The north and south nodes of Jupiter can vary as much as a sign from opposition. The north and south nodes of Mars can vary as much as two signs from opposition. The north and south nodes of either Venus or Mercury can have any aspect with each other, including conjunction. The geocentric nodes for planets outside the Earth's orbit oscillate around their corresponding heliocentric nodes. The geocentric nodes for Mercury and Venus, however, move forward through the zodiac at a varying rate, completing a revolution in about a year.

Table 3 lists the celestial longitudes for both heliocentric and geocentric planetary nodes for January 1, 1980.

Nodical Month: See DRACONIC PERIOD.

Nodical Period: See DRACONIC PERIOD.

Nonagesimal (or **Zenith Projection**): The point of the ECLIPTIC that is above the HORIZON and 90° from the ASCENDANT; the ZENITH projected onto the ecliptic by an AZIMUTH circle that passes through the north and south ecliptic poles; in the Equal House System of HOUSE DIVISION, the Tenth-House cusp. The nonagesimal should not be confused with the MIDHEAVEN, with which it rarely coincides.

Noon Date: See PROGRESSION AND DIRECTION.

Northern Angle: See IMUM COELI; MIDHEAVEN.

North Node: See NODES.

North Point: See HORIZON.

Nostradamus consulting the stars; anonymous popular engraving. (Photo by Larousse.)

Nostradamus (Latin name of Michel de Notredame; December 14, noon, St. Remy, France–July 2, 1566, Salon, France): French physician and astrologer. In 1555 he published a book of rhymed prophecies under the title *Centuries*, which has been frequently reprinted and is the subject of many commentaries. He correctly predicted the manner of death of Henry II of France, gained the favor of Catherine de Médicis, and was physician to Charles IX.

Notredame, Michel de: See NOSTRADAMUS.

Occult (from the Latin *occultus*, hidden): Hidden, mysterious, not comprehensible to the uninitiated. The occult arts (alchemy, astrology, magic, necromancy, geomancy, cartomancy, numerology, palmistry, and so on) were believed to be concerned with supernatural forces and the methods of bringing these under control. Some of these arts—for example, alchemy and astrology—were once widely regarded as sciences. Since the Renaissance, however, science has been concerned more with observation and measurement and less with meaning or value, and is wary of any association with the supernatural. If a body of knowledge is widely published and scientifically established, it ceases, by definition, to be occult, for science is that which is known. As this volume goes to press, the Western world is witnessing an extraordinary revival of the occult teachings, whose ultimate consequence may be the disappearance of the distinction.

Occultation: See ECLIPSE.

Octile: See SEMISQUARE.

Official Astrologers: In spite of the suspicion with which the majority of Christian theologians regarded astrology, most of the great personages of the Middle Ages and the Renaissance had their official appointed astrologers. Pope Sylvester II, the German emperor Frederick II, and Alphonse X of Castile are a few examples among many. In France, it was during the reign of the Valois that astrologers were first received at court. After Charles V, who took as his astrologer Thomas de Pisan, father of the poet Christine de Pisan, the post was created of "physician-astrologer to the king," which after the sixteenth century became simply "astrologer to the king." The Bourbons continued the tradition, and it was not until 1682 that Louis XIV abolished the post.

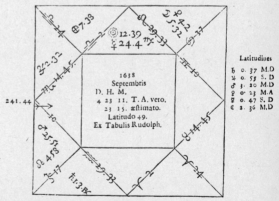

Horoscope of Louis XIV, cast by Jean-Baptiste Morin.

Although the day of official astrologers in Europe and the leading developed countries is long since past, political figures continue to consult astrologers and prophets. The role of Mme. de Thebes behind the scenes of the Third French Republic has often been cited, and in 1975 in Argentina, President Isabel Perón unleashed a storm of protest when she appointed a prime minister who practiced astrology. It also created a scandal when Mme. Sirimavo, prime minister of Sri Lanka, confided in astrologers, though politicians in the East in fact consult astrologers with great frequency. Of course, Theodore Roosevelt always kept a weather eye on his chart.

What is less well known is the use that was made of astrology during World War II. The most important Nazi leaders under Hitler—Rosenberg, Himmler, and Hess—frequently consulted astrologers. Goebbels was undoubtedly more skeptical about astrological predictions, but he did exploit them in the interests of propaganda against the Allied forces. After the mysterious flight into England of Hess, the German leader most closely connected in occult circles, on May 10, 1941, most of the leading German astrologers were arrested, including Reinhold Ebertin and the Swiss Karl Ernst Krafft. After a year's imprisonment Krafft was set to work by Goebbels's Propaganda Ministry preparing reports on the charts of the Allied military leaders. He died in the Oranienburg prison on January 8, 1945.

History has it that in April 1945 Goebbels and Hitler sent for some

The Astrologer Speaks: fresco in the Château de Villeneuve-Lembron. (Photo by Giraudon.)

astrological reports that had been prepared in 1933 based on the charts of the Führer and the German Republic of 1918. These reports correctly predicted the outbreak of war in 1939, the German victories until 1941, the subsequent reversals, the peace of August 1945, and the dramatic postwar recovery. The astrologer responsible for these remarkable predictions is not known.

In the Allied camp, astrology was also enlisted into the war effort. Louis de Wohl, a Hungarian astrologer who became an officer in the British Intelligence Service, prepared reports on the charts of the leading Nazis and anticipated the kind of advice they would be receiving from their astrologers.

Opposition (symbol ☍): One of the major aspects recognized by classical astrology, in which planets or important points are opposite each other in the zodiac, or separated by half the circle, an angle of 180°. The Sun and Moon form an opposition approximately once a month at the time of the Full Moon. Except for Mercury with Venus, or either with the Sun, any two planets can be in opposition.

The opposition has traditionally been regarded as MALEFIC, though less so than the SQUARE. This is presumably because whereas the square usually unites signs of different polarities—for example, fire and water, or earth and air—the opposition usually unites signs of the same polarity—for example, fire and air, or earth and water. Alan LEO points out that the opposition places planets in a diametrical relation and may be considered "an aspect of perfect hatred, or on the other hand, of perfect balance." Opposites may repel, but they also attract. There may be greater tension at the time of the Full Moon, but there is also greater illumination: Oppositions are associated with both separation and objectivity. Modern astrologers tend to view the opposition as a challenge to growth through awareness of conflicting tendencies within the personality.

People with oppositions tend to alternate between the extremes represented by the two planets and signs until awareness of their seesaw behavior leads to greater understanding. For example, a woman born at the Full Moon, with Sun and Moon in opposite signs and houses, will feel pulled in opposite directions. The dictates of the ego, her conscious goals and self-image, will sometimes be in conflict with her unconscious drives and emotional needs. But this very conflict and the tension it creates provide an opportunity for growth, and as the opposition is resolved, her life is enriched. A chart without oppositions lacks motivation and objectivity.

By transit, oppositions provide opportunities to work on existing problems by shedding light on them. Orbs for oppositions vary according to the speed of the planets involved; but according to some astrologers, orbs of 6° to 8° are acceptable, with even greater allowances in the case of faster-moving planets such as Mercury and the Moon (see ORB).

Opposition Midpoint: See MID-POINT.

Orb: A spherical space of variable size surrounding a planet or important point within which its influence or receptivity with respect to other bodies is considered to operate; the radius within which an aspect is considered to be potent. (For a discussion of the orbs allowed for the different planets and aspects, see ASPECT.)

Orbit: The path of a heavenly body, called a *satellite*, in its revolution around another heavenly body, called a *primary*. The Earth and the other planets in our solar system are satellites describing orbits around the Sun, which is the primary. The Moon is a satellite describing an orbit around the Earth, which in this case is the primary. The orbital path of a satellite is elliptical and can be measured either by its mean distance from the primary or by its revolutionary period. An intersection of the plane of one orbit with that of another is called a *node* (see NODES). The Earth's orbit is called the ECLIPTIC.

Outer Planets: See MODERN PLANETS.

Out-of-Sign Aspect: See ASPECT.

Ox (or **Buffalo**): The second sign of the Chinese zodiac, including all persons born between

February 19, 1901, and February 8, 1902 (metal)
February 6, 1913, and January 26, 1914 (water)
January 25, 1925, and February 13, 1926 (wood)
February 11, 1937, and January 31, 1938 (fire)
January 29, 1949, and February 17, 1950 (earth)
February 15, 1961, and February 5, 1962 (metal)
February 3, 1973, and January 23, 1974 (water)
January 21, 1985, and February 9, 1986 (wood)

Natives of the sign of the Ox are easy to get along with, even-tempered, courteous, and discreet. Their level-headed manner inspires confidence, and they immediately win the sympathy of others, although the intelligence behind their somewhat unpolished facade sometimes goes unrecognized. They say little, but they can be eloquent when their interests are at stake. Their calm appearance is not a pose; yet their wrath is terrible when they feel they have been betrayed. Precise, methodical, and stubborn in their professional life, they are just as successful in manual as in intellectual work. Their horror of waste is proverbial, and they make excellent managers.

On the emotional level, they can be tender and even sensual, but never romantic or passionate. Their reserve may cause them many disappointments in love and marriage.

Compatible signs: Cat, Cock, Monkey, Pig, Serpent.

Neutral signs: Dog, Horse, Rat.

Incompatible signs: Dragon, Goat, Ox, Tiger.

Famous Oxen include Aristotle, Johann Sebastian Bach, William Blake, Edgar Cayce, Charles Chaplin, Walt Disney, Adolf Hitler, Machiavelli, Margaret Mead, Napoleon, Pundit Nehru, Pierre Renoir, Peter Paul Rubens, Henry David Thoreau, Vincent van Gogh, Daniel Webster, and William Butler Yeats. (See CHINESE ASTROLOGY.)

Pallas (glyph ♀): One of the four largest ASTEROIDS, discovered in 1802. Zipporah Dobyns associates it with politics and the women's movement; Eleanor Bach with craftsmanship, discipline, and government.

Pancratos: See BYZANTIUM, ASTROLOGY IN.

Parallel (or **Parallel of Declination**): An aspect in which two planets have the same DECLINATION on the same side of the CELESTIAL EQUATOR. Opinion is divided on its significance, but most astrologers who use it consider it similar to the conjunction, but of longer duration. A *rapt parallel* is a parallel formed by primary direction (see PROGRESSION AND DIRECTION).

The parallel of declination was introduced by Placidus. Long neglected by astrologers, it is currently enjoying a revival. Cosmobiologist Reinhold Ebertin has written a major work on the subject and includes parallels and midpoints of declination in all his studies.

A *contraparallel* is an aspect in which the planets have the same declination on opposite sides of the celestial equator. Some astrologers consider contraparallels as similar to conjunctions, others to oppositions. (See ANTISCION.)

Paran (or **Paranatellon**): A relationship between two planets that simultaneously cross the same ANGLE or two different angles in a birth chart. For example, if Venus crosses the Midheaven at the same time that Saturn crosses the Ascendant, there is a paran between the two planets. It is not necessary that the planets be on the angles at the time of birth—only that they are coordinated to cross the angles simultaneously. If the crossing occurs *after* the birth moment, it will be by TRANSIT within a few hours and by *direction* (see PROGRESSION AND DIRECTION) sometime in the native's life. PTOLEMY took parans into account, and it is likely that they were used by the ancient Babylonians, who were observing the heavens constantly and—using the foregoing example—would not fail to notice that Venus was culminating at the same moment that Saturn was rising. Unfortunately modern astrologers, who consult EPHEMERIDES instead of observing the heavens, must, in order to find parans, use a rigorous procedure that involves spherical trigonometry and takes into account the two planets' CELESTIAL LONGITUDE, CELESTIAL LATITUDE, RIGHT ASCENSION, and DECLINATION. However, some reputable computer services offer as an option the calculation of parans.

Pars Fortunae: See PART OF FORTUNE.

Partial Eclipse: See ECLIPSE.

Partile Aspect: Exact aspect; the term is seldom used by modern astrologers.

Part of Fortune (also called **Pars Fortunae**, **Fortuna**, or **Lunar Ascendant**; symbol ⊕): The best-known of the Arabian parts and the only one widely used by modern astrologers. The Part of Fortune is obtained by adding the CELESTIAL LONGITUDES of the Moon and the Ascendant and subtracting from the result the longitude of the Sun. Thus the Part of Fortune represents the position of the Moon if the chart were rotated so that the Sun were on the Ascendant; in other words, the position of the Moon on a solar chart. According to some authorities, the Part of Fortune should be calculated along the celestial equator rather than the ecliptic, that is, in RIGHT ASCENSION. The Part of Fortune is represented by a circle containing a cross, a symbol that is also used by astrologers and astronomers to represent the planet Earth. De Vore points out that it is also the ancient Chinese symbol *Tien*, "field," which was used by the Egyptians to signify territory.

In chart interpretation Fortuna, as its name suggests, has long been regarded as extremely BENEFIC. PTOLEMY associates it with inherited wealth and general good fortune; modern astrologers see it as positive, but their approach is more psychological. Since it represents a relationship between Sun (ego), Moon (instinct), and Ascendant (body), it seems to be a point of integration. The activities associated with the sign and house in which it occurs are those in which the native will be able to express himself most easily and naturally and are consequently those in which he is most likely to succeed. (See ARABIAN PARTS.)

Penumbra: See ECLIPSE.

Penumbral Eclipse: See ECLIPSE.

Peregrine: Literally, "foreign"; term used to describe a planet occupying a sign where it is neither dignified nor debilitated (see DEBILITY; DIGNITY). It is seldom used today, except in HORARY ASTROLOGY.

Perigee (from the Greek *peri*, near, and *gaia*, Earth): The point in the Moon's ORBIT that is closest to the Earth, or the moment when the Moon is at that point. (See APOGEE.)

Perihelion (from the Greek *peri*, near, and *helios*, Sun): The point in a planet's ORBIT that is closest to the Sun, or the moment when the planet is at that point. (See APHELION.)

Period: See ANOMALISTIC PERIOD; DRACONIC PERIOD; SIDEREAL PERIOD; SYNODIC PERIOD; TROPICAL PERIOD.

Personal Points: In the URANIAN SYSTEM and COSMOBIOLOGY, a term used to refer to Sun, Moon, Midheaven, and Ascendant, which can be considered the most important and individualized factors in a birth chart.

Pig: The twelfth and last sign of the Chinese zodiac, including all persons born between

February 11, 1899, and January 31, 1900 (earth)
January 30, 1911, and February 18, 1912 (metal)
February 16, 1923, and February 5, 1924 (water)
February 4, 1935, and January 24, 1936 (wood)
January 22, 1947, and February 10, 1948 (fire)
February 8, 1959, and January 28, 1960 (earth)
January 27, 1971, and February 15, 1972 (metal)
February 13, 1983, and February 2, 1984 (water)

The Chinese do not regard the pig as the symbol of uncleanliness, as we do in the West. Natives of this sign are obliging, chivalrous, and tolerant, both good sports and good losers. However, their gentleness is only on the surface; underneath, they have authoritarian tendencies. Eager to increase their knowledge and omnivorous readers, they are born intellectuals. They are conscientious and hardworking and are very well suited to business, medicine, architecture, and literature.

They are often disappointed in love, the victims of their own naiveté. They must learn to choose their partners carefully. They make good mates and parents.

Compatible signs: Dog, Goat, Monkey, Ox, Pig, Rat, Tiger.

Neutral signs: Cat, Cock, Dragon, Horse.

Incompatible sign: Serpent.

The founders of the three great financial dynasties, Meyer Amschal

Rothschild, John D. Rockefeller, and Henry Ford, were all Pigs. Other famous Pigs include Otto von Bismarck, Oliver Cromwell, Mahalia Jackson, Henry Kissinger, Federico García Lorca, Ignatius Loyola, Marshall McLuhan, and Marcel Marceau. (See CHINESE ASTROLOGY.)

Piscean Age: See AQUARIAN AGE.

Pisces (glyph ♓): The twelfth sign of the zodiac, which the Sun transits during the last month of winter, from about February 21 to about March 20. The symbol for this sign is two fishes. Its POLARITY is negative, its element is water (see ELEMENTS), its quality is mutable (see QUALITIES), its modern ruler is Neptune, its traditional ruler is Jupiter (see RULERSHIP), and its NATURAL HOUSE is the Twelfth.

In Pisces the emotionality of water, the impressionability of mutability, and the mysterious influence of Neptune combine to produce a creature who seems not quite of this world, a "fish out of water." The two fishes of the glyph are swimming in opposite directions, duality compounded by ambivalence. Ever conscious that they are half body, half spirit, Pisceans—who include not only Sun-sign Pisceans, but all in whose charts the sign is emphasized—are pulled this way and that, never exactly sure where they are headed but vaguely sensing that this world is not their real home.

♓ Pisces

The image of the sea provides a clue to the Pisces personality. For even as all streams, rivers, and separate bodies of water must ultimately flow into the sea, so Pisces people long to merge their being with another's or lose themselves totally in mystical communion with nature or with God. Poets and dreamers, they relate to the ideal more easily than to the real. They may try to make the world come closer to their vision through dedicated service; they may express their rich dream life through art, music, or the theater; or they may choose to retreat into meditation, solitude, or drugs.

Pisces children are of all others the most addicted to make-believe and magic and will prolong the delightful fantasies of childhood as long as they possibly can. They also have a profound love and understanding of music, which seems to strike a sympathetic chord almost from birth and will be a source of joy and comfort all their lives. If they suffer more than other children from the pettiness of life, they also have a greater capacity for pleasure and for laughter.

Pisceans' ready sympathy, innocent credulity, and instinctive tendency to see the best in people usually bring them some difficult lessons before they learn to stand up for themselves and be more discriminating in their choice of companions. For most Pisces people, learning to say no is a lifelong project. Their instinct is to trust without question and to give without thought of reward. These traits are the root of their religious depth, but they do not always make for satisfying personal relationships. Yet the "unluckiness" and "self-undoing" sometimes associated with Pisces is by no means inevitable. They can do anything, once they learn to take responsibility for their lives. For as the last sign in the zodiac, Pisces' potential for spiritual evolution is unlimited. At their best, these natives are capable of being "in the world, but not of it": combining a profound understanding of the material world with an inspired vision of ultimate reality, a clear perception of time with an ecstatic experience of eternity.

In love, Pisces idealism and self-effacement can lead to some curious partnerships. They may be drawn to those who are handicapped in some way; or on the other hand, they may seek a solid support for their own delicate nature. They make highly erotic partners and devoted parents. Their most compatible signs are Cancer, Scorpio, Capricorn, and Taurus; Aquarius, Aries, Leo, and Libra are neutral; while Gemini and Sagittarius are apt to be difficult. With another Pisces, there may be a deep psychic bond. With Virgo, their polar opposite on the zodiac, there will be both tension and attraction; but ultimately the question of COMPATIBILITY can be answered only by careful comparison of two whole charts.

In work, Pisceans will seldom be motivated by a desire for money or fame. However, they often achieve both, especially in the arts, the theater, poetry, music, or dance. Although shy, their love of illusion and their ability to get inside other people's skins sometimes draws them to the stage or the cinema. Their openness to other levels of reality makes them temperamentally suited to mediumship, psychic healing, and the ministry. In hospitals, prisons, and social reform they can find a constructive outlet for their spirit of self-sacrifice. Their theoretical intelligence and universal perspective lend themselves to philosophy, astronomy, mathematics, and physics. This sign also has an affinity for professions involving the sea, fish, liquids (including wine and oil), chemicals, or plastics, all of which are ruled by Neptune. Famous Sun-sign Pisceans include W. H. Auden, Meher Baba, Elizabeth Barrett Browning, Michelangelo Buonarroti, Edgar Cayce, Frederic Chopin, Nicolaus Copernicus, Albert Einstein, Galileo Galilei, Victor Hugo, Henrik Ibsen, Jack Kerouac, Edna St. Vincent Millay, Michel de Montaigne, Ralph Nader, Vaslaw Nijinsky, Rudolph Nureyev, and Elizabeth Taylor. (See BIRTHSTONES; COLORS; DAYS OF THE WEEK; METALS.)

Placidean Arc: See PROGRESSION AND DIRECTION.

Placidus de Titus (1603, Perugia, Italy—1668, Pavia, Italy): Italian monk, mathematician, and astrologer; author of a revolutionary system of HOUSE DIVISION that bears his name and that is still used by the majority of modern astrologers. Placidus also developed the technique of primary directions (see PROGRESSION AND DIRECTION).

The widespread use of the Placidean system may be attributed in large measure to the inclusion of Placidus tables of houses in *Raphael's Ephemeris*, which until recently has been the most widely available ephemeris in the world. Many other systems exist, and that of Placidus has been severely criticized on mathematical grounds. Margaret Hone recalls that when it was first brought to England, the Placidus system was vehemently rejected. In 1711 a certain Gibson denounced it in scathing terms, saying, "Here is nothing but Egyptian Absoluteness [a reference to PTOLEMY] and the power of monkish infallibility, zealously urged in Billingsgate rhetorick, all of which I could not read without just abhorrence and detestation." (See RAPHAEL.)

Placidus System: See HOUSE DIVISION.

Planetary Cycles: See CYCLE.

Planetary Nodes: See NODES.

Planetoids: See ASTEROIDS.

Planets (from the Greek *planasthai,* to wander): In ancient astronomy and astrology, the seven seemingly "wandering" celestial bodies, as distinguished from the fixed stars—that is, Moon, Mercury, Venus, Sun, Mars, Jupiter, and Saturn; in modern astronomy, all celestial bodies with no light of their own, except comets and meteors, which revolve around the Sun of our solar system—that is, Mercury, Venus, Earth, Mars, Jupiter, Saturn, Uranus, Neptune, Pluto, and the ASTEROIDS. Modern astrologers usually retain the traditional terminology and refer to the Sun and Moon as planets, although they are well aware that the first is a star and the second a satellite. Hence they work with ten "planets": Sun, Moon, Mercury, Venus, Mars, Jupiter, Saturn, Uranus, Neptune, and Pluto; heliocentric astrologers include the Earth as well.

The planets whose orbits lie inside the Earth's orbit—Mercury and Venus—are called *inferior*; those whose orbits lie beyond the Earth's—Mars, Jupiter, Saturn, Uranus, Neptune, and Pluto—are called *superior*.

Planets are also classified according to their speed of motion. Those that take less than 2 years to complete their orbits around the Sun—Mercury, Venus, and Mars—are called *fast-moving*; those that take more than 2 years—Jupiter, Saturn, Uranus, Neptune, and Pluto—are called *slow-moving*, or *heavy*.

The ancients were aware only of those planets visible to the naked eye. Uranus was discovered in 1781 by William Herschel as a direct result of the invention of the telescope; Neptune was discovered in 1846 as a result of the calculations of the French mathematician, Urbain Leverrier, who had determined the

planet's position before it was observed in a telescope. A third modern planet, Pluto, was discovered in 1930 by Clyde Tombaugh as a result of research started in 1905 by Dr. Percival Lowell.

Astrology is based on the premise that the motions of the planets are related in a significant, observable manner to events on Earth. Astrologers believe that the positions of the planets at the birth of an individual constitute a symbolic language that provides important information about that individual's personality, character, and probable behavior. The basic elements of this symbolic language for each planet are its position with respect to the zodiac (sign), its position with respect to the Earth's rotation on its axis (house), and its position with respect to other planets (aspects).

Each planet is associated with one (and in some cases two) signs of the zodiac, which it is said to rule. When placed in such a sign, it is said to be at home, or in DOMICILE; when placed in the sign opposite its domicile, it is said to be in DETRIMENT. Each planet is also associated with a sign in which it is regarded as particularly powerful and where it is said to be exalted, or in EXALTATION. When placed in the sign opposite its exaltation, it is said to be in FALL.

The ancients classified the planets as *masculine*, *feminine*, and *androgynous*. Sun, Mars, Jupiter, and Saturn were masculine; Moon and Venus were feminine; and Mercury was androgynous. They also classified the planets as *benefic* (favorable), *malefic* (unfavorable), or *common* (neutral). Jupiter and Venus, known respectively as the *Greater Fortune* and the *Lesser Fortune,* were considered benefic; Saturn and Mars, known respectively as the *Greater Infortune* and the *Lesser Infortune,* were considered malefic; and Sun, Moon, and Mercury were regarded as common, that is, either benefic or malefic, depending on the aspects they formed with other planets. Many modern astrologers ignore these categories, which reflect an outmoded determinism, and regard the planets as representing different energies that can be either positive or negative, depending on how they are used.

The essential meanings of the planets, unlike many other parts of astrological doctrine, is an area of basic agreement among astrologers worldwide. These meanings have been confirmed to a remarkable degree by the statistical studies of Michel and Françoise GAUQUELIN and John ADDEY. (Further information about the planets is included under the individual entries for SUN, MOON, EARTH, MERCURY, VENUS, and so on.)

Platic Aspect (from the Greek *platykos,* broad): An aspect that is wide, but operative, that is, within ORB of exactitude; the term is seldom used by modern astrologers. (See PARTILE.)

Plato (ca. 427–347 B.C.): The greatest of the Greek philosophers. Plato is believed to have lived for a period in Egypt and to have studied astrology, among other occult teachings, with priests. Like PYTHAGORAS, Plato taught that man is a MICROCOSM, that is, a miniature version of the universe, to which he is connected by many affinities and correspondences, an idea that is inherent in classical astrology. (See GREEKS, ASTROLOGY AMONG THE.)

Pletho, Gemistus: See BYZANTIUM, ASTROLOGY IN.

Plotinus (A.D. 205?–270): Roman philosopher, the most important of the Neoplatonists. Plotinus was born in Egypt and studied at Alexandria, an ancient center for the teaching of Egyptian alchemy, astrology, magic, and medicine. Plotinus believed in astrology but argued against a fatalistic interpretation of celestial influence. The Neoplatonists of Alexandria were chiefly responsible for the survival of serious astrology in the West.

Pluto (glyph ♀ or ♇): The most remote known planet of our solar system, discovered in 1930 by Clyde Tombaugh as a result of research started in 1905 by Dr. Percival Lowell. Pluto is remarkable for the eccentricity of its orbit, which sometimes comes inside Neptune's and has an inclination to the ECLIPTIC of 17°9'. Its diameter is probably no greater than 4,000 miles, its mean distance from the Sun is 3,670 million miles, and its SIDEREAL PERIOD is 248.4 tropical years.

In astrology, Pluto is not generally classified as either BENEFIC or MALEFIC. Like the other modern planets, Uranus and Neptune, Pluto is seen as representing a powerful transforming energy whose positive or negative value depends on the way it is used. Pluto bears the name of the Greek god of the underworld, counterpart of the Roman Dis.

Regarded as a "higher octave" of Mars, Pluto has been assigned RULERSHIP of the sign of Scorpio, whose traditional ruler was Mars. Hence it is in DOMICILE in that sign and in DETRIMENT in the opposite, Venus-ruled sign of Taurus. The sign of Pluto's EXALTATION has not been determined; some astrologers believe it will prove to be Aquarius, which would place its FALL in Leo.

The attributes of the modern planets are deduced by careful observation, over a period of time, of cultural trends that appear around the time of their discovery. Some of the most important events of the 1930s were the rise of Nazism and fascism in Europe; the discovery of atomic energy; the laboratory perfection of television equipment and the rise of mass media; the growing public acceptance of psychoanalysis; and the sudden prevalence of cancer. Astrologers are beginning to associate Pluto with a subtle but powerful underground force that lies dormant within various collective systems and bursts forth volcanically at a given moment: the power of the masses and the collective unconscious; the invisible power of the atom; the power of the unconscious, forcing to the surface repressed memories locked within the cells; the dark, proliferating force of cancer that works insidiously within the body until it is diagnosed.

Pluto's qualities are power, elimination, latency, eruption, annihilation, transformation, renewal, regeneration. It rules atomic, cellular, and collective phenomena; the masses, mass movements, the media, especially television; networks, chains; the collective unconscious, mob psychology, anonymity, crowds; gangs, terrorism, fascism, holocausts, genocide; cataclysms, volcanoes, land mines, submarines; atomic energy, nuclear fission, cell division; physics, chemistry, synthetics, plastics; cancer; birth, death, rebirth; sexuality, the orgasm, the *kundalini*, psychic energy, the chi; healing, purging, cleansing, recycling; the return of the repressed, therapy, bioenergetic therapy; psychic healing, the occult, and ESP. When afflicted, Pluto is associated with compulsion, a drive for power, a need for control, repression, and violence.

If the kind of power Pluto represents seems destructive, this is probably because it is so new—or has so recently impinged on our consciousness—that the human race has not yet learned to understand or control it. Like the underworld after whose lord it was named, the realm of Pluto inspires the fear of the unknown. But the unknown may hold help as well as horrors. Thus Pluto rules not only death but the transcendence of death: reincarnation, communication with the dead, and immortality.

The following delineations are offered to show some of the ways Pluto may operate in the signs and houses. It should be remembered that they are merely suggestions and that their accuracy in any given case depends on the overall strength and condition of Pluto in the chart as a whole, especially the aspects it forms with other planets and important points.

Because of its highly eccentric orbit, Pluto's period of transit is variable: It may spend from 12 to 31 years in a sign. Its impact is more obvious on an entire generation than on a single individual. However, individuals in whose birth charts Pluto is angular or closely aspected by Sun, Moon, or Ascendant may be more closely attuned to its energy in that particular sign and may express it in a more conspicuous way. Bear in mind that the planet is simultaneously influencing the present, through cultural patterns and world events, and the future, through the children born during those years.[1] (See MUNDANE ASTROLOGY.)

PLUTO IN THE SIGNS

Pluto in Scorpio (1735/36–1746/47): excavation of Herculaneum (sister city of Pompeii); first successful appendectomy (1736). *Contributions of this generation*: inventors James Watt and Joseph Guillotin, astronomer William Herschel, revolutionaries Patrick Henry and Thomas Paine.

Pluto in Sagittarius (1746/47–1762): the skeptical philosophy of David Hume reduces all cognition to ideas and impressions and undermines the notion of causality. *Contributions of this generation*: the candid naturalism of Goya; the antirationalism of Goethe and Blake, precursors of the romantic movement.

Pluto in Capricorn (1762–78): Rousseau's *Social Contract* undermines the authority of the state; British trade laws stir American colonists to rebellion. *Contributions of this generation*: Malthus's law of population and scarcity; John Dalton's understanding of the atomic structure underlying nature.

Pluto in Aquarius (1778–97/98): French Revolution; Industrial Revolution underway in Britain; first steam engine; Thomas Paine's *Rights of Man*; Kant's philosophy lends validity to scientific observation. *Contributions of this generation*: Shelley's atheism; Michael Faraday's work on electromagnetism; Samuel Morse's invention of the first magnetic telegraph.

Pluto in Pisces (1797/98–1822/23): Romantic movement challenges Age of Reason; invention of the steamboat. *Contributions of this generation*: transcendentalists Alcott, Emerson, and Thoreau; the tragic vision of Pushkin; the humanity of Victor Hugo; the melancholy of Poe; the renunciation of Kierkegaard; the dark romanticism of the Brontës; the morbid sensibility of Baudelaire.

Pluto in Aries (1822/23–1851/53): first railroad; Greek War of Independence; Belgian independence from the Netherlands; social reforms in Britain. *Contributions of this generation*: rebels such as Ulysses S. Grant, Henrik Ibsen, Leo Tolstoi, Emily Dickenson, Émile Zola.

Pluto in Taurus (1851/53–1882/84): prosperity; *Realpolitik*; skepticism, materialism; rise of Marxism; building of first subway; discovery of petroleum; agrarian reform. *Contributions of this generation*: the Curies and the radioactive decay of matter; Max Planck and the confusion between matter and energy.

Pluto in Gemini (1882/84–1912/14): breakthroughs in communication;

development of aircraft; development of psychoanalysis; discovery of X rays; explicit sex in literature. *Contributions of this generation*: James Joyce and D. H. Lawrence and the exploration of the psyche in the novel.

Pluto in Cancer (1912/14–1937/39): rise of new dictators who stress glory of the homeland; isolation of the nuclear family; female suffrage; bottle feeding. *Contributions of this generation*: high respect for the "establishment"; deep unconscious ties to home, mother, and country; sexual guilt, breast fetishism, nationalism; drive to accumulate material things as an expression of emotional insecurity.

Pluto in Leo (1937/39–1956/58): collapse of the British and French colonial empires; rise of new nation states; growth of the entertainment industry; introduction of television to the market (1945). *Contributions of this generation*: the "hippies"; the pleasure principle, "be here now," Woodstock nation, drugs, sexual freedom, sanctity of the individual, life as theater; the Beatles, Bob Dylan, and the renaissance in popular music.

Pluto in Virgo (1956/58–1971/72): health food movement; growing power of labor unions; introduction of psychedelic drugs; new methods of birth control. This generation has not been heard from yet, but they are being influenced by the prevalent ideas of natural healing, concern for the environment, conservation of resources, and the antinuclear movement.

Pluto in Libra (1971/72–1983/84): resumption of diplomatic relations between U.S. and China; birth control, rape, and abortion legislation; euthanasia legislation; radical changes in marriage and relations between the sexes, consciousness-raising groups, the Equal Rights Amendment, equal opportunity laws, the gay rights movement, encounter and dialogue therapies.

PLUTO IN THE HOUSES

Pluto in the First House: powerful personality, psychic or healing ability, connection to collective unconscious, potential for self-transformation, sexual orientation, reclusive tendencies.

Pluto in the Second House: resourcefulness, drive to acquire material things, transformation of values, talent as healer or psychic.

Pluto in the Third House: penetrating mind, psychological insight, intense communication, lonely childhood, probing of early experiences.

Pluto in the Fourth House: strong attachment to home, mother, and the land; deep unconscious drives, potential for radical self-transformation, possibility of much repression and armoring.

Pluto in the Fifth House: compulsion to create, powerful bonds with children, intense sexuality, great capacity for pleasure.

Pluto in the Sixth House: compulsive worker, vocation as healer, obsession with health, diet, or cleanliness.

Pluto in the Seventh House: charisma, possibility of influencing large numbers of people, attraction to powerful people, tendency to be dominated in relationships.

Pluto in the Eighth House: interest in the occult, powerful personality, healing powers, strong sexuality, intense experiences, strength in crisis, understanding of death.

Pluto in the Ninth House: intellectual leadership; drive to learn, travel, or teach; spiritual transformation, religious fanaticism.

Pluto in the Tenth House: strong public image, charisma, dominating father, immoderate ambition, understanding of power, crises in career, spectacular comebacks, authoritarian tendencies.

Pluto in the Eleventh House: drive to transform society, tendency to dominate friends and groups, group therapy, attraction to communal living.

Pluto in the Twelfth House: intense inner life, therapy, psychic ability, reclusive tendencies, power behind the scenes, celibacy or secret affairs.

Polarity: One of the basic ways in which signs are classified; a sign's polarity is either *positive* or *negative*. The fire and air signs belong to the positive polarity; the water and earth signs to the negative polarity. The order of the signs through the zodiac is one of alternating polarity—that is, every positive sign is followed by a negative one, and vice versa. Signs of the positive polarity are characterized by extraversion and activity; those of the negative polarity by in-

troversion and receptivity.

The polarities are sometimes referred to as *masculine* and *feminine*, after PTOLEMY, who also called them *diurnal* and *nocturnal*, and *fortunate* and *unfortunate*. "An alternating order was assigned to [the signs] because day is always yoked to night and close to it, and female to male. Now as Aries is taken as the starting-point . . . and as the male likewise rules and holds first place, since also the active is always superior to the passive in power, the signs of Aries and Libra were thought to be masculine and diurnal. . . ."

The sexism implicit in Ptolemy's terminology—especially his identification of masculine with fortunate and feminine with unfortunate—is rapidly falling out of style. In 1947 de Vore wrote, "For some untenable reason, the ancients deemed the negative signs to be unfortunate. . . . Nevertheless it can readily be seen that for objective results, public acclaim, and personal glamor, the fire and air signs hold a certain advantage over the more self-contained and introspective earth and water signs." And Margaret Hone, writing in 1951, gives the *coup de grâce* to this antiquated notion: "The word negative . . . does not carry the somewhat derogatory meaning now given to it conversationally. People with more strength of earth and water in their charts have a receptivity from which they can again give out. They may therefore gain what the self-expressive person is too busy to notice."

Political Astrology: See MUNDANE ASTROLOGY.

---

[1] For some of the delineations of Pluto in the signs we are indebted to the following: Robert Hand, *Planets in Youth* (Rockport, Mass.: Para Research, 1977); Marcia Moore and Mark Douglas, *Astrology, The Divine Science* (York Harbor, Me.: Arcane Publications, 1971); Frances Sakoian and Louis Acker, *The Astrologer's Handbook* (New York: Harper & Row, 1973).

Porphyry System: See HOUSE DIVISION.

Posited (from the Latin *ponere*, *positum*, to place): Placed; as of a planet in a house.

Positive Signs (also called **Masculine**, **Diurnal**, or **Fortunate Signs**): The signs of the fire and air triplicities, namely, Aries, Gemini, Leo, Libra, Sagittarius, and Aquarius (see POLARITY).

Precessional Age (or **Astrological Age**): The length of time it takes for the VERNAL POINT to move backward through one constellation of the sidereal zodiac, as a result of the "wobble" of the Earth's axis about the ecliptic pole, or approximately 2,150 years. A precessional age is approximately one-twelfth of the time it takes for the vernal point to precess through the entire zodiac, which is 25,800 years, known as the *precessional year*. (See PRECESSION OF THE EQUINOXES.)

The precessional ages have a striking relevance to the history of civilizations, especially their religious orientation. Margaret Hone speculates that the Leonian Age (about 10,000 B.C.) may have coincided with the legendary "golden age" of Sun worship; the Cancerian Age (about 8000 B.C.) may have been the time of the great flood and Moon worship; the Geminian Age (about 6000 B.C.) probably saw the development of writing and was definitely characterized by the worship of twin gods. There is considerable existing evidence that the Taurean Age (about 4000 B.C.) was characterized by bull worship (the biblical "golden Calf") and by the building of pyramids and temples. The Arian Age (about 2000 B.C.) was a time of exploration and conquest, when Jewish ritual included the sacrificial offering of lambs. Mithras, the Persian god who had been the "Sacred Bull," became the Slayer of the Bull, while the Assyrian god Ashur, formerly "Great Bull," became a Martian god of war. The Greeks venerated Pallas Athene, dressed in armor with ram's horns on her helmet, and Roman soldiers wore ram's horns on their uniforms.

The dawn of the Piscean Age at the beginning of the Christian era represented the beginning of a new zodiacal cycle, a new precessional year. The Piscean Age coincides with the Christian era, and Christian religion is permeated with Piscean symbolism. The early Christians identified themselves by the fish; Christ chose fishermen for his disciples, calling them "fishers of men"; Christianity emphasizes the value of altruism, suffering, and otherworldliness—all Piscean ideals.

As humankind approaches the year A.D. 2000, the decline or transformation of many of the values and institutions of Western civilization seems to indicate that the world stands on the threshold of a new age (see AQUARIAN AGE).

Precessional Year: See PRECESSION OF THE EQUINOXES.

Precession of the Equinoxes: The continuous shift of the EQUINOXES backward through the SIDEREAL ZODIAC, as a result of the slow revolution of the Earth's axis of rotation

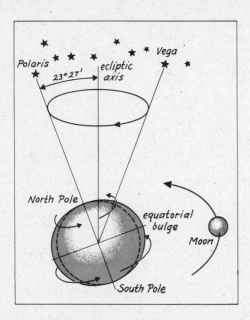

Figure 49. Precession of the equinoxes. The magnetic effect of the Moon on the Earth's equatorial bulge causes the Earth's rotational axis to revolve around the ecliptic axis, which in turn causes the phenomenon of precession.

about the ecliptic pole, itself caused by the gravitational attraction of the Sun and Moon on the Earth's equatorial bulge (see figure 49). The phenomenon of precession is said to have been discovered by the Greek astronomer Hipparchus in 130 B.C., but recent findings of archeoastronomy strongly indicate a knowledge of precession in preliterate peoples millennia before Egyptian civilization.

Because of precession the Earth's North Pole is oriented toward different stars in different epochs. For the past several centuries the North Star has been Polaris. The Earth's axis is pointed at a spot less than a degree from that star in 1980 and will point

most directly at it in A.D. 2095, after which time it will gradually recede. Over the millennia there have been many North Stars: α Lyrae (Vega) about 12,200 B.C., τ Herculis about 10,000 B.C., ι Herculis about 7300 B.C., ι Draconis about 4500 B.C., α Draconis (Thuban) about 2700 B.C. (see EGYPT, ASTROLOGY IN), β Ursae Minoris (Kochab) about 1000 B.C., α Ursae Minoris (Polaris) about A.D. 2000; and there will be many more. At present the Earth's South Pole is not oriented toward any star, but in other epochs there have been and will be South Stars, some of them quite a bit brighter than Polaris.

One complete revolution of the vernal equinox through the entire zodiac of constellations takes about 25,800 years, a span of time known as the *precessional year,* or *great year.* The time it takes for the VERNAL POINT to move backward through one of the twelve constellations is approximately 2,150 years, a period known as a *precessional age,* or *astrological age.* Each precessional age has been given the name of the constellation where the vernal point occurred. Thus the period when the vernal point occurred in Aries (about 2000 B.C. to the time of Christ) is known as the Age of Aries, or the Arian Age. The following period, (from the time of Christ to the present) in which the vernal point occurred in the constellation of Pisces, is known as the Age of Pisces, or the Piscean Age. At the present time the vernal point occurs somewhere between the bright stars in the constellation of Pisces and those in the constellation of Aquarius. The uncertainty is due to the fact that the constellations, unlike the signs of the zodiac, are of unequal size and have no clearly defined boundaries. They are simply groupings of unrelated stars, the boundaries of which were established by astronomers in 1930 for their own convenience.

The precession of the equinoxes has been a favorite weapon of critics of astrology, from Voltaire to twentieth-century astronomers. The argument runs that due to precession, which astrologers are presumed to ignore, the signs of the TROPICAL ZODIAC no longer express the "real" positions of the planets; that is, an Aries is no longer an Aries, but really a Pisces, and so on. The fact is that astrologers have been aware of the phenomenon of precession since before the time of PTOLEMY. They would reply that the signs of the zodiac do not pretend to coincide with the constellations, which have no natural integrity or special reliability as a frame of reference. In a vast sea of space in which all the bodies are constantly shifting at varying rates of speed, the zodiac is a frame of reference based on the most important celestial event in terms of life on Earth: the intersection of the Sun's apparent path with the CELESTIAL EQUATOR at the two points that mark the change in seasons for the planet. The 30° segment of the ecliptic that follows the Sun's position at the spring equinox is Aries; the 30° segment that follows that is Taurus, and so on. Thus the signs of the zodiac are relative references; and they situate a planet or point in relation to the equinoxes rather than in relation to the CONSTELLATIONS, with which

they have nothing in common but their names. (See AQUARIAN AGE.)

Precision: The amount of exactitude in a statement of measurement. The degree of precision increases with the number of *significant figures* used. For example, 12°51′22″ (six significant figures) is more precise than 12°51.4′ (five significant figures), which in turn is more precise than 12°51′ (four significant figures). Astrologers are often misled by the extremely precise values usually given in an EPHEMERIS or TABLE OF HOUSES, erroneously assuming that maintaining this level of precision in chart calculation will make the chart more accurate. In fact, no greater accuracy can be obtained by employing calculations that are more precise than the least precise value entering the calculations. This least precise value is generally the BIRTHTIME, which at best is rounded to the nearest minute.

Unless the birth second is recorded from a clock synchronized with government-broadcast time signals, the calculated local sidereal time (see TIME) should be rounded to the nearest minute. Interpolation for time in the table of houses, which ordinarily presents cusps at 4-minute intervals, should therefore be figured in nothing more precise than quarter intervals. A minute of time amounts to a difference of 15′ of CELESTIAL LONGITUDE on the MIDHEAVEN and can make a difference of up to 27′ on the ASCENDANT at the birth latitude of New York City, 40′ at the latitude of London, and 50′ at the latitude of Edinburgh. Thus, precision finer than rounding to the nearest degree on house cusps is questionable and depends on latitude and sidereal time; at best no greater precision than the nearest quarter degree should be used.

A minute of time amounts to a difference of 30″ to 36″ of celestial longitude in the Moon's position; clearly any precision finer than the nearest minute of longitude—for example, figuring the Moon's position as 8°33′41″ Taurus—is meaningless when the birthtime has been rounded to the nearest minute. On the other hand, each minute of time amounts to a difference of only 2.3″ to 2.6″ of longitude in the Sun's position; therefore, precision to the nearest tenth of a longitude minute for the Sun—for example, rounding the Sun's position to 18°21.6′ Cancer—is still relevant and is certainly helpful in calculating a solar return.

TERRESTRIAL LONGITUDE and LATITUDE are also often used with excessive precision. Listings for these coordinates are accurate for some central location in a city or town, such as the city hall or main post office; but big cities stretch over several miles, and the actual birthplace may be as much as 15 miles from the central location. (The same may be true of small-town births, which may actually have occurred in outlying rural areas.) However, even when the precise coordinates are not known, the resulting error is negligible compared with the imprecision deriving from birthtimes rounded to the minute. For example, a distance of 5 miles east or west of London's official longitude of 0W05 will only make a difference of 7′ of longitude, or 28

seconds of time. A difference of 5 miles north or south is slightly more than 4′ of latitude. The resulting difference on the Ascendant is not as great as that resulting from a 1-minute difference in time. In fact, even when extremely precise terrestrial coordinates for the actual place of birth are known, they will not render the chart more accurate if the birthtime has been rounded to the minute. Longitude and latitude rounded to the nearest quarter degree are sufficiently precise. Interpolation for latitude in the table of houses, like interpolation for time, should be figured for quarter intervals.

On the other hand, a case can be made for calculating with whatever precision is available so that when one attempts to rectify the birthtime, one will have a clear idea of one's starting point. In other words, if the place at least is known accurately, then one only has the dimension of time to worry about. (See RECTIFICATION.)

For appropriate precision in calculating with birthtimes more vague than to the minute, see CHART CALCULATION.

Pre-Columbian Astrology: The vandalism of the early conquerors and the excessive zeal of such missionaries as Father Landa, who burned the Mayan library of Yucatán, are responsible for the rarity of ancient documents on the astrology practiced by the Aztecs and Mayas. However, thanks to people like Fray Antonio de Marchena, who accompanied Christopher Columbus on his second voyage, and above all José d'Acosta,

Mayan observatory in Yucatán, Mexico. (The Bettman Archive.)

a sixteenth-century Spanish missionary, we have some indication of Pre-Columbian astrology. In addition, archaeological findings such as the recently discovered solar observatory in Chaco Canyon, New Mexico, indicate that the early inhabitants of the American continent had a detailed and sophisticated knowledge of celestial cycles.

Early American astrologers had several zodiacs. The first contained twelve signs, like the European zodiac, with which it has a symbolic correspondence. The names of the signs that have survived are the Splendor of the Lamb (Aries), the Powerful Male (Taurus), the Joined Stars (Gemini), the Sleeping Snake (Cancer), the Return of the Lance of the Hidden and Rampant Lion (Leo), the Divine Mother (Virgo), the Ladder (Libra), the Eager Stag (Capricorn), the Age of Waters (Aquarius). The names of the signs corresponding to Scorpio, Sagittarius, and Pisces are not known.

However, an older zodiac based on the sacred year was very widely known. The secular year, which consisted of 365 days, was divided into 18 months of 20 days each, to which there were added 5 so-called "useless" days. Each day of the year was devoted to a different divinity, whose feast was accompanied by numerous sacrifices. The sacred year, which consisted of 260 days, was divided into 20 months of 13 days each based on a zodiac attributed to the god Quetzalcoatl.

Bernardino de Sahogun, a Spanish Franciscan monk and contemporary of d'Acosta, lived in Mexico, where he learned the language of the inhabitants and recorded their customs. He was able to shed some light on this zodiac, although it is still impossible to determine the beginning and end of each sign.

The Swordfish, the first sign of the sacred year, was extremely benefic, bringing honors and wealth. The second, the Jaguar, was much less auspicious. The third, the Stag, was ambiguous, good or bad according to the day of birth. The fourth, the Flower, indicated an unhappy life; it was usually the sign of women who went into prostitution. The fifth, the Reed, endowed the native with an unstable character. The sixth, Death, was less macabre than its name would indicate; during the time ruled by this sign it was forbidden to beat one's slaves under pain of being enslaved oneself. The seventh, Rain, a sign of ill omen, corresponded to the time during which criminals were executed. Natives of the first day of this sign were doomed to celibacy. The eighth, the Creeper, was no cause for rejoicing; although it foretold the birth of many children, none of them could hope to live beyond the first years of adolescence. The ninth, the Snake, was just the opposite, happy and prosperous. The tenth, the Rock, was a sure indication of competence. The eleventh, the Monkey, granted the highest honors, but only at the price of a premature death. The twelfth, the Leopard, bestowed the gift of perfect health. The thirteenth, Movement, was a neutral sign, neither good nor bad, whose meaning had to be clarified by the observation of lunar eclipses. The fourteenth, the Dog, was particularly auspicious, although it was during this period that judges pronounced death sentences. The fifteenth, the House, was the most unfortunate of all, whereas the sixteenth, the Vulture, distributed all manner of felicity. The seventeenth, Water, caused a neurasthenic temperament, while the eighteenth, Wind, incited to treason. The nineteenth, the Eagle, was not to be trusted, for its destiny was slander. The twentieth, the Rabbit, was industrious and economical.

According to Alexandre VOLGUINE, one of the few contemporary astrologers who have compiled the scattered information on Pre-Columbian astrology, it was the day of birth within the sign, rather than the sign itself, that was significant. For example, the ninth day of each sign was distinctly unfortunate; the third as well as the last four were favorable; the fourth and the seventh were neutral.

Mayan astrology was essentially religious. The planets, like the constellations of fixed stars that the Sun passed through in the course of its annual cycle, were part of Pre-Columbian mythology. Max-Pol Fouchet, who has written a scholarly study on the subject, writes, "The Bacabs,

gods of the four cardinal points, the gods and goddesses of the Sun (Kinich Aham), the Moon (Ixchel), the Rain (Chac), Death (Ahpuch), and the Polar star (Xaman Ek), made up a vast pantheon to which divinities from other places were often welcomed. . . . The world was composed of thirteen upper heavens and nine lower heavens, each of which was ruled by a divinity. These gods without number, great or small, good or bad, lived with the Maya, and presided over every moment of their lives."

Prenatal Chart: See CONCEPTION CHART.

Prenatal Epoch: See CONCEPTION CHART.

Primary: See ORBIT.

Primary Arc: See PROGRESSION AND DIRECTION.

Primary Direction: See PROGRESSION AND DIRECTION.

Primary Point: An important or SENSITIVE POINT in a birth chart, such as the position of a planet, angle, node, or the Part of Fortune; as distinguished from a MIDPOINT, a point located halfway between two primary points.

Prime Vertical: The GREAT CIRCLE passing through the EAST POINT, ZENITH, WEST POINT, and NADIR. Since it is perpendicular to both the HORIZON and the MERIDIAN, it defines the third dimension to a location on the Earth's surface. The prime vertical coincides with the 90° azimuth circle in the east and the 270° azimuth circle in the west. Some systems of HOUSE DIVISION use the prime vertical as the reference circle, dividing it into twelve equal sectors and projecting the divisions onto the ECLIPTIC to determine the house cusps. (See AZIMUTH; COSMOGRAPHY.)

Prodome, Theodore: See BYZANTIUM, ASTROLOGY IN.

Progression and Direction: Two closely related systems for timing events or predicting future conditions for a given individual based on the motions of the Earth and other planets in the days following (and sometimes preceding) birth. In both systems the positions of the planets, Ascendant, and Midheaven in the natal chart are moved forward (or backward) in time according to a given formula.

For example, in *secondary progressions* (sometimes called secondary directions), the system most widely used by modern astrologers, the formula is "a day for a year." This means that each day following birth is regarded as equivalent to a year in the life of the native, and the positions of the planets on the thirtieth day after birth, for example, as well as the aspects they form with natal planets, are regarded as symbolic of conditions during the thirtieth year. In *primary directions*, on the other hand, the formula is "a degree for a year"; that is, a degree of RIGHT ASCENSION is regarded as equivalent to a year in the life of the native. According to this system, the number of degrees a planet or point must

travel in order to form an exact aspect with a natal planet is translated into years of age in the life of the native.

Progression is based on the actual orbital motions of the planets along the ECLIPTIC, whereas direction is based on the apparent motions of the planets as a result of the Earth's rotation on its axis. Thus in progressions, the bodies move at different rates of speed and sometimes in different directions (that is, they can be RETROGRADE), whereas in directions, the bodies move at the same rate of speed and in the same direction.

There are three main types of progressions: *secondary,* or *major, progressions; tertiary progressions;* and *minor progressions.* These three types represent ratios between the three basic motions of the Earth: its daily rotation on its axis; its annual revolution around the Sun; and its monthly revolution, with the Moon, around their common center of mass, which is about 3,000 miles from the Earth's center—a period of 27.32 days.

In secondary progressions, a day in the ephemeris is considered equivalent to a year of life, a ratio of 1 to about 365. (The exact ratio used by most modern astrologers is 1 to 365¼, based on the solar day. However, two outstanding technical astrologers of modern times, Cyril FAGAN and L. E. JOHNDRO, used the sidereal day, giving a ratio of 1 to 366¼.)

In tertiary progressions, a day in the ephemeris is considered equivalent to a lunar period, a ratio of 1 to 27.32. In minor progressions, a lunar period is considered equivalent to a year of life, a ratio of 27.32 to 365, or 1 to 13.368.

It will be seen that planets progressed by the secondary method move relatively slowly, yielding fewer aspects than those formed by the faster-moving tertiary and minor progressions. However, those aspects that are formed are generally considered to be more significant, just as transits of the slower-moving outer planets are considered more significant than those of the faster-moving inner planets. The method of tertiary progressions was developed in the twentieth century by the German astrologer Edward Troinski.

Finally, bodies may be "regressed" as well as progressed. In *converse secondary progressions,* a day *before birth* in the ephemeris is considered equivalent to a year of life. These converse directions are regarded as significant, but less potent.

The calculation of secondary progressions is greatly simplified by the use of the *Adjusted Calculation Date* (*ACD,* sometimes called Noon Date, a confusing expression that should be avoided). To find it, one translates the difference between the birthtime and the time given in the ephemeris from hours and minutes into months and days. Secondary progressions are based on the formula "a day for a year." Since 24 hours are considered equivalent to 12 months, it follows that 2 hours are equivalent to 1 month, 120 minutes are equivalent to 30 days, and 4 minutes are equivalent to 1 day.

For example, let us find the ACD for a birth occurring September 11, 1950, at 2:24 P.M. GMT. Assuming that we are using a midnight ephemeris, this is 14 hours 24 minutes after the prior midnight. But 14 hours cor-responds to 7 months, and 24 minutes corresponds to 6 days; so the ACD is 7 months and 6 days prior to the birth date, or February 5. If we wish to find the progressed positions of the planets for a date during the thirtieth year, we count 30 days after birth date in the ephemeris—that is, October 11, 1950. The positions listed for that day are the progressed positions for February 5, 1980. To calculate their positions for dates other than the ACD, find each planet's daily motion, divide by twelve, multiply by the number of months between the ACD and the desired date, and add or subtract that interval to or from the ACD. In the case of converse progressions, one works with the converse ACD, which is found by adding instead of subtracting the correct interval from the birth date.

The progressed positions of the planets for a given date are sometimes entered on an outer wheel of a natal chart like transits, for comparison with their natal positions; but sometimes the astrologer calculates a new chart, called the progressed horoscope. To find the progressed Ascendant, one can either find the local sidereal time (see CHART CALCULATION) for the day that corresponds to the year in question or one can add to the natal Midheaven a value known as the *solar arc.* The solar arc is the amount of longitude the Sun has traveled between the birthday and the day that corresponds to the year for which the planets are being progressed. To find the solar arc for the thirtieth year, for example, simply subtract the Sun's longitude on the birthday in the ephemeris from the Sun's longitude 30 days later in the ephemeris. In calculating a progressed Ascendant, many astrologers use the latitude of birth, but some use the latitude of the place the native now resides, as in solar and lunar returns.

Secondary progressions are based on the theory that there is a meaningful relationship for the human psyche between the Earth's diurnal rotation on its axis and its annual orbit around the Sun. Thus the motions of the planets in the days following birth and the aspects that the transiting planets form to the natal planets in those postpartum days are believed to represent the native's inner development in the corresponding years. For example, in July 1925 Margaret Mead's natal Sun at 23°57′ Sagittarius had moved by progression to 18° Capricorn, where it was exactly conjunct natal Ascendant and Jupiter and closely applying to a conjunction with progressed Saturn. The Sun represents the creative self, the Ascendant the physical body, and Saturn, responsibility and duration; in addition, Saturn is the ruler of Mead's chart. This was the time that she first set sail for Samoa, thus beginning her career as an anthropologist. The configuration of progressed planets at the outset of this adventure indicates that this young woman was launched on a voyage that would take her far; that although only twenty-three, she had found not only herself but her life's work.

There are three main types of directions: *primary directions* (also called *primary arcs, equatorial arcs,* and *Placidean arcs*), which are measured along the CELESTIAL EQUATOR in right ascension; *solar arc directions*, which are measured along the ecliptic in CELESTIAL LONGITUDE; and *solar declination arc directions*, which are measured in DECLINATION. To illustrate all three types, imagine that it is the first day of spring in the Northern Hemisphere, with the Sun at exactly 0°00′ Aries, and that it is true local noon, so that the Midheaven is also at 0° Aries. Now let 10 days pass. In that time the Sun will have moved 9°02′ along the equator by primary arc and 9°50′ along the ecliptic by solar arc, and its declination will have increased from 0°00′ to 3°54′ north. These are the three arcs that can be added to all bodies in order to direct them. Of the three methods, primary directions are the most difficult to calculate and depend for their accuracy on a precise birthtime; an error of 4 minutes can throw off predictions by as much as a year. For these reasons they are often neglected by modern astrologers. However, solar arc directions are easy to calculate and unaffected by errors in the birthtime; they are widely used by modern astrologers, especially in Europe.

In solar arc directions, the solar arc is added to all the planets, but not to the Ascendant or Vertex. The method of finding the progressed Ascendant has already been described; the progressed Vertex is found by adding the solar arc to the Imum Coeli, using the result as the Midheaven, and looking up the Ascendant for the colatitude of the birthplace (see VERTEX).

The difference between the natal and the progressed Ascendant for the birth latitude is called the *Ascend-*

ant arc; the difference between the natal and progressed Vertex for the birth colatitude is called the *Vertical arc.* All bodies may be directed in turn by these two arcs, in declination as well as in longitude; these methods are known as *Ascendant arc directions* and *Vertical arc directions.* It is also possible to move bodies backward in time by primary, solar, and declination arc; these methods are known as converse directions.

Radix directions are a form of solar arc directions in which the Midheaven, Sun, and planets are moved forward at the rate of 0°59′8⅓″ per year, which is the Sun's mean diurnal motion, known as the *major,* or *Naibod, arc.* The Moon is moved forward at the rate of 13°11′ per year, which is its mean diurnal motion, known as the *minor arc.*

Symbolic directions are a form of directions used by Charles CARTER based on formulas that have no apparent basis in astronomy. The exception, according to Charles JAYNE, is the formula by which the Midheaven, Sun, and planets are moved forward at the rate of ¼° per year, which represents the extra quarter of a day in both the sidereal and the tropical year.

The concept of direction is at least as old as PTOLEMY. De Vore points out that ancient astrologers did not have access to written ephemerides, and progressing or directing planets was a way of obtaining approximate information. The technique of primary direction was expounded by Ptolemy and further developed in the seventeenth century by PLACIDUS DE TITUS. Because of their mathematical rigor and their dependence on exact birth information, primary directions have been largely abandoned as a predictive tool in favor of transits, progressions, solar arc directions, and the SOLAR RETURN. However, precisely because of their exactitude, directions are a potentially important tool for astrologers; and with the advent of modern calculators and computers, it is once again practicable to put these often neglected methods to empirical test. Existing texts on directions include Simmonite's *Arcana,* Pearce's *Textbook of Astrology,* De Luce's *Complete Method of Prediction,* and Jayne's *Progressions and Directions.*

Promittor (archaic **Promissor**): Literally, "one who promises"; in classical astrology, a planet that promises good or ill according to its sign, house, and aspects in the natal chart and fulfills that promise when another planet or important point, called a SIGNIFICATOR, forms an aspect to it by progression, direction (see PROGRESSION AND DIRECTION), or TRANSIT. The distance the significator must travel to form an aspect to a promittor is called the *arc of direction.* The terms are used mainly in directions and in horary astrology. (See HORARY ASTROLOGY.)

Psellus, Michael Constantine: See BYZANTIUM, ASTROLOGY IN.

Psychoanalysis: The therapeutic method developed by Sigmund Freud; its concepts and terminology are often used by modern astrologers in interpreting birth charts. It is generally agreed that the unconscious

and dream life are ruled by the Moon
and Neptune; the ego, or conscious
self, corresponds roughly to the Sun;
and the superego is ruled by Saturn,
and to some extent the Midheaven.
Saturn also governs the reality principle and repression. The sex drive
and aggression are ruled by Mars,
and the sexual energy itself by Pluto.
The id seems to partake of both
Moon and Mars, and to some extent
the Imum Coeli. Neurosis and psychosis are associated with HARD AS-
PECTS, especially when numerous or
when involving the Sun or Moon.

Ptolemy, Claudius (A.D. 100–178):
Greek astronomer and astrologer
who lived in Alexandria. Ptolemy
was one of the greatest scholars of
antiquity, with an encyclopedic
knowledge that embraced mathematics, geography, music, optics, and
the art of making sundials. In his
Mathematiké Syntaxis, which the Arabs called the *Almagest,* he not only
catalogued three hundred new stars
but gave an explanation of the motions of the planets that was generally accepted until the sixteenth century. According to the so-called
Ptolemaic system, which developed
and systematized the ideas of previous thinkers, especially Appolon-
ius and HIPPARCHUS, the Earth was
the fixed center of the universe
around which the Sun, stars, and
planets revolved in concentric orbits
called spheres. This geocentric conception, which was attacked by COP-
ERNICUS, does not invalidate Ptolemy's astrological ideas; in astrology
what matters is not the actual positions of the planets in the sky but the

Claudius Ptolemy Inspired by Astronomy: sixteenth-century German engraving illustrating
Reisch's *Margarita Philosophica.* In the left fore-
ground is an armillary sphere. (Photo by Viol-
let.)

angular relationships they have from
the viewpoint of Earth.

Ptolemy's main astrological work
is the *Tetrabiblos,* a treatise in which
he compiled the knowledge of the
ancients and tried to make it into a
unified whole. He classified the aspects, established the system of rulership, and explained the fundamen-
tals of judgment. He also attempted
to explain how astrology works in
terms of the astronomy and physics
of his day. The fact that his understanding of celestial dynamics was
limited to APPARENT MOTION led him
to some curious contradictions; and
his RULERSHIP system, based on the
theory of the ELEMENTS, now seems
somewhat arbitrary. His theory of
POLARITY inspired de Vore to com-

pare him to Freud "in that he seemed bent on reducing everything to terms of sex." Despite these shortcomings, his contribution to astrology is considerable, especially in view of the meager tools at his command. Not only did he organize a vast and heterogeneous body of information; he helped to establish ethical principles by stressing the proper use of astrology, the value of experience in forming judgments, and the necessity of weighing such nonastrological factors as education and environment. (See GEOCENTRIC SYSTEM; GREEKS, ASTROLOGY AMONG THE.)

Pythagoras (ca. 580–500 B.C.): Greek philosopher, mathematician, and astronomer, founder of the Pythagorean school. Pythagoras and his followers were the first to conceive of the Earth as a sphere, self-supported in empty space, revolving with the other planets around the Sun. Thus they anticipated the heliocentric theory of the universe, and COPERNICUS acknowledges his debt to their ideas. The Pythagoreans developed the concepts of equation and proportion, which are common to all branches of mathematics. For making this contribution to the scientific method, the *Encyclopedia Britannica* calls Pythagoras "fully comparable to Descartes."

Pythagoras is believed to have traveled widely in search of wisdom, probably to Egypt, since he apparently introduced to the West the ancient Eygptian doctrine of *metempsychosis*, or the transmigration of souls. About 530 B.C. he settled in Crotona, a Greek colony in southern Italy. Pythagoras left nothing in writing, and his doctrines are known only through his disciples. The best known of these is the MUSIC OF THE SPHERES, the idea that the intervals between the spheres of the planets correspond to the tones of the musical scale and that the movements of the planets along these spheres produce an ethereal harmony. Pythagoras also believed that the human being is a MICROCOSM, or miniature version of the universe, and is connected to it by numerous affinities and correspondences. These last two doctrines are intimately related to astrology. While it is not known whether Pythagoras taught or practiced astrology, belief in the influence of the heavenly bodies on human affairs is implicit in much of Pythagorean doctrine, and astrologers throughout history have been influenced by his ideas. Pythagoras' ideas on the meaning of numbers are taking on renewed importance in the light of harmonic theory and the development of an integral astrology by John ADDEY and others.

Qabbala (or **Qabbalah**): See CABALA.

Qarra, Thâbit ibn: See ISLAM, ASTROLOGY IN.

Quadrant (from the Latin *quattuor*, four): One of the four quarters of a horoscope, defined by the cusps of the four ANGULAR houses, and in many systems of HOUSE DIVISION, by the intersecting axes of MERIDIAN and HORIZON. Each quadrant contains three houses.

Quadrant System: See HOUSE DIVISION.

Quadruplicity: A group of four signs belonging to the same quality (see QUALITIES); there are three quadruplicities, corresponding to the three qualities. For example, the cardinal quadruplicity consists of Aries, Cancer, Libra, and Capricorn.

Qualities: (also called **Modes** or **Quadruplicities**): The three types of energy—*cardinal*, *fixed*, or *mutable*—which provide one of the two primary classifications of the signs of the zodiac, the other being the ELEMENTS. The cardinal signs are Aries, Cancer, Libra, and Capricorn; the fixed signs are Taurus, Leo, Scorpio, and Aquarius; and the mutable signs are Gemini, Virgo, Sagittarius, and Pisces. The cardinal signs are characterized by outgoing energy and initiative; the fixed signs by persistence and resourcefulness; and the mutable signs by adaptability and service. Some astrologers have made an analogy with physics, in which the cardinal quality corresponds to centrifugal force, or to energy itself; the fixed quality corresponds to centripetal force, or to matter; and the mutable quality corresponds to wave motion, or to information.

Quartile: See SQUARE.

Querent: See HORARY ASTROLOGY.

Quincunx: (symbol ⊼): A minor aspect that may have been discovered by MORIN; it combines planets five signs apart, or 150°. Opinion is divided as to whether it is favorable or unfavorable, potent or negligible. Since it brings together signs whose elements are not in harmony, its energies may be difficult to integrate. Lying as it does midway between the trine (120°, an aspect of understanding) and the opposition (180°, an aspect of objectivity), it is sometimes associated with a kind of offbeat wisdom. It is considered by many astrologers to have a connection with health. There are probably as many qualities of quincunxes as there are combinations of signs, and it is to the particular blend in question that one should look for clues to its meaning. Thus the Leo-Pisces quincunx is dramatic; the Gemini-Capricorn quincunx, scientific, and so on. The quincunx is usually assigned an ORB of 2°; slightly more if the Moon is involved. (See DOUBLE QUINCUNX.)

Quintile (symbol ★): A minor aspect introduced by KEPLER that combines planets separated by one-fifth of the zodiac, or 72°. The quintile is generally regarded as favorable; it has been associated with both talent and power. It is usually given an ORB of 1° to 2°.

Radical: Pertaining to the RADIX, that is, the original chart; as, the radical positions of the planets.

Radical Chart: See BIRTH CHART.

Radix: Literally, "root." The original chart, the foundation of all astrological study for a given individual, event, etc., as distinguished from a directed or progressed chart for the same individual or event at a later date (see PROGRESSION AND DIRECTION).

Radix Direction: See PROGRESSION AND DIRECTION.

RAMC: See MERIDIAN, RIGHT ASCENSION.

Raphael (born R. C. Smith): Publisher of an EPHEMERIS that first appeared in 1800 and is still the best known in the world. Originally included in an almanac of mixed information, the astrological section was eventually published separately. *Raphael's Ephemeris* is now issued annually and contains not only planetary positions, lunar nodes, aspects, lunations, ingresses, eclipses, and sidereal time, but also tables of houses for the latitudes of London, Liverpool, and New York based on the system of HOUSE DIVISION of the Italian monk PLACIDUS DE TITUS. Indeed, the widespread use of the Placidean system can be attributed in large measure to the success of *Raphael's Ephemeris*, which lent it a certain authority and introduced it to many areas where no other tables were available.

Rapt Parallel: See PARALLEL.

Rat: The first sign of the Chinese zodiac, including all persons born between

January 31, 1900, and February 19, 1901 (metal)
February 18, 1912, and February 6, 1913 (water)
February 5, 1924, and January 25, 1925 (wood)
January 24, 1936, and February 11, 1937 (fire)
February 10, 1948, and January 29, 1949 (earth)
January 28, 1960, and February 15, 1961 (metal)
February 15, 1972, and February 3, 1973 (water)
February 2, 1984, and January 21, 1985 (wood).

Nervous, anxious, meddling, and aggressive, natives of the sign of the Rat manage to atone for these faults with their devastating charm. Lovers of pleasure, good food, and gambling, they have a tendency to take advantage of those around them, which sometimes gets them in trouble. On the positive side, their greatest virtues are their fundamental honesty, their analytical minds, and their creativity. A great many of these natives are tradespeople, civil servants, accountants, businesspeople, or writers. Capable of placing their personal happiness after that of the people they love, sentimental without being affected, they make perfect lovers.

Compatible signs: Monkey, Pig, Rat, Serpent.

Neutral signs: Cock, Dragon, Ox.

Incompatible signs: Cat, Dog, Goat, Horse, Tiger.

Famous Rats include Lucretia Borgia, Marlon Brando, Charlotte Brontë, Truman Capote, Pablo Casals, Galileo Galilei, Heinrich Himler, Henrik Ibsen, Richard Nixon, Georges Sand, William Shakespeare, Leo Tolstoi, George Washington, and Émile Zola. (See CHINESE ASTROLOGY.)

Rational Horizon: See HORIZON.

Reception: In classical astrology, condition of a planet occupying a sign not its own; such a planet is said to be "received" by the ruler of that sign. For example, when Mercury is in Aries, it is received by Mars. (See MUTUAL RECEPTION.)

Reci, Abraham ben: See HEBREWS, ASTROLOGY AMONG THE.

Rectification: A procedure designed to correct an uncertain birthtime by working backward from known events in the native's life or known traits of his or her personality. Given times of birth can be very inaccurate (see BIRTHTIME). An error of only 4 minutes of time will shift the Midheaven by 1°, which in many modes of direction represents about a year of time! It is obvious that if the birthtime is inaccurate, it will be difficult to interpret the chart correctly and still more difficult to forecast with it.

Many methods of rectification are employed, all of them controversial, subject to error, and highly dependent on the skill and experience of the astrologer. Many modern astrologers study transits, progressions, and directions to and by the Ascendant and Midheaven in an attempt to isolate sensitive degrees that recur with significant frequency at the time of major events (see PROGRESSION AND DIRECTION; TRANSIT). Such events include honors, promotions, changes of residence, marriage, birth of children, death of parents, accidents, operations, and illnesses. The followers of Alfred Witte's URANIAN SYSTEM and Reinhold Ebertin's COSMOBIOLOGY make much use of midpoints and planetary pictures in combination with solar arc directions. Charles JAYNE includes the VERTEX among the angles to be considered and recommends the use of solar arc directions in longitude, since they are unaffected by errors in birthtime. He also finds adverse events to be more useful, especially the deaths of parents, which are most often associated with hard aspects of Saturn (men) and Pluto or Neptune (women).

Jayne, who has been rectifying charts for over thirty years, calls rectification "probably the single most important technique an astrologer can master." However, it is an extremely complex and demanding operation that should be attempted only by those with an advanced working knowledge of astrology. Two good texts are Gustav Schwickert's *Rectification* and Charles Jayne's *The Technique of Rectification*.

Recurrence Cycle: See CYCLE.

Regiomontanus (born Johann Müller; June 6, 1436, Königsberg— July 6, 1476, Rome): German mathematician, astronomer, and astrologer. Regiomontanus founded an observatory and printing press in Nuremberg, where he observed the comet afterward known as Halley's comet. He published some of the earliest EPHEMERIDES, including those used by Columbus; indeed, they were those most widely used until RAPHAEL. Pope Sixtus IV summoned him to Rome to assist in reforming the calendar. He translated Ptolemy's *Almagest* and is credited with originating a system of HOUSE DIVISION widely used until about 1800.

Regiomontanus System: See HOUSE DIVISION.

Reincarnation: The belief that the soul survives death and is reborn in other bodies, each of these different lifetimes constituting an incarnation. The doctrine is implicit in much of astrological thought, especially that of the esoteric school. Some astrologers regard the NODES of the Moon as clues to reincarnation, especially

to karmic relationships that persist over several lifetimes. (See ESOTERIC ASTROLOGY.)

Relationship Chart: See COMPOSITE CHART.

Relativity, Theory of: A physical view of the universe whereby the concepts of time and space are not regarded as absolute entities but as interdependent variables in a cosmic fabric known as *space-time*. The idea was originally proposed by Albert Einstein in 1905 and later expanded by him into a general theory. According to relativity, it cannot be demonstrated in any absolute sense that one object is stationary while another object moves about; all motion is relative to one's local frame of reference. What appears to be gravitational "force" is merely a local deviation in the geometry of space-time. Objects follow paths (such as planetary orbits) not because of some mysterious force but because the geometry of the region necessitates such paths (which are called *world lines*, or *geodesics*).

For example, a massive body such as the Sun produces a curvature in the geometry of its region of space-time; a less massive object nearby, such as the Earth, follows a geodesic in that curved region. Relativity overthrows Euclidean geometry, which asserts that the most efficient path is always a straight line. Each region has its own special geometry, and the most efficient path in that region is the geodesic special to that region. It is always possible to regard the Earth as stationary if we do not adhere to Euclidean geometry.

But the implications of relativity lend more support to astrology than a mere justification of a geocentric frame of reference. Pre-Einsteinian physics asserted that the more massive an object was, the more force it would have and that that force would diminish with increasing distance from the object. One of the principal criticisms directed against astrology is that it presupposes that a small planet, such as Mercury, or a remote planet, such as Pluto, might have as much influence on the Earth as a massive planet, such as Jupiter, or a close planet, such as Mars. Experiments verifying relativity have demonstrated that photons—particles of light—bombarding the Earth exhibit the same energy irrespective of the mass or distance of their source.

Renaissance, Astrology in the: The fifteenth and sixteenth centuries were the golden age of astrology in the West. Contributing factors were the revival of classical culture, which was now no longer confined to Aristotle as interpreted by Averroes; the invention of the printing press, which permitted the publication of astrological treatises; and the advances in astronomy. One should also mention the decline in the power of the Church and a new sense of independence that ignored the ancient condemnations. Among the great minds of this age there were few who were not convinced of the validity of astrology. Tycho BRAHE (1546–1601), the great Danish astronomer who vastly improved the art of observation, was a practicing astrologer and an outspoken champion of astrology. And his student Johannes

Illustration for the sign of Taurus from the *Shepherds' Almanac*, published in 1491.

KEPLER (1571–1630), who discovered the laws governing the elliptical orbits of the planets and is regarded as the father of modern astronomy, made his living as an astrologer. Intellectuals sympathetic to astrology included philosophers Giordano Bruno (1548–1600) and Pierre Gassendi (1592–1655), physician Michael Servetus (1511–53), and writers François Rabelais (1494–1553) and Pierre de Ronsard (1524–85).

However, astrology was not simply a phenomenon of philosophers, scholars, or artists. It was also popular among ordinary people. There was a great proliferation of astrological almanacs, including the famous *Great Kalendar and Compost of Shepherds*, published in 1493 and reprinted countless times. This craze, which was accompanied by magical practices of all kinds, assumed such proportions that King Francis I of France passed an edict against the printers of almanacs that was upheld by the Estates General of Orléans (1560), Blois (1579), and Bordeaux (1583). These measures had very little effect, as did the banning of astrological treatises and the condemnation of astrology in 1563 by Popes Sixtus V (*Constitutio Coeli et Terrae*) and Urban VIII (*Constitutio inscrutabilis*). However, these attempts at suppression were much more concerned with the current tendency to combine astrology with magic or sorcery than with the art of casting horoscopes, provided allowance was made for man's free will.

The Protestants, too, were divided on the issue of astrology: Luther and Melanchthon were in favor, Calvin opposed. Luther wrote a preface to an astrological work in which he remarked, "the signs in the sky and on the earth should not be overlooked, since they are the work of God and the angels." By the end of the Renaissance, astrology, having survived the intermittent disapproval of the Church, would have to face a much more formidable enemy, one that succeeded in undermining her respectability and paralyzing her progress for 200 years: the rise of rationalism, skepticism, and materialism, and the advance of modern science.

Research in Astrology: See STATISTICS AND ASTROLOGY.

Retrograde: A term used to describe a planet that appears from the Earth to be moving backward through the zodiac, from east to west, against the order of the signs. This phenomenon, which is inexplicable as long as the Earth is regarded as stationary, gave rise to all sorts of theories. In

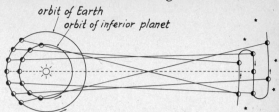

Figure 50. Retrogradation of an inferior planet.

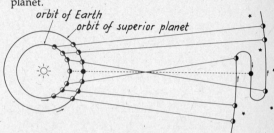

Figure 51. Retrogradation of a superior planet.

fact, the backward motion is an illusion created by the revolution of the planets and the Earth in their concentric orbits around the Sun (see figures 50 and 51). A similar illusion often occurs on a train when another train that is moving less rapidly than that of the observer appears to be moving backward.

In chart interpretation, retrogradation was traditionally regarded as a *debility*, a weakening of the planet's influence. Many modern astrologers associate it with delay or confusion in the activities ruled by the planet. For example, since Mercury rules communication and business, it is not recommended to sign contracts or undertake writing projects when Mercury is retrograde. These are the periods when letters go astray, appointments are missed, and communication breaks down. Another theory, advanced by Dane RUDHYAR, is that retrograde planets operate on a subconscious level; and a third, presented by Martin Schulman, associates what he calls the "retrograde personality" with altered perception of time. However, before placing undue emphasis on the interpretation of a planet's retrograde motion, students should bear in mind that the three outer planets are retrograde over 40 percent of the time. Thus such interpretations can only be of a very generalized kind. (See DIRECT; STATIONARY.)

Return: A planet's completion of its cycle, that is, the time it takes the planet to make a complete circuit of the zodiac; as, the Saturn return (see CYCLE).

Revolution: See ANOMALISTIC PERIOD; DRACONIC PERIOD; SIDEREAL PERIOD; SYNODIC PERIOD; TROPICAL PERIOD.

Rhazes: See ISLAM, ASTROLOGY IN.

Right Ascension: (Usually abbreviated RA, α, or R.) Angular distance measured along the CELESTIAL EQUATOR in an eastward direction from the VERNAL POINT in units either of degrees, minutes, and seconds of arc or of hours, minutes, and seconds of sidereal time (see TIME). The right ascension of the vernal point is considered to be 0°0'0", or 0 hours 0 minutes 0 seconds. A *meridian of right ascension* or sidereal time is a GREAT CIRCLE perpendicular to the celestial equator at a point a certain amount of right ascension or sidereal time from the vernal point. For example, the star Alphecca (as of 1980) is on the right-ascension meridian of 233°27'36" (or 15 hours 33 minutes 50 seconds), even though it is remote

from the celestial equator (its DECLINATION is 26°46'47" north). Right ascension and declination are the principal CELESTIAL COORDINATES used in astronomy for locating objects in the sky. Right ascension is used in astrology for the compilation of tables of houses (see TABLE OF HOUSES) or the technique of primary direction (see PROGRESSION AND DIRECTION). What is generally needed in such calculations is the right ascension of the local upper MERIDIAN, referred to as the *RAMC* (right ascension of the MIDHEAVEN). Actually, local sidereal time is defined as the right ascension (expressed in hours, minutes, and seconds) that is crossing the local upper meridian. Right ascension and meridians of right ascension should be distinguished from CELESTIAL LONGITUDE and meridians of celestial longitude, respectively, which are measured along the ECLIPTIC.

Rising Point: See CELESTIAL LATITUDE.

Romans, Astrology among the: The early Romans believed that in certain special cases the gods would communicate with them; hence the abundance of methods of divination. However, astrology did not become popular until the third century B.C., through contact with the Greek colonies of southern Italy. It was Greek slaves who brought astrology to the lower classes. Its success was spectacular; the poet Ennius (239–169 B.C.) raged against the quack astrologers who set up their stands in the streets of Rome.

The astrologers, who were known as "mathematicians" or "Chal-

Fragment of a Roman representation of the zodiac. (Collection of Pierre Chaumeil.)

deans," had no monopoly on the art of prediction. They often had to compete for business with the official augurs and soothsayers of the state. Cicero (106–43 B.C.) attacked astrologers violently in *De Divinatione* ("Were all those slain at Cannae born under the same star?"), as did Lucretius (96?–55 B.C.) and Juvenal (A.D. 60?–140?); the latter commented that some people could neither bathe nor dine without first consulting an astrologer. The rigorous determinism of Oriental astrology was diametrically opposed to the philosophical ideas professed by most Romans, who were attached to the idea of their personal freedom. To be sure, divination was supposed to reveal the future, but this future was conceived as a possibility that could be influenced by one's free will.

It was among the Stoics that astrology counted its greatest number of ardent defenders, because it accorded with their conception of a world that was organized by divine plan and characterized by universal sympathy. Like the ancient Chaldeans, the Stoics believed that astrology could help human beings to decipher the will and purpose of the

gods. Stoic philosophy urged resignation to fate. Vettius Valens, one of the first astrologers to attempt statistical observations, considered the ordinary pagan worship of his day to be useless: "It is impossible to defeat by sacrifice that which has been established from the beginning of time." Though such a fatalistic interpretation of astrology would later be denied by PLOTINUS (A.D. 205–70), it remained a vital enough part of the astrological canon to earn the disapproval of the Church (see CHRISTIANITY AND ASTROLOGY).

The Oriental campaigns and trade with Asia brought foreign religions and new attitudes to Rome, and under the Roman Empire astrology was almost officialized. Caesar, Crassus, and Pompey had already shown their confidence in it; after them most of the emperors had their official astrologers. Theogenes the Greek was astrologer to Augustus; Babilius was astrologer to both Claudius and Nero. Tiberius studied astrology himself and enlisted the services of Thrasyllus, among others (Juvenal referred to his "herd of Chaldeans"); but according to Seutonius, at one point the emperor banished the "mathematicians" and did not allow them to return until they promised to abandon their art. Domitian fully accepted divine stellar rule but banished the astrologers in A.D. 89 after they predicted the time of his death. In A.D. 70 Pliny complained that practically everyone believed in astrology.

By the early third century A.D. the superficial astrology of street fortune-tellers was losing its appeal for the masses, who were increasingly embracing various Oriental religions of salvation—some of which had incorporated astrological ideas. For example, Mithraism, probably the chief competitor of Christianity, stressed an all-powerful and eternal God, who was identified with heavenly motion, especially the Sun. Heliogabalus and later Aurelian established Sun worship in Rome: The Sun was seen as a giant, intelligent master who directed the motions of its servants, the planets.

Rooster: See Cock.

Royal Stars (also called **Watchers of the Heavens**): The four stars used by the ancient Sumerians in the third millennium B.C. to mark the EQUINOXES and SOLSTICES by the Sun's TRANSIT in front of them. Aldebaran marked the vernal equinox, Regulus the summer solstice, Antares the autumnal equinox, and Fomalhaut the winter solstice. Regulus can still be considered *the* Royal Star. The eclipse of August 22, 1979, immediately preceding the assassination of "that most royal of all European princes," Lord Mountbatten, was in 29' conjunction to Regulus.

Rudhyar, Dane (March 23, 1895, 12:42 A.M., Paris–): American astrologer, author, and composer; founder of humanistic astrology. Dane Rudhyar came to the United States in 1916 and settled in California, where a deep interest in Oriental philosophy led to his study of astrology. Between 1933 and 1976 he wrote monthly articles for several astrological magazines, including Paul

Dane Rudhyar. (Photo by Betty Freeman.)

Clancy's *American Astrology* and *Horoscope*. He has also written some thirty books, which include a majority on astrological subjects, but also works on music, art, and philosophy, two novels, and two volumes of verse.

Rudhyar's most famous work is *The Astrology of Personality*, which, since its appearance in 1936, has seen three editions, has been translated into Dutch, German, and French, and is generally acknowledged to be a classic. To Rudhyar, writing in the 1930s, traditional European astrology with its piecemeal approach to interpretation and its emphasis on the prediction of events seemed dominated by Greek intellectualism and spiritually bankrupt. In *The Astrology of Personality*, which is dedicated to its original publisher, Alice Bailey, Rudhyar called for a reformulation of astrological principles in the light of contemporary depth psychology and holistic philosophy. Rudhyar believes that astrology should concern itself primarily with people rather than with events; this is why he calls his approach humanistic. He sees astrology not as an empirical science but as a symbolic language like mathematics, and the planets not as transmitters of physical influence but as symbols of personality functions and ways of measuring cycles (see CYCLE). Astrology is "the algebra of life," whose goal is "the alchemy of personality," in other words, integration, the binding of parts into wholes, the discovery of meaning.

In *The Lunation Cycle* (1967) Rudhyar studied the soli-lunar relationship and described eight personality types corresponding to eight stages in this cycle: New Moon, Crescent Moon, First Quarter, Gibbous Moon, Full Moon, Disseminating Moon, Last Quarter, and Balsamic Moon. Other books include *The Pulse of Life* (1943), *The Practice of Astrology* (1968), *The Planetarization of Consciousness* (1970), and *The Sun Is Also a Star: The Galactic Dimensions of Astrology* (1975). In 1969 Rudhyar founded the International Committee for Humanistic Astrology.

Rudhyar's approach makes no use of the methods of investigation of empirical science, such as statistics; he has held aloof from the movement to demonstrate the scientific validity of astrology (see MODERN ASTROLOGY). However, he has repeatedly suggested that the most fundamental research astrology can undertake is to examine in detail the psychology and lives of large numbers of people born at the same time in large cities. Such studies would enable astrologers to discover the range of possi-

bilities inherent in one birth moment.

Rudhyar sees astrology as the practical application to human life and the development of consciousness of a cosmic philosophy based on the concept of cycle and the search for meaning. Through astrology, the deeper meaning of life events can be communicated to persons baffled by changes and uncertain how to cope with the problems they present. A recent book, *Beyond Individualism*, outlines a new psychology in which individual growth at four successive levels of actualization is related to the cyclic development of societies and their culture. (See CHIRON; ETHICS; HUMANISTIC ASTROLOGY; MUNDANE ASTROLOGY; URANUS.)

Rulership: The system whereby each sign of the zodiac is said to be "ruled" by one of the planets or luminaries. The traditional system of rulership was limited to the seven planets observed by the ancients; in more modern times, it has been revised to include the newly discovered planets, Uranus, Neptune, and Pluto. The following is the system observed by most modern astrologers:

Aries	Mars
Taurus	Venus
Gemini	Mercury
Cancer	Moon
Leo	Sun
Virgo	Mercury
Libra	Venus
Scorpio	Mars/Pluto
Sagittarius	Jupiter
Capricorn	Saturn
Aquarius	Saturn/Uranus
Pisces	Jupiter/Neptune

The traditional system of rulerships is generally attributed to PTOLEMY, who in turn ascribes it to the ancients. In the *Tetrabiblos* Ptolemy explains how his predecessors assigned the signs (then confusingly called "houses") to the planets on the basis of "familiarity," or affinity. Cancer and Leo, the signs occupied by the Sun during the northern summer, being the most powerful, were assigned to the luminaries: Leo, being masculine, to the Sun, and Cancer, being feminine, to the Moon. Capricorn and Aquarius, the opposite signs and those occupied by the Sun during the northern winter, were assigned to Saturn, since it was the most distant and therefore the coldest of the planets. The remaining signs were divided equally between Jupiter, Mars, Venus, and Mercury, in accordance with similarities in their nature. Jupiter, being BENEFIC, was given the signs in trine to the signs of the luminaries, that is, Sagittarius and Pisces; Mars, being MALEFIC, those in square to the signs of the luminaries, that is, Scorpio and Aries; Venus, being benefic and closer to the Sun, those in sextile to the signs of the luminaries, that is, Libra and Taurus; and Mercury, being closest to the Sun, those adjacent to the signs of the luminaries, that is, Gemini and Virgo.

The rulership system has been criticized by many modern astrologers, including Charles CARTER, Cyril FAGAN, L. E. JOHNDRO, and Geoffrey Dean. Its critics point out that it is arbitrary, irrelevant to the Southern Hemisphere, and outmoded by the discovery of the modern planets—Uranus, Neptune, and Pluto—and that there is no real evidence that it works. Rulerships are not used in the Ebertin midpoint system, and seldom by Uranian astrologers (see COSMOBIOLOGY; URANIAN SYSTEM).

Sagittarius (glyph ↗): The ninth sign of the zodiac, which the Sun transits during the last month of autumn, from about November 22 to about December 20. The symbol for this sign is the archer. Its POLARITY is positive, its element is fire (see ELEMENTS), its quality is mutable (see QUALITIES), its ruling planet is Jupiter (see RULERSHIP), and its NATURAL HOUSE is the Ninth.

In Sagittarius, the self-confidence of fire and the restlessness of mutability are joined with the genial influence of Jupiter to create an expansive nature that cannot be confined. The archer of the symbol is really a centaur, a mythological creature who was half man and half horse. Thus the Sagittarian nature is double: one-half rooted in animal instinct, the other half aiming at the stars. Like its polar opposite, Gemini, Sagittarius wants to know, but this knowing must go further. Where Gemini is content to think, Sagittarius must experience; where Gemini will let the mind wander, Sagittarius wants the body to travel; and where Gemini likes to accumulate facts, Sagittarius wants to construct theories, to fit all the separate pieces of information into an all-encompassing world view. This paradoxical sign can produce both the athlete who goes as far as his body will take him and the philosopher who explores the ultimate nature of reality.

Sagittarians—who include not only Sun-sign Sagittarians, but all in whose charts the sign is emphasized—are eager to share their experience with others. Their expression ranges from arrogant bombast to rarified abstraction, from devastating satire to evangelical fervor. Whatever their genre, their motive is to convince, which makes them better talkers than listeners. They must be free to pursue their truth unhampered, but once they have arrived at it, they may forget the winding path that led them there in their desire to spread it around. Indeed, this Jupiterian tendency to self-righteousness and arrogance makes Sagittarius the least mutable of the mutable signs. But Jupiter is also responsible for their best qualities, which are their faith, their optimism, and their sense of humor.

Most Sagittarian infants are very active and hate being confined; even cuddling or diapering may send them into fits of claustrophobia. They are usually early walkers and runners and, because of their hunger for

♐ Sagittarius

knowledge, probably early talkers as well. They love roughhousing and horseplay, but they are also the easiest children to travel with. They are entertaining guests and have no trouble sleeping in a strange bed.

In love, Sagittarians are capable of some curious extremes. They can be passionate to the point of exhaustion, treating sex as an indoor sport in which they must prove their skill and endurance, or they may be so engrossed in philosophical abstraction or a spiritual path that they forget all about human love. Their insatiable appetite for experience coupled with their idealism often produces Don Juans, driven to endless variety in the restless search for the perfect mate. Their partners must respect their need for freedom and give them a long rein. Their most compatible signs are Aries, Leo, Libra, and Aquarius; Scorpio, Capricorn, Taurus, and Cancer are neutral; and

Virgo and Pisces are likely to be difficult, although with the latter they share a universal perspective through the rulership of Jupiter. With another Sagittarius, there may be more energy than stability. With Gemini there will be both attraction and tension, the outcome depending, as with all combinations, on how the two charts interact in their entirety, and not on the COMPATIBILITY of Sun signs alone.

This sign is traditionally associated with the professions, and Sagittarians are often drawn to teaching, philosophy, religion, and the law. Theirs is also the sign of the free-lancer, and they should be independent, if not actually self-employed. They need to move around and are at their best when selling or preaching. Publishing, advertising, traveling, lecturing, entertaining (especially as comedians), sports, exploring, hunting, and working with animals, especially horses and dogs, all come naturally. Some famous Sun-sign Sagittarians include Louisa May Alcott, Ludwig van Beethoven, William Blake, Winston Churchill, Noel Coward, Sammy Davis, Jr., Charles de Gaulle, Emily Dickinson, Emmett Kelly, Claude Lévi-Strauss, Margaret Mead, John Milton, Pope John XXIII, George Santayana, Frank Sinatra, Alexander Solzhenitsyn, Baruch Spinoza, Jonathan Swift, James Thurber, and Mark Twain. (See BIRTHSTONES; COLORS; DAYS OF THE WEEK; METALS.)

Saros Cycle: See ECLIPSE.

Satellite: See ORBIT.

Satellitium: See STELLIUM.

Saturn (glyph ♄): The most remote planet known to the ancients, sixth in order from the Sun, and distinguished from the others by its remarkable system of rings. Saturn is next in size to Jupiter, its diameter being about 72,000 miles. Its mean distance from the Sun is 886 million miles, and its SIDEREAL PERIOD is 29.46 tropical years.

In astrology, Saturn was traditionally known as the "Greater Infortune," the "Lesser Infortune" being Mars; thus its nature was regarded as extremely MALEFIC. The planet was named after the Roman god of seed sowing, who became officially identified with the Greek god Kronos. Kronos was erroneously regarded as the god of time by confusion of his name with *chronos,* the Greek word for time. Whatever its source, the association with time is relevant to astrology, as we shall see. Saturn rules the sign of Capricorn and is traditional ruler of the sign of Aquarius, which most modern astrologers now assign to Uranus (see RULERSHIP). Thus it is in DETRIMENT in the opposite signs of Cancer and Leo. Saturn is exalted in Libra (see EXALTATION) and in FALL in Aries.

As the planet whose orbit circumscribed the known world, Saturn was regarded as the ruler of the material plane and was identified with the laws of time and space that govern it. In chart interpretation, Saturn stands for boundaries, definition, limitation, restriction, authority, discipline, and responsibility. Its qualities are seriousness, stability, conservation, practicality, economy, duration, crystallization, and cold. It rules order, form, structure, organization, government, policemen, the letter of the law; duty, debts, work, teachers, authority figures (especially fathers); older people in general, old age, death, mortality; the skeleton, the skin, the hair; asceticism and fasting; the superego and the reality principle; science, especially geometry and geology; earth, dirt, land, rocks, jewels, minerals, mountains, caves, agriculture, and real estate. When afflicted, Saturn is associated with anxiety, inhibition, delay, isolation, depression, rigidity, stinginess, poverty, starvation, and famine.

The following delineations are offered to show some of the ways Saturn may operate in the signs and houses. It should be remembered that they are merely suggestions and that their accuracy in any given case depends on the overall strength and condition of Saturn in relation to the chart as a whole, especially the aspects it forms with other planets and important points.

SATURN IN THE SIGNS

Saturn in Aries: determination, ambition, aggression, defiance, impatience, tension.

Saturn in Taurus: patience, perseverence, industriousness, conservatism, economy, miserliness.

Saturn in Gemini: intellectual discipline, aptitude for science, linguistic ability, overly analytical or theoretical mind.

Saturn in Cancer: teaching ability, stern disciplinarian, moral principles, defensiveness, guilt.

Saturn in Leo: loyalty, creative discipline, pride, rigidity, selfishness, authoritarianism.

Saturn in Virgo: shyness, thoroughness, perfectionism, industriousness, self-criticism, penny-pinching, asceticism.

Saturn in Libra: deliberation, fairness, aesthetic sense, talent for architecture or the law, caution, lack of spontaneity.

Saturn in Scorpio: penetrating mind; gift for physics, chemistry, or archaeology; authority; secretiveness; sarcasm.

Saturn in Sagittarius: theoretical intelligence, spiritual discipline, religious orthodoxy, benevolent despotism.

Saturn in Capricorn: organizing ability, strong sense of responsibility, seriousness, ambition, high standards, teaching ability, isolation.

Saturn in Aquarius: democratic leadership, responsibility to the future, understanding of technology, loyalty, stubbornness.

Saturn in Pisces: self-sacrifice; devotion to fellow humans; talent for music, poetry, or dance; yoga; meditation; shyness; isolation.

SATURN IN THE HOUSES

Saturn in the First House: seriousness, responsibility, authority, sense of limitation, effort, obstacles, delays, pessimism.

Saturn in the Second House: financial problems, hard work, feelings of deprivation, conservation of resources, fear of poverty.

Saturn in the Third House: mental discipline, conscientious student, talent for writing or teaching, responsibility for siblings or in neighborhood.

Saturn in the Fourth House: family responsibilities, parental discipline, isolation in later years or longevity.

Saturn in the Fifth House: artistic ambition, love for older people, responsibilities involving children or lack of children.

Saturn in the Sixth House: industriousness, work in science or medicine, possibility of health problems from overwork.

Saturn in the Seventh House: stable relationships, marriage to older person or teacher, marriage delayed, many responsibilities to other people, celibacy.

Saturn in the Eighth House: strength in crisis, responsibilities for other people's money or resources, sexual repression, morbid fear of death.

Saturn in the Ninth House: continuing education, spiritual aspiration, professional ambition, travel for business, lack of travel.

Saturn in the Tenth House: ambition, achievement of recognition as a result of hard work and effort, leadership, authority, reversals in fortune.

Saturn in the Eleventh House: deep sense of responsibility to friends or to society, long-lasting friendships, friends who are older or who are teachers, isolation from friends.

Saturn in the Twelfth House: responsibility behind the scenes, scientific research, work for institutions, isolation, chronic illness.

Schools of Astrology: See MODERN ASTROLOGY.

Scientific School: See MODERN AS-
TROLOGY.

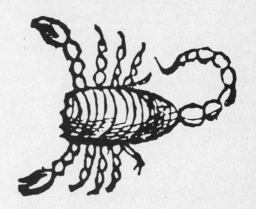

ᛑ Scorpius

Scorpio (glyph ᛑ): The eighth sign
of the zodiac, which the Sun transits
during the second month of autumn,
from about October 23 to about November 22. The symbol for this sign
is the scorpion. Its POLARITY is negative, its element is water (see ELE-
MENTS), its quality is fixed (see QUAL-
ITIES), its modern ruler is Pluto, its
traditional ruler is Mars (see RULER-
SHIP), and its NATURAL HOUSE is the
Eighth.

In Scorpio the resourcefulness of
fixity and the emotionality of water
are combined with the invisible
power of Pluto to create a nature of
profound depth and dramatic intensity. Fixed water suggests a dam, an
iceberg, or an underground pool,
and all the images are apt, for in
Scorpio a great deal is going on under the surface; energy is being held
in reserve. Water stands for emotion,
and emotion can be fixed only if it is
not expressed, which only increases
its intensity. Thus love may be poi-
soned with jealousy, and anger may
harden into hate.

The symbol for Scorpio is the scorpion, a creature that travels by night
and is feared for its deadly sting.
Though all Scorpio people are by no
means venemous and cruel, the symbol conveys the qualities of secretiveness, penetration, and power that do
characterize the natives of this sign.
(Incidentally, Scorpio people include
not only Sun-sign Scorpios, but all in
whose charts the sign is emphasized.) It should be noted that the
ancient esoteric symbol for Scorpio is
the eagle, one of the biblical four

beasts of the Apocalypse (Rev. 4:7)
who represent the four fixed signs of
the zodiac. The eagle kills too, but it
also soars high above the ground and
thus symbolizes not only power but
transcendence.

Pluto was the Roman god of the
underworld, and Scorpio is the sign
of death. It is also the sign of birth
and sexuality—in short, the critical
moments of human existence that involve a release of the ego and contact
with the ultimate mysteries. Besides
the strong sexuality for which they
are famous, Scorpio people have an
awareness of death that is often not
fearful, for this is also the sign of
reincarnation. They have a natural
affinity for occult studies: *Occult*
means "hidden," and Scorpios like
to pry into dark corners. All the
water signs are psychic, but many
Scorpios will actually explore areas
like ESP, psychic healing, and mediumship and develop the powers
that are latent in all of us but of which
many people are afraid. Indeed, if

they are afraid of anything at all, it is of being known as deeply as they wish to know. Their ability to penetrate and probe may be channeled constructively into research or healing or it may be used to manipulate people in personal relationships.

Scorpio children are sometimes hard to fathom because of their emotional intensity. Deeply sensitive, they seem to understand their parents' unspoken feelings even before they have acquired language. The trauma of being displaced by a new sibling can be particularly painful for them, although the pain may be partly alleviated by giving them responsibility around the house.

Relationships are very important to Scorpios, and sex is usually involved, for these natives have a magnetic appeal that is almost universal. They tend to focus on their partner's reactions as a way to avoid facing their own. They seem to attract crises and may put themselves through infernos of jealousy and rage before they learn to stop trying to control people. Their most compatible signs are Cancer, Pisces, Virgo, and Capricorn; Libra, Sagittarius, Aries, and Gemini are neutral; Leo and Aquarius are apt to be difficult. With another Scorpio there would probably be too much intensity. With Taurus there will be both attraction and tension, as the irresistible force meets the immovable object; but in all cases the success of the relationship will depend on how the two charts interact and not on the COMPATIBILITY of Sun signs alone.

Scorpios excel in any activity that involves going deeply into things: psychology, detective work, investigation, research, chemistry, physics, astronomy, archaeology, history, oceanography, plumbing, dentistry, surgery, hypnotism, and all forms of healing. Scorpio artists and writers tend to focus on sex or death or may have a gift for satire. The Scorpio charisma draws many to the stage or to politics. Famous Sun-sign Scorpios include Sarah Bernhardt, Benvenuto Cellini, Marie Curie, Fëdor Dostoevski, Indira Gandhi, W. S. Gilbert, Edmund Halley, Katharine Hepburn, Sir William Herschel, William Hogarth, Chiang Kai-shek, Robert Kennedy, Anton von Leeuwenhoek, Joseph McCarthy, Charles Manson, Jawaharlal Nehru, Pablo Picasso, Sylvia Plath, Ezra Pound, Theodore Roosevelt, Herman Rorschach, Jonas Salk, Dylan Thomas, Norman Thomas, and Voltaire. (See BIRTHSTONES; COLORS; DAYS OF THE WEEK; METALS.)

Seasonal Year: See TROPICAL YEAR.

Secondary Direction: See PROGRESSION AND DIRECTION.

Secondary Progression: See PROGRESSION AND DIRECTION.

Semiarc: See HOUSE DIVISION.

Semidecile (also called **Vigintile**): A minor aspect of 18°; half a DECILE (36°). It is regarded as mildly favorable and given an ORB of 1°.

Semiquartile: See SEMISQUARE.

Semiquintile: See DECILE.

Semisextile (or **Dodecile**; symbol ⟇): A minor aspect, said to have been introduced by MORIN, combining planets separated by one-twelfth of the zodiac circle, or 30°; half a sextile (60°), and the geometric supplement of the quincunx (150°). The semisextile is generally classified as neutral or ambiguous. De Vore describes it as "rhythmically favorable, but involving planets in inharmonious signs." Modern astrologers tend to regard it as an aspect of opportunity, like the sextile, but less potent. The usual ORB is 2°.

Semisquare (or **Octile**; symbol ∠): One of the strongest of the minor aspects, introduced by KEPLER, combining planets separated by one-eighth of the zodiac circle, or 45°. Since it is half a square, it is traditionally regarded as mildly MALEFIC; modern astrologers classify it with the HARD ASPECTS, which are associated with the stress or tension that precipitates events. The usual ORB is 2°; however, the German cosmobiologists consider it a major aspect, and allow up to 5° when personal points are involved.

Sensitive Point: 1. In a birth chart, a point of personal significance such as the longitude of the Sun, Moon, or Ascendant.

2. A point that is the result of a mathematical relationship between two or three other bodies or points. There are three general types of sensitive points: $A + B - C = D$, in which the sensitive point is equal to the sum of the first two points minus a third (for example, the Part of Fortune); $A + A - B = C$, in which the sensitive point is equidistant with a given body from a given point but on the opposite side (for example, the

antiscion); and $A + A - B = B$, in which the sensitive point is the midpoint between, or half sum of, two bodies. The first type is used in traditional astrology; all three types are used in Uranian astrology.

Separating Aspect: See APPLYING ASPECT.

Serpent (or **Snake**): The sixth sign of the Chinese zodiac, including all persons born between

February 4, 1905, and January 25, 1906 (wood)
January 23, 1917, and February 11, 1918 (fire)
February 10, 1929, and January 30, 1930 (earth)
January 27, 1941, and February 15, 1942 (metal)
February 14, 1953, and February 3, 1954 (water)
February 2, 1965, and January 21, 1966 (wood)
February 18, 1977, and February 7, 1978 (fire)
February 6, 1989, and January 27, 1990 (earth)

In the Far East this animal is not an object of abhorrence, as it is elsewhere. Associated in Japan with Benten, goddess of Love, Beauty, and the Sea, the Serpent brings to its natives subtlety, independence, elegance, and fluency of speech. These people know how to captivate their audience with their humor, which is usually the key to their success. However, they have a selfish streak and often use their intelligence and intuition to further their own ends. When they have the means, they enjoy study and are particularly interested in philosophy. They have little talent for the arts but succeed very

well in business or teaching and are attracted to the occult sciences. Neither borrowers nor lenders, they would much rather spend other people's money than their own, but by no means can they be accused of stinginess.

Their love lives are in a perpetual state of agitation. They are restless types whose behavior is always causing scenes, tears, and breakups. They are jealous and keep their partner on a tight rein.

Compatible signs: Cat, Cock, Dragon, Horse, Ox, Rat.

Neutral signs: Goat, Monkey.

Incompatible signs: Dog, Pig, Tiger.

Famous Serpents include Pierre Charles Baudelaire, Johannes Brahms, John Calvin, Casanova, Nicolaus Copernicus, Bob Dylan, Mary Baker Eddy, Gustave Flaubert, Indira Gandhi, Greta Garbo, Johann Wolfgang von Goethe, Grace Kelly, Pope John XXIII, John F. Kennedy, Henri Matisse, Montaigne, Gamel Abdul Nasser, Jacqueline Kennedy Onassis, Pablo Picasso, and Mao Tse-Tung. (See CHINESE ASTROLOGY.)

Sesquare: See SESQUISQUARE.

Sesquiquadrate: See SESQUISQUARE.

Sesquisquare (also **Sesquiquadrate** or **Sesquare**; symbol ⌑): A minor aspect, introduced by KEPLER, combining planets separated by 135°. The sesquisquare is a square (90°) and a half, and thus the geometric supplement of the semisquare. It is traditionally regarded as mildly MALEFIC and similar to the semisquare. In modern astrology the semisquare

and sesquisquare are regarded as HARD ASPECTS of less importance than the square and are allowed orbs of 2°. However, the German cosmobiologists consider them to be major aspects and allow orbs of up to 5° when personal points are involved.

Sextile (from the Latin *sex*, six; symbol ⚹): One of the major aspects recognized by classical astrology, bringing into relationship planets or important points separated by one-sixth of the zodiac circle, half a trine, or an angle of 60°. The sextile is regarded by ancients and moderns alike as a harmonious aspect, because it unites signs of the same *polarity*—that is, earth and water, which both belong to the negative polarity, or fire and air, which both belong to the positive polarity. Alan Leo considered the sextile to be generally stronger and more favorable than the trine, because it requires more effort on the part of the native. For example, a person with Mercury in Virgo sextile Uranus in Scorpio is likely to be more highly motivated to use and develop his or her intelligence than, say, a person with Mercury in Cancer in trine to the same Uranus, who may simply rely on inherent intuitive gifts.

Orbs for sextiles vary; most authorities allow 4° to 6°, though some as much as 8°, depending on the condition of the planets involved (see ORB).

Shad Bala: See INDIA, ASTROLOGY IN; VOLGUINE, ALEXANDRE.

Shodasavarga: See INDIA, ASTROLOGY IN; NAVAMSA.

Short Ascension: See ASCENDANT; ASCENSION, LONG OR SHORT.

Sidereal Cycle: See CYCLE; SIDEREAL PERIOD.

Siderealists: See SIDEREAL ZODIAC.

Sidereal Month: See MOON.

Sidereal Period (from the Greek *sidus*, star): The time it takes a celestial body to make one complete round in its orbit, or to return to a given point in its orbit, measured by its recurrent alignment to a star. The sidereal periods of the planets, rounded to the nearest day, are as follows:

Mercury	88 days
Venus	224 days
Earth	365 days
Mars	1 year 322 days
Jupiter	11 years 315 days
Saturn	29 years 167 days
Uranus	84 years 5 days
Neptune	164 years 290 days
Pluto	248 years 157 days

(See CYCLE; MOON; SIDEREAL YEAR; SYNODIC PERIOD; TROPICAL PERIOD.)

Sidereal Time: See TIME.

Sidereal Year: The SIDEREAL PERIOD of the Earth; the time it takes the Earth to complete one revolution around the Sun and realign itself to any given star. The sidereal year is 365 days 6 hours 9 minutes 9.5 seconds. (See TROPICAL YEAR.)

Sidereal Zodiac (abbreviated **SZ**; also called **Fixed Zodiac**): The zodiac based on the twelve constellations intersected by the ECLIPTIC plane; as distinguished from the TROPICAL ZODIAC, which is based on the seasons and composed of equal divisions of the ecliptic called signs, which have the same names as the constellations. The sidereal zodiac is probably more ancient than the tropical zodiac. It is still used by Hindu astrologers and has been adopted by a school of Western astrologers called *siderealists* pioneered by Cyril FAGAN, Donald Bradley (alias Garth Allen), Rupert Gleadow, and Brigadier R. C. Firebrace, among others.

The sidereal zodiac is referred to as fixed because within the time frame of hundreds of thousands of years the constellations appear unaltered. The tropical zodiac is referred to as moving because, owing to PRECESSION OF THE EQUINOXES, the VERNAL POINT, which is its starting point, moves backward against the fixed zodiac of constellations about 1° every 72 years. According to Fagan, the two zodiacs were momentarily aligned in A.D. 221, but the discrepancy between them—which Hindu astrologers call the *ayanamsa*—has been increasing at the rate of approximately 50.25″ of CELESTIAL LONGITUDE per year ever since. By now, the ayanamsa amounts to slightly more than 24°, almost an entire sign; thus, most people who are Arians according to the tropical zodiac would be regarded by the siderealists as natives of Pisces. Unlike its tropical counterpart, the sidereal zodiac has no obvious beginning point. Siderealists take one or another star as a marker, or *fiducial*, from which they gauge the ayanamsa, which they then subtract from tropical celestial longitude to arrive at sidereal celestial longitude. However, the sidereal longitude given to a fiducial is open to controversy. Bradley proposed a more refined marking point, called the *synetic vernal point,* which he claimed is the sidereal longitude of the vernal point. Ephemerides have been compiled that list the ever-precessing position of the synetic vernal point at selected intervals, usually every 10 days.

In interpreting charts, siderealists put more emphasis on aspects and proximity to angles than they do on constellations or houses. Natal chart interpretation appears to be much less important to them than prediction of events; they concentrate on solar and lunar returns, which have, of course, been corrected for precession.

Significator: Literally, "one who signifies," or "one who has meaning"; broadly, any planet in a horoscope is a significator of the matters connected with the house it rules or occupies. For example, the ruler of the sign on the cusp of the Second House, or a planet placed in the Second House, is a significator of money or possessions. In classical astrology, the term was specifically applied to Sun, Moon, Ascendant, Midheaven, and sometimes the Part of Fortune. The strongest planet in a birth chart, usually the ruler of the Ascendant, is regarded as the significator of the native. Significators are especially important in HORARY ASTROLOGY and in the predictive technique of *primary direction,* where they are distinguished from PROMITTORS. (See PROGRESSION AND DIRECTION.)

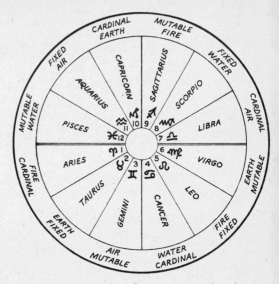

Figure 52. The zodiac wheel.

Signs of the Zodiac: Twelve 30° segments of the ECLIPTIC, the Sun's apparent path around the Earth, measured from the point where the ecliptic intersects the CELESTIAL EQUATOR, called the VERNAL POINT and expressed as 0° Aries. The signs of the zodiac were named after the constellations that are located along the zodiac but otherwise bear no relationship to them. Unlike the signs, the constellations are of unequal size and have no clearly defined boundaries. The Sun passes through the twelve signs of the zodiac in the course of a year. Its entry into a given sign occurs at a precise moment which varies from year to year. The following timetable is approximate; for more accurate information, consult an EPHEMERIS for the year in question.

Aries   Mar. 21–Apr. 20
Taurus   Apr. 21–May 20
Gemini   May 21–June 20

Cancer	June 21–July 22
Leo	July 23–Aug. 22
Virgo	Aug. 23–Sep. 22
Libra	Sep. 23–Oct. 22
Scorpio	Oct. 23–Nov. 22
Sagittarius	Nov. 23–Dec. 21
Capricorn	Dec. 22–Jan. 20
Aquarius	Jan.21–Feb. 20
Pisces	Feb. 21–Mar. 20

The signs of the zodiac are classified according to *quality* and according to *element*. The three qualities are *cardinal* (outgoing), *fixed* (indrawing), and *mutable* (variable). The four elements are *fire* (spirit), *earth* (matter), *air* (mind), and *water* (feeling). There are four signs belonging to each of the three qualities, and three signs belonging to each of the four elements. In other words, each of the twelve signs is a combination of one of the elements and one of the qualities.

The qualities and elements recur around the zodiac in a regular order. For the qualities this order is cardinal, fixed, mutable; for the elements it is fire, earth, air, water. Thus the first sign is cardinal fire, Aries; the second sign, fixed earth, Taurus; the third sign, mutable air, Gemini; and so on around the wheel. Because of the order in which the qualities and elements recur around the wheel, signs opposite each other on the zodiac will always be of the same quality and of harmonious elements. (See figure 52.)

The signs are also classified according to *polarity*. The two polarities are *positive* (active) and *negative* (reactive). The fire and air signs belong to the positive polarity; the earth and water signs to the negative polarity.

The polarities alternate around the wheel, starting with Aries, which, being a fire sign, is positive.

(For additional information about the signs, see AIR; ASCENSION, LONG AND SHORT; CARDINAL; DOUBLE SIGNS; EARTH; EQUINOCTIAL SIGNS; FIRE; FIXED; MUTABLE; POLARITY; RULERSHIP; SIDEREAL ZODIAC; TROPICAL SIGNS; TROPICAL ZODIAC; WATER; ZODIAC; and the entries for the individual signs.)

Sinister Aspect: See DEXTER ASPECT.

Sky Map: See BIRTH CHART.

Smith, R. C.: See RAPHAEL.

Snake: See SERPENT.

Soft Aspects: In modern astrology, the trine and sextile; and according to some authorities, the semisextile, the quincunx, and the quintile group; the *hard aspects* are the square, opposition, semisquare, and sesquisquare. (See ASPECT.)

Solar Arc: See PROGRESSION AND DIRECTION.

Solar Arc Direction: See PROGRESSION AND DIRECTION.

Solar Chart: A chart obtained without calculating an ASCENDANT, and in which the cusp of the First House is the degree of CELESTIAL LONGITUDE occupied by the Sun at noon on the day of birth. Cusps of the succeeding houses are at regular 30° intervals from the First-House cusp, according to the Equal House system (see HOUSE DIVISION). Such houses are known as *solar houses*. The solar chart is generally used to study the mutual aspects of the planets in cases where the time of birth is unknown. It should not be confused with the *sunrise chart*, in which the cusp of the First House is the degree occupied by the Sun at sunrise at the latitude of the birthplace and in which the other cusps are generally based on a quadrant system rather than on the Equal House system.

Solar Declination Arc: See PROGRESSION AND DIRECTION.

Solar Eclipse: See ECLIPSE.

Solar Houses: See SUN-SIGN ASTROLOGY.

Solar House System: See HOUSE DIVISION.

Solar Return (also called **Solar Revolution**): The moment when the Sun, in its APPARENT MOTION along the ECLIPTIC, returns to the exact degree of CELESTIAL LONGITUDE that it occupied at an individual's birth; also, a horoscope cast for this moment. The solar return will not necessarily fall on the calendar birthday; it may be a day earlier or later. A solar return chart is usually cast for the place of residence at the time it occurs rather than for the place of birth.

An ancient technique—NOSTRADAMUS mentions it in his letters—the solar return is currently enjoying a revival. It is used in much the same way as progressions and transits are, to analyze trends and anticipate probable events during the coming year. Since the Sun will, by definition, have the same sign position as in the natal chart, particular attention is paid to the Sun's house position, the Moon's sign and house position, the signs on the Ascendant and Midheaven, and aspects to these. Other elements are interpreted as in a natal chart, with constant reference to and comparison with the natal chart in question.

To cast a solar return, it is necessary to determine the moment when the Sun returns to its natal longitude. For example, let us say that we want to cast a solar return for Margaret Mead for 1926, the year of her twenty-fifth birthday. Mead was born December 16, 1901, in Philadelphia; her natal Sun is at 23°57' Sagittarius. Looking at *The American Ephemeris* for December 1926, we see that the Sun's longitude at midnight GMT was 23°17' Sagittarius on December 16 and 24°18' Sagittarius on December 17. Thus the Sun's diurnal motion for the day in question was 1°1', or 61'. To find the Sun's motion between midnight and the time of the return, we subtract its longitude at the prior midnight from its natal longitude: 23°57' − 23°17' = 40'. To determine how long it takes the Sun to travel 40', we multiply 40/61 by 24 hours, which gives approximately 16 hours. Sixteen hours after midnight is 4 P.M. GMT. A chart may now be cast for this moment, expressed in the standard time and at the latitude of New York City, where Mead was living at that time.

Mead's solar return for 1926 has the Sun and Venus in the Tenth House of honors and profession and Jupiter rising in Aquarius in the Twelve House of research, conjunct her natal Moon. Mercury and Saturn are conjunct and elevated in Sagittarius in the Ninth, the sign and house of teaching and publishing. This was the year that Mead began her association with the American

Museum of Natural History, which provided her with a base of operations for her professional life for the next 52 years.

The casting of a solar return is greatly facilitated by the use of a simple calculator or a book providing tables of diurnal planetary motion, such as the one published by the American Federation of Astrologers.

It is also possible to calculate a chart for the moment when the Moon returns to its exact radical position. Such a chart is known as a *lunar return* and is considered to reveal the mood of the month. Both solar and lunar returns are widely used by siderealists, who calculate them allowing for the amount of PRECESSION that has occurred since birth (see SIDEREAL ZODIAC).

An authoritative text on solar returns is Alexandre VOLGUINE's *The Technique of Solar Returns.*

Solar Revolution: See SOLAR RETURN.

Solar Time: See TIME.

Solar Year: See TROPICAL YEAR.

Soli-Lunar Year: See LUNAR YEAR.

Solstice Points: See ANTISCION.

Solstices (from the Latin *sol,* sun, and *sistere, statum,* to stand still): The two moments during the year when the Sun, in its apparent path along the ECLIPTIC, is farthest from the Equator, either north, causing the longest day in the year in the Northern Hemisphere, or south, causing the longest night in the year; so called because the Sun then "stands still" in its apparent northward or southward motion. These two moments occur when the Sun enters the sign of Can-

cer at the beginning of summer, about June 21 (called the *summer solstice*), after which the days grow shorter again, and when the Sun enters the sign of Capricorn at the beginning of winter, about December 21 (called the *winter solstice*), after which the days grow longer again. At the summer solstice the noon Sun is at the ZENITH at the Tropic of Cancer; at the winter solstice the noon Sun is at the zenith at the Tropic of Capricorn.

The term *solstices* also refers to the two points where the ecliptic is farthest from the CELESTIAL EQUATOR. The solstitial points are known by astrologers and astronomers alike as 0° Cancer and 0° Capricorn. Cancer and Capricorn are sometimes called the *solstitial,* or *tropical, signs.* Charts cast for the Sun's entry into the summer and winter solstices are considered of great importance by mundane astrologers. (See ANTISCION; COSMOGRAPHY.)

Solsticial Signs: Cancer and Capricorn; see SOLSTICES.

Southern Angle: See MIDHEAVEN; IMUM COELI.

Southern Hemisphere: Most tables of houses are designed for northern terrestrial latitudes. To find the house cusps for a birth that took place in the Southern Hemisphere, add 12 hours to the sidereal time of birth, look up the cusps as if the latitude were north, and then reverse the sign of all the cusps found—in other words, add 180° to the degrees of CELESTIAL LONGITUDE listed (see CHART CALCULATION). Since the terrestrial longitudes of the planets are calculated in relation to the Greenwich Meridian, they are the same for births in the Southern or Northern Hemisphere.

In the chart for a birth south of the Equator, the MIDHEAVEN—the Sun's position at noon—is in the north instead of in the south, as it is on a Northern Hemisphere birth chart. Technically, the ASCENDANT (the east) should therefore be on the right, but most southern astrologers observe the northern orientation, keeping the Ascendant on the left. The Sun enters Aries on or near March 21, but in the Southern Hemisphere this is the autumnal equinox. There has been no attempt to adapt sign meanings, which have evolved in northern latitudes, where Aries represents the first thrust of life, Leo the height of summer when the Sun is king, and so on, to the southern situation. Some astrologers advocate using opposite signs for the Southern Hemisphere so that the Sun would enter Aries on or about September 23 and correspond to the southern spring. But this solution introduces a serious dilemma for casting charts of births on or near the Equator, and, more importantly, does not seem in any way justified by the experience of astrologers working in the Southern Hemisphere.

Southern Latitudes: See SOUTHERN HEMISPHERE.

South Node: See NODES.

South Point: See HORIZON.

Spring Equinox: See EQUINOXES; VERNAL POINT.

Spring Ingress: See INGRESS.

Square (symbol □): One of the five major aspects recognized by classical astrology, bringing into relationship planets or important points separated by one-fourth of the zodiac circle, or an angle of 90°; in modern astrology, perhaps the strongest of the HARD ASPECTS.

In classical astrology, the square was regarded as MALEFIC. Most modern astrologers see the square as stressful or challenging but not harmful unless the conflicting energies it represents are misused or ignored. The stress associated with the square may be explained by the fact that it unites signs of inharmonious elements. For example, if Mars is at 15° Aries and the Moon is at 15° Cancer, Mars and the Moon are said to be in square. Aries is a fire sign, and Cancer is a water sign; fire and water are inharmonious ELEMENTS; fire and water are always three signs apart, and therefore in square.

In chart interpretation, fire represents action and water represents emotion. A man with the Moon in Cancer squared by Mars in Aries in his natal chart would often feel at cross-purposes with himself, as if his extreme sensitivity and need for security were keeping him from asserting himself and going after his goals; and he would have to cope with a great deal of anger. He would probably have a difficult relationship with his mother (ruled by the Moon) and might take out his resentments on other women. His passionate temperament could find an outlet in rage, self-pity, or alcohol, could be bottled up as depression, or could be channeled into physical exercise or artistic creativity.

The difficult aspects are the building blocks of character, because they force one to become aware of inner conflict. A chart without squares may lack the energy necessary to personal growth. Squares are important not only in natal charts but by transit. For example, if the man with the Moon-Mars square received a square to his natal Moon from transiting Saturn in the sky, the period when this aspect was in orb would be one in which his emotional maturity would be put to the test. Such a period could be fraught with frustration but could also be an opportunity to take a quantum leap in self-awareness.

Squares are usually given an ORB of 5° to 6°, depending on other factors involved.

Standard Time (ST): See TIME.

Standard Time Meridian: See TIME.

Star: A self-luminous celestial body, as distinguished from a planet, which shines by reflected light. In astrology, the word has traditionally been used with a wider range of meanings than that recognized by astronomers. Thus, the planets and the Moon are sometimes referred to loosely or poetically as stars, as in Shakespeare's "The fault, dear Brutus, is not in our stars, / But in ourselves, that we are underlings."

The term *fixed stars* refers to stars in the astronomical sense: incandescent, gaseous celestial bodies such as our Sun. They are not fixed at all, but because of their great distance from the Earth their motion—both actual and apparent—is so small that it cannot be detected by observation with the naked eye. The ancients distinguished the "fixed stars" from the "wandering stars" or "goat stars" (goats being notorious for wandering). The latter, of course, were the planets, which appear to travel from constellation to constellation, come to a stop, and perversely travel backward for a while.

From the very beginning, astrologers have assigned importance to fixed stars, in both natal and mundane astrology. HIPPARCHUS was the first to establish a list of them (about 130 B.C.), including several hundred whose names later appeared in PTOLEMY's *Almagest.* The *Palomar Star Survey,* used by American astronomers, lists positions for 1.3 billion stars.

Of this number, fewer than a hundred are occasionally included in a birth chart. Most modern astrologers ignore them altogether. Those who do use stars regard them as significant only when they seem to form a close CONJUNCTION or PARALLEL with a planet or one of the angles of the chart. A star of the first magnitude (brightness) conjunct the Midheaven or Ascendant at birth is said to be an indication of fame.

However, calculations of a star's aspects are subject to gross error because most astrologers confine themselves to a single dimension: CELESTIAL LONGITUDE. For example, let us consider an aspect of Pluto to the star Canopus in the birth chart of Harry Belafonte (born March 1, 1927). The celestial longitude of Canopus was then 13°57' Cancer, while that of Pluto was 13°55' Cancer. It seems reasonable to regard the two as conjunct until we consider a second dimension: CELESTIAL LATITUDE. Canopus's latitude was 75°50' south, while Pluto's was 01°20′ south. The difference between them is 74°30′, which is within ORB of a QUINTILE, a totally different aspect.

The actual motion of a star consists of its orbital revolution around the center of the GALAXY (a journey that takes our solar system, traveling a million miles in slightly more than 2 hours, or 135 miles a second, about 225 million years), and its swings above and below the galactic plane. This motion, which gradually alters the shapes of the constellations, does not affect a star's CELESTIAL COORDINATES within the time frame of a few centuries. (The mean motion of a star relative to other stars in its constellation is 1° every 120,000 years, though closer stars may move considerably faster.) However, a star's apparent motion, which is based on the PRECESSION OF THE EQUINOXES and is part of the shifting of the constellations relative to the celestial coordinates, is important and measurable.

Some astrologers believe that certain degrees of the zodiac possess specific qualities and influences of their own, even in the absence of a planet—and even without regard to the sign of which the degree is a unit. Some of these DEGREE MEANINGS reflect the ancient reputations of the stars currently or recently located at these celestial longitudes. However, these degree systems are not updated to keep pace with the gradual shifting of the stars that correspond to the degrees.

The positions of all the stars in table 4 are for 1980. For years after 1980 add 50¼″ per year (approximately 5′

for every 6 years) to the celestial longitude; for years before 1980, subtract. Change in celestial latitude is negligible.

In the following alphabetical list, each of these fifty stars is described briefly, identified as to constellation, and given its astrological interpretation, which consists of its nature (that is, its affinity to one or more planets according to Ptolemy) and its traditional meaning. In considering stars in a birth chart, the following guidelines should be kept in mind: Very small orbs (less than 1°) should be allowed for aspects between stars and planets or angles, although a star of the first magnitude may have a greater orb than a dimmer star (see ORB). The meaning of a star has more weight if the star is aspecting a planet whose nature it shares. A star is more significant if the planet it aspects is emphasized in the birth chart, for example, if it is the focal point of a T-SQUARE. Finally, a star assumes greater importance if its associations are corroborated by indications in the birth chart as a whole. (For more information on stars, consult Vivian E. Robson, *The Fixed Stars and Constellations in Astrology* [New York: Samuel Weiser, 1969], which was a major source for this entry.)

Acrux: Brightest star in the constellation of the Southern Cross; Jupiterian in nature; associated with a love of display. Because of its great celestial latitude, astrologers should be cautious in figuring aspects to it.

Agena: Second star in the constellation of Centaurus; Venusian and Jupiterian in nature; a significator of success.

Table 4. Fifty Important Stars

Celestial Longitude	Proper Name	Catalog Name	Magnitude	Celestial Latitude
02♈18	Difda	β Ceti	2	20S46
14♈01	Alpheratz	α Andromedae	2	25N41
00♉07	Mirach	β Andromedae	2	25N56
03♉41	Sharatan	β Arietis	3	08N29
07♉22	Hamal	α Arietis	2	09N58
14♉02	Menkar	α Ceti	2½	12S35
25♉53	Algol	β Persei	V*	22N25
29♉42	Alcyone	η Tauri	3	04N02
09♊30	Aldebaran	α Tauri	1	05S28
16♊33	Rigel	β Orionis	1	31S08
20♊40	Bellatrix	γ Orionis	2	16S50
21♊34	Capella	α Aurigae	1	22N55
22♊17	El Nath	β Tauri	2	05N23
23♊12	Alnilam	ε Orionis	2	24S32
28♊17	Polaris	α Ursae Minoris	2	66N05
28♊28	Betelgeuze	α Orionis	1	16S02
13♋59	Sirius	α Canis Majoris	1	39S35
14♋41	Canopus	α Argus	1	75S50
19♋58	Castor	α Geminorum	2	10N05
22♋57	Pollux	β Geminorum	1	06N40
25♋31	Procyon	α Canis Minoris	1	16S00
08♌26	South Asellus	δ Cancri	4	00N04
27♌00	Alphard	α Hydrae	2	22S23
29♌33	Regulus	α Leonis	1	00N28
11♍02	Zosma	δ Leonis	2	14N20
21♍20	Denebola	β Leonis	2	12N16
09♎40	Vindemiatrix	ε Virginis	2	16N12
23♎33	Spica	α Virginis	1	02S03
23♎57	Arcturus	α Boötis	1	30N47
11♏36	Acrux	α Crucis	1	52S52
12♏00	Alphecca	α Coronae Borealis	2	44N20
14♏48	South Kiffa	α Librae	3	00N20
19♏05	North Kiffa	β Librae	2½	08N30
21♏46	Unukalhai	α Serpentis	2½	25N25
23♏33	Agena	β Centauri	1	44S09
29♏18	Bungula	α Centauri	1	42S34
02♐54	Graffias	β Scorpii	3	01N01
09♐29	Antares	α Scorpii	1	04S34
11♐40	Rastaban	β Draconis	3	75N17
22♐10	Rasalhague	α Ophiuchi	2	35N51
29♐28	Sinistra	ν Ophiuchi	3	13N41
15♑02	Vega	α Lyrae	1	61N44
19♑31	Deneb	ζ Aquilae	3	36N12
01♒29	Altair	α Aquilae	1	29N18
03♒32	Giedi	α Capricorni	4	06N58
03♒46	Dabih	β Capricorni	3	04N36
03♓34	Fomalhaut	α Piscis Australis	1	21S08
05♓04	Deneb Adige	α Cygni	1	59N55
23♓12	Markab	α Pegasi	2	19N24
29♓05	Scheat	β Pegasi	2	31N08

* Variable.

Alcyone: See "Pleiades, the," below.

Aldebaran: Brightest star in the constellation of Taurus; Martian in nature; associated with public or military honors and courage. The Sumerians of the third millennium B.C. considered Aldebaran one of the ROYAL STARS, since at that time it marked the position of the vernal equinox. Aldebaran is regarded as the *fiducial*, or marking star, by some modern siderealists (see SIDEREAL ZODIAC).

Algol: Variable star in the constellation of Perseus (marking Medusa's severed head); Saturnian and Jupiterian in nature; said to foreshadow violence and violent death.

Alnilam: Brilliant white star in the constellation of Orión; Jupiterian and Saturnian in nature; an indication of short-lived success.

Alphard: Orange star, first in the constellation of Hydra; Saturnian and Venusian in nature; associated with immorality. Alphard was the South Star about 3000 B.C. (see PRECESSION OF THE EQUINOXES).

Alphecca: Brightest star in the constellation of Corona Borealis; Venusian and Mercurial in nature; associated with artistic talent.

Alpheratz: Double star system, white and violet, first in the constellation of Andromeda; Jupiterian and Venusian in nature; regarded as an indication of good fortune, wealth, honors, freedom, and love.

Altair: Pale yellow star, first in the constellation of Aquila; Martian and Jupiterian in nature; associated with immoderate ambition.

Antares: Double star system, fiery red and emerald green, brightest in the constellation of Scorpio; Martian and Jupiterian in nature; associated with rashness, imprudence, and violent death. The Sumerians in the third millennium B.C. considered Antares one of the ROYAL STARS, since at that time it marked the position of the autumnal equinox. Antares is regarded as the *fiducial*, or marking star, by some modern siderealists (see SIDEREAL ZODIAC).

Arcturus: Golden yellow star, brightest in the constellation of Boötes; Martian and Jupiterian in nature; associated with fame and honors.

Bellatrix: Somewhat variable pale yellow star in the constellation of Orion; Martian and Mercurial in nature; associated with marriage for money and honors followed by reverses.

Betelgeuze: Somewhat variable orange star, brightest in the constellation of Orion; Martian and Mercurial in nature; said to be a harbinger of wealth.

Bungula: Double star system, white and yellow, brightest in the constellation of the Centaur; Venusian and Jupiterian in nature; associated with friendship and refinement. Bungula (α Centauri) is the closest star to Earth other than the Sun; its distance is 4.2 light-years (2.47×10^{13} miles, or 265,818 times as far from us as the Sun).

Canopus: White star, brightest in the constellation of Argo; Saturnian and Jupiterian in nature; considered a bad omen for sea voyages. Canopus was the South Star about 12,100 B.C. and will be again about A.D. 13,700 (see PRECESSION OF THE EQUINOXES). Because of its great celestial latitude, astrologers should be cautious in figuring aspects to it.

Capella: White star, brightest in the constellation of Auriga; Martian and Mercurial in nature; reputed to augur wealth, honors, and friends in high places.

Castor: Double star system, bright white and pale white, in the constellation of Gemini; Mercurial in nature; associated with guile and duplicity.

Dabih: Double star system, yellow orange and light blue, in the constellation of Capricorn; Venusian and Saturnian in nature; indicating a tendency to melancholy.

Deneb: Green star in the constellation of Aquila; Martian and Jupiterian in nature; indicating authority.

Deneb Adige: Brilliant white star, brightest in the constellation of Cygnus; Venusian and Mercurial in nature; associated with a love of study. Because of its great celestial latitude, astrologers should be cautious in figuring aspects to it.

Denebola: Blue star in the constellation of Leo; Saturnian and Venusian in nature; reputed to portend misfortune and regrets.

Difda: Yellow star in the constellation of Cetus; Saturnian in nature; associated with illness, misfortune, and violence against the self.

El Nath: Double star, brilliant white and pale gray, in the constellation of Taurus; Martian in nature; reputed to be an indication of success.

Fomalhaut: Reddish star in the constellation of Pisces; Venusian and Mercurial in nature; traditionally associated with fame. The Sumerians of the third millennium B.C. considered Fomalhaut one of the ROYAL STARS, since at that time it marked

the position of the winter solstice.

Giedi: Triple star system—yellow, gray, and light purple—in the constellation of Capricorn; Venusian and Martian in nature; associated with piety and self-sacrifice.

Graffias: Triple star system, pale white and light purple, in the constellation of Scorpio; Martian and Saturnian in nature; associated with malice and sometimes with cruelty.

Hamal: Brightest star in the constellation of Aries; Martian and Saturnian in nature; associated with brutality and cruelty.

Markab: White star, brightest in the constellation of Pegasus; Martian and Mercurial in nature; associated with wounds.

Menkar: Orange star, brightest in the constellation of Cetus; Saturnian in nature; associated with illness and ruin.

Mirach: Yellow star in the constellation of Andromeda; Venusian in nature; associated with good fortune, beauty, and lasting marriage. Mirach entered the sign Taurus in the summer of 1971.

North Kiffa (also called *Zubeneschamali*): Light green star, brightest in the constellation of Libra; Jupiterian and Mercurial (according to later sources, Jupiterian and Martian) in nature; associated with success and happiness.

Pleiades, the: Group of fixed stars in the constellation of Taurus, centered around the greenish yellow star Alcyone; lunar and Martian in nature; traditionally considered MAL-EFIC. Alcyone is regarded as the *fiducial*, or marking star, by some siderealists (see SIDEREAL ZODIAC). By the year 2000 the Pleiades will be entering the sign of Gemini.

Polaris: Double star system, yellow and white, in the constellation of Ursa Minor; Saturnian and Venusian in nature; associated with illness, disgrace, and ruin. For the past few centuries, Polaris has marked the north celestial pole, being about 50′ from it. It will come closest in A.D. 2095 (see COSMOGRAPHY; PRECESSION OF THE EQUINOXES). Because of Polaris's great celestial latitude, astrologers should be cautious in figuring aspects to it.

Pollux: Orange star in the constellation of Gemini; Martian in nature; associated with audacity and cruelty.

Procyon: Double star system, white and yellow, brightest in the constellation of Canis Minor; Mercurial and Martian in nature; associated with vigorous activity verging on violence.

Rasalhague: Blue star, brightest in the constellation of Ophiuchus; Saturnian and Venusian in nature; associated with perversion and depravity.

Rastaban: Double yellow star system in the constellation of Draco; Saturnian and Martian in nature; associated with accidents. Because of its great celestial latitude, astrologers should be cautious in figuring aspects to it.

Regulus: Triple star, white and blue, in the constellation of Leo; Martian and Jupiterian in nature; regarded as BENEFIC; associated with generosity and ambition. The Sumerians of the third millennium B.C. considered Regulus one of the ROYAL STARS, since at that time it marked the position of the summer solstice. In A.D. 2012 Regulus will leave the tropical sign of Leo and enter Virgo.

It is regarded as the *fiducial*, or marking star, by some siderealists (see SIDEREAL ZODIAC).

Rigel: Double star system, pale blue, in the constellation of Orion; Jupiterian and Saturnian in nature; associated with fame, wealth, and originality.

Scheat: Irregularly variable yellow star in the constellation of Pegasus; Martian and Mercurial in nature; regarded as an omen of violent death. Scheat is due to enter the sign of Aries in 2046.

Sharatan: White star in the constellation of Aries; Martian and Saturnian in nature; associated with violence.

Sinistra: Small star in the constellation of Ophiuchus; Saturnian and Venusian in nature; associated with depravity. Sinistra will enter Capricorn in 2018.

Sirius: Double star system, white and yellow, brightest in the constellation of Canis Major; Jupiterian and Martian in nature; regarded as a harbinger of fame. It was known to the Egyptians as Sothis, and its HELIACAL rising, which coincided with the annual flooding of the Nile, marked the beginning of the year (see EGYPT, ASTROLOGY IN). Sirius is one of the closest stars to Earth; its distance is only 8.7 light-years (550,623 times as far as the Sun).

South Asellus: Beige star in the constellation of Cancer; Martian and Solar in nature; associated with fever and the risk of blindness.

South Kiffa (also called *Zubenelgenubi*): Double star system, light yellow and light gray, second brightest in the constellation of Libra; Saturnian and Martian in nature; associated with misfortune.

Spica: Brilliant white double star system, brightest in the constellation of Virgo; Venusian and Martian in nature; regarded as an indication of success and associated with love of the arts and sciences. Spica is also known as Arista. It is regarded as the *fiducial,* or marking star, by some siderealists (see SIDEREAL ZODIAC).

Unukalhai: Yellow star in the constellation of the Serpent; Saturnian and Martian in nature; associated with accidents and violence.

Vega: Light blue star in the constellation of Lyra; Venusian and Mercurial in nature; associated with wealth and pretentiousness. Vega was the North Star in 12,200 B.C. and will be again in A.D. 13,500 (see PRECESSION OF THE EQUINOXES). Because of its great celestial latitude, astrologers should be cautious in figuring aspects to it.

Vindemiatrix: Brilliant yellow star in the constellation of Virgo; Saturnian and Mercurial in nature; associated with deceit and difficult ordeals.

Zosma: Triple star system—yellow, blue, and violet—in the constellation of Leo; Saturnian and Venusian in nature; associated with selfishness, immorality, and a propensity to drug addiction.

Star Time: See TIME.

Station: See STATIONARY.

Stationary: A term used to describe a planet that appears from Earth to be standing still in its orbit prior to reversing its motion, either from DIRECT to RETROGRADE (called *stationary retrograde*) or from retrograde to direct (called *stationary direct*). The effect is, of course, an illusion. In the case of the *inferior planets* (those inside the Earth's orbit), the illusion is produced when the planet is momentarily moving directly toward the Earth (stationary retrograde) or directly away from the Earth (stationary direct). In the case of the *superior planets* (those outside the Earth's orbit), the situation is the same, except that it is the Earth that moves toward or away from the planet. The Sun and Moon can never be stationary.

The point in the planet's orbit where it seems to stand still is called its *station*. According to some astrologers, the length of time that a planet's station can be considered operative is inversely proportional to the speed of its motion; that is, the slower it moves, the longer its station. According to this theory Mercury's station is operative for 1 day, Venus's for 2 days, Mars's for 3 days, Jupiter's for 4 days, Saturn's for 5 days, Uranus's for 7 days, and Neptune's and Pluto's for 8 days each.

In a natal chart, the influence of a planet is held to be greatly intensified by its being stationary, especially if it is stationary direct (retrograde motion is associated with the past or the unconscious). For example, a stationary-direct Mercury in a horoscope would be one indication of a strong and active intelligence. Mercury stationary retrograde might indicate an equally acute mind, but of a more introspective sort. By transit, Mercury stationary direct would be an excellent time to sign a contract, while Mercury stationary retrograde would be a good time to begin psychotherapy.

Statistics and Astrology: The use of statistics to validate various aspects of astrological theory seems appropriate, since most astrologers agree that astrology deals with probabilities rather than certainties, and statistics rests upon the theory of probability. However, there are certain built-in problems, as we shall see.

Early attempts to correlate birth data with observable effects were made in the 1920s by the French astrologer Paul CHOISNARD (outstanding ability, violent death) and in the 1930s by the Swiss astrologer Karl Krafft (choice of profession as a clergyman). Although the work of Krafft and Choisnard has been criticized (for example, by French statistician Michel GAUQUELIN) on the grounds of inadequate samples and faulty methods, it did draw the attention of other astrologers, and Krafft in particular found early evidence for harmonics that anticipates the independent work of John ADDEY. But the use of statistics in astrology really came alive in the 1950s with the pioneering work of Donald Bradley in America, Michel and Françoise Gauquelin in France, and John Addey in England.

In analyzing the planetary positions of 2,593 clergymen whose birthdates he compiled from *Who's Who*, Bradley found no significant correlations with Sun signs—at least for the tropical zodiac—but his data when further analyzed did reveal a wave-like curve that Addey later identified as the seventh harmonic (and replicated, using birth data for British clergymen). Meanwhile the Gauquelins, intrigued by an experiment conducted by French astrologer Léon Lasson, began compiling vast amounts of birth data and analyzing birth charts with respect to angular planets and choice of profession, with highly significant results. And in England John Addey embarked on 20 years of research that led to the discovery and exploration of harmonics. The statistical experiments of both the Swiss psychologist C. G. JUNG (comparative positions of Sun, Moon, and Ascendant in the charts of married couples) and the American psychologist Vernon CLARK (ability of astrologers to match birth charts with biographies) also occurred in the 1950s.

To date, statistical studies have almost consistently failed to find correlation between Sun position and observable data; the exception is the work done by Mayo and Eysenck on extraversion and introversion and the positive and negative signs of the zodiac. However, they have confirmed the traditional meanings of angularity and the planets (Gauquelin) and the ability of astrologers to perform above chance level in blind matching tests, where control groups of nonastrologers performed at chance (Clark); and they have revealed significant correlations of profession with subdivisions of the zodiac heretofore unknown to traditional Western astrology, which invite further investigation (Addey).

The drawbacks of statistical research are, first, that it is time-consuming and expensive. The Gauquelins have shown the importance of large samples, which virtually require the use of the computer. Then there is the problem posed by the multiplicity of factors considered by astrology and the necessity of isolating one variable out of a complex whole made up of interdependent parts. No two charts are alike. The positions of the planets do not repeat themselves for hundreds of thousands of years; yet they are nonrandom, so that orbital characteristics must be taken into account. Intelligently constructed tests require a knowledge of astrology; yet if astrologers are in charge, results are not taken seriously by the scientific establishment. Few professional statisticians are interested in astrology—the Gauquelins are the exception—and until recently, astrologers have been blissfully ignorant of the principles of the scientific method or the importance of adequate sample, control groups, and replication. However, the gap is now being closed by a new generation of astrologers who are at home with technology, computers, and statistics, and judging from what has been accomplished in the last 30 years, the future possibilities for this field are promising indeed.

Stellium (or **Satellitium**): A cluster of several planets in the same sign or house. De Vore specifies five or more; Hone accepts three, citing the common example of Sun, Mercury, and Venus in the same sign. Since each planet reinforces the influence of the others, such a planetary grouping gives that sign or house major importance in the interpretation of the chart. For example, the stellium of five planets plus south node in Capricorn in the birth chart of novelist Horatio Alger helped to make his name synonymous with the "rags to riches" story that typifies Capricornian ambition.

Succedent (from the Latin *succedere,* to follow): A term used to describe the HOUSES in a horoscope that follow the ANGULAR houses, proceeding in a counterclockwise direction, or planets occupying such houses. The succedent houses are the Second, Fifth, Eighth, and Eleventh; they correspond to the FIXED signs, and planets in those houses are associated with preservation and resources. A planet in a succedent house is said to be weaker than if it were angular—that is, placed in one of the houses following the angles of the chart—but not so weak as if it were CADENT—that is, placed in one of the houses preceding the angles of the chart.

Summer Solstice: See SOLSTICES.

Summer Time: See TIME.

Sun (glyph ☉): The luminous celestial body whose light constitutes our day (and the lack of whose light, our night). Once thought to be a planet revolving around the Earth; now known to be a star, the central body of our solar system around which the Earth and other planets revolve, by which they are held in their orbits, and from which they receive light and heat. Its mean distance from the Earth is 93 million miles, and its diameter is 865,370 miles, or over a hundred times that of the Earth. (See GEOCENTRIC SYSTEM; PTOLEMY.)

In Western astrology, the Sun is sometimes classified as BENEFIC, if favorably aspected, and sometimes as neutral. Only in Eastern astrology, which is based on a lunar zodiac, is the Sun traditionally regarded as MALEFIC. The Sun rules the sign of Leo (see RULERSHIP) and is therefore in DETRIMENT in the opposite, Saturn-ruled sign of Aquarius. The Sun is exalted in Aries (see EXALTATION) and in FALL in Libra.

In chart interpretation the Sun stands for vitality, consciousness, spirit, creativity, identity. Its qualities are visibility, power, grandeur, nobility, honor, dignity, generosity, authority, and leadership. It rules the ego, individuality, self-image; career, fame, public life (as distinguished from private life, which is ruled by the Moon); will, ideals, destiny, purpose, future; yang energy (yin energy is ruled by the Moon); persons in authority, fathers, husbands, and men in general; and the general health and constitution of the native. When afflicted, the Sun is associated with pompousness, ostentation, despotism, egotism, self-centeredness, and pride.

The following delineations are offered to show some of the ways the Sun may operate in the signs and houses. It should be remembered that they are merely suggestions and that their accuracy in any given case depends on the overall strength and condition of the Sun in relation to the chart as a whole, especially the aspects it forms with other planets and important points. Although the Sun sign is of major importance in a birth chart, its influence is modified by other factors such as Moon, Ascendant, or a strong emphasis in another sign. (For fuller descriptions of the signs of the zodiac, especially in re-lation to the Sun, see the entries for the individual signs.)

SUN IN THE SIGNS

Sun in Aries: pioneering spirit, courage, impulsiveness, strength, aggression, competition, impatience, selfishness.

Sun in Taurus: patience, perseverence, loyalty, nurturing instinct, stamina, sensuality, conservatism, rigidity, materialism, greed.

Sun in Gemini: intelligence, curiosity, writing ability, versatility, changeability, restlessness, diffusion, nervousness, amorality, superficiality.

Sun in Cancer: sensitivity, maternal instinct, empathy, psychic ability, love of home, shyness, indirectness, tenacity, moodiness, possessiveness, defensiveness.

Sun in Leo: creativity, dramatic sense, love of pleasure, dignity, generosity, romanticism, childlike quality, egotism, pride.

Sun in Virgo: craftsmanship, service, humility, love of detail, interest in health and diet, perfectionism, fastidiousness, skepticism, criticism, worry.

Sun in Libra: fairness, unselfishness, aesthetic sense, pacifism, interest in law, need for partner, indecisiveness, weak identity.

Sun in Scorpio: resourcefulness, penetrating insight, strength in crisis, healing ability, psychic power, charisma, strong sexuality, interest in occult, secretiveness, jealousy.

Sun in Sagittarius: independence; optimism; love of sports, travel, and the outdoors; sense of humor; talkativeness; theoretical mind; self-righteousness.

Sun in Capricorn: responsibility, ambition, thoroughness, seriousness, forethought, executive ability, caution, anxiety.

Sun in Aquarius: group consciousness, idealism, inventiveness, unpredictability, detachment, dogmatism.

Sun in Pisces: impressionability, compassion, sensitivity, artistic gifts, mysticism, meditation, spirituality, mediumship, escapism, dependency, masochism.

SUN IN THE HOUSES

Sun in the First House: self-confidence, energy, good health, leadership, optimism, initiative, dignity, individualism, ambition, self-centeredness.

Sun in the Second House: interest in money and possessions, talent, creative ability, possibility of wealth and of prodigality.

Sun in the Third House: good student, interest in communication, writing or teaching ability, curiosity.

Sun in the Fourth House: strong attachment to home and family, love of houses, late development, reclusive tendencies.

Sun in the Fifth House: creativity; love of pleasure, theater, and children; romanticism; passion.

Sun in the Sixth House: concentration on work, interest in health and diet, service or healing profession, possibility of overwork.

Sun in the Seventh House: interest in other people, need for partner, outgoing personality, objectivity.

Sun in the Eighth House: ability to handle other people's resources, healing ability, strength in crisis, interest in the occult, intense experiences, awareness of sex.

Sun in the Ninth House: interest in higher education and spiritual growth, love of travel, professional success, strong sense of values.

Sun in the Tenth House: fame or recognition in chosen profession, worldly success, leadership, political power, ambition.

Sun in the Eleventh House: leadership in group activities, many friends, friends in high places, interest in the future, idealism.

Sun in the Twelfth House: working behind the scenes, identification with schools or institutions, interest in research, reclusive tendencies.

Sun-Sign Astrology: A form of astrology, necessarily oversimplified, which deals only with Sun signs. Although the term can apply to valid astrological works that happen to focus on the Sun, it is usually used by serious astrologers to refer disparagingly to the watered-down astrology found in the syndicated "Daily Horoscopes" in newspapers and the astrology columns in popular magazines.

The principal tool of Sun-sign astrology is the technique of *solar houses*, in which the native's Sun sign is regarded as the cusp of the First House, the following sign as the cusp of the Second House, and so on around the wheel. For example, all people born with Sun in Leo would have their second solar house ruled by Virgo, their third solar house by Libra, and so on. The current transits of the planets through the houses of this imaginary horoscope are used as the basis for predictions which, of course, will be identical for all Sun-sign Leos for a given period of time.

The advantage of this technique is that it can be used in the absence of specific information regarding time or place of birth and thus without the necessity of casting a chart.

But although the Sun is one of the most important elements in a birth chart, any attempt to describe character or predict events on the basis of the Sun's sign position alone, thus ignoring the myriad complexities of individual birth charts, is usually either naïve or irresponsible. How rough a sketch of individual personality the Sun sign alone represents can be seen by the fact that each sign encompasses one-twelfth of the human race. Sun-sign astrology survives, and indeed flourishes, for the simple reason that it is the easiest kind to commercialize. Most people know their birthday and can thus easily discover "what sign they are"—that is, what sign the *Sun* was in at their birth. Any further refinements require the services of a competent astrologer and are thus beyond the scope of those who would capitalize on the perennial gullibility of the public and the current popularity of astrology.

Note: Solar houses should not be confused with the Solar House System of HOUSE DIVISION, in which an actual chart is cast, based on the celestial longitude of the Sun. Like the Solar House System, solar houses may be a valid technique aside from their use in commercialized Sun-sign astrology.

Sun House System: See HOUSE DIVISION.

Sunrise Chart: A chart calculated for sunrise on the day of birth at the latitude of the birthplace. The cusp of the First House is therefore the degree of CELESTIAL LONGITUDE occupied by the Sun at sunrise and is generally treated as a true ASCENDANT, generating the MIDHEAVEN and intermediate cusps according to one of the quadrant systems of HOUSE DIVISION. The sunrise chart is generally used to study the mutual aspects of the planets in cases where the time of birth is unknown. It should not be confused with the *solar chart,* in which the cusp of the First House is the degree occupied by the Sun at noon on the day of birth.

Sun Sign: The sign of the zodiac that the Sun was transiting at the time of an individual's birth; sometimes called *birth sign*. (See SUN-SIGN ASTROLOGY.)

Superior Conjunction: A CONJUNCTION of the Sun and an inferior planet (Mercury or Venus) in which the planet is on the opposite side of the Sun from the Earth; as distinguished from an *inferior conjunction,* in which the planet is between the Earth and the Sun. (See ELONGATION.)

Superior Planet: A planet whose orbit lies outside that of the Earth; the superior planets are Mars, Jupiter, Saturn, Uranus, Neptune, and Pluto.

Symbolic Direction: See PROGRESSION AND DIRECTION.

Symbolist School: See HUMANISTIC ASTROLOGY; MODERN ASTROLOGY.

Synastry: See CHART COMPARISON.

Synchronicity (from the Greek *syn*, together, and *chronos*, time): JUNG's theory of meaningful coincidence; the idea, developed by him in the 1940s, that some events are connected by significance rather than by causality. In *Synchronicity: An Acausal Connecting Principle* (1952), Jung explores the relationship of this acausal concept to astrology. (See HORARY ASTROLOGY.)

Synetic Vernal Point: See SIDEREAL ZODIAC; VERNAL POINT.

Synodic Cycle: See CYCLE.

Synodic Month: See SYNODIC PERIOD.

Synodic Period (from the Greek *sunodos*, copulation, a reference to the New Moon, when the Sun and the Moon are conjoined): The time it takes a celestial body to make one complete round in its orbit, measured from one conjunction with the Sun to the next. The mean synodic period of the Moon, the *synodic month*, from one New Moon to the next, is 29 days 12 hours 44 minutes 2.7 seconds. The synodic periods of the planets, rounded to the nearest day, are as follows:

Mercury	116 days
Venus	1 year 220 days
Mars	2 years 289 days
Jupiter	1 year 34 days
Saturn	1 year 13 days
Uranus	1 year 4 days
Neptune	1 year 2 days
Pluto	1 year 2 days

The synodic period is distinguished from the *synodic cycle*, which is the interval between two successive conjunctions of any two planets, not one planet with the Sun. The synodic cycle is used in MUNDANE ASTROLOGY to measure important developments in world history. (See CYCLE; MOON; SIDEREAL PERIOD; TROPICAL PERIOD.)

Synthesis (from the Greek *syn*, with, and *tithenai*, to place): Literally, "putting together"; the art of weaving all the separate indications contained in a horoscope into a unified whole; the final stage or end product of interpretation. Synthesis is (or should be) distinguished from *delineation*, which is the interpretation of a specific influence, such as a planet's position in sign or house, an aspect, and so on. All of these separate delineations are part of the overall process of CHART INTERPRETATION, but the last step is the most difficult, and the ability to arrive at a meaningful synthesis is the mark of an experienced astrologer.

Syzygy: Literally, "a joining together"; an archaic term defined broadly as a CONJUNCTION or OPPOSITION of any two celestial bodies, or more particularly as a conjunction or opposition of a planet with the Sun, or of the Sun and Moon; PTOLEMY uses it as a synonym for LUNATION.

Table of Houses: A table showing the degrees of the signs of the zodiac on the cusps of the houses for various terrestrial latitudes for every degree of right ascension (every 4 minutes of sidereal time), or every celestial-longitude degree on the MIDHEAVEN, according to one of several systems of HOUSE DIVISION. In casting a horoscope, this reference tool is necessary for the beginner and very helpful to the astrologer, sparing him or her the necessity of performing complex and tedious calculations of spherical trigonometry. Among the best-known and most widely available tables of houses are Dalton's and Raphael's, based on the system of Placidus. For instructions in the use of tables of houses, see CHART CALCULATION. A sample page from a table of houses can be found on page 49.

Taurus (glyph ♉): The second sign of the zodiac, which the Sun transits during the second month of spring, from about April 21 to about May 20. The symbol for this sign is the bull. Its POLARITY is negative, its element is earth (see ELEMENTS), its quality is fixed (see QUALITIES), its ruling planet is Venus (see RULERSHIP), and its NATURAL HOUSE is the Second.

In Taurus the stability of earth and the perseverance of fixity are blended with the aesthetic sense of Venus to produce a slow, steadfast nature with a deep appreciation of the wealth and beauty of this planet. The symbol for Taurus is the bull, an image of brute force and calm endurance. While not all Taureans are bullish or bovine, many do have the quiet strength and stamina of this animal. If Arians are the pioneers and discoverers of the land, Taureans—who include not only Sun-sign Taureans, but all in whose charts the sign is emphasized—are the settlers and cultivators. They are the ones who roll up their sleeves and till the soil and build houses, bridges, and towns. Aries is the force of nature; Taurus the force of civilization.

Earth is the slowest-moving of the elements, and Taurus, being fixed earth, is the earthiest of the earth signs. Its natives have a special intimacy with the land and a deep understanding of and respect for all forms of matter. They value natural resources and want to conserve them; they value their bodies and usually take good care of them; and they value the fruits of their labor,

♉ Thaurus

grance. This delicacy, combined with their legendary persistence, has given the world some great artists and writers who illustrate the truth of the saying that genius is 1 percent inspiration and 99 percent perspiration.

Taureans are slow to take offense, but once their anger is aroused, they are implacable. Better face a Sherman tank than a Taurus on the warpath! But being children of Venus, they are fundamentally peace-loving souls who enjoy all the good things of life, especially eating, drinking, music, art, and making love.

Indeed, with their affectionate nature and slow sensuality, Taurus people are among the finest lovers of the zodiac. They make devoted partners and caring parents, though they are both possessive and overprotective. Their most compatible signs are Virgo, Capricorn, Pisces, and Cancer; Aries, Gemini, Libra, and Sagittarius are neutral; and Leo and Aquarius may be difficult. With another Taurus there would be more stability than passion. With Scorpio there will be both attraction and tension; but ultimately the question of COMPATIBILITY can be answered only by careful comparison of two whole birth charts.

Work comes naturally to Taureans, but they will do best at activities that involve building, growing, nurturing, cooking, conserving, or handling money or possessions. They make fine carpenters, gardeners, farmers, breeders, teachers, conservationists, naturalists, ecologists, economists, bankers, and businessmen. Their keen perception and pa-

whether these be food, money, or possessions. They tend to be fixed in their ideas, which are often conservative.

Taurean infants are characteristically content and regular in feeding and sleep patterns. They may be remarkably slow in reaching each successive developmental milestone, but once they reach it, they will persevere until it has been passed. The typical Taurus child has a solid-looking body and a strong sense of "mine." They must be gently taught to share their toys, for when Taureans are insecure, their love of material things can harden into greed. Like Cancers, they are loyal and protective toward their siblings, dolls, and playmates.

Taurus has a reputation for being dull and unimaginative, but actually this sign is often emphasized in the charts of highly creative people. Taurus rules the five senses, and these natives are tuned in to the subtlest nuances of color, sound, and fra-

tient dedication may also contribute to accomplishment in scholarship and the arts. Famous Sun-sign Taureans include John James Audubon, Honoré de Balzac, Johannes Brahms, Sigmund Freud, Martha Graham, William Randolph Hearst, Adolf Hitler, Immanuel Kant, Sören Kierkegaard, Nikolai Lenin, Karl Marx, John Stuart Mill, John Muir, Vladimir Nabokov, Henri Rousseau, Bertrand Russell, Benjamin Spock, Sir Arthur Sullivan, Rabindranath Tagore, Pierre Teilhard de Chardin, Harry S Truman, and Max Weber. (See BIRTHSTONES; COLORS; DAYS OF THE WEEK; METALS.)

T-Cross: See T-SQUARE.

Terrestrial Latitude: Angular distance of locations on the Earth's surface, measured in degrees, minutes, and seconds north or south of the Earth's Equator, whose latitude is 0°. Maximum terrestrial latitude is at the Earth's North Pole (90° north) and South Pole (90° south). Other locations are said to be on *parallels of latitude*; for example, Philadelphia, at 40° north terrestrial latitude, usually written 40N, is on the 40th Parallel. Above latitude 23N27 (the Tropic of Cancer) and below latitude 23S27 (the Tropic of Capricorn), the Sun is never directly overhead. Above 66N33 (the Arctic Circle) and below 66S33 (the Antarctic Circle), there are times during the year when the Sun does not set and other times when it does not rise. The sea-level distance between one terrestrial latitude and the next is slightly over 69 miles.

Local terrestrial latitude for the

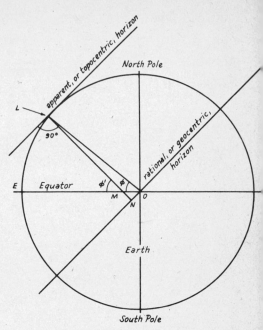

Figure 53. Geocentric versus geographic latitude. The Earth has greater diameter at the Equator than it does at the Poles. A plumb line from any location on the surface, **L**, extends down toward the nadir, **N**, which does not usually coincide with the Earth's center, **O**. **LM** is the plumb line from the surface, and **EM** is the plumb line from the Equator; the angle formed at their intersection, ϕ', is the geographic latitude. The angle forced by the intersection of **LO**, location to center, and **EO**, Equator to center—that is, ϕ—is the geocentric latitude. The horizon, either apparent or rational, is perpendicular to **LM** (the plumb line), not to **LO**.

birthplace is one of the two terrestrial coordinates an astrologer must know in order to calculate a birth chart; the other is TERRESTRIAL LONGITUDE. Terrestrial latitude determines the AsCENDANT, DESCENDANT, and (in most systems of HOUSE DIVISION) all the other house cusps except the Fourth and the Tenth.

Geographic latitude, which is given in atlases, is the terrestrial latitude determined by measuring the angle between an idealized plumb line (with topographical irregularities not taken into consideration) at the location and an idealized plumb line at the Equator. *Geocentric latitude* is the terrestrial latitude determined by measuring the angle formed at the Earth's center between the line extending to the surface at the location and the line extending to the surface at the Equator (see figure 53). There is a small difference between the two latitudes (never more than 12′) due to the fact that the Earth has greater diameter at the Equator than it does at the Poles (7,927 miles and 7,900 miles, respectively). Since the Ascendant is defined geocentrically, Charles JAYNE has advocated using geocentric latitude. But Robert Hand argues against its use because the HORIZON (which generates the Ascendant) is defined as the plane perpendicular to the plumb line. (See COSMOGRAPHY; PRECISION.)

Terrestrial Longitude: Angular distance of locations on the Earth's surface, measured in degrees, minutes, and seconds along the Earth's Equator from the Greenwich Meridian (that is, the longitude of Greenwich, England, which is 0°). Terrestrial longitude is measured for 180° from the Greenwich Meridian in both an eastward and a westward direction.

A *meridian of terrestrial longitude* is a GREAT CIRCLE perpendicular to the Equator at a point a certain number of longitude degrees east or west of the Greenwich Meridian. For example, Denver, Colorado (longitude 105° west, usually written 105W), is on the 105th Meridian. The local terrestrial meridian projected onto the CELESTIAL SPHERE is the local (celestial) meridian or, simply, the MERIDIAN. (See RIGHT ASCENSION.)

The sea-level distance between one terrestrial longitude degree and the next varies with TERRESTRIAL LATITUDE, becoming shorter the farther one is from the Equator. At the Equator the distance is about 69 miles; at 20° latitude (north or south) it is about 65 miles; at 40° it is about 53 miles; at 60° it is about 34 miles; at 80° it is about 12 miles. At the Poles (90° north or south latitude) there is no distance: All the longitudes meet.

Terrestrial longitude determines *mean solar time* at a given location. The *local mean time* (LMT) for each degree of longitude west of Greenwich is 4 minutes earlier than Greenwich mean time (GMT), and for each degree east of Greenwich it is 4 minutes later than GMT. Thus when it is noon in GMT, the LMT in New York City (longitude 74W) is 7:04 A.M. (74 × 4 = 296 minutes, or 4 hours 56 minutes earlier).

Standard Time (ST) is the LMT at legally instituted *Standard Time Meridians*, usually at 15° (1-hour) intervals east or west of the Greenwich Meridian. Locations within an ST zone more or less centered on the ST Meridian observe the same Standard Time.

The local terrestrial longitude for the birthplace is one of the two coordinates an astrologer must know in order to calculate a birth chart; the other is terrestrial latitude. Local longitude determines local mean time (LMT); from LMT can be derived *local sidereal time* (LST), which determines the positions of the MIDHEAVEN, ASCENDANT, and intermediate house cusps. (See PRECISION; TIME.)

Tertiary Progression: See PROGRESSION AND DIRECTION.

Theogenes the Greek: See ROMANS, ASTROLOGY AMONG THE.

Thrasyllus: See ROMANS, ASTROLOGY AMONG THE.

Tiger: The third sign of the Chinese zodiac, including all persons born between

February 8, 1902, and January 29, 1903 (water)
January 26, 1914, and February 14, 1915 (wood)
February 13, 1926, and February 2, 1927 (fire)
January 31, 1938, and February 19, 1939 (earth)
February 17, 1950, and February 6, 1951 (metal)
February 5, 1962, and January 25, 1963 (water)
January 23, 1974, and February 11, 1975 (wood)
February 9, 1986, and January 29, 1987 (fire)

Symbol of the power of faith among the Buddhists, the Tiger possesses a magnetism that few can resist. Natives of this sign like to do things with style and can put on quite a show when they want to dazzle, but their coldness, indifference, and pride make them plenty of enemies. They despise established values and hate to answer to anyone, although they themselves have a strong desire to dominate. A great many captains of industry, leaders, and revolutionaries are born under this sign. They work like demons, have big ideas, and are not afraid to take risks.

In love, they make a great show of passion and are possessive without being faithful themselves, which often makes them unhappy. They are the epitome of the unsatisfied Don Juan.

Compatible signs: Cat, Dog, Dragon, Monkey, Pig, Tiger.

Neutral signs: Cock, Goat, Horse.
Incompatible signs: Ox, Rat, Serpent.

Famous Tigers include Ludwig van Beethoven, Emily Brontë, William Burroughs, Charles de Gaulle, Emily Dickinson, Dwight D. Eisenhower, Allen Ginsberg Ho Chi Minh, Joe Louis, Stephane Mallarmé, Karl Marx, Marilyn Monroe, Vaslav Nijinsky, Rudolf Nureyev, Arthur Rimbaud, Jonas Salk, Dylan Thomas, and Alan Watts.

Time: The first step in calculating a birth chart is to adjust the recorded clock time of birth to the time reference used by a particular EPHEMERIS. Without this adjustment, the planetary positions in the emphemeris are imprecise, and determination of the MIDHEAVEN, ASCENDANT, and house cusps is impossible. Precise calculation requires that the astrologer be familiar with different types of time.

Solar time is time measured with reference to the Sun. *Apparent solar time* is based on the *apparent solar day*, the interval between two successive appearances of the Sun at either the upper MERIDIAN (Midheaven) at noon or the lower meridian (Imum Coeli) at midnight. Ordinarily the apparent solar day is said to begin when the Sun crosses the Imum Coeli. Apparent solar time is the time measured on sundials and is often referred to as "God's time." *Mean so-*

lar time is based on the *mean solar day*, and compensates for variation in the Sun's apparent speed (resulting from the Earth's orbit not being a perfect circle). For example, the apparent solar day of December 23 is about 51 seconds longer than the apparent solar day of September 23. Clocks measure mean solar time.

Local mean time (LMT) is the mean solar time at any given location. LMT for one location is ahead of LMT for locations to the west of it and behind LMT for locations to the east. The difference amounts to 4 minutes of time for each 1° of TERRESTRIAL LONGITUDE, or 1 hour of time for each 15° of longitude. (For all 360° of longitude—180° west and 180° east—the difference is 24 hours, or 1 day. In other words, once all 360° of longitude have passed beneath the Sun's direct rays as the Earth spins, 1 solar day will have elapsed.) Thus local mean noon in New York City (longitude 73W57) occurs 5 minutes of mean solar time before local mean noon in Philadelphia (longitude 75W11). *Greenwich mean time (GMT)*, or—when expressed in 24-hour notation—*Universal Time (UT)*, is the LMT at Greenwich, England (whose terrestrial longitude is 0°). *True local time (TLT)* is the *apparent*, not mean, solar time—the sundial time—at any given location, determined by adding or subtracting a specific number of minutes to or from the LMT. TLT is not used to determine sidereal time and therefore is irrelevant to chart calculation.

Sidereal time (or *star time*; from the Latin *sidus, sideris*, constellation, or star) is time measured with reference to the Earth's rotation on its axis. Unless noted otherwise, it is always considered local, but to avoid misunderstanding we will use the term *local* with it. The principal unit of sidereal time is the *local sidereal day*, the true period of one complete rotation, or the interval between two successive transits of any particular star over the meridian of any given location. When the VERNAL POINT—that is, 0° of celestial longitude or 0° Aries—crosses the Midheaven, the local sidereal day is considered to begin. At that moment local sidereal time is 0 hours 0 minutes and 0 seconds (usually expressed as 0h 0m 0s, or 00:00:00). The star Aldebaran will cross the upper meridian 4 hours and 33 minutes of sidereal time later—that is, local sidereal time will then be 4h 33m. Aldebaran will cross the meridian *every* day at 4h 33m; in fact, that local sidereal time is a permanent celestial coordinate of that star, called its RIGHT ASCENSION. The same is true of any other star. *Greenwich sidereal time (GST)* is the local sidereal time at Greenwich, England.

Both the local sidereal day and the mean solar day are divided into 24 hours, each of which is divided into 60 minutes, each of which is divided into 60 seconds. But the 24-hour local sidereal day is 23 hours 56 minutes and 4.09 seconds of mean solar time. Conversely, a 24-hour mean solar day is about 24 hours 3 minutes and 56 seconds of local sidereal time (LST). For this reason the ephemeris will show an increase of about 3 minutes and 56 seconds of GST for each day at either noon or midnight in GMT. Thus Aldebaran (or any other

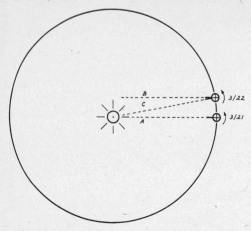

Figure 54. The difference between solar time and sidereal time. On March 21 when New York City's Empire State Building had its greatest orientation toward the Sun (see line **A**, the local meridian), it was noon in apparent solar time in New York City. (The building can never actually point toward the Sun, since the Sun is never overhead at the terrestrial latitude of New York City.) After 24 hours of local sidereal time, the Earth had completed one rotation on its axis and the Empire State Building was again oriented in the same direction, but the Sun was not yet crossing the local meridian (line **B**). After another 3 minutes and 56 seconds of local sidereal time, the Empire State Building again had its greatest orientation toward the Sun, the Sun was crossing the local meridian (line **C**), and it was noon—24 hours of apparent solar time after the previous noon. (For purposes of illustration, apparent solar time has been used instead of mean solar time, and the arc of the Earth's daily motion and its angles of orientation have been greatly exaggerated.)

star) will cross the meridian 3 minutes 56 seconds of LMT earlier each day. The difference between LST and mean solar time, which amounts to 1 complete sidereal day each year, is due to the Earth's revolution around the Sun. The Sun is very close to us relative to the other stars (more than 265,000 times closer than the next nearest star, Alpha Centauri). After one complete rotation of the Earth (1 sidereal day) the Earth has moved

through about 1/365 of its annual orbit around the Sun. The angular difference in the Earth's orientation toward a star (other than the Sun) is negligible, but the difference in its orientation toward the Sun is considerable. It takes a bit longer each day (3 minutes 56 seconds of LST) for the local meridian to line up with the Sun (see figure 54).

Ephemeris Time (*ET*) is a uniform solar time reference that takes into account variations in planetary orbits due to gravitation. It is currently several seconds in advance of GMT. Astrological ephemerides list the GST at either midnight or noon in GMT (0 hours or 12 hours in UT). Until recently most astrological ephemerides also listed the positions of the Sun, Moon, and planets at midnight or noon in GMT, but recently published ephemerides generally list them at 0 hours (midnight) of ET.

Standard, or *Zone*, *Time* (*ST*) was introduced by law at the end of the nineteenth century as a matter of convenience in commerce, transportation, and long-distance communication. (Until then train schedules listed arrivals and departures for each location in its own local apparent solar time. Trying to determine how long a train trip would take for passengers or businessmen who needed to move freight was next to impossible.) Every 15° of terrestrial longitude east or west of Greenwich (0° longitude) is a *Standard Time meridian*. (There are a few intermediate ST meridians as well—see table 5.) All clocks within a *time zone* more or less centered on an ST meridian are set to the LMT of the ST meridian.

For example, Boston, New York City, Philadelphia, and Detroit are in the Eastern Standard Time (EST) zone, whose ST meridian is 75° west longitude, usually written 75W. EST is defined as that longitude's LMT, which is 5 hours earlier than GMT. All clocks in the EST zone are set to that time. Thus, at noon GMT, clocks throughout the EST zone read 7:00 A.M. But the LMT of Boston is really 7:16 A.M., of New York City is 7:04 A.M., of Philadelphia is 6:59 A.M., and of Detroit is 6:28 A.M.

Daylight Saving, Summer, or *War Time (DST* or *WT)* has been used in the summer months in many localities since World War I. When this time is in effect, clocks are advanced 1 hour (in some places ½ hour) later than ST. (In Great Britain in World War II during summer months, clocks were 2 hours in advance of ST— which is GMT there. This was called *Double Summer Time.)* The original purpose of Daylight Saving Time was to take advantage of surplus summer daylight in order to increase industrial output. During war years DST was sometimes continued year-round. Also, during energy crisis periods DST has been used in winter so that less energy would be needed for light and heat at the end of regular work shifts to accommodate those working overtime. (For general guidelines to determine where and when DST was in effect, see table 6.)

An accurate birthtime is essential for the calculation of the Midheaven, Ascendant, and house cusps. This time is almost always expressed in *clock time,* which may be ST or DST. In some methods of CHART CALCU-LATION, recorded clock time must be converted to LMT and then to LST according to specific rules. It is crucial to know whether clock time is ST or DST and which ST meridian was in effect.

Time Acceleration: In the so-called LMT method of CHART CALCULATION, a correction to account for the difference between the sidereal time and the mean solar time that has elapsed since the Greenwich sidereal time (GST) listed in the EPHEMERIS (see TIME). Time acceleration is one of the adjustments necessary to convert GST to local sidereal time (LST). It amounts to an additional 10 seconds for each hour of elapsed mean solar time. For example, consider a birthtime of 3:15 A.M. local mean time (LMT). If the GST is found from a midnight ephemeris, the elapsed mean solar time is 3 hours 15 minutes, or 3.25 hours. The time acceleration is 10 × 3.25 = 32.5 seconds, rounded to 33 seconds. If the GST is found from a noon ephemeris, we must consider the mean solar time elapsed since the previous noon, which is 12 hours + 3.25 hours = 15.25 hours. Multiplying by 10 seconds per hour, we get 152.5 seconds, rounded to 153 seconds, or 2 minutes 33 seconds.

The reason for time acceleration is as follows: For every 24 hours of mean solar time there are 24 hours 4 minutes of sidereal time. Dividing the extra 4 minutes (240 seconds) by 24 hours, we arrive at 10 seconds, which must be added to the sidereal time for each hour of elapsed mean solar time.

Table 5. ST Meridians (Time Zones) in
the English-speaking World.

American Samoa	
traditionally	172W30
by 1965	165W00
Andaman Islands	97E30
Anguilla	60W00
Antigua	75W00
Ascension Island	
to 1946	15W00
1946–	14W15
Australia[a]	.
Western Australia	120E00
Northern Territory,	
South Australia	142E30
Canberra, New South	
Wales, Queensland,	
Tasmania, Victoria	150E00
Bahamas	75W00
Baker Island	165W00
Barbados	60W00
Belize	90W00
Bermuda	60W00
Botswana	30E00
British North Borneo	120E00
British Solomon Islands	165E00
British Virgin Islands	60W00
Brunei	120E00
Canada[a]	
Newfoundland ST	52W30
Atlantic ST	60W00
Eastern ST	75W00
Central ST	90W00
Mountain ST	105W00
Pacific ST	120W00
Yukon ST	135W00
Canal Zone	75W00
Cayman Islands	75W00
Chagos Islands	75E00
Cook Islands	159W06
Corn Islands	90W00
Cyprus	30E00
Danger Islands	165W00

Dominica	60W00
Eire	
1916–68	00W00
1968–	15W00
Ellice Islands	180W00
Falkland Islands	60E00
Fiji Islands	180E00
Gambia	
1912–18, 1933–	15W00
1918–33	00W00
Ghana	00W00
Gibraltar	00W00
Gilbert Islands	165W00
Grenada	60W00
Guam	150E00
Guyana	56W15
Hong Kong	120E00
Howland Island	165W00
India	87E30[b]
Jamaica	75W00
Jarvis Island	165W00
Johnston Island	157W30
Kenya	45E00[c]
Kermadec Islands	180E00
Kingman Reef	157W30
Lesotho	30E00
Lord Howe Island	150E00
Mawali	30E00
Malaysia[d]	112E30[e]
Maldives	73E30
Malta	15E00
Mariana Islands	135W00
Marshall Islands	150E00
Mauritius	60E00
Midway Islands	
to 1947	157W30
1947–	150W00
Montserrat	60W00
Nauru	172E30
Navassa Island	75W00
Nevis	60W00
New Guinea[f]	150E00

New Hebrides	165E00	Trinidad and Tobago	60W00
New Zealand		Tristan da Cunha	
to 1946	172E30	to 1972	15W00
1946–	180E00	1972–	00W00
Nicobar Islands	97E30	Tuvalu	180E00
Nigeria	15E00	Uganda	41E15[h]
Norfolk Island	168E00	Union of South Africa	30E00
Palmyra Island	157W30	United Kingdom	00W00[i]
Papua	150E00	United States[a]	
Pitcairn Island	150W00	Eastern ST	75W00
Puerto Rico	60W00	Central ST	90W00
Rodrigues Island	60E00	Mountain ST	105W00
Ryuku Islands	135E00	Pacific ST	120W00
Sabah	120E00	Yukon ST	135W00
St. Christopher	60W00	Alaska-Hawaii ST[j]	150W00
		Bering ST[k]	165W00
St. Helena		U.S. Virgin Islands	60W00
to 1972	05W45	Wake Island	180E00
1972–	00W00	Western Samoa	165W00
St. Lucia	60W00	Zambia	30E00
St. Vincent	60W00	Zanzibar	45E00[l]
Sand Island	157W30	Zimbabwe Rhodesia	30E00
Sarawak			
to 1926, 1942–	120E00		
1926–42	112E30		
Savage Island	170E00		
Seychilles	60E00	[a] Time zone boundaries subject to change over the years.	
Sierra Leone		[b] Confusion before 1947.	
to 1972	15W00	[c] Confusion before 1960.	
1972–	00W00	[d] Except Sabah and Sarawak.	
Singapore		[e] Confusion before 1972.	
to 1965	110E00	[f] Except Solomon Islands.	
1965–	105E00	[g] Confusion before 1972 between 45E00 and 41E15.	
Somali Republic	45E00	[h] To 1928—LMT observed; on Jun 31, 1928, 45E00 adopted; on Jan 1, 1930, 37E30 adopted; by 1948 41E15 observed nationwide.	
Sombrero	60W00		
South Georgia			
to 1972	31W45		
1972–	30W00	[i] Between Feb 18, 1968, and Nov 1, 1972, 15E00 adopted.	
South Sandwich Islands	30W00	[j] Called Central Alaska ST until 1967; Hawaii observed 157W30 until Jun 8, 1947.	
Sri Lanka	82E30		
Swan Islands	90W00		
Swaziland	30E00	[k] Called Nome ST until 1967.	
Tanzania	45E00[g]	[l] Confusion before 1972 between 37E30 and 41E15.	
Tonga Islands	175W00		

Table 6. Observance of Daylight Saving (Summer) and War Time in the English-speaking World.
(Changes at 2 A.M. unless otherwise specified)

Non-U.S. Places Not Observing

American Samoa, Andaman Islands, Anguilla, Antigua, Ascension Island, Baker Island, Barbados, Bermuda, Botswana, British North Borneo, British Solomon Islands, Brunei, Canal Zone, Caroline Islands, Cayman Islands, Chagos Islands, Cook Islands, Corn Islands, Cyprus, Danger Islands, Dominica, Ellice Islands, Fiji Islands, Gambia, Ghana,[a] Gilbert Islands, Grenada, Guam, Guyana, Howland Island, Jamaica, Jarvis Island, Johnston Island, Kenya, Kermadec Islands, Kingman Reef, Lesotho, Lord Howe Island, Mawali, Malaysia,[b] Maldives, Mariana Islands, Marshall Islands, Mauritius, Midway Islands, Montserrat, Nauru, Navassa Island, Nevis, New Guinea,[c] New Hebrides, Nicobar Islands, Nigeria, Norfolk Island, Palmyra Island, Papua, Pitcairn Island, Puerto Rico, Rodrigues Island, Ryuku Islands, Sabah, St. Christopher, St. Helena, St. Lucia, St. Vincent, Sand Island, Savage Island, Seychilles, Singapore, Somali Republic, Sombrero, South Georgia, South Sandwich Islands, Sri Lanka,[d] Swan Islands, Swaziland, Tanzania, Tonga Islands, Trinidad and Tobago, Tristan da Cunha, Tuvalu, Uganda, Union of South Africa,[e] Virgin Islands, Wake Island, Western Samoa, Zambia, Zanzibar, Zimbabwe.

Australia
1917	Jan 1–Mar 25
1918–41	NO
1942	Jan 1–LSI Mar, LSI Sep–LSI foll-Mar
1943	Oct 3–LSI foll-Mar
1945–71	NO
1972–	LSI Oct–1SI foll-Mar[f]

Bahamas
1970–71	Year-round
1972–	Same as Canada

Belize
1918–	1SI Oct–2SI foll-Feb

Canada
1918	Apr 14–Oct 31
1942–45	Feb 2[g]–Sep 30, 1945
1972–	LSI Apr–LSI Oct[h]

Alberta
1919	Apr 13–May 27
1920–41	NO[i]
1946–47	Most places NO
1948–71	NO

British Columbia
1919–41	NO (except Victoria 1921–23)
1946	NO (except Vancouver and Victoria)
1946–47	Most places NO
1948–71	NO

Labrador
1919–35	NO
1936–41	Questionable
1946–50	NO

1951–59	LSI Apr–LSI Sep
1960–	LSI Apr–LSI Oct

Manitoba
1916	NO (except Brandon and Winnepeg)
1919–41	NO (except Beausejour 1937)
1946–63	Questionable
1964–65	LSI Apr–2SI Sep
1966	Questionable
1967–	LSI Apr–LSI Oct

New Brunswick
1919–65	Questionable
1966–72	LSI Apr–LSI Oct

Newfoundland
1917	NO (except St. John's)
1919–50	NO (except St. John's)
1951–59	LSI Apr–LSI Sep
1960–	LSI Apr–LSI Oct

Northwest Territories: NO

Nova Scotia
1916	NO (except Halifax)
1919–41	Most places NO
1946–71	Questionable

Ontario
1916	NO (except Hamilton)
1919–71	Questionable

Prince Edward Island
1919–41	NO
1946–61	NO (except Charlottetown 1946–47 and Summerside 1947)
1962–	LSI Apr–LSI Oct

Quebec
1919–67 Questionable
1968–   LSI Apr–LSI Oct
Saskatchewan
1919–41 Most places NO
1946   Questionable
1947   LSI Apr–LSI Sep
1948–58 Questionable
1959   LSI Apr–LSI Oct
1960–61 Questionable
1962–   NO

Yukon: NO

Eire: Same as United Kingdom, except
1925 ends Oct 4 and Double Summer
Time never observed.
Falkland Islands
1937–42 LSI Sep–3SI Mar (change at
         0 hr.)
1943–   Questionable
Hong Kong
1961   3SI Mar–Oct 29
1962   3SI Mar–Oct 28
1963   3SI Mar–Nov 3
1964   3SI Mar–Nov 1
1965   3SI Mar–Oct 31
1966–   3SI Apr–3SI Oct
India
1941   Questionable
1942–45 Sep 1–Oct 15, 1945
1946–47 Questionable
1948–   NO
Malta
1916–20 Questionable
1921–39 NO
1940–45 Jun 15–Sep 30, 1945
1946–65 NO
1966–71 May 23–Sep 25
1972–   NO
New Zealand
1927   Nov 6–Mar 4, 1928
         (advanced 1 hour)
1928–33 2SI Oct–3SI foll-Mar
         (advanced ½ hour)
1934–39 1SI Sep–LSI foll-Apr
         (advanced ½ hour)
1940–46 Sep 1–Jan 18, 1946 (advanced
         ½ hour)
1947–73 NO
1974–   Same as Australia (advanced
         1 hour)
Sarawak
1935–42 Sep 14–Dec 14 (advanced 20
         minutes)

1943–   NO
Sierra Leone
1936–42 Jun–Sep (advanced 40
         minutes)
1943–59 Questionable
1960–   NO
United Kingdom
1916   May 21–Oct 1
1917   Apr 8–Sep 17
1918–19 LSI Mar–LSI Sep
1920   LSI Mar–LSI Oct
1921   Apr 3–Oct 3
1922   Mar 26–Oct 8
1923   Apr 22–Sep 16
1924   Apr 13–Sep 21
1925   Apr 19–Oct 4
1926   Apr 18–Oct 3
1927   Apr 10–Oct 2
1928   Apr 22–Oct 7
1929   Apr 25–Oct 6
1930   Apr 13–Oct 5
1931   Apr 19–Oct 4
1932   Apr 17–Oct 2
1933   Apr 9–Oct 8
1934   Apr 22–Oct 7
1935   Apr 14–Oct 6
1936   Apr 19–Oct 4
1937   Apr 18–Oct 3
1938   Apr 10–Oct 2
1939   Apr 16–Oct 19
1940–45 Feb 25–Oct 7, 1945
         (advanced 1 hour, except
         when Double Summer Time)
1941   May 4–Aug 10 (Double
         Summer Time, advanced 2
         hours)[j]
1942   Apr 5–Aug 9 (Double
         Summer Time, advanced 2
         hours)[j]
1943   Apr 4–Aug 15 (Double
         Summer Time, advanced 2
         hours)[j]
1944   Apr 2–Sep 17 (Double
         Summer Time, advanced 2
         hours)[j]
1945   Apr 2–Jul 15 (Double
         Summer Time, advanced 2
         hours)[k]
1946   Apr 14–Oct 6
1947   Mar 16–Nov 2 (Apr 13–Aug
         10, advanced 2 hours)
1948   Mar 14–Oct 31
1949   Apr 3–Oct 30
1950   Apr 16–Oct 22

1951	Apr 15–Oct 21
1952	Apr 20–Oct 26
1953	Apr 19–Oct 4
1954	Apr 11–Oct 3
1955	Apr 17–Oct 2
1956	Apr 22–Oct 7
1957	Apr 14–Oct 6
1958	Apr 20–Oct 5
1959	Apr 19–Oct 4
1960	Apr 10–Oct 2
1961	Mar 26–4SI Oct
1962	Mar 25–4SI Oct
1963	Mar 31–4SI Oct
1964	Mar 22–4SI Oct
1965	Mar 21–4SI Oct
1966	Mar 20–4SI Oct
1967	Mar 19–4SI Oct
1968–71	NO
1972–	3SI Mar–4SI Oct

United States
1918–19	LSI Mar–LSI Oct
1942–45	Feb 9–Sep 30, 1945
1967–73[1]	LSI Apr–LSI Oct
1974[1]	Jan 6–LSI Oct
1975[1]	Feb 23–LSI Oct
1976–[1]	LSI Apr–LSI Oct

Connecticut from 1938 (1938 ends Oct 2); Chicago 1922–35, 1946–66; Colorado 1966; Delaware 1966; rest of Illinois from Jul 1, 1959; Iowa 1966; Maine from 1955; Maryland from 1959 (except 1963 LSI Apr–LSI Sep); New Jersey from 1946; New York City; rest of New York State from 1955; Philadelphia and Pittsburgh; rest of Pennsylvania 1966; Rhode Island from 1949; Vermont from 1955; West Virginia 1966
1920	LSI Mar–LSI Oct
1921–54[m]	LSI Apr–LSI Sep
1955–66	LSI Apr–LSI Oct

Massachusetts; New Hampshire from 1937
1920	LSI Mar–LSI Oct
1921–37	LSI Apr–LSI Sep
1938	LSI Apr–Oct 1
1939–53[m]	LSI Apr–LSI Sep
1954–66	LSI Apr–LSI Oct

California; Nevada; Portland, Oregon, from 1951 (except 1961 ends Oct 1); rest of Oregon 1951, 1963–66; Washington from 1961 (1962 LSI Apr–LSI Sep)
1948–49	Mar 14–Jan 1, 1949
1950–61	LSI Apr–LSI Sep
1962–66	LSI Apr–LSI Oct

District of Columbia from 1947 (1947 May 11–Sep 21; 1948 begins May 2); St. Louis, Missouri
1946–55	LSI Apr–LSI Sep
1956–66	LSI Apr–LSI Oct

Wisconsin
  1957–64 LSI Apr–LSI Sep
  1965–66 LSI Apr–LSI Oct

U.S. Places Not Observing, 1967–
  Alaska (until 1969[n]); Arizona (except 1967[n]); Hawaii; parts of Indiana (except 1969–71[n]); parts of Kentucky (1967); parts of Michigan (1967–68); all of Michigan (from 1969)

U.S. Places Not Observing, 1920–41, 1946–66
  Alaska; Arizona; Arkansas; California through 1947; Colorado (except 1966, *and* Aspen 1964, Denver 1920–21); District of Columbia 1920–21, 1923–46; Florida (except Pensacola and Eglin AFB 1946–66); Georgia (except Albany and Atlanta 1938–40); Hawaii; Iowa through 1941 (except Davenport); Kansas through 1965; Kentucky through 1941; Louisiana (except Kenner and New Orleans 1946); Maryland through 1941; Minnesota through 1956 (except Duluth 1946); Mississippi; Missouri through 1941; Montana through 1941; Nebraska through 1965 (except Ainsworth and Valentine 1955–56); Nevada through 1947; New Hampshire through 1936; New Mexico through 1952; North Carolina through 1941, 1947–66 (except Wilmington 1957); North Dakota through 1951, 1961–66; Oklahoma (except Bartlesville 1962); Oregon through 1948, 1952–62 (except Portland); South Carolina; South Dakota through 1965 (except Jefferson, Vermillion, Yemkton 1964); Tennessee through 1946, 1957–65 (except Chattanooga 1920 and Nashville 1920, 1940); Texas; Utah; Vermont through 1937; Virginia through 1941; Washington 1946–47, 1953–60 (except Richland 1956); West Virginia through 1936; Wisconsin 1920, 1924–56 (except Walworth and Zenda 1955–56); Wyoming

Note: Places and times not covered are questionable.
  LSI = last Sunday in
  1SI = first Sunday in
  2SI = second Sunday in
  3SI = third Sunday in
  4SI = fourth Sunday in
  foll = the following
  NO = not observed

[a] Except 1936–42 (Sep 1–Dec 31).
[b] Except Sarawak.
[c] Except Solomon Islands from 1974, which observes Daylight Saving Time like Australia.
[d] Except 1942–45 (Jan 5–Aug 31, advanced ½ hour; Sep 1–Oct 16, 1945, advanced 1 hour).
[e] Except 1942 (questionable) and 1943 (Sep 19–foll-Mar 19).
[f] Except Northern Territory and Victoria, which did not observe Daylight Saving Time.
[g] Ontario and Quebec began at 0 hr. on Sep 29, 1940.
[h] Except Saskatchewan.
[i] Except Edmonton: 1920 (LSI Apr–LSI Oct), 1921–23 (LSI Apr–LSI Sep).
[j] For the rest of the year time advanced 1 hour.
[k] For the rest of the year, until Oct 7, time advanced 1 hour.
[l] Exceptions listed separately below.
[m] Except 1942–45; see main United States listing.
[n] See main United States listing.

Tombaugh, Clyde: See PLUTO.

Topocentric Cosmography: See COS-MOGRAPHY.

Topocentric Horizon: See HORIZON.

Topocentric System: See HOUSE DIVISION.

Total Eclipse: See ECLIPSE.

Traditional Astrology: See CLASSICAL ASTROLOGY.

Transit (from the Latin *transire, transitum,* to go or pass over): **1.** The passage of a planet through a sign of the zodiac (for example, the Sun's transit of Aries occurs between March 21 and April 20).
2. The passage of a planet over the position of a planet or important point in a natal, progressed, or horary chart, or over any degree where it forms an aspect to such a planet or important point. Transits are found by referring to an EPHEMERIS of the planets' positions for a given year and comparing this information with the positions of the planets and important points in the natal chart.

For example, if natal Mercury is at 27° Scorpio, it may receive transits by conjunction, as when a planet in the sky reaches 27° Scorpio; or by aspect, as when a planet in the sky reaches 27° Taurus (opposition), 27° Leo or 27° Aquarius (square), 27° Cancer or 27° Pisces (trine), or 27° Virgo or 27° Capricorn (sextile). In the study of transits, the minor aspects are generally ignored. The strongest transits are those in which the transiting planet forms a conjunction with the natal planet or point. The next most powerful transits are squares, which are associated with stress and motivation, and oppositions, which are associated with both objectivity and separation. Trines and sextiles from transiting planets are associated with opportunities, those by sextile generally requiring more effort on the part of the native than those by trine.

Thus transiting Uranus conjunct natal Mercury can have an electrifying effect on the native's mind, bringing new ideas, breakthroughs in communication, and often sleeplessness through overstimulation of the nervous system. The opposition would be similar but less intense, and there would be more objectivity than with the conjunction. The square, on the other hand, might be more uncomfortable; the native might feel that he was being forced to change his ideas almost against his will or that he had to oppose rigid thinking in others. The trine might bring brilliant insights that he would not necessarily do anything about; the sextile might mean opportunities from unexpected quarters that could galvanize him into activity.

The quality of the transit depends not only on the nature of the aspect but on the nature of the transiting planets. Transits from Jupiter and Venus were traditionally regarded as fortunate, and transits from Saturn and Mars as unfortunate. However, these categories are breaking down, and many modern astrologers regard all transits as opportunities for learning and growth. The first rule in interpreting transits, which is stressed by all authorities, is that nothing can happen by transit that is not "promised" in the natal chart. In other words, a transit cannot "cause" a person to behave out of character; it can only activate energies already present within the native and ready to be released. Thus transiting Jupiter conjunct natal Sun will not necessarily cause a shy adolescent Pisces to take the lead in the school play, but it may give her the courage to take a bit part.

To get an idea what to expect when a transiting planet forms an aspect to a natal planet, the astrologer studies the relationship between the two planets in the natal chart. Thus if transiting Uranus is forming a square to natal Mars, an aspect associated with accidents, the astrologer will look to see what aspect, if any, Mars and Uranus make in the natal chart before becoming alarmed. If they are in easy aspect, or if there is no aspect, the native may simply be more energetic, more creative, and more interested in sex during that period. If they are in difficult aspect natally, there would still be no reason to hide under the bed; the astrologer would probably tell the client to expect a period when his or her impatient streak would be more pronounced.

The transit of a planet through a house in a horoscope will activate the affairs of that house. For example, Sun transiting the First House may bring physical energy and an enhanced self-image; Jupiter transiting the Second House may expand financial opportunities; and Saturn transiting the Third House may restrict communication with the im-

mediate environment or improve concentration.

Transits vary in intensity according to their duration, which depends on the rate of motion of the transiting planet. Transits from the Moon and Mercury are over almost before they've begun; they represent the little swings and dips of mood and energy that characterize our day-to-day existence. An exception to this rule occurs when a fast-moving planet is about to make its station before going RETROGRADE or resuming DIRECT motion, in which case its transit has greater duration (see STATIONARY). Slower-moving planets, such as Jupiter and Saturn, may be within a degree of exact aspect to another planet or point for weeks at a time; hence their transits are usually more profound. Transits from the outer planets—Uranus, Neptune, and Pluto—are associated with periods of transformation that may be significant within the context of a whole lifetime.

Most astrologers agree that the strength of a transit is greatest as it approaches exactness and tapers off rather quickly afterward. Reinhold Ebertin finds that the effect of most transits is over *before* they reach exactness. An ORB of 1° is generally used.

A philosophical definition of transit is given by Dane RUDHYAR, who writes, "A transit is the focused manifestation of the unending pressure applied by Nature upon the natal, archetypal structure of our selfhood. It pits the power of the universe of change—and of the collective, social factors in individual experience which constitute 'human nature'—against the integrity of the individual; thus it pits the ephemeris against the birth chart!"

Transits are one of the primary tools astrologers use to anticipate future conditions, the others being progressions, directions, and the SOLAR RETURN. (See PROGRESSION AND DIRECTION.)

Translation of Light (also called **Borrowed Light**): In a horoscope, a transfer of energy between two planets not within ORB of aspect by the agency of a transiting planet that is separating from an aspect to the first while applying to an aspect to the second. For example, if Mars is at 4° Taurus and Saturn is at 14° Virgo, the two planets are not within orb of a trine. However, if transiting Jupiter is at 9° Taurus, thus separating from a conjunction with Mars and applying to a trine with Saturn, it "translates the light" from Mars to Saturn and makes the trine operational. Translation of light can also occur within a natal chart. Thus in the foregoing example if natal Jupiter were at 9° Capricorn, it would tie the three planets into a grand earth trine, even though the other two are not strictly in orb. Similarly, translation of light can often serve to tie together a series of planets in conjunction and integrate them with the rest of the chart.

Trans-Neptunian Planets: See URANIAN SYSTEM.

Trans-Saturnian Planets (also called **Extra-Saturnian Planets**): See MODERN PLANETS.

Trigonalis: See CYCLE.

Trine (from the Latin *tres, tria,* three; symbol △): One of the major aspects recognized by classical astrology, bringing into relationship planets or important points separated by one-third of the zodiac circle, or an angle of 120°. The trine has traditionally been regarded as highly BENEFIC, not only because it unites signs of the same element but because it divides the circle by the mystical number of three. Three trines (or a GRAND TRINE) form an equilateral triangle, symbol of perfection. Sepharial calls it "the most perfect of all the aspects."

Recently, however, doubt has arisen as to the unqualified desirability of the trine. If, as some esoteric astrologers believe, the trine represents a reward for good deeds done in previous lifetimes, then it may have a negative influence by failing to motivate the native to work toward personal growth in this lifetime. Many modern astrologers (for example, Alan LEO) consider the trine weaker and less favorable than the SEXTILE, an aspect of 60° that combines signs of different but harmonious elements and seems to call for more effort on the part of the native. The trine is associated with ease and advantages, whereas the sextile is associated with opportunity. For example, a man with Moon in Sagittarius trine Jupiter in Leo may have a wonderful optimism, but he could also be complacent or arrogant, unless this aspect were offset by other factors in the chart. However, a man with Moon in Sagittarius sextile Jupiter in Libra would tend to make the most of his opportunities and would probably be better able to see another person's point of view.

The consensus seems to be that one or two trines in a chart are helpful but that too many trines can be an embarrassment of riches.

By transit, the trine is deemed less powerful than the conjunction, the opposition, or the square and is more associated with states of consciousness than with the triggering of events.

Orbs for trines are smaller than those allowed for squares, but larger than those for the minor aspects. Average orbs are 3° or 4°, but orbs always depend on the condition of the planets involved. (See ASPECT; ORB.)

Triplicity: A group of three signs belonging to the same element; there are four triplicities, corresponding to the four ELEMENTS. For example, the fire triplicity consists of Aries, Leo, and Sagittarius.

Tropical Period: The time it takes a celestial body to make one complete round in its orbit, measured from the VERNAL POINT, as distinguished from the *sidereal period*, the time it takes a celestial body to realign itself with a given star. Because of PRECESSION OF THE EQUINOXES, the tropical period is slightly shorter than the sidereal period. The Earth's tropical period is known as a *tropical year* and takes 365 days 5 hours 48 minutes and 46 seconds in mean solar time—about 20 minutes shorter than the sidereal year.

Tropical Signs (from the Greek *tropos*, turning): Cancer and Capricorn;

so called because upon entering them, the Sun apparently reverses its direction north or south of the Equator. (See SOLSTICES.)

Tropical Year (also called **Astronomical Year, Equinoctial Year, Natural Year, Seasonal Year,** or **Solar Year**): The TROPICAL PERIOD of the Earth; the period between one vernal equinox and the next. It is the tropical year that the *civil*, or *calendar*, year attempts to approximate through the addition of an extra day every 4 years. The tropical year is 365 days 5 hours 48 minutes 46 seconds in mean solar time (see TIME). This span is about 20 minutes shorter than the *sidereal year*, the actual time it takes the Earth to make one complete revolution in its orbit. The discrepancy is due to the PRECESSION OF THE EQUINOXES.

Tropical Zodiac (abbreviated **TZ;** also called **Moving Zodiac**): The zodiac based on a twelvefold equal division of the Earth's orbit in space (the ECLIPTIC) or the year in time, beginning with the VERNAL POINT (spring equinox); each of its twelve segments contains 30° of CELESTIAL LONGITUDE and is called a sign. Each of the four seasons, which begin when the Sun is at one of the cardinal points on the ecliptic—vernal equinox, summer solstice, autumnal equinox, and winter solstice—is composed of three signs, the first CARDINAL, the second FIXED, and the third MUTABLE. Taken as a unit, the tropical zodiac is a twelve-part sequential cycle of maturation.

Many Western astrologers are unaware of any other zodiac than the tropical one and may be surprised and disconcerted to learn, for example, that on the first day of spring, when the Sun enters the sign of Aries, it is actually in front of the stars in the constellation of Pisces. The signs did temporarily correspond to the constellations about two millennia ago, but because of PRECESSION OF THE EQUINOXES, the tropical zodiac is continuously moving backward in relation to the "fixed" zodiac of constellations. There is a school of Western astrologers called *siderealists* who spurn the tropical zodiac and use the actual constellations as the backdrop against which they calculate the planetary positions (see SIDEREAL ZODIAC); Hindu astrologers have adhered to the constellations for thousands of years (see INDIA, ASTROLOGY IN).

On the other hand, most Western astrologers who are aware of the precessional displacement still adhere to the tropical zodiac as a system relevant to life on the Earth. The signs, after all, derive a good deal of their meaning from the seasons—at least in the Northern Hemisphere. And whereas individual stars at important points in a birth chart may give deeper meaning to the chart (see STAR), the constellations themselves are arbitrary, subjectively perceived patterns of stars physically unrelated to one another. Moreover, in spite of siderealists' attempts to define and equalize them, the constellations do not have definite boundaries: They overlap and are greatly varying in size and shape. (See SIGNS OF THE ZODIAC.)

True Local Time (TLT): See TIME.

True Nodes: See NODES.

Trutine: See CONCEPTION CHART.

T-square (or **T-cross**): A MAJOR CONFIGURATION in which two planets are in OPPOSITION to each other, with a third planet at their MIDPOINT, forming SQUARES to both ends of the opposition. The T-square has been found to be an extremely potent and dynamic pattern, combining as it does the restlessness of the square with the objectivity of the opposition. It can generate considerable tension, especially at the beginning of the life, as the opposing tendencies represented by the two ends of the opposition are forced on the native's awareness through the squares. The planet at midpoint is the focal point of the configuration, and represents the means by which the polarized tendencies are resolved. Although initially an uncomfortable formation, the T-square is perhaps the most motivating of any of the major configurations. It is frequently found in the charts of people who achieve a great deal, particularly when the planets are in the cardinal signs. With the mutable T-square the energies can be diffused, and with the fixed they can become crystallized into repetitive patterns; many astrologers feel that fixed T-squares are harder to resolve. But in all three cases the potential for integration is good.

In the chart of Jack Kerouac there are three T-squares, two in mutable signs and the third in a combination of cardinal and mutable. The best example is the one in which the Moon, which is rising in Virgo in the Twelfth House, opposes Uranus in Pisces in the Sixth House, the opposition being squared by Mars in Sagittarius in the Third House. Rebelliousness, inspiration, and emotional instability are all suggested by the opposition, with the wanderlust, spirituality, and volubility of Mars in Sagittarius in the Third House of communication providing the outlet.

This T-square, together with the others, helped to galvanize the volatile energies in the chart into the prolific and charismatic creativity of the author of *On the Road* and the spokesman for the Beat Generation.

Two Fortunes, the: See FORTUNES, THE.

Two Infortunes, the: See INFORTUNES, THE.

Ultimate Dispositor: See DISPOSITOR.

Unfortunate Signs: See FEMININE SIGNS; POLARITY.

Universal Time (UT): See TIME.

Upper Culmination: See MERIDIAN.

Upper Meridian: See MERIDIAN.

Uranian Astrology: See URANIAN SYSTEM.

Uranian House Systems: See HOUSE DIVISION.

Uranian Planets: See URANIAN SYSTEM.

Uranian System (or Hamburg School): A school of astrology founded by Alfred Witte (1878–1943) and Friedrich Sieggrün (1877–1951) in which extremely concise delineations are applied to complexes of midpoints known as *planetary pictures*. Uranian midpoint theory is derived from Witte's observation that *hard aspects* have much greater significance than *soft aspects*. Hard aspects include the opposition (one-half circle), the square (one-fourth circle), the semi-square (one-eighth circle), the sesquisquare (three-eighths circle), and the following angles: 22½° (one-sixteenth circle), 67½° (three-sixteenths circle), 112½° (five-sixteenths circle), and 157½° (seven-sixteenths circle). Hard aspects are in fact successive midpoints of the circle. In order to perceive these angles more clearly than is possible on an ordinary birth chart, Witte invented the 90° dial (see CHART FORM). He later realized that the midpoint of any angular separation between two planets was a potent focus for the planets' energies.

As developed by Witte, Sieggrün, and others, the Uranian system now considers midpoints not only between two planets but between a planet and a primary point (such as the ASCENDANT, MIDHEAVEN, the two lunar NODES combined into a single nodal axis, the VERTEX, the EAST POINT, and the VERNAL POINT), between two primary points, between a planet and a midpoint, between a primary point and a midpoint, and between two midpoints. Adding to the complexity are eight hypothetical Uranian, or trans-Neptunian, planets postulated by Witte and Sieggrün—Cupido, Hades, Zeus, Kronos, Appollon, Admetos, Vulkanus, and Poseidon—for which precise ephemerides have been compiled. Thus in any single chart there are thousands of factors that must be taken into consideration, although much confusion can be avoided by reducing the size of the orbs. Several Uranian house systems, most of them variations on the Equal House system, are used to emphasize one or another of these factors. Witte's system, except his house systems, hypothetical planets, and more complicated "sensitive points," was adopted by Reinhold Ebertin in the 1930s and refined into the system known as COSMOBIOLOGY. (See HOUSE DIVISION.)

Uranus (glyph ⛢, ♅, or ♅): The first major planet after Saturn, discovered March 13, 1781, by Sir William Herschel and originally called Herschel in his honor. Uranus would not have been discovered were it not for the invention of the telescope, since it is barely visible to the naked eye. Its mean diameter is 29,500 miles, its mean distance from the Sun is 1,783 million miles, and its SIDEREAL PERIOD is 84.02 tropical years. It has four satellites—Ariel, Umbriel, Titania, and Oberon—and was recently found to have rings.

Since Uranus was not known to the ancients, it is exclusively a planet of modern astrology, the first of the so-called trans-Saturnian, or modern, planets. Thus it has no traditional classification as BENEFIC or MALEFIC, although soon after its discovery it was sometimes regarded as malefic. The current tendency is to view Uranus, Neptune, and Pluto as planets of social, cultural, and spiritual transformation that transcend these categories; Dane RUDHYAR calls them "ambassadors from the galaxy." In Greek mythology, Uranus was the personification of heaven, the husband (or son) of Gaia, the goddess who personified the Earth.

Regarded as a "higher octave" of Mercury, Uranus has been assigned RULERSHIP of the sign of Aquarius, whose traditional ruler was Saturn. Hence it is in DOMICILE in Aquarius and in DETRIMENT in the opposite, Sun-ruled sign of Leo. Many astrologers consider its sign of EXALTATION to be Scorpio and hence its FALL to be Taurus.

The attributes of the modern planets have been deduced by careful observation, over a period of time, of cultural trends that appeared around the time of their discovery. Uranus first impinged on human consciousness around the time of the American Revolution, the French Revolution, the harnessing of electricity, the Industrial Revolution, and numerous inventions of far-reaching consequences, such as steam-driven machinery. Before its discovery, the social hierarchy was more or less fixed; but the Industrial Revolution resulted in the rise of the middle class, greater social mobility, and the idea of the classless society. Astrologers have come to associate this planet with revolution, invention, innovation, sudden change, the unexpected. Its qualities are originality, individuality, independence, rebelliousness, inventiveness, unconventionality, and amorality. It rules inspiration, imagination, intuition, insight, genius; art, iconoclasm, bohemianism, the avant-garde; homosexuality, bisexuality,, asexuality, unisex, group sex; androgyny; grandparents; science, and astrology. It rules the technology that is new at the time. Thus in the early twentieth century it ruled electricity, radio, aviation; now it rules electronics, circuitry, and computers. Uranus has been called the Awakener and is regarded as a force for dynamic change, the principle that opposes ideas and institutions that have become rigid and outmoded, thus effectively challenging the tyranny of Saturn. When afflicted, Uranus is associated with intractability, eccentricity, fanaticism, anarchy, explosion, and violence.

The following delineations are offered to show some of the ways Uranus may operate in the signs and houses. It should be remembered that they are merely suggestions and that their accuracy in any given case depends on the overall strength and condition of Uranus in relation to the chart as a whole, especially the aspects it forms with other planets and important points.

Since Uranus remains in a sign for approximately 7 years, its influence is more obvious on an entire generation than on a single individual. However, individuals in whose birth charts Uranus is ANGULAR or closely aspected by Sun, Moon, or Ascendant may be more closely attuned to its energy in that particular sign and may express it in a more conspicuous way. Bear in mind that the planet is simultaneously influencing the present through cultural patterns and world events, and the future through

the children born during those years.[1]

URANUS IN THE SIGNS

Uranus in Sagittarius (1897/98–1904): first Zeppelins, Wright brothers; William James's *The Varieties of Religious Experience*; John Dewey and modern education; founding of Shintoism; founding of anthroposophy. *Contributions of this generation*: breakdown of ethnocentrism, intellectual freedom (Margaret Mead, George Orwell).

Uranus in Capricorn (1904–12): Einstein and Rutherford revolutionize concepts of structure of matter and space-time; behaviorism; cubism. *Contributions of this generation*: rebellion against authority, lasting change (B. F. Skinner, Simone de Beauvoir, Jean-Paul Sartre, Marshall McLuhan).

Uranus in Aquarius (1912–19/20): Bolshevik Revolution, women's suffrage, development of world federalism, IWW. *Contributions of this generation*: reformers, humanitarians (Eugene McCarthy, J. F. Kennedy, Indira Gandhi).

Uranus in Pisces (1919/20–1927): Prohibition, rise of radio and cinema, invention of TV. *Contributions of this generation*: idealism (Judy Garland, Robert F. Kennedy, Pete Seeger, George McGovern).

[1] For some of the delineations of Uranus in the signs we are indebted to the following: Robert Hand, *Planets in Youth* (Rockport, Mass.: Para Research, 1977); Marcia Moore and Mark Douglas, *Astrology, The Divine Science* (York Harbor, Me.: Arcane Publications, 1971); Frances Sakoian and Louis Acker, *The Astrologer's Handbook* (New York: Harper & Row, 1973).

Uranus in Aries (1927–34/35): pioneering in technology, including first digital computer, cyclotron, Charles Lindbergh's flight. *Contributions of this generation*: nonconformism (Jacqueline Onassis, Andy Warhol, Yoko Ono, Günter Grass).

Uranus in Taurus (1934/35–1941/42): the New Deal, rise of socialism and communism; invention of nylon. *Contributions of this generation*: revolution in values, rejection of materialism (Jane Fonda, Joan Baez, Ken Kesey).

Uranus in Gemini (1941/42–1948/49): splitting of the atom, computer technology, phototypesetting, transistor. *Contributions of this generation*: reintegration of science and values; this generation may succeed in reinstating astrology as a science.

Uranus in Cancer (1948/49–1955/56): TV invades the home; the pill; liberation of women in Communist China; frozen foods. This generation has not been heard from, but they seem to have new ideas about intimacy, question the nuclear family and other establishment values, and are drawn to psychic research.

Uranus in Leo (1955/56–1961/62): beatniks; rise of rock 'n' roll, happenings; sexual permissiveness; individualism and eccentricity.

Uranus in Virgo (1961/62–1968/69): student rebellions, civil rights movement; health food movement, awakening about pollution.

Uranus in Libra (1968/69–1974/75): women's movement, increase in divorce, coeducational dormitories, introduction of ERA, abortion reform.

Uranus in Scorpio (1974/75–1981): sexual revolution, new attitudes toward death and dying; particle theory in physics; DNA; exposing scandals in government; renaissance of the occult; new discoveries about psychic phenomena and life after death.

URANUS IN THE HOUSES

Uranus in the First House: conspicuous individuality, eccentricity, need for freedom, love of change, unusual appearance or mannerisms.

Uranus in the Second House: rapid changes in financial affairs, unusual talent, unconventional values, technical skills.

Uranus in the Third House: intuitive, original mind; erratic education; talent for writing, teaching, or science.

Uranus in the Fourth House: unconventional background, many changes of residence, disrupted or broken home, emotional instability.

Uranus in the Fifth House: unusual or gifted children, original self-expression, creativity, bizarre romances.

Uranus in the Sixth House: need for independence in employment, many changes of employment, unusual diet, potential health problems.

Uranus in the Seventh House: attraction to unusual people, offbeat relationships, need for freedom in relationships, intuitive communication, possibility of divorce.

Uranus in the Eighth House: healing ability, strong attraction to the occult, propensity to unexpected crises.

Uranus in the Ninth House: unorthodox religious or philosophical ideas, original scholarship, biofeedback, much travel, spiritual consciousness.

Uranus in the Tenth House: unusual profession, sudden fame, unorthodox reputation, technical or scientific work, astrology or art, sudden changes in fortune.

Uranus in the Eleventh House: utopian and revolutionary ideas, interest in the future and technology, unusual friends, creative stimulation from friends and groups.

Uranus in the Twelfth House: psychic experiences, brilliant research, creative solitude, possibility of mental illness if afflicted.

Venus (glyph ♀): The third brightest body in the heavens after the Sun and Moon, slightly smaller than the Earth, moving in an orbit between those of Mercury and Earth, and remarkable for the extreme density of its atmosphere. Its diameter is 7,610 miles, its mean distance from the Sun is 67 million miles, and its SIDEREAL PERIOD is 224.7 days.

In astrology, Venus was traditionally known as the Lesser Fortune, the Greater Fortune being Jupiter; thus its nature was held to be BENEFIC, though less so than Jupiter's. Both planets were believed to confer fame, wealth, favors, success, and happiness; but whereas with Jupiter the emphasis is on expansion, importance, and grandeur, with Venus it is on charm, pleasure, and beauty. This is in keeping with the name of the planet, which is that of an ancient Italian goddess of fertility and beauty who was later identified with the Greek Aphrodite and became universally known as the Roman goddess of love.

Venus rules the signs of Taurus and Libra (see RULERSHIP); thus it is in DETRIMENT in the opposite, Mars-ruled signs of Scorpio and Aries. It is exalted in Pisces (see EXALTATION) and in FALL in Virgo.

In chart interpretation Venus stands for love, friendship, relationship, affinity, and values. Its qualities are affection, gentleness, sociability, peacefulness, harmony, balance, elegance, grace, and sensuality. It rules sympathy, taste, likes and dislikes, attraction, magnetism, and appeal; art, beauty, aesthetic sense, comfort, pleasure, jewelry, ornaments, perfumes, luxury, and fashion; and Platonic or romantic love, as distinguished from sexual love, which is ruled by Mars. When afflicted, Venus is associated with laziness, vanity, and overindulgence, especially in sweets.

The following delineations are offered to show some of the ways Venus may operate in the signs and houses. It should be remembered that they are merely suggestions and that their accuracy in any given case depends on the overall strength and condition of Venus in relation to the chart as a whole, especially the aspects it forms with other planets and important points.

VENUS IN THE SIGNS

Venus in Aries: a taste for the primitive, enthusiasm, impulsiveness, sexual orientation, aggression, tactlessness.

Venus in Taurus: warmth, sensuality, nurturing impulse, aesthetic refinement, loyalty, possibility of financial success.

Venus in Gemini: lively personality, changeable tastes, love of learning, talent for communication, sociability, diffusion.

Venus in Cancer: love of home and children, deep affections, empathy, intimacy, loyalty, shyness, possessiveness.

Venus in Leo: love of luxury and display, generosity, popularity, creativity, star complex, laziness.

Venus in Virgo: discriminating tastes, critical faculty, loyalty, undemonstrative nature, reluctance to make a commitment.

Venus in Libra: refined pleasures, outgoing personality, charm, diplomacy, love of justice, aesthetic sense, laziness.

Venus in Scorpio: seductiveness, subtlety, shrewdness, secretiveness, suspicion, jealousy, tendency to manipulate others.

Venus in Sagittarius: self-confidence, sense of humor, love of travel and the outdoors, optimism, arrogance, self-righteousness.

Venus in Capricorn: loyalty, seriousness, attraction to older people, social aspirations, ambition, austere beauty.

Venus in Aquarius: gregariousness, democratic tastes, liberal values, collective art, detachment.

Venus in Pisces: unselfish love, universal compassion, appreciation of music or poetry, gullibility, emotional dependence, masochistic tendencies.

VENUS IN THE HOUSES

Venus in the First House: good loooks, charm, opportunities, sociability, love of pleasure, laziness, overindulgence.

Venus in the Second House: love of material things, artistic talent, possibility of financial success.

Venus in the Third House: good education, intellectual tastes, love of learning, talent for writing.

Venus in the Fourth House: comfortable home, possibility of inherited wealth, love of entertaining, happy old age.

Venus in the Fifth House: love of children; artistic ability; romantic personality; love of theater, parties, and pleasure.

Venus in the Sixth House: love of work, work involving art or beauty, social life and business life inseparable.

Venus in the Seventh House: happy marriage, successful relationships, popularity, social skills, social butterfly.

Venus in the Eighth House: ability as counselor or therapist, sexual orientation, interest in the occult, possibility of inheritance, freeloading.

Venus in the Ninth House: friends in foreign countries; love of travel, religion, and philosophy; high ideals; graduate school; scholarship.

Venus in the Tenth House: financial success, success in the arts or the entertainment world, talent for publicity, famous beauty or wealth.

Venus in the Eleventh House: many friends, artistic friends, good fortune through group activities, high ideals.

Venus in the Twelfth House: love of solitude, shyness, secret relationships, mediumistic tendencies, social conscience.

Vernal Equinox: See EQUINOXES; VERNAL POINT.

Vernal Ingress: See INGRESS.

Vernal Point (or **First Point of Aries**): The beginning of the TROPICAL ZODIAC (0° Aries); the vernal, or spring, equinox, the point on the ECLIPTIC where the Sun is on the first day of spring in the Northern Hemisphere; one of the two points where the ecliptic intersects the CELESTIAL EQUATOR, the other being the *autumnal equinox*. The vernal point marks the beginning of measurement of RIGHT ASCENSION on the celestial equator (0°0'0", or 0 hours 0 minutes 0 seconds) or of CELESTIAL LONGITUDE on the ecliptic (0°0'0"). The vernal point is continuously moving backward in relation to the constellations (see PRECESSION OF THE EQUINOXES), and the equatorial and ecliptic CELESTIAL COORDINATES move along with it. The siderealist Donald Bradley has attempted to quantify the moving position of this point, which he calls the *synetic vernal point* (see SIDEREAL ZODIAC). According to his findings, the position of the synetic verbal point on January 1, 1980, was 5°32'-22" in the constellation of Pisces. The vernal point is also considered by Uranian astrologers to be one of the primary points in a chart (see URANIAN SYSTEM).

Vertex: In a birth chart, the point where the PRIME VERTICAL intersects the ECLIPTIC in the west; the *Antivertex* is the point where the prime vertical intersects the ecliptic in the east. In midlatitudes the Vertex is always within two signs of the Descendant.

To find the Vertex, first determine the *colatitude*. Subtract the terrestrial latitude from 90°. Then consider the Imum Coeli as the Midheaven and look up the Ascendant in a table of houses under this new "Midheaven" for the colatitude. For example, in Margaret Mead's chart (see CHART INTERPRETATION), the birth latitude is 40N; the colatitude, then, is 90 − 40 = 50N. Her Midheaven is 11°43' Scorpio; thus the new "Midheaven" is 11°43' Taurus. Looking up the Ascendant for 11°43' Taurus at 50N, we find her Vertex to be 23°44' Leo.

The Vertex was discovered independently by L. E. JOHNDRO and Charles JAYNE. Johndro considered it and the Antivertex as electrostatic release points of the Earth at the birth moment, and connected them with Uranus. Jayne regards the Vertex as the most impersonal angle in the chart: the most fated, the least conscious or voluntary, and having to do with the past (as distinguished from the Ascendant, which is the most personal angle, the least fated, the most conscious and voluntary; and has to do with the future). (See EAST POINT.)

Vertical Arc: See PROGRESSION AND DIRECTION.

Vertical Circle: See AZIMUTH.

Vespertine (or **Vesperal**; from the Latin *vesper*, evening): A term used to describe a planet that sets just after the Sun; opposite of *matutine*.

Vesta (glyph ⚶): One of the four largest ASTEROIDS; discovered in 1807. Zipporah Dobyns associates it with personal devotion, isolation, and possible health problems; Eleanor Bach with security and tradition.

Via Combusta (Latin): Literally, "the path of combustion"; an area of the zodiac, usually the first 15° of Scorpio, but sometimes 15° Libra to 15° Scorpio or 15° Libra to 30° Scorpio, held by the ancients to be particularly unfortunate. The Moon *in via combusta* was considered just as afflicted as if in eclipse. The negative influence was probably derived from association with certain fixed stars such as Antares, which have now moved by precession into the sign of Sagittarius. The term is still used in HO-RARY ASTROLOGY.

Vigintile: See SEMIDECILE.

Villefranche, Morin de: See MORIN, JEAN-BAPTISTE.

Virgo (glyph ♍): The sixth sign of the zodiac, which the Sun transits during the last month of summer, from about August 23 to about September 22. The symbol for this sign is the virgin. Its POLARITY is negative, its element is earth (see ELEMENTS), its quality is mutable (see QUALITIES), its ruling planet is Mercury (see RULERSHIP) and its NATURAL HOUSE is the Sixth.

In Virgo the practicality of earth and the adaptability of mutability are combined with the intelligent influence of Mercury to produce a modest yet discriminating nature that is oriented toward service. The maiden in the symbol for this sign is usually shown holding an ear of corn, thus combining the idea of purity with that of fertility. In northern latitudes, the Sun's passage through Virgo coincides with the harvest, the time when farmers gather the fruits of their labor and separate the grain from the chaff. Like the other earth signs, Virgo people like to work with the earth and its products, not so much in a spirit of ownership (like Taurus) or ambition (like Capricorn) as in a desire to be useful.

Virgo shares this spirit of service with its polar opposite, Pisces, but it is very unlike Pisces in that it takes nothing on faith. Virgoans—who include not only Sun-sign Virgos, but all in whose charts the sign is emphasized—are distinguished by their highly developed critical and analytical faculties. They are able to make fine discriminations and they distrust things that do not hang together logically or people who are too emotional. Their fussiness can be infuriating, but their ability to focus on detail and their willingness to do something over until it is right make them the craftsmen of the zodiac. If Leo is the sign of the artist, Virgo is the sign of the craftsman and critic.

There is a humility in Virgo that inspired Isabel Hickey to call it "the sign of the hidden Christ." Christianity, with its emphasis on sacrifice, is ruled by Pisces, sign of the fisherman and the fish; but the potential for Christlike service is ruled by Virgo, sign of the lowly carpenter—and of the Virgin Mary.

In the human body Virgo corresponds to the intestines and the eliminatory system, and there is a special concern in this sign for health, diet, and cleanliness. Mercury's rulership of the nervous system indicates a high-strung temperament, and what with worrying about details that others would not notice, Virgos are prone to nervous indigestion. Their preoccupation with cleanliness and order can sometimes be obsessive; the "anal retentive" personality is a negative manifestion of Virgo energy.

As children they are apt to be shy and picky eaters but may actually enjoy tasks such as helping with the dishes, laundry, or cleaning up their rooms. They are neat and conscientious students, though somewhat lacking in self-esteem.

The same qualities that make Virgos such good workers can cause them unhappiness in their personal lives. They are painfully conscious of all the imperfection in the world, in themselves as well as in others, and as a result they are often dissatisfied. They sometimes have trouble learning to trust, and they are slow to make a personal commitment, which has earned them a reputation for being standoffish. However, once they have made a choice—usually a sensible one—they are devoted partners. They have all the sensuality of the other earth signs, with more than

a dash of anal eroticism. Their most compatible signs are Taurus, Capricorn, Cancer, and Scorpio; Leo, Libra, Aquarius, and Aries are neutral; Gemini and Sagittarius are likely to be difficult. With another Virgo, there could be intellectual rapport. With Pisces there will be both attraction and tension, the outcome depending, as with all combinations, on how the two charts interact and not on the COMPATIBILITY of Sun signs alone.

Virgo people like to work with their hands and are often more comfortable in subordinate positions. They excel in all crafts, especially those requiring precision, such as carpentry, jewelry making, watch repair, or sewing. Virgos take naturally to gardening, teaching, writing—especially criticism—scholarship, clerical work, health or service occupations, or work involving sanitation, nutrition, or diet. Famous Sun-sign Virgos include Antonin Artaud, Jean-Louis Barrault, Ingrid Bergman, Theodore Dreiser, Queen Elizabeth I (the "Virgin Queen"), Greta Garbo, Johann Wolfgang von Goethe, Samuel Johnson, D. H. Lawrence, Maria Montessori, Grandma Moses, Orville Prescott, Walter Reed, Walter Reuther, Margaret Sanger, William Saroyan, Upton Sinclair, and Leo Tolstoi. (See BIRTHSTONES; COLORS; DAYS OF THE WEEK; METALS.)

Void of Course: A term used to describe a planet that will form no major aspect before leaving the sign it occupies. The term is most often applied to the Moon, and its interpretation is similar to that for the phenomenon of RETROGRADE—that is, a void-of-course Moon is associated with confusion, failure to materialize, and delay. The concept has been widely used in HORARY ASTROLOGY, but recently it is enjoying a revival in NATAL and MUNDANE ASTROLOGY. Void-of-course Moon ephemerides are published by astrologer Al Morrison and are included in the *American Ephemeris*, published by Astro Computing Services (for an example, see page 48).

Volguine, Alexandre (March 3, 1903, 5:30–6:00 A.M., Novaya-Praha, near Alexandria, Russia–June 1977): French astrologer and author, generally considered to be the greatest French astrologer of the twentieth century. Volguine came to astrology in 1917. Brought to France at an early age after the Russian Revolution, he was uprooted again during World War II, when he was arrested by the Nazis and placed in a concentration camp. He is perhaps best known as the founder (in 1937) of *Les Cahiers Astrologiques*, the distinguished French journal of astrology which is highly regarded by astrologers all over the world. Volguine edited *Les Cahiers Astrologiques* from 1937 until his death in 1977, in spite of war, the Nazi occupation, strikes, economic problems, illness, and hospitalization. In addition, he wrote many original works on astrology, including *L'astrologie lunaire* (*Lunar Astrology*, 1936), *La technique des révolutions solaires* (*The Technique of Solar Returns*, 1937), and *Le maître de nativité* (*The Ruler of the Nativity*, 1945), which have been translated into English; and *Les parts astrologiques* (*The Arab Parts*), *Les encadrements planétaires*

(*Planetary Containment*), and *L'interprétation astrologique des rêves* (*Astrological interpretation of Dreams*, 1953), soon to be published in English translation by ASI of New York.

Volguine is one of the few modern astrologers who have investigated foreign and occult traditions such as the Hindu, Arab, Chinese, Hebrew, and Pre-Columbian (see especially his *Lunar Astrology; The Ruler of the Nativity; The Arab Parts;* and *L'astrologie chez les Mayas et les Aztèques,* 1946). He criticized his contemporaries for neglecting such important tools as the Arabian parts, decanates, and navamsas, and for their rigid adherence to the five Ptolemaic aspects. His own broad approach to aspect theory—he believed that all planets are in aspect—is related to ADDEY's theory of HARMONICS. Volguine stressed the importance of treating the chart as a whole. An example of his holistic approach to chart interpretation is his concept of *encadrement,* or planetary containment, which pays special attention to the sequence of the planets around the wheel and especially to the planets that flank such significators as Sun, Moon, Ascendant, and Midheaven. He also emphasized the importance of assessing the relative strengths of the planets. In *The Ruler of the Nativity* he presents a highly sophisticated system for determining the ruling or dominant planets in a chart that is really a modern reinterpretation of the Hindu doctrine of *shad bala,* or strengths (see INDIA, ASTROLOGY IN). His *Technique of Solar Returns* is still the authoritative work on that important tool of prediction (see SOLAR RETURN).

Waning: See CYCLE.

War Time (WT): See TIME.

Water: According to HERMETIC THEORY, one of the four ELEMENTS, under which the signs Cancer, Scorpio, and Pisces, known as the *water triplicity* or *water trigon*, are classified. In astrology water stands for emotion, sensitivity, and fluidity. An overemphasis of water signs in a chart is associated with emotional instability and hypersensitivity to the psychic environment. A lack of water is associated with emotional coldness and an inability to empathize, qualities that may be considerably offset by a well-placed, well-aspected Venus or Moon. (Also see CHINESE ASTROLOGY.)

Water Signs: See WATER.

Water Trigon: See WATER.

Water Triplicity: See WATER.

Waxing: See CYCLE.

Western Point: See EAST POINT.

West Point: The point where the western HORIZON intersects both the CELESTIAL EQUATOR and the PRIME VERTICAL; in some systems of HOUSE DIVISION, the cusp of the Seventh House. The West Point should not be confused with the Descendant, which is the point where the western horizon intersects the ECLIPTIC. (See COSMOGRAPHY, EAST POINT.)

Winter Solstice: See SOLSTICES.

Witte, Alfred: See URANIAN SYSTEM.

Yod: See DOUBLE QUINCUNX.

Zariel System: See HOUSE DIVISION.

Zenith: The point of the CELESTIAL SPHERE directly overhead at any location on the Earth's surface, where the upper MERIDIAN intersects the PRIME VERTICAL; the opposite of *nadir*. The zenith should not be confused with the MIDHEAVEN, which is the point where the upper meridian intersects the ECLIPTIC. (See COSMOGRAPHY.)

Zenith Horoscope: See LOCATIONAL ASTROLOGY.

Zenith Projection: See NONAGESI-MAL.

Zenith System: See HOUSE DIVISION.

Zodiac: Literally, "circle of animals"; an imaginary belt in the heavens extending some 8° or 9° of CELESTIAL LATITUDE on either side of the ECLIPTIC to include the orbits of the Moon and planets (except Pluto). The zodiac is divided into twelve 30° divisions called signs, which bear the names of animals, human beings, and mythological creatures, after the constellations that are located along this band and through which the Sun passes in its apparent path around the Earth.

A distinction should be made between the TROPICAL ZODIAC, which is oriented in relation to the equinoxes, and the SIDEREAL ZODIAC, which is oriented in relation to the stars. Because of PRECESSION OF THE EQUINOXES, the tropical zodiac moves backward in relation to the sidereal zodiac. The two zodiacs are considered by some astrologers, particularly Cyril FAGAN, to have coincided temporarily in A.D. 221 but now to be more than 24° apart—the tropical behind the sidereal.

The origin of the zodiac is obscure, but it is generally associated with the rise of civilization in the Middle East. The earliest zodiacs were probably sidereal. The traditional division into twelve signs reflects the ancient division of the year into twelve lunar months, for which the shifting constellations provided a calendar. Ancient zodiacs were probably lunar; modern Hindu, Chinese, and Arab zodiacs are still based on cycles of the Moon. (See CONSTELLATIONS; LUNAR MANSIONS; SIGNS OF THE ZODIAC.)

Zone Time: See TIME.

Bibliography to the English-language edition

Andrews, E. J. "Moon Talk: The Cycle Periodicity of Postoperative Hemorrhage." *Journal of the Florida State Medical Association* 46 (1961): 1362–66.

Bach, Eleanor. *Ephemerides of the Asteroids: Ceres, Pallas, Juno, Vesta, 1900–2000.* Brooklyn, N.Y.: Celestial Communications, Inc., 1973.

Bailey, Alice. *Esoteric Astrology: A Treatise on the Seven Rays.* New York: Lucis Publishing Company, 1951.

Bradley, Donald A. *Solar and Lunar Returns: How They Affect You According to the Sidereal Zodiac.* St. Paul, Minn.: Llewellyn Publications, 1973.

Bridgwater, William, and Kurtz, Seymour, eds. *The Columbia Encyclopedia.* 3d ed. New York and London: Columbia University Press, 1963.

Case, Paul Foster. *The Tarot: A Key to the Wisdom of the Ages.* Richmond, Va.: Macoy Publishing Company, 1947.

Cooper, Michael and Weaver, Andrew. *An Astrological Index to the World's Famous People.* Garden City, N.Y.: Doubleday and Company, 1975.

Cornell, H. L. *Encyclopaedia of Medical Astrology.* New York: Samuel Weiser, 1972.

Cumont, Franz. *Astrology and Religion among the Greeks and Romans.* New York: Dover, 1960.

Dean, Geoffrey, comp. *Recent Advances in Natal Astrology: A Critical Review 1900–1976.* Subiaco, Western Australia: Analogic, 1977.

The Encyclopaedia Britannica. 11th ed. New York: The Encyclopaedia Britannica Company, 1910; Chicago, 1974.

De Luce, Robert. *Constellational Astrology according to the Hindu System.* Los Angeles: De Luce Publishing, 1963.

De Vore, Nicholas. *Encyclopedia of Astrology.* Totowa, N.J.: Littlefield, Adams & Co., 1977 (1st ed. 1947).

Dobyns, Zipporah. *Asteroid Ephemeris 1883–1999.* Los Angeles: TIA Publications, 1977.

Ebertin, Reinhold. *The Combination of Stellar Influences.* Translated by Alfred G. Roosedale and Linda Kratzch. Aalen, Germany: Ebertin-Verlag, 1972.

Edmands, Dodie and Allan. *Child Signs.* London: Hutchinson & Co., 1979. (*The Children's Astrologer.* New York: Hawthorn Books, Inc., 1978.)

Erlewine, Michael and Margaret. *Astrophysical Directions.* Ann Arbor, Mich.: Heart Center, 1977.

———. "Our Roots in the Sun: The New Helio Astrology." *Astrology Now* 3, whole number 19 (February 1978): 32–39.

Erlewine, Stephen. *The Circle Book of Charts.* Ann Arbor, Mich.: Circle Books, 1972.

Ernst, Br., and de Vries, Tj. E. *Atlas of the Universe.* Translated by D. R. Welsh. Edited by H. E. Butler. New York: Thomas Nelson, 1961.

Gauquelin, Michel. *The Cosmic Clocks: From Astrology to a Modern Science.* Chicago: Henry Regnery Company, 1967.

———. *Cosmic Influences on Human Behavior: The Planetary Factors in Personality.*

Translated by Joyce E. Clemow. New York: ASI Publishers, Inc., 1978.

———. *The Scientific Basis of Astrology: Myth or Reality*. Translated by James Hughes. New York: Stein and Day, 1970.

Hand, Robert. "Astrology's Second Dimension: Declination and Latitude." *Astrology Now* 4, no. 1, whole number 25 (April–May 1979): 72–78.

———. "Geocentric Latitude: Some Second Thoughts." *Journal of Geocosmic Research* 2, no. 1, pp. 49–52.

———. *Planets in Composite: Analyzing Human Relationships*. Rockport, Mass.: Para Research, 1975.

———. *Planets in Youth: Patterns of Early Development*. Rockport, Mass.: Para Research, 1977.

———. "Science and Symbolism in Astrology." *Geocosmic News* 5, no. 1 (September 1979): 1.

Hickey, Isabel M. *Astrology: A Cosmic Science*. Bridgeport, Conn.: Altieri Press, undated.

Hone, Margaret E. *The Modern Text-Book of Astrology*. London: L. N. Fowler, 1951.

Hoyle, Fred. *Astronomy*. Garden City, N.Y.: Doubleday, 1962.

Jayne, Charles. *An Introduction to Locality Astrology*. Monroe, N.Y.: Astrological Bureau, 1978.

———. *A New Dimension in Astrology*. Monroe, N.Y.: Astrological Bureau, 1975.

———. *Progressions and Directions*. Monroe, N.Y.: Astrological Bureau, 1972.

Jayne, Vivia. *Aspects to Horoscope Angles*. Monroe, N.Y.: Astrological Bureau, 1975.

Johndro, L. E. *The Earth in the Heavens: Ruling Degrees of Cities, How to Find and Use Them*. New York: Samuel Weiser, 1973.

Jones, Marc Edmund. *The Guide to Horoscope Interpretation*. Stanwood, Wash.: Sabian Publishing Society, 1967.

Jung, C. G. *Synchronicity: An Acausal Connecting Principle*. New York: Pantheon Books, 1955.

Koster, Heinz. *Astrological House Systems*. Concord and Still River, Mass.: Bannister Associates, 1976.

Kurtz, Paul, ed. "A Note from the Editor." *The Humanist* 35, no. 5 (September–October 1975): 3.

Landscheidt, Theodor. *Cosmic Cybernetics: The Foundations of a Modern Astrology*. Translated by Linda Kratzch. Aalen, Germany: Ebertin-Verlag, 1973.

Leo, Alan. *The Complete Dictionary of Astrology*. Edited by Vivian Robson. New York: Astrologer's Library, 1978.

———. *Esoteric Astrology*. London: L. N. Fowler, 1967.

Lorenz, Dona Marie. "How Much Accuracy Do We Really Need?" *Astrology Now* 1, no. 8 (November 1975): 5, 31–33.

———. *Tools of Astrology: Houses*. Topanga, Calif.: Eomega Grove Press, 1973.

Mayo, Jeff. *The Astrologer's Astronomical Handbook*. 3d ed. Romford, Essex, England: L. N. Fowler, 1976.

McCaffery, Ellen. *Graphic Astrology*. Richmond, Va.: Macoy Publishing Company, 1931.

Meyer, Michael R. *A Handbook for the Humanistic Astrologer*. Garden City, N.Y.: Doubleday, 1974.

Moore, Marcia, and Douglas, Mark. *Astrology, The Divine Science*. York Harbor, Me.: Arcane Publications, 1971.

Munkasey, Michael. "The Houses: The Measurement View—Twenty Different Systems." *Astrology Now* 1, no. 8 (November 1975): 1, 17–20.

Neilson, William Allan, ed. *Webster's New International Dictionary of the English Language*. 2d ed. Springfield, Mass.: G. & C. Merriam, 1953.

Nelson, J. H. *Cosmic Patterns: Their Influence on Man and His Communications*. Washington, D.C.: American Federation of Astrologers, 1974.

Norton, Arthur P., and Inglis, J. Gall. *A Star Atlas and Reference Handbook (Epoch 1950) for Students and Amateurs*. Edinburgh and London: Gall and Inglis, 1969.

Polich, Vendel. *The Topocentric System with Tables of Houses and Oblique Ascension for All Latitudes 0°–90°*. Buenos Aires: Editorial Regulus, 1975.

Ptolemy, Claudius. *Tetrabiblos*. Edited and translated by F. E. Robbins. London: William Heinemann, 1964.

Robson, Vivian E. *The Fixed Stars and Constellations in Astrology*. New York: Samuel Weiser, 1969.

Rudhyar, Dane. *The Astrology of Personality*. Garden City, N.Y.: Doubleday, 1970 (1st ed. 1936).

———. *The Lunation Cycle*. St. Paul, Minn.: Llewellyn Publications, 1967.

———. *The Practice of Astrology*. Baltimore, Md.: Penguin Books, 1970.

Sakoian, Frances, and Acker, Louis. *The Astrologer's Handbook*. New York: Harper & Row, 1973.

Schulman, Martin. *Karmic Astrology: Retrogrades and Reincarnation*. New York: Samuel Weiser, 1977.

Sepharial. *New Dictionary of Astrology*. New York: Arco Publishing Company, 1964.

Townley, John. *Astrological Cycles and the Life Crisis Periods*. New York: Samuel Weiser, 1977.

Volguine, Alexandre. "Les Encadrements de l'Ascendant et du Milieu du Ciel." *Les Cahiers Astrologiques*, no. 150 (January–February, 1971), pp. 1–10.

———. *The Ruler of the Nativity*. New York: ASI Publishers, Inc., 1973.

———. *The Technique of Solar Returns*. New York: ASI Publishers, Inc., 1976.

Webster's Biographical Dictionary. Springfield, Mass.: G. & C. Merriam, 1963.

West, John Anthony, and Toonder, Jan Gerhard. *The Case for Astrology*. New York: Coward-McCann, 1970.

White, Harold J. "House Systems: How They Fare in High Latitudes—A Critical Discussion." *CAO Times* 3, no. 3 (1978): 30 ff.

Witte, Alfred, and Lefeldt, Hermann. *Rules for Planetary Pictures: The Astrology of Tomorrow*. Translated by Ludwig Rudolph. Hamburg: Witte-Verlag, 1974.

Zolar. *The History of Astrology*. New York: Arco Publishing Company, 1972.